CROSS-CULTURAL HARLEM

SANDHYA SHUKLA

CROSS-CULTURAL HARLEM

Reimagining Race and Place

Columbia University Press / *New York*

Columbia University Press
Publishers Since 1893
New York   Chichester, West Sussex
cup.columbia.edu
Copyright © 2024 Columbia University Press
All rights reserved

Library of Congress Cataloging-in-Publication Data
Names: Shukla, Sandhya Rajendra, author.
Title: Cross-cultural Harlem : reimagining race and place / Sandhya Shukla.
Description: New York : Columbia University Press, [2023] |
Includes bibliographical references and index.
Identifiers: LCCN 2023049707 (print) | LCCN 2023049708 (ebook) |
ISBN 9780231208468 (hardback) | ISBN 9780231208475 (trade paperback) |
ISBN 9780231557443 (ebook)
Subjects: LCSH: Harlem (New York, N.Y.)—Race relations—History. |
Harlem (New York, N.Y.)—Ethnic relations—History. | New York (N.Y.)—
Race relations—History. | New York (N.Y.)—Ethnic relations—History. |
Cultural fusion—New York (State)—New York—History.
Classification: LCC F128.68.H3 S48 2023 (print) | LCC F128.68.H3 (ebook) |
DDC 305.80097471—dc23/eng/20231103
LC record available at https://lccn.loc.gov/2023049707
LC ebook record available at https://lccn.loc.gov/2023049708

Cover design: Noah Arlow
Cover image: *Harlem, 1956*, Keystone-France/Getty Images

CONTENTS

An Introduction to Harlem: Theory, Method, and Material   1

  1 Langston Hughes's Harlem: "Spanish Blood" and Geographies of Blackness   45

  2 Mapping Place: The Facts and Fictions of Claude McKay's Harlem Imaginary   93

  3 Crossings at Home and in the World: Vito Marcantonio's Working-Class Cosmopolitanism   137

  4 Selfhood and Difference: Piri Thomas and Aladdin on the Streets of Harlem   185

A Coda for the Stories: Futures for Harlem   239

Acknowledgments 247

Notes 251

Index 305

CROSS-CULTURAL HARLEM

AN INTRODUCTION TO HARLEM

Theory, Method, and Material

Who could forget the *Life* magazine image of a fatally wounded Malcolm X?[1] The photograph circulated long after he was shot and killed in 1965, along paths carved by painful memories of Black death—the promise of liberation extinguished—as well as in ruts worn down by countless tabloid clichés of violence in the popular press.[2] To gaze at the picture is to witness and feel loss, through the layers of time between the Civil Rights movement and our complicated political present. And when we are transported into the scene of the Audubon Ballroom, a now-repurposed building that has for so long conjured up Harlem and its racial politics because Malcolm X died there (even though it stands within the formal bounds of Washington Heights), we cannot help but compare the spectacularized vulnerability of a human life with the precarity of Black places.

Varying perspectives bring the photograph into a different kind of presence. We could start from the top right of the frame and settle into the intimate physical gesture of a young Japanese American woman, Yuri Kochiyama, cradling Malcolm X's head. Kochiyama was not there accidentally—though her ethnic identity does not feature prominently in contemporary discourses about who and what Harlem was, she was a

AN INTRODUCTION TO HARLEM

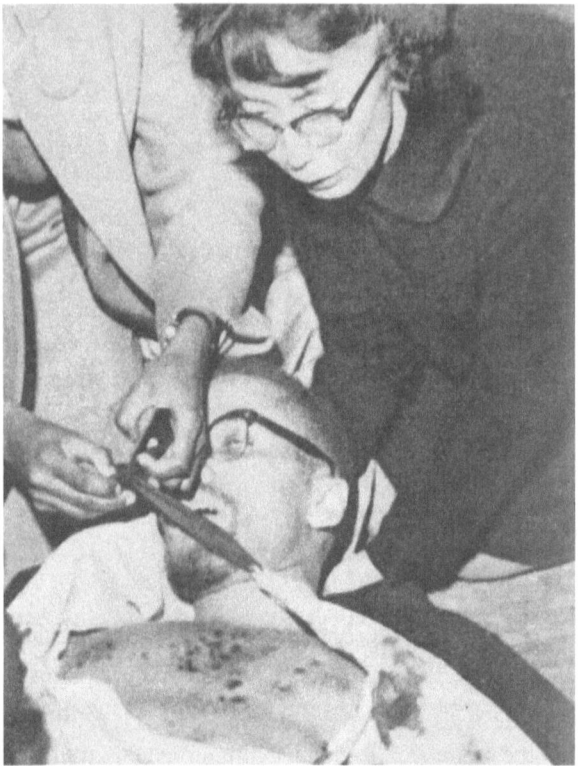

FIGURE 0.1 Malcolm X and Yuri Kochiyama in the Audubon Ballroom, 1965.

Photo by Earl Grant.

proud resident of the area and was deeply affiliated with its cultures and peoples. And she and Malcolm X had a relationship that reflected a political intimacy that Asian and Black peoples in Harlem have drawn on in the many years since.[3]

The paths that Kochiyama and Malcolm X took to Harlem had some uncannily common themes of racialization and globalism. Born exactly four years apart on the nineteenth of May, both were children of migrants. Kochiyama's parents had come from Japan, Malcolm Little's mother from

AN INTRODUCTION TO HARLEM

Grenada. Foreignness made these families targets of hostility: Kochiyama's father was arrested for having pictures of Japanese ships in his possession and being friendly with an ambassador; the Littles were continually hounded by the KKK through the Midwest for their activities in support of Marcus Garvey. Such alienating childhood experiences alone might have caused them to develop a wariness about what it meant to belong to the United States. Their confinements at the hands of the U.S. state—Kochiyama's internment in a camp during World War II and Malcolm X's imprisonment for theft just afterward—surely made the limits of belonging even more apparent. Given their personal histories, it seems inevitable that the two would come to embrace transnational struggles like antiwar and anti-imperial movements, Pan-Africanism and Black Islam.[4]

The convergence of Kochiyama's and Malcolm X's histories on the bloodied floor of the Audubon Ballroom is part of an archive that *Cross-Cultural Harlem: Reimagining Race and Place* cracks open. In this book I bring to the surface interactions, collisions, and borrowings that have been submerged in many accounts of a legendary site of race and class formation. From the turn of the twentieth century until the present the symbolic and geographic territory of Harlem has been made by relations among African Americans, West Indians, Africans, Puerto Ricans, Italians, Mexicans, Asians, and others who had nowhere else to go and who sought and carefully built a sense of community that expressed a critical relationship to a dominant "America." Those crossings have had spatial effects: even if groups of people came to settle en masse in particular regions of Harlem, "central" or "west" or "east," their movements, their languages, and their social exchanges would not be restricted by neighborhood blocks.

Harlem has been the capital of the global Black diaspora since the 1920s and has also been a space for other experiences and identities that brought race, ethnicity, and class together.[5] A Little Italy formed uptown in the late 1800s, predating its better-known counterpart on the lower east side of Manhattan. The Jewish population of Harlem from the 1870s until the 1930s was the third largest in the world. The eastern part of Harlem was the location for the legendary El Barrio, built by Puerto Rican migrants

AN INTRODUCTION TO HARLEM

beginning in the early twentieth century and becoming especially populous in the 1940s to 1960s. And in more recent years Little Senegal has encompassed a concentration of Francophone West African immigrants.[6] Political representation on the local, state, and national levels has been based in Harlem's different communities; many African Americans, Latinos, West Indians, and Italians have served on the city council or in state or national legislatures, advocating for the neighborhoods they came from. No less importantly, Harlemites have accumulated sustenance from both formal and underground economies, owning property, running small businesses, and developing social organizations. Black, Italian, Jewish, and Puerto Rican Harlems may be held together in one formulation but distinguished in another through their relative racializations, reinforcing not only the plurality of urban forms but also multiple ways of knowing. Further complicating the picture is that formations of peoplehood, such as "Blackness," "Latinoness," "Asianness," and "whiteness," have always been constituted by heterogeneous groups and flexible identifications. And all these entanglements produce intimacy and friction, experienced on the street, in a grocery store, or at someone's home.

In that spirit, *Cross-Cultural Harlem* asks how to reconcile the power of race with its ever-present multiplicity. Underlying such a question is a refusal of ideological choices between racial identity and diversity, or between accommodating change in the shape of late capitalist development or submitting to something called the status quo. Global trends of rising real estate prices and the cultural cachet of the city for middle- and upper-class populations have provoked a crisis about the meaning and life of this place amid so many claims. Fears about a changing neighborhood or the disappearance of Black Harlem are often processed through informal assessments of new peoples moving in and older populations having no choice but to leave. As we grapple with the significance of declines in the African American population in greater Harlem over the years, what is the relationship of the "Blackness" of Harlem to the number of its comprising peoples?[7] Can we even speak of the symbolic potential of a place like Harlem without attending to the impact of economic crises on poor and working-class residents? And can we think more expansively about identity, provisional and incomplete though it may be, in terms of solidarity (without resorting to facile critiques of "identity politics")?

These predicaments acquire shape in a context in which many racialized peoples can no longer call Harlem home, and the place may thus be evacuated of its referents.[8] All the regions of Harlem—central, west, and east—contend with this trend. Life in East Harlem's barrio and Central Harlem's African communities dramatizes the contemporary struggle to survive, when bodegas and ethnic markets cannot find a footing in neoliberal economies, and in the refrain of the progeny of immigrants that they cannot afford to live where they grew up. Developers' claims that expensive housing will have positive effects in diversifying Harlem ring hollow for activists of color, who call out this corporate multiculturalist mantra as an alibi for displacement. The influx of African American moneyed people who seek to connect with Harlem's storied Black past, or the desire of well-meaning liberal artists and cultural producers to create a vibrant creative zone on New York's northern edge, significantly complicates the picture of gentrification, though it hardly reverses its course.[9] And if longtime Puerto Rican residents have made "Spanish Harlem" their physical and symbolic home, more recently arrived Mexicans and Central Americans expand on Latino ethnicity, but with a rather different claim to settlement, especially when some of them are undocumented. Wecquaesgeek Indians originally traded Harlem's territory for beads in a 1626 agreement with the Dutch West India Trading Company. This indigenous history of loss is tapped by contemporary accounts of Latin American migrants in the area who speak Mixtec but not Spanish and endure multiple forms of linguistic and cultural disempowerment.[10] More layers of difference can be unearthed through the example of Garifuna peoples of mixed African and indigenous ancestry, who have come mostly from coastal areas of Honduras, Belize, and Guatemala and who move in and out of Harlems that are Black, Latino, and/or Caribbean.[11]

This book considers stories of encounters across regions, identities, and community spaces, with the weight of recurrent anxieties about Harlem "as we know it" changing.[12] Encounters are never merely harmonious: they often reflect power differentials, too. But when we look closely at the pushes and pulls of identification, when people come together, surprising intimacies are revealed. Both the composition and the affective charge of place cannot be rendered only by discourses of "race relations," given how that approach has fixed groups. The stories that follow range quite widely, revisiting familiar life-worlds of canonical Black and Puerto Rican writers, excavating lesser-known performances such as a one-man show by a Bangladeshi comedian, and attending to accounts of deep investment in what Harlem does and can mean. Nonetheless, this book's curation discovers a shared sensibility that is recalcitrant to capture by a liberal managerial ethos of groups sitting side by side, to explain living *in* difference rather than just *with* difference.

Harlem remains exceptional, if not unique, in the measure that its racialized urban geography has both sustained and been sustained by an extraordinary internal sociocultural and political heterogeneity built of minoritization. In simplest terms, this is a majority-minority space structured, since the late nineteenth century, by relations among migrants from the U.S. South, the Caribbean, Puerto Rico, and southern and eastern Europe who settled in adjacent uptown neighborhoods. On the one hand, there was containment in formal jurisdiction of policing and real estate, in the informal naturalization of racial categories such as "Black" and "white," and in the popularization of spatial discourses for the "ghetto" or "enclave." But on the other, the development of community has followed the fluidity of social relationships, with shifting residences, connections to and through the experience of being disenfranchised, hybrid ethnic cultures, language pluralism, and more. Porous boundaries can be seen between and inside group formations.[13]

Cross-Cultural Harlem brings these diversities together to shift how the space *as a whole* is conceived of, and what it could mean for the goal of a different kind of recognition and ownership. Harlem is not just a physical site: it is also an idea that many people relate to for consolation, compensation, and transcendence, in those uptown blocks and around the world. Planners and developers may try to organize and define territories, community members may seek to draw boundaries to prescribe membership, but Harlem cannot be owned. Its meanings spin through and out of the place.

And so too the stories escape their canonical boxes, asking to be recognized, identified with, or rejected. Creative repertoires for making sense of Harlem express belonging and alienation, submission and resistance. And the resulting contradictions, in turn, develop new possibilities for interpretation and resistance to dominant representation.

TO MAP HARLEM

This book develops a racial geography that maps physical, social, psychic, and symbolic terrain. It remains alive to that difference between a Harlem that can be contained by a conventional city planning document or regional or ethnic taxonomies and one that cannot, as it gains meaning from practice and the imagination. Harlem's peoples have been partly (though never fully) brought into being through their identifications with neighborhoods such as Italian Harlem or Little Senegal and/or regions such as Black Central Harlem or El Barrio in the east. The interpretive balancing act involves using those organizational categories while understanding them to be provisional. A critical reference point can be found in the scholarship on Chinatowns, which has carefully attended to how classifications have been built through racist and colonial othering and also illuminated dense social and political experience.[14] Another set of influential works has theorized Black spaces of contestation and hybridization developed out of slavery's aftermaths.[15] What *Cross-Cultural Harlem* shares with those interventions from Asian Pacific American Studies and Black Studies is a fundamental concern with race and space and how the relationship between them is established, lived, and challenged. This is one way to ask what the following map—any map—projects, holds, and misses, in order to, as geographers Katherine McKittrick and Clyde Woods have put it, "move us away from territoriality, the normative practice of staking a claim to space," with the goal of finding a "new or different perspective on the production of space."[16]

One Harlem emphasizes a form with identifiable physical and social units, in the broad swath of upper Manhattan territory that extends between

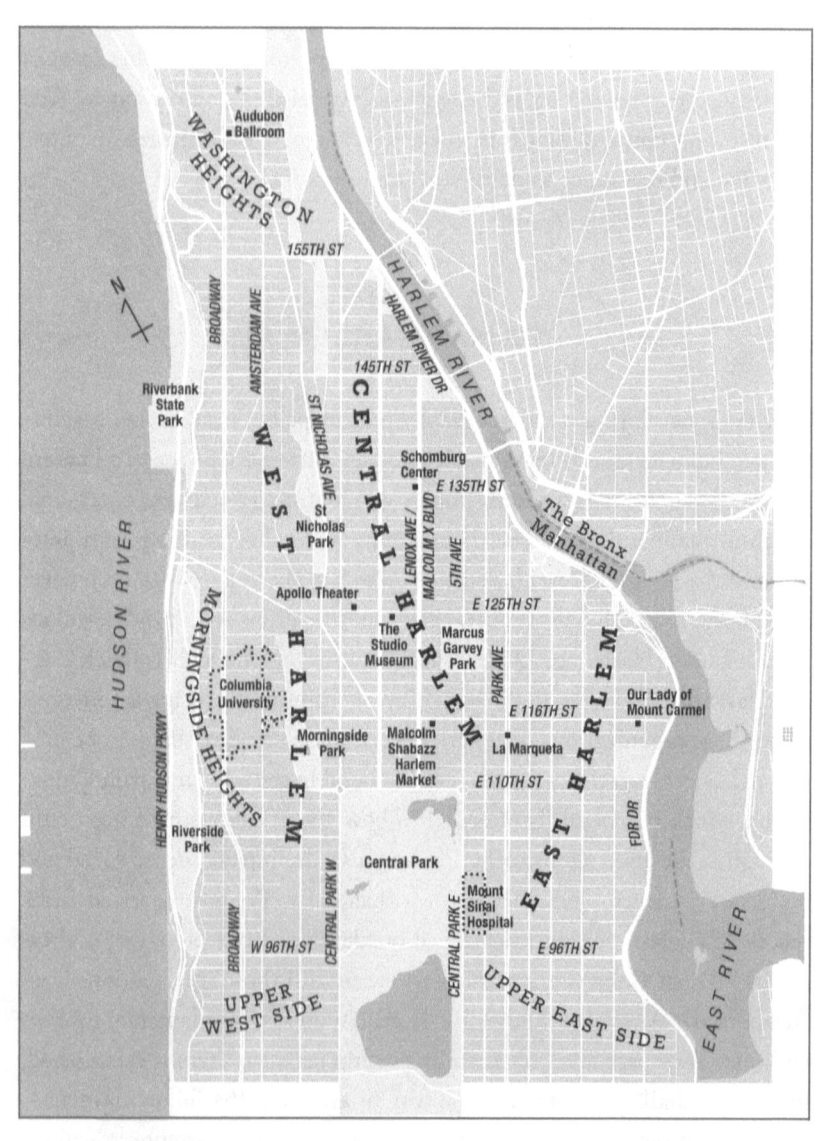

FIGURE 0.2 Harlem.

Map by Nat Case, INCase, LLC. Map data © OpenStreetMap contributors.

the East and Hudson Rivers and from 96th and 110th Streets in the south up north to 155th Street. We can begin with Kevin Lynch's template for city space, containing elements of "paths," "edges," "districts," "nodes," and "landmarks."[17] Paths find form in the central arteries of 125th and 116th Streets, cutting across east-to-west expanses and moving through different, and shifting, districts. Beginning almost at the Hudson River, an area once occupied by warehouses and other commercial enterprises, and reaching to the East River—passing the Harlem Metro-North train station on the block between Park and Madison Avenues (a node for people to come into Harlem and travel north out of the city) and leading to an entrance to Route 278 and the Grand Central Parkway, which accesses another transit hub, the New York LaGuardia Airport—125th Street is alive with the commerce of small shops and large retail stores, restaurants, churches, beauty salons, and offices for social organizations.

When Lynch noted that "people observe the city while moving through it, and along these paths the other environmental elements are arranged and related,"[18] he was directing interpreters to touch down into particular loci and pay attention to the narratives that emerge. If one were to walk across 125th Street, a main street of Harlem, he or she would engage with landmarks such as the Studio Museum and the Hotel Theresa to access various imaginaries of Blackness that link the past and present. Here, as elsewhere, history bears down heavily on material culture. The Apollo Theater, on West 125th Street between Seventh and Eighth Avenues (now renamed Adam Clayton Powell Jr. and Frederick Douglass Boulevards, respectively), exists as both symbol and weathervane, reflecting transformations of Harlem that include the complex interplay between white patronage and Black cultural life.[19] Also on West 125th Street is the old Blumstein's Department Store, the site of protests against racist hiring policies in the 1930s and an institution that evolved to have Harlem's first Black Santa Claus in 1958.[20]

The somewhat less iconic 116th Street weaves through a number of districts and their ethnic communities. It starts at the East River in what was once, actively in the late 1800s to 1930s, Italian Harlem. At least some of the contestations over culture and identity for Italian and other residents of East Harlem settled around the iconic Catholic Church of Our Lady of Mount Carmel on 116th Street between Pleasant and First Avenues, which served as a cornerstone of the district;[21] its annual celebration and yearly *festa*, or procession of the statue transplanted from Italy to East Harlem, mapped the dreams and anxieties of many Italians who understood themselves to belong to the place just as it traveled through always-changing neighborhoods.[22] Slightly to the west, "Lucky Corner" on Lexington Avenue was the site for political speeches during the congressional campaigns of Fiorello La Guardia in the 1920s and throughout the career of La Guardia's protégé, Vito Marcantonio, into the 1950s. As Puerto Ricans put down roots in East Harlem from the 1940s on, they began to share the eastern section of 116th Street. When their population was on the wane, in 1982, the portion of the street between Second and Fifth Avenues was renamed Luis Muñoz Marín Boulevard after the first governor of Puerto Rico. Senegalese and other West African migrants began arriving in Harlem in the 1980s, and the area of West 116th Street between Morningside and Fifth Avenues became known as Little Senegal. If gentrification has thinned out residential concentrations, important businesses and social organizations such as the Senegalese Association of America remain there, and on the street there is the optic of people in African clothing and the sound of French and Wolof being spoken.[23] Both major thoroughfares, 125th and 116th Streets, differ in their purchase on the popular imagination: the first largely conjures up U.S. Blackness, while 116th continues to be associated with multiple ethnic populations.[24]

Another porous social formation is signaled by the Jewish Community Center on West 118th Street and, just a bit to the west, the Chabad of Harlem, then further north, the Old Broadway synagogue.[25] Recent Jewish populations diverge in religious and political inclinations, as they may step into or eschew participation in these institutions, but housed therein are spectral memories of robust Jewish presences in West and East Harlems. When I took a walking tour of Central Harlem that explored mostly landmarks of the Black experience, a woman remarked at the very end, and quietly, "Oh, my Jewish grandfather lived here."[26] In that moment, she was registering ambivalence rather than any proud claim to place. How could

AN INTRODUCTION TO HARLEM

she not, in a historical context of Jewish–Black exchanges full of both conflicts and intimacies?[27] If the constructions of whiteness for ethnic groups subjected to (racial) minoritization, both nationally and globally, have been profoundly vexed, local spaces logically bear associated anxieties. And that field of already difficult identification may not flexibly accommodate difference, as we see when we consider the Black Jews of Harlem, a relatively small group in terms of population but still present in a number of accounts.[28] Tellingly, by and large their history does not feature prominently in either Jewish or Black place-stories.

In another orientation, different points of convergence and contestation become visible. On the east side of Harlem, on its Pleasant and First Avenues, there are traces of Italian culture and consumption, exemplified by Patsy's Pizzeria (which has undergone many revisions, and is now owned by an Albanian immigrant and his son, both local residents). A bit further west, Third Avenue connected areas of greater Puerto Rican settlement and expression, a landmark of which was the Eagle Theater, where jazz and mambo musician Tito Puente used to play. A principal focal point of Black Harlem has been Lenox Avenue, also named Malcolm X Boulevard, which runs from West 110th Street to 147th Street.[29] Located on Lenox are the now-shuttered Savoy Ballroom and still-bustling Sylvia's Restaurant (both on the itineraries of "cultural" walking tours for tourists), as well as the Schomburg Center for Research in Black Culture, an enduringly vital center for African American intellectual and cultural life in Harlem since the 1920s. Marcus Garvey's Universal Negro Improvement Association offices were nearby from 1918 to 1927. Through the 1920s and 1930s, West 130th to 138th Streets between Fifth and Seventh Avenues were lined with jazz and dance clubs where interracial and gay social life flourished. The Rockland Palace, further north on West 155th Street and Frederick Douglass Avenue, was especially famous for the Hamilton Lodge Ball drag performances, as well as for being the place where Black religious-political leader Father Divine received then mayoral candidate Fiorello La Guardia in 1933.[30] The immensely influential Abyssinian Baptist Church on West 138th Street illuminates a deep history of Black religious and political movements, including the lengthy 1940s to 1970s career of Central Harlem congressman (and minister) Adam Clayton Powell, Jr.. Back in the east of Harlem, just below 116th Street, lies the iconic La Marqueta, built from the old Park Avenue Market that Mayor LaGuardia launched in 1936 to contain largely Italian and Jewish pushcarts in a minimally physical glass and steel-beamed structure, but also preserve some semblance of its street life experience at the time. As the surrounding area became more Puerto Rican, the market acquired its ethnically resonant name. It has been many years since La Marqueta was vibrant, but it has continually been part of private and city-sponsored development plans. To its south, on East 105th Street, is Saint Cecilia Church, built in 1873 by the Irish for the Irish and welcoming successive waves of migrants from Puerto Rico, the Philippines, Mexico, and the Dominican Republic, as well as African Americans from the neighborhood, to this day.

Returning to the other side of Harlem, in the late 1980s and early 1990s African migrant vendors gave a central section of 125th Street a distinct texture. Mayor David Dinkins attempted but failed to disperse the informal shopping concentration, when a variety of local storeowners and community groups defended the vendors' right to the space. But his unapologetically neoliberal successor Rudolph Giuliani launched an all-out assault by focusing on illegality, ostensibly regarding the sellers' lack of formal licenses, but certainly raising a vision of what commerce should look like. West African merchants in particular responded by relocating to West 116th Street, near the Malcolm X/Malcolm Shabazz *masjid* (mosque). An uptick in business in the African market on 116th Street during the African American holiday of Kwanzaa and the continued presence of sellers of African goods on 125th Street, despite Giuliani's efforts, testify to the impossibility of maintaining tidy containers for race and ethnicity, the persistent heterogeneity of "Blackness," and the shifting geographic borders of "community." If there are resemblances in the origins of La Marqueta and the Malcolm Shabazz African Market, of intentionality in locating ethnic commerce, the stories of development find their contrasts in history, the easier cosmopolitanism of East Harlem in the early twentieth century and increasingly tight control over compartments of identity and peoplehood in later twentieth-century multicultural America. These are overlapping complexities of any spatial account of Harlem and they animate *Cross-Cultural Harlem*.

Another kind of market story that crystallizes more recent tensions of gentrification began even before the 1999 opening of a Pathmark chain grocery store on East 125th Street amid smaller "mom and pop" establishments, bodegas, and other minority-owned shops. There have always been different visions of the space, but in the 1990s disputes about aspiration reached a high pitch as changing incomes and rapid development stoked a fundamental uncertainty about what communities needed and wanted.[31] Cultural and economic ownership over a commercial street in the very symbolic center of Harlem may have been one way to think about life there, and access to consumption, simply eating and wearing what others could, was another. The sale of the property in late 2015 to a developer intending to build luxury condominiums, however, completed a rather simpler arc, from minoritized space (Black, Latino, and working-class) to high-end real estate for white and other residents from outside of Harlem, toward a more thoroughly late capitalist future. And the upscale Whole Foods grocery established in 2017 at the corner of West 125th Street and Lenox Avenue catered to a significantly wealthier contingent of the area than the Pathmark supermarket or, certainly, the smaller local stores had earlier.

Like many urban landscapes, Harlem's has historically contained a range of commercial and residential properties and, to a lesser extent, small green areas, and the mix, the relative proportions, has often been at issue. Public housing, beginning when the Harlem River Houses went up in 1937 and the East River Houses in 1941 and continuing through the 1960s and 1970s, pulls one thread across and up and down Harlem, and boxy buildings along the way mark vexed relationships between neighborhoods and the state.[32] That undocumented peoples cannot access government-sponsored residences is a socioeconomic reality (and source of ethnic differentiation) that lies just beneath that web. Throughout the neighborhood, dilapidated housing, trash spilling out onto the streets and people without resources fill out other pictures, journalistic photography especially, associated with this city space.[33] The constancy of some of those images of impoverishment does not fully contradict their shifting meanings throughout history, from the intense effects of the Great Depression to the recession and accompanying urban crisis of the 1970s and 1980s to a crack epidemic and more. Since the 1930s working-class jobs in Harlem have given way to largely service-based occupations, all without social safety nets. Manufacturing and large government sectors of the city infrastructure began to erode in the 1970s. Meanwhile, urban centers across the globe saw an increasing concentration of capital from outside investors. This, and renewed desires for middle- and upper-class city life, found physical expression in the razing or upscale renovation of old buildings and the construction of expensive high-rise condominiums across east, west, and central Harlem. The verticality of the city changed, and all around were the sights and sounds of massive displacement.[34]

To draw the shape of Harlem is to establish edges and illuminate spaces of spillover and its consequences. At the western boundary with Columbia University, a town–gown conflict is always deeply felt.[35] In an extended history of strained relations, 1968 stands out. That year, Columbia's release of plans to build a gymnasium in Morningside Park unleashed long-simmering tensions.[36] Local protests grew from the student politics of the era, from civil rights, exclusions, and representation at universities, and from the global and domestic tensions of the Vietnam War (and an awareness of whose bodies were on the line there). Their broader critique of power clarified the dynamics of an elite educational institution closely adjacent to poor and working-class Black communities. Indeed, blueprints for the building distilled spatial issues: they envisaged "community" residents having access from a lower floor, while Columbia students and faculty would enter from the top floor, at the main level of the university. The eventual failure of that proposal may have had something to do with the crude coding of difference, which echoed Jim Crow segregation as it made even more apparent the divides of a regional map. But Columbia University's projects to remake Manhattanville, the section of Harlem between 125th and 135th Streets west of Broadway, have been inexorable. And Harlem residents' accusations of land-grabbing have always mingled with support in some quarters for development that has the potential to create jobs and revitalize a neighborhood.[37]

AN INTRODUCTION TO HARLEM

Similar frictions have existed on the border between the Upper East Side and East Harlem. The contrast there, like those at every edge of Harlem, is viewed in class and race terms. There are analogues, too, in the relationships between community formation and outside institutions. Mount Sinai Hospital, for example, is located on the Upper East Side and Metropolitan Hospital in East Harlem proper. All of their properties (laboratories, offices, residences) threaten to engulf local life unrelated to the hospitals, just as Columbia overwhelms its neighbors. East 96th Street has long symbolized the divide between two very different worlds. When the Islamic Cultural Center, located on Third Avenue between East 96th and 97th Streets, was being planned in the late 1970s, it was seen, as a reporter for the *New York Times* baldly put it, to "soften the edge of East Harlem."[38]

An ambiguity about the ends of Harlem further deepens in the location of Malcolm X's death. Many people in New York and elsewhere think of Washington Heights as Dominican, a destination for migrants from the Dominican Republic.[39] The discernable presence of those peoples in West Harlem, across a soft boundary, variegates Blackness there, Caribbean Blackness especially, and serves as a reminder that "Spanishness" cannot be relegated to East Harlem, where many Puerto Ricans settled. For several decades now, Broadway and Amsterdam Avenue have featured Dominican businesses and restaurants, as well as, more recently, evangelical churches, which have shaped the linguistic and cultural character of the area.

This is one backdrop for transformations at the Audubon Ballroom, located on Broadway between West 165th and West 166th Streets. After Malcolm X's assassination, the Audubon became known as the San Juan Theater, shifting from a symbol of Black cultural life (and political injury) to a Latino community space. Seized by the city in 1980 because of unpaid taxes and bought by Columbia University in 1983, the future of the building generated increasingly brittle negotiations, with local political groups anxious that the university's plans for demolition were a harbinger of even further encroachment into Harlem and Washington Heights. The eventual 2005 compromise, in the form of a conjoined Mary Woodard Lasker Biomedical Research Building (in the back) and Malcolm X and Dr. Betty Shabazz Memorial and Educational Center (in the front), self-presents with visible hybridities and historicities that cannot easily be made sense of by urban development language of "adaptive reuse."[40] This point of apparent convergence, like any edge, boundary, or corner, dramatically calls into question what it means to live with others, and also reminds us that practices of respectful accommodation must acknowledge the pull of disparate attachments in any register of collective experience.

Lines in a diagram cannot always show what is unevenly contained inside the formed blocks or indicate whether one feature of the space is more or less important than the other, but those very asymmetries reveal critical hierarchies of power and interest. Numbers undoubtedly matter, but how depends a great deal on comparative and historical context. Beginning in the early 1900s, when East Harlem was beginning to be associated with immigrants, first Italian and then Puerto Rican, the continued presence of African Americans, measured in significant percentages of the resident population there, have testified to the permeability of territorial boundaries between different peoples. When census tracts identify a rise in the African American population across Harlem from the 1910s through the 1930s and 1940s, it supports our understanding of this as a Black place. It is hardly surprising that shifts in the relative proportions of Black and other peoples would engender a deep crisis in always-fragile neighborhood identities associated with race, just as they draw attention to the insufficiency of any mapping that cannot account for dense experience.

HARLEM AS THEORY: CROSS-CULTURALITY, RACE, AND URBAN SPACE

Geography's possibilities and limits, made ever so clear in the cartographic practice illuminated above, are given another kind of texture with cross-culturality: exchanges, heterogeneities, and translations that define the Harlem of *Cross-Cultural Harlem* and also construct a model for analyzing race and urban space. Without denying the good use that many scholars and critics have put to the more common frame of multiculturalism, particularly in fields where there has been an ignorance of perspectives from marginalized groups, I propose an interpretive shift that can be partly seen in the prefixes "multi" and "cross."[40] Guyanese novelist and critic Wilson Harris, who famously expressed in all of his work an attention to overlapping histories of movement and ensuing processes of racialization, explicitly distinguished the approaches: "Cross-culturality differs radically from multiculturality. There is no creative and re-creative sharing of dimensions in multiculturality. The strongest culture in multiculturality holds an umbrella over the rest, which have no alternative but to abide by the values that the strongest believe to be universal. Cross-culturality is an opening to a true and variant universality of a blend of parts we can never wholly encompass."[41]

This critical *and* political objection to multiculturalism's reinscription of familiar patterns resonates in majority-minority Harlem, where whiteness must be decentered. Cross-culturality, instead, stresses how the contacts among differentially minoritized racial and ethnic groups have made Harlem in a way that attends both to the power of identity and the dynamic blends that defy easy categorization. Harris refused a teleology that reinforces the popular wisdom that cities and nations, and their cultures, are becoming more complex when he averred, "Cross-culturalism can no longer be evaded because the whole world has been built on it for centuries."[42] Such a layered historicity derives from Guyana's mix of indigenous and migrant peoples, with specific ecological and social experiences over time—conquest and settlement, slavery and indenture, colonialism and diasporas, resource exploitation—but it is one that has a purchase on minoritized peoples throughout the Americas and other continental and regional formations.[43]

Moreover, the critical associations of cross-culturality point to its possibilities for the arguments in *Cross-Cultural Harlem*.[44] Cross-cultures bring to mind Martinican critic Édouard Glissant's idea of "relation," a way of interpreting the Caribbean as a space of interactions shaped by slavery and colonialism, those that resulted in unpredictable ways of being in and of the world.[45] There are also echoes of earlier work by Fernando Ortíz, who in 1947 advanced "transculturation" to describe the "extremely complex transmutations of culture" that emerged from interactions between different groups of people in Cuba.[46] Glissant's understanding of "rooted errantry," building on the notion of the rhizome in the work of Gilles Deleuze and Felix Guattari, maintains the importance of the Caribbean, in which "each and every identity is extended through a relationship with the Other" and provides yet another path through the deeply referential languages for thinking about space and identity.[47]

These particular models (and there are others) lead us to ask whether Harlem is *like* the Caribbean. One answer would be that in Harlem, as in Caribbean countries, there has been a blend of peoples who have been ethnicized by the state and also racialized by histories of conquest, slavery, colonialism, and imperialism, making a space in which whiteness is not the dominant form of peoplehood even while it is omnipresent as a force. A number of historians have put the two places into a geographic relationship through a map of the "extended Caribbean," in which Harlem has been connected by economics, migration, and politics to island nations.[48] In this move, Harlem is reimagined as a place with its own logic, a kind of island, not just a part of the United States or Manhattan; we can also cast it as the heart and soul of diasporas that challenge race and class formations of the nation-state. The issue of sovereignty obviously presents limits and possibilities for analogy: Harlem cannot be politically independent in the ways individual nations can after decolonization, and yet the *regional* imaginary of the Caribbean understands autonomy somewhat differently. Jamaican-British thinker Stuart Hall critiqued generalizations of "pluralism" in the Caribbean, when he considered historical systems of stratification within particular societies. Hall's careful discussions of the simultaneity of shared racial pasts and divergent experiences for identity, to which I will return in subsequent chapters of this book, point to yet more complications in any project of comparison.[50]

We can hardly forget that diasporic understandings of political and social possibility, which many migrants were shaped by and brought with them, are central to any treatment of Caribbeanness and Harlem together. The most famous of those may be Garveyism, but they also include Caribbean radical and independence movements from the period before and extending through the Harlem Renaissance.[49] At play were rather different perspectives on race in Harlem: many people believed that Blackness could be a source of solidarity, and that it was also necessarily more heterogeneous than U.S. dichotomies dictated.[50] Language has always dug one deep fault line: English-speaking Caribbean migrants from, for example, Jamaica or Trinidad, have (been) associated with African American Blackness, and Spanish Caribbean groups such as Puerto Ricans or Dominicans have filled out another formation, even when they have thought of themselves as "Black."[51]

What is at stake is how we imagine Harlem as a place and, more richly, deeply, and differentially, as global. In Martinican novelist Patrick Chamoiseau's words, place is a "multi-transcultural, multi-translingual" space from which "one lives the world community."[52] Importantly for this book, place dislodges nation and effectively its discrete identities of the multicultural. It will become clear in these pages that, indeed, Harlem cannot be fully seen inside the nation-state. Its critical relationship to the United States has as much to do with racial experience as it does with the ideological effects of dwelling in a space that is multiply constituted.[53] The sensation of being Black or Puerto Rican in America is saturated by an anxiety of belonging. Thus, constitutive racial meanings, even inside particular geographic bounds—Blackness or Latino-ness or Jewishness—gain energy from diasporic, postcolonial, and hemispheric articulations. Metropolitan life has long been associated with cosmopolitanism, the openness to and citizenship of the world that Immanuel Kant proposed, exceeding parochialism, and also, rather differently, articulating to intense localism. As he wrote in the 1798 preface to *Anthropology from a Pragmatic Point of View*, "A city such as *Königsberg*, on the River Pregel—a large city, the center of a state, the seat of the government's provincial councils, the site of a university (for cultivation of the sciences), a seaport connected by rivers with the interior of the country, so that its location favors traffic with the rest of the country as well as with neighboring or remote countries having different languages and customs—is a suitable place for broadening one's knowledge of man and of the world. In such a city, this knowledge can be acquired even without traveling."⁵⁴ To embrace the kind of understanding of place articulated by Kant, Chamoiseau, and others is to break down scholarly and popular oppositions between globality and locality.⁵⁵

By now it should be evident that in *Cross-Cultural Harlem* "global" means much more than the space outside of the nation. To point to how the global cannot be reduced to the effects of economic globalization is to pull the term away from capitalist modernity's hold.⁵⁶ Globality highlights multiplicity, the crossing of borders, and an expansive imagination. It is bigness, but it is densely constituted heterogeneous bigness especially. In the case of Harlem, globality obtains energy from its close quarters; a space might be carved up into regions and communities, yet be simply unable to maintain a balkanization of interests. The invocation of globality and its frequent conceptual companion, cosmopolitanism, often conveys a privileged mobility, the ability to travel across borders and thus, effectively, diminish the importance of living in place. But to further unsettle scalar registers, I want especially to maintain that globality enables an understanding of the particular ("small") and racialized and classed encounters of Harlem. This place has so often been represented on an edge—the edge of New York, of the United States, even of world history. To the north of a busy downtown financial center and a commercial midtown, Harlem was seen in the late nineteenth century as an escape from the density of urban life. Later it received peoples who would not be accommodated elsewhere in the city because of racism. To argue for its fundamentally global nature is not to overshadow U.S. racial dynamics that shape what is possible and desirable for individuals or their communities, but to highlight the hyperlocalized and transoceanic crossroads at which so many kinds of encounters converge.

KOCHIYAMA AND MALCOLM X IN HARLEM

Consider more closely Yuri Kochiyama's exchanges in Harlem. The front cover photo of her autobiography shows her sitting with two Black activists; the back cover features a sign for the 125th Street stop of the subway.⁵⁷ Symbolic

AN INTRODUCTION TO HARLEM

Blackness visually bookends the representation of Kochiyama's life story, and the text inside the volume develops the deep affiliations by which she feels she is formed. After describing her limited contact with Black Americans during her childhood and young adulthood in California, she notes, about arriving on the East Coast: "How glad I was to . . . have my first experience with Black people. I enjoyed it a great deal, and I learned so much about the South and the racism there since many of my co-workers were from the South."[60] But a more personal evolution began when she settled in Harlem alongside Latino and African American families: in her words, "it was in this new neighborhood that at the age of forty, my political activism began to take shape."[58] The inspiration of Black Harlem even radiates through her family; she notes her children as being "influenced by the different aspects of Afro-American culture: its music (jazz, blues, spirituals, freedom songs); its dance (African, Caribbean); its literature (W. E. B. DuBois, Richard Wright, James Baldwin); and its sports figures (Paul Robeson, Jesse Owens, Jackie Robinson). It was the best place. . . . Harlem was a university without walls."[59] It is hard to miss the resemblance of the terms "university," which Kochiyama

FIGURE 0.3 Yuri Kochiyama speaking in New York with two activists.

Photo courtesy of the Kochiyama family and UCLA Asian American Studies Center.

FIGURE 0.4 Yuri Kochiyama at the 125th Street subway station, Harlem.

Photo courtesy of the Kochiyama family and UCLA Asian American Studies Center.

uses to refer to a space for *racial* learning, and "universality," raised as an ideal by writers such as Harris and Chamoiseau.

Reading these comments as psychic projections is a complicated task, not least because Kochiyama does not presume to be an insider, yet rarely questions her ability to belong. Such apparently paradoxical elements might be resolved in a return to the scene of the Audubon Ballroom. When shots were fired, many of the audience members must have fled the area, but Kochiyama remembers marching right up to the stage: "I just picked up his head and just put it on my lap. I said, 'Please, Malcolm! Please, Malcolm! Stay alive!'"[60] Both the evocation of strong feeling (the repetitive "please") and the extraordinary physical gesture of Kochiyama lifting Malcolm X's head and putting it on her lap are remarkable for their lack of self-consciousness and professed ease ("just"). But the moment is much more comprehensible when we approach it with the sensibility of cross-cultural solidarity that enabled a quasi-kinesthetic experience for these two very different people.

We might also situate Kochiyama's relationship to Harlem's Blackness via another place and through other political experiences. That story begins in San Pedro, California, where Kochiyama was born and where she lived until her evacuation to a Japanese internment camp as a young woman. She identifies San Pedro as a "white working-class neighborhood" and this racial-economic definition of place is also, it turns out, a social and cultural one, central to a life trajectory.[61] Kochiyama offers the crucial detail that her best friend growing up was named Vivian Martinez, a "Hispanic," and she also describes working at a settlement house for Mexicans in the area. Moreover, she carefully identifies the white population as diverse, composed of Slovenians and Italians who worked in the local fishing industry. The children that she interacted with, Kochiyama points out, had parents who did not speak English well, much like her own.

And so, like Harlem, San Pedro is part of Kochiyama's political origin story. Of a meaningful inflection point, she writes: "As much as I enjoyed growing up in a friendly cosmopolitan small town, I needed to leave it and grow up, open myself to new ideas, meet new people, learn from life's experiences. My provincial mentality and apolitical ideas needed to change and develop."⁶² The yoking of "cosmopolitan" and "small town" may be dissonant to modern ears, trained as we are in the elite presumptions of worldliness.⁶³ While proposing that cosmopolitanism exists in working-class and small places outside of major cities like New York or Paris, Kochiyama also puts the newness of ideas, peoples, and experiences outside (this) locality. Moreover, she distinguishes between different kinds of cosmopolitanism: on the one hand, the cultural-linguistic one of San Pedro, on the other, the political one of the world. Given that we know the end point, of Kochiyama in Harlem and its insurgent Blackness, it is not too much of a stretch to build a trajectory toward a more modern cosmopolitanism.

Through her many moves—physical, political, and philosophical—Kochiyama is very much a Japanese American subject. Of course, this was first established, cruelly, in San Pedro, where the FBI suspected Kochiyama's father of treason just after the bombing of Pearl Harbor and imprisoned him. He died just after being released in 1942, and then Kochiyama and the rest of her family were taken to a camp and interned for three years.⁶⁴ In reflecting on the trauma of those experiences, Kochiyama is alive to comparison: "I see the parallel between the way African Americans were treated in the segregated South and the way Japanese Americans were evacuated and relocated."⁶⁵ In a sense, then, so much personal history and self-imagining inform what is possible in any exchange, and that psychic truth preceded Kochiyama's even stepping foot in Harlem while also shaping her experience there.

Not surprisingly, given what Malcolm X meant for the world, their relationship had an outsize importance for her. In 1963, Kochiyama approached him in a Brooklyn courthouse to discuss ideas about integration after they had both attended a Congress of Racial Equality (CORE) protest—a politically intentional rather than serendipitous encounter. Kochiyama continued the conversation, writing letters to Malcolm X, and he responded by sending postcards to her and her family from Africa. She gives this exchange a deeper expression in a chapter of her memoir that returns readers to her Harlem apartment, a space where the domestic and the public could meet, and where she explored the complex currents of racial identity in intimate terms. Though she was both insider (Harlem resident) and outsider (non-Black), Kochiyama foregrounds her Japanese-ness as she recounts facilitating a reception for writers who had survived the atomic bomb and were arguing against nuclear proliferation as part of the Hiroshima/Nagasaki World Peace Study Mission. Indicating that movements between different forms of racialization are never seamless, Kochiyama delicately points out in the 2004 autobiography that she and the others were uncertain about whether Malcolm X would accept an invitation to attend. But earlier, in a 1972 interview, Kochiyama was even more direct about the difficulty of relation and identification, recalling a rawer emotional experience: "Why would he go to a strange place and to an Asian home?"[66]

In Kochiyama's telling, such anxieties were put to rest by Malcolm X himself, who also seemed invested in crossing over to, embracing, and being changed by difference. He did come to the reception and described to the assembled group how he had read Asian history while in prison and become convinced of the comparison between the colonizations of Africa and Asia. In this fashioning, he found a fulcrum of shared political territory with Asian American activists, saying that "the struggle of Vietnam is the struggle of the whole Third World: the struggle against colonialism, neocolonialism, and imperialism."[70] If the *Life* magazine photo communicated one-way movement, from Kochiyama to Malcolm X, it bears emphasis that in a Harlem apartment, an "Asian home" no less, we can see a kind of reciprocity, movement from politicized Japanese-ness to and through Blackness, as well as from African American subjectivity through anticolonial and anti-imperial projects in Africa and Asia.

The cross-culturality of Malcolm X's Black internationalism went back years before that moment. It is worth remembering that when he arrived in Harlem in 1943, he had already had a familial experience with Pan-Africanism. And in 1950 before he left prison, he had written a letter to Harry Truman opposing the Korean War, one early instance of his opposition to U.S. interventions in Asia.[67] A trip to Mecca and travels across northern and sub-Saharan Africa constituted another field of influence, in which we can see a racial politics that would have to accommodate heterogeneity and alliance. No doubt Malcolm X had read works by other political thinkers such as W. E. B. DuBois, who much earlier in the century had touted solidarity between Asian and Black peoples.[68] When this expansive perspective came into contact with Kochiyama's, the effect was to globalize Harlem, too, taking a space often rendered as peripheral to the nation, to world capitalism, and to geopolitical developments, and remaking it into a central site for the modern political imagination.[69]

But Malcolm X's commitment to the particularities of Blackness resonated for Kochiyama; as she notes admiringly, he "always stressed things like, if you don't know who you are and where you come from, meaning your heritage and history, how can you know in which direction to go?"[70] In fact, all of Kochiyama's representations of Malcolm X encompass the fundamental and productive tension between difference and sameness within Blackness. So when she writes about how Black history and politics shaped her own subjectivity, she is expressing affiliation but also engagement, subjectively, in dialogue. Instead of flattening the landscape, Kochiyama's experience in Harlem only sharpened a sensibility that echoed what Harris has described: "It's a threshold into wholeness. It means one faction of humanity discovers itself in another, not losing its culture but deepening itself. One culture gains from another; both sides benefit from opening themselves to a new universe . . . you can advance, see things you never saw before, move out of boundaries that have been a prison."[71] Herein, then, the interpretive distance between roots and routes is collapsed.[72] By the time Kochiyama circulated her memoir she was already a canonical hero of Asian American history. Her exchange with Malcolm X adds another textual valence, of two legendary political figures coming together, their pasts and perhaps their futures being tracked in conversation.

The space of minoritization in which Kochiyama's and Malcolm X's exchange took shape is more than backdrop: its constitution directs an approach to the encounter. Harlem may have accommodated peoples that were disempowered and rendered as other in a range of societies, but it cannot be considered a minority space, as Blackness has shaped a majority population, with major symbolic effects. And yet the core term "minor" is especially generative for conceiving of cultural and political forms, from "minor literature" to "minor transnationalism."[73] Such formulations critique hegemonic projects and point to lateral, sideways perspectives on relationships among peoples who have been disempowered and rendered as other in a range of societies.[74] Resulting engagements might also be illuminated with the critical category of diaspora, to account for histories of displacement and identifications outside of the nation-state. Many versions of the latter, including Paul Gilroy's Black Atlantic, challenge narratives of modernity and race itself.[75] Even further, those associations cut through other categories: the broader "Harlem" and regionally specific "East Harlem" or "West Harlem" may all signify ideas and experiences that extend far beyond geographic coordinates.

With an eye to the many important debates on spatiality—its production and representation throughout the social sciences and humanities—*Cross-Cultural Harlem* foregrounds racialization.[76] But this book's consideration of race shifts weight to the interpretive and political resistance of the exchanges among minoritized peoples. And attending specifically to the minoritization of and in Harlem—political, cultural, economic, social—reorders the coordinates, such that Harlem becomes central to broader narratives in which it has often been rendered as marginal. What would it mean to suggest that Harlem and its encounters—which have been at the edges of so many discourses and formations—say something deeply significant about twentieth- and twenty-first-century global cultural diversity? At the very least, the spatiality produced geographically, socially, and affectively by cross-cultural Harlem develops a theory that helps us approach other cases. That is to say, as a place where racialized and ethnic subjects together constitute a majority, Harlem offers lessons on the multiplicity of an alternative modernity.[77]

HARLEM AS METHOD: SOCIAL LIFE, REPRESENTATION, AND TRANSLATION

Just as the cross-cultural makes porous the boundaries of identity formation, it also breaks down divides between disciplinary techniques. I have looked in particular to conceptions of exchange that have been able to hold together social and imaginative modes that often exist in separated areas of critical thought and practice (in the social sciences on the one hand and literary and cultural studies on the other). And therein I have found instructions for the method of *Cross-Cultural Harlem*, and for the method that Harlem itself can offer. The Caribbean that inspires cross-culturality also has its political struggles, national–state projects, and discursive (and oppressive) regimes of containment in the form of racialization and racism. All these facts "on the ground" express a recursive relationship to the past as well as a vision of the future. Wilson Harris frequently noted that his own wildly imaginative fiction was the logical outcome of and a vehicle for a theorization of culture.[78] A similar kind of mutual mediation constitutes the Harlem that this book seeks to illuminate—it would simply be impossible to think about life there without invoking the myth, symbol, and imaginary of this legendary place. At its simplest, stories of Harlem, those that appear in forms such as novels or films or that are told through political solidarities or represented by major cultural formations such as the Harlem Renaissance, have made people feel a certain way. Discourses, ideas, and images develop affective maps based in Harlem's neighborhood blocks. Often bearing little resemblance to either planners' blueprints for urban life or critics' understandings of the boundaries of identity and community, these living maps create meaning not only for Harlem residents, but also for those in worlds beyond.

Harlem offers different ways of observing, interpreting, and imagining: it compels interdisciplinary method.[79] This is more than a *protocol* brought to the wide set of cultural forms to address how the power dynamics inherent in social, even physicalized structures such as bounded community enclaves or maps intersect with the expressions of difference and hierarchy in aesthetic expression.[80] More to the point, this critical reading practice is a methodological *response* to the Harlem stories of this book, the engagements and exchanges across communities, in and through categories that cannot remain segregated. Specific chapters will elaborate how these stories operate through some generic conventions and implode others and how, above all, they point to the basic inextricability of representation and social life. Another way of thinking about the shift made here is through a critique of the referentiality that draws a line from an object to representation, which has informed even some rigorous works on literary environments and cultural history. In discussions of minority or subaltern cultures, we often see a compulsion to realism: a novel by an African American writer is seen to describe social facts of Black populations or postcolonial fiction to contain political allegories.[81] Scholars have challenged these tendencies, arguing for the autonomy and creative freedom of those literatures.[82] Similar issues emerge especially for representation that must contend with the proliferation of social scientific discourse on the urgent realities of city life. But here a commitment to maintaining the contingency of form may lead us to something more open, even unpredictable: what Harris referred to as the "unfinished genesis of the imagination."[83]

This book's ambition to capture the lived and imagined worlds of Harlem confronts an always-debated ethnographic impulse. Methods appropriate to anthropology and cultural geography—narrative description, participant observation, the tracking of movements through multiple sites and temporalities—can help us to understand aspects of Harlem stories.[84] But rather than creating knowledge of peoples or descriptions of where and how they live, I set out a different kind of ethnography, one driven by a hermeneutic rather than a community. Part of what has often eluded the "community study," and what this book develops, is a keen attention to shifting internal and external boundaries to which a set of crossings are articulated: a relationship to an unstable material and symbolic presence. Thus my own assembly indicates critical-conceptual choices rather than an appraisal of which meaning-making practices figure most prominently in social life. And the texts, figures, and events critique narrower definitions of place and representation.[85] The writers Langston Hughes, Claude McKay, and Piri Thomas saw and interpreted Harlem in their storytelling, and politician Vito Marcantonio conveyed fine-grained understandings of his congressional constituencies throughout his speeches and participation in solidaristic formations. One might also think about how collectivities, organized around identities such as Blackness or through enclave formations such as El Barrio process social experiences of racialization (and containment) and dreams of transcendence in the forms of artistic expressions, movements for particular causes, and community histories. So, putting

AN INTRODUCTION TO HARLEM

our feet on the ground—the convention of the engaged researcher—may mean paying attention to a range of echoes and disagreements between the written text and other authorized narratives, plans for space, cultural canons, and political performances.

As I have gathered a range of materials (both "data" and "texts") that emerge from place-making practices, I have had my own relationship to Harlem. It is no surprise that I have returned again and again to neighborhood blocks for inspiration and resources (if not revelations). This project, like others that invoke lived experience, must be self-conscious about implicatedness, in a space that is constantly under a gaze from outside with regard to those who are aware of that dynamic. These dilemmas were especially vivid at the very beginning of a "Historic Harlem" walking tour when children on a playground yelled at the assembled group: "Welcome to Harlem—these are black kids."[86] Not surprisingly, the tensions of racialized life and a high level of consciousness about gentrification have radiated through social relations for many years. On the same day, as I walked to the meeting place for that tour near the Schomburg, I overheard a woman remarking to her companion, "They want to move us out of here." Was she speaking in general or about my presence there? One of the first conversations I had when conducting research for this book was with a South Asian woman who had moved to West Harlem in the mid-1990s amid protests about the scope and content of economic development in the neighborhood. She insisted that she was not a gentrifier, that she was politically, even racially, affiliated with longtime African American and Dominican residents, and yet, of course, it was *so* difficult to make that known in daily life, walking down the street or in a shop. Her relationship to the contours of minoritization mirrored some of my own. When I have talked to people in Harlem, I have been aware of myself as a racially ambiguous subject: not African American, nor Puerto Rican, but also not white. When Spanish has been spoken to me casually in various spaces, with assumptions based on complexion, and I have answered in that language, the danger of misrecognition is close at hand. And I began my research when I worked at Columbia University, yet another affiliation that complicated my presence in Harlem.

AN INTRODUCTION TO HARLEM

How, indeed, are we to establish solidarities and identifications? One answer lies in how the first-person "I" and "we" are employed, with varying levels of authority, reflexivity, and collectivity. It is clear that many mistakes can be made with both the individual perspective in autoethnography and the shared assumptions of the collective critics.[87] My own response related to method has, again, to do with the kinds of stories discussed here. They are chosen and presented as occasions for interpretation, and so the "I" does read and reflect on Harlem. But cross-cultures extend beyond individuals into some murkier philosophical territory of democratic participation—"we" are all part of this world of exchange. The points that Harris made about becoming transformed by difference emerged from presence, too, though he might not have termed it as such; he was a land surveyor and, as he mapped the interior of Guyana, he interacted with a range of peoples. Other ideas about crossings, relations, and more, I would argue, have developed out of a desire to understand something of human experience.

Any account of Harlem, even of an overwhelming present, cannot be fully understood without a rigorous attention to structuring pasts, and any method that Harlem compels must thus integrate a subtle and complicated sense of history. Experiences of slavery, imperialism, segregation, economic depression, and/or cultural struggle press on every moment of articulation; as memory, they saturate individual subjectivity and community identities of place, not only when they are consciously excavated. The cross-culturality of any text's border-crossing is situated in a particular set of contemporary conditions, but also exudes the power of Harlem's pasts. So *how* this book is historical differs from other formal histories of Harlem. *Cross-Cultural Harlem* reads residents' anxiety that Harlem is experiencing a transformation that could lead to extinction back in time to point to a political-economic concern of many periods. In fact, this is a way of relating to place that thematizes every moment of social life. In an introductory essay to a 2003 collection of photographs on gentrification by Alice Attie, significantly titled *Harlem on the Verge*, Robin Kelley recalls that in 1925, at the height of the Harlem Renaissance, James Weldon Johnson asked in an article for *Survey*, "Are the Negroes going to be able to hold Harlem?"[88]

AN INTRODUCTION TO HARLEM

And a character in Nella Larsen's 1929 novel *Passing* remarks, with astonishing prescience, about white people coming in hordes to Harlem to socialize: "Pretty soon the colored people won't be allowed in at all, or will have to sit in Jim Crow sections."[89]

This perspective is about the past, a concern of history, yes, but even more than that, it emphasizes how change is processed. We may understand this historical imagination as marked by a temporality somewhat different from that of dominant accounts, or at least fired by events and movements that exist at the periphery. We can read Langston Hughes not just vis-à-vis his major works in the Harlem Renaissance, but also through his writings about traveling to visit his father in Mexico and his awareness of interethnic tensions under the surface of representations of community in place. Most certainly the overwhelming experience and repetitive practices of race destabilize assumptions about history and the creative process: no fact or articulation can be untethered from a much longer in-formation collectivity, however fragile and fractured. And the archive that is drawn on to begin to address that and other topics must necessarily be conceived of in expanded fashion. There is no doubt that a study focusing on the novels of Harlem would yield similar insights about the porousness of form and the possibilities of encounter, but this project's consideration of materials that self-present with less apparent closure provides what I understand to be a more direct path into interdisciplinary questions about the inseparability of representation and social life.

The spaces, texts, and figures of *Cross-Cultural Harlem* thus ride a broadly historical arc, explicitly engaging key moments during the 1930s and continuing through to the present. They also access the deep memory of earlier migrations from the U.S. South and other countries. My choice not to begin with the Harlem Renaissance and rather to focus on works that came afterward stems in part, first, from a sense that so much important scholarship already exists on that period, and, second, a desire to outline the contours of modernity (and postmodernity) in Harlem as a consequence of the dramatic changes of the 1920s.[90] I use the term modern here, and throughout the book, to effectively put Harlem at the center of debates about twentieth-century economic, political, and cultural formations, and also to contest the idea that the experience we have of this urban space, that everything is changing, is not original. Hughes's cross-cultural imagining in the 1930s may in fact enable a reconsideration of the Harlem Renaissance, not only to suggest that it was more multiethnic and multiracial than ordinarily thought, but also to pursue *how* it was a Black project, to engage in a different way with influential discussions of the Black–white encounters of that period, for example.[91] While identity does not disappear from view, it is certainly complicated and interrogated, especially in those instances when overrelied on for interpretation.

Harlem as method, shaped by ideas of cross-culturality and a sensibility of the global, entails interpreting across and through multiple modes of the literary, ethnographic, and historical in a way that could be called translational. Such an operation is based on an understanding of language as encompassing more than linguistic systems. This allows a scholar to capture a broader range of expression, more akin to what Mikhail Bakhtin famously termed heteroglossia.[92] If Bakhtin was specifically concerned with the work of the novel, I wish to suggest here that the idea of heteroglossia travels well, its proposal of simultaneity and varied forms of expression a helpful way to frame the more interdisciplinary project of *Cross-Cultural Harlem*. Practices of translation, too, are refined when we ask what language depicts and whether it is possible to move fluidly and fluently across differences of convention, authority, or style.

Throughout this book's chapters, I ask whether there is a place-based vernacular that could be seen as not a subset or version of a language but, instead, a set of expressions for intimacies and conflicts based in knowing and communication—the materials of translation—to express the fullness of presence. Congressman Marcantonio's political addresses in Spanish, for example, may have been imperfect, integrating many Italian words and grammatical constructions and spoken with a heavy Italian accent, but the understanding he communicated to and received from his Spanish-speaking listeners emerged out of solidarities forged in the cultures and politics of 1930s and 1940s East Harlem, not least of which was a vision of an independent Puerto Rico.[93] Translations thus may have been signaled in the first instance by language use, but involved epistemological and social phenomena in a city-space articulated to other registers of region, nation, and globe.

STORIES OF HARLEM

All of the contested points of a Harlem racial geography enable the organization, search, and retrieval of information for residents and interpreters alike. Memories (both feeling and insight) of place can only be accessed through recalling them in a particular way. Territorial markers or castings of peoplehood freeze a moment for ideological effects, which include commemoration of loss, establishment of community, or delineation of belonging. But the discourses about them are dynamic—a given narrative of the Harlem Renaissance as constituting of a kind of Blackness, for example, or a local neighborhood meaning various things to people all over the world. Represented pasts can be said to be in our present.[94] At play here is the force of how people narratively relate to a history thematized by transformation. Ask anyone to describe a place that he or she knows intimately and you will hear of change, that one group of people has moved out because another has moved in, how buildings that used to be important are no longer there, how the texture of life has become less recognizable. It is to be reminded of Michel de Certeau's dictum that "what the map cuts up, the story cuts across."[95]

Culture is front and center in popular representations of Harlem, as well as those of this book. For so many people, Harlem conjures up the arts, literature, and music. That is one reason that the Harlem Renaissance resonates for both inhabitants and observers, living in popular memory as encapsulating a relationship to place.[96] No doubt important writers and musicians have found great inspiration in the neighborhood blocks, especially but not only for their close association with Blackness and other ethnic and racial formations. But the resulting forms—expressive, representational, symbolic designs meaningful to those who have lived and worked in Harlem as well as to their relatives, comrades, correspondents, and critics abroad (both in other countries and simply beyond the bounds of a formal geography)—are cultural in the complex manner that scholars and critics in the British cultural studies tradition, beginning with Raymond Williams and continuing into the present, have clearly established.[97] Therein lies another explicit iteration of the interdisciplinarity of *Cross-Cultural Harlem*'s stories, which capture both the aesthetic and the everyday of this place.[98]

Stories are associated with literary studies, but in organizing my own inquiry, I wish to highlight what can slip under the radar of discipline-bound, as well as community- and geography-bound, scholarship. I am interested in more than the forms of narration, character development, and plot, or even setting. The stories of this book do not present as artifacts or repositories of meaning, but instead open up epistemes. In charting the movements, crossings, and encounters that have remade cartographic coordinates, not only of the place we call Harlem but of all places, real and symbolic, I engage with de Certeau again, and his reminder that "every story is a travel story—a spatial practice."[99] The language of travel enables more interpretive movements across familiar literary divides of realism and lyricism or, even more importantly for Harlem, which lives on the street and in the imagination, nonfiction and fiction as flexible resources.

The frames of the chapters of *Cross-Cultural Harlem* can be named by genres—the fictional short story, the sociological story, the political story, and the autobiographical story—though genres can only partially enfold the boundary-crossing cultures of Harlem to which they give life. The representative case of Yuri Kochiyama and Malcolm X illustrates as much.[100] And so all of the following chapters of this book will manifest a consciousness of the limits of any single form as they pursue the production, consumption, and circulation of Harlem as idea and site. As such, they engage what I would maintain are both social *and* literary questions, and they draw for "evidence" on observations and conversations, unfinished works, and documents from archives, as well as published materials. There is no question that a wealth of stories of Harlem exist to choose from, but I have highlighted a number that challenge ideas about race and identity while being especially alive to the experience of deep habitation. Together, these chapters build a multimodal inquiry into how peoples have lived together and how a consequent relationality has defined Harlem over time, into the present.

The first chapter, "Langston Hughes's Harlem: 'Spanish Blood' and Geographies of Blackness," focuses our attention on the possibility of an imagined intimate encounter between "Black" and "Spanish" Harlems. Hughes's critically understudied 1934 short story "Spanish Blood" depicted a mixed African American–Puerto Rican character navigating the complicated racial divides of Harlem. "Spanish Blood" can be understood as emerging partly from Hughes's own travels, linguistic fluencies, and consciousness of his position as a Black writer. And in opening up interesting transferences between author and protagonist, the story invites readers to engage in cultural translation as they move among various represented social and regional worlds. Its characters and Hughes himself effectively ask who and what Black and Spanish are, and thus interrogate the organization and ownership of space in Harlem. The publication of "Spanish Blood" only slightly predated a 1935 riot in Harlem that began after a shop manager accused a teenager named Lino Rivera of stealing. The ethnicity of the boy was occluded by African American protesters and disavowed by Puerto Ricans, and so a contemplation of the story of an Afro-Latino who sits uneasily in the world of Harlem generates questions about Hughes's broad ethnographic imagination and what he understood the relationship of fiction and experience to be.

Chapter 2, "Mapping Place: The Facts and Fictions of Claude McKay's Harlem Imaginary" considers McKay's representation of place in *Harlem: Negro Metropolis*, a work that I argue should be seen as a Harlem *story* like the others of this book, constructed with passion and perspective, exceeding boundaries of space and time, as well as the formalistic limits of the "sociological study." This chapter is deeply concerned with how, in a text hidden in plain sight—like "Spanish Blood," *Harlem: Negro Metropolis* has not garnered much attention from literary critics or social scientists—multiple modes of seeing, interpreting, and narrating combine to develop a Black geography for Harlem. *Harlem: Negro Metropolis* vividly reveals how a racial consciousness, misunderstood by some of McKay's contemporaries as separatist, is built from exchanges that are remarkably open to difference and contestation. Thus this chapter helps to elucidate the cross-culturality of *Cross-Cultural Harlem* to be not only about ethnic diversity, but even more so a deeper affect of place.

Chapter 3, "Crossings at Home and in the World: Vito Marcantonio's Working-Class Cosmopolitanism," moves the discussion to less literary but still imaginative dimensions in the politics of an Italian American congressman from East Harlem. Marcantonio represented the area from the middle 1930s until 1951. As a working-class socialist politician, he brought a special kind of attention to Harlem and also, remarkably, crossed its ethnic and racial divides by relating to and feeling for peoples who were not like him. Here, the larger argument of the book can be understood through expressions of *solidarity* born of working-class cosmopolitanism and left-wing critique. This chapter considers a range of discourses—public speeches, constituent letters, newspaper coverage, and interviews—as well as a number of historical events that elaborate how this figure lived multiplicity. I suggest that Marcantonio's linguistic fluencies enabled a practice of cultural translation in place. With the exception of one trip to Puerto Rico to support nationalists there, he never traveled outside of the United States. Unlike those of Hughes or McKay, Marcantonio's movements seem to be deeply circumscribed within limited neighborhood blocks; nonetheless they similarly embody a global transgression of ethnic and racial boundaries.

Identity experiments are contemplated in Chapter 4, "Selfhood and Difference: Piri Thomas and Aladdin on the Streets of Harlem." Piri Thomas published *Down These Mean Streets* in 1967, and over time this autobiographical work has come to represent the gritty life of the barrio and Puerto Rican experience. But even more than that, this chapter argues, it brings to light various crossings and mixtures that defy easy categorization and that also reveal the limits of Harlem's racial geography. Aladdin, a Bangladeshi comedian from East Harlem, might be seen as an inheritor of Thomas's cultural imagination: he performs lives on the stage that further reorder coordinates of space and time by creatively drawing on locality, religious-racial formation, and diaspora. For these self-styled outsider figures who have been witness to many important political junctures, including the Civil Rights and Nuyorican movements, literary censorship campaigns, gentrification, and post-9/11 nationalism, the streets have enabled dwelling and belonging. The project of tying selfhood to place in life stories also has us rethink forms through the performative nature of the written autobiography or the dramatic one-man play.

Even though each of these chapters has its own logic, together they form a constellation, assembling ideas in relation to one another to understand different perspectives, sometimes from one ethnic or racial group or one region, other times in combinations.[101] *Cross-Cultural Harlem*'s narrative force takes shape through a loose, even kaleidoscopic pattern of intertextuality. Hughes fictionally represents the dilemmas of identity with an Afro-Latino figure who can be seen to be speaking to the autobiographical subject that Thomas constructs in a depiction of crossing territories of Black Harlem to which McKay gave detail and life, and those works that fictionalize multiple affiliations resonate strongly with the cosmopolitan political articulations of Marcantonio in the public sphere. Another strand that acquires heft through the book has to do with an immanent critique of any unqualified celebration of cross-cultures. A predictable gendered mobility surfaces as an implicit theme across the exchanges explored here. Many instances of the cross-cultural point to a masculine genre, yet Kochiyama and her domestic home suggest an alternative at the margins. And the mother figure in "Spanish Blood," Hattie, might be read as centrally important for Hughes's imagination and evidence of a critique of the gendered formations of diaspora. The basic fact of friction accompanying intimacy is brought out if we know where to look: in the gendered mixtures of Blackness and Spanishness of "Spanish Blood," in the solidarities expressed by McKay in *Harlem: Negro Metropolis*, in Marcantonio's affiliation to Italianness and Puerto Ricanness simultaneously, in Thomas's problems with a father he cannot psychically leave behind and Alaudin "Aladdin" Ullah's changing family dynamics over time.

Some attention should be paid to the specific techniques of representation or, at the very least, to what it means to put them together. Can the devices of a fictional short story be compared to the shape-shifting possibilities of autobiographical expression? Do references in interviews with Harlem residents to quotidian "real" life employ literary modes? Answers to these sorts of questions illuminate the pauses, even ruptures, in the project of interdisciplinarity, never a seamless ride. As with any conceptual approach, this book reflects the author's inclinations and experience. As a writer, teacher, and scholar, I have moved continuously through academic disciplines: American Studies, African American studies, Asian American studies, diaspora studies, anthropology, English literature, U.S. history. Some of these have been sites of sustained activity, others mere way stations, but all of these fields, ways of organizing knowledge, have made their marks on my intellectual work and on this project.

Issues of scale are everywhere apparent in *Cross-Cultural Harlem*, as the occasions of these chapters have emerged from both centers and edges, sometimes familiarly and sometimes as the product of deeper excavation. They ask us to ponder canonicity in relation to Harlem—what figures, what literary works, what historical events, and what ideas have been crucial to the imagining of this place? The flip side of that line of inquiry has to do with how a story from the periphery, Kochiyama's and Malcolm X's exchange or Hughes's understudied story, might reveal important meanings about Harlem. This is not to jettison what came before—I cannot emphasize enough that there already exist many wonderful books on Harlem, to which *Cross-Cultural Harlem* pays homage and on which it seeks to build—but rather to expand our view with an alternative grouping and resituating of materials and foregrounding of a different approach. Most of all, from the outlining of general community and spatial formations to the deep dive into specific cultural expressions, the moves across varied views of Harlem exceed generic concerns to highlight the overarching rubric of place.

Still, without making any claims to comprehensiveness, I might ask about the status of different kinds of sources. Is being "of Harlem" to walk its streets? Is it to write about how the place makes us feel? Is it to identify with one cause or another? Scholarly investments in Harlem have a great deal to do with which materials are considered and what is foregrounded. When I have discussed this project with colleagues in literary studies. anthropology, urban studies. and African American and comparative ethnic studies, they have asked how I am going to address the Harlem that they know, in some cases the literary field, in others a place of extreme poverty or a space of aspiration. These are not simply disciplinary inclinations: they reveal the subjective nature of place. And this dilemma finds an analogue in contemporary life as inhabitants and noninhabitants alike struggle to square their hopes, dreams, and anxieties about Harlem with all the stories that give life to that level of consciousness, but also fall short in the face of what they perceive either to be "real life" or what makes sense to them.

There are many gaps, pauses, and moments for reflection in any account of who and what a place is. Narrativization itself always involves shaping, inclusion, and exclusion, almost a kind of violence to all the possibilities that did not make it in; it can also be overwhelming in its claims of totality. I hope that in *Cross-Cultural Harlem* there are spaces in which to breathe as potential exchanges open up new possibilities of interpretation. For example, if each chapter seems at first glance to concentrate on one ethnicity or form of racialization (say, Hughes's Blackness, or Marcantonio's Italianness), an attention to encounter, with otherness outside of a particular formation of identity, opens up another vector for thinking about belonging. The political project, as philosophers Deleuze and Guattari convey it, lies in explaining the consequences of flows and displacements that complicate the constitution of spaces while also building something new: deterritorialization and reterritorialization at once.[102] It is crucial to add that multiplicity does not imply completeness: While *Cross-Cultural Harlem* tells a big story, plenty has been left out. Many ethnic groups appear on the edges of the stories considered here, but do not figure prominently in the texts considered in the chapters of this book. Race and class dynamics are central to Harlem and its stories, yet I do not present a study of Harlem poverty, which other works have already done so well.[103]

Given how spatial practice has been understood to be potentially liberating, if negotiated, its story form carries ethical stakes. What we bring to places, and what we want them to be, are constitutive. The stories of this book, then, are not just about Harlem: they are the Harlem I want to convey, one built of exchanges and the power of racial history in the production of space. They comprise culture, in that expanded sense, and they do cultural work that has to do with political, economic, and psychic interests. Rendering modernity from the standpoint of difference, the stories of this book are situated in a moment defined, again and again and over time, by newness, as well as by social questions of the relationship of the individual to the community and philosophical concerns about the particular vis-à-vis the universal.

GRIEF AND HOPE: A PLACE TO BEGIN

Any story of living in difference cannot but be countered by one of dying in difference. When encountering the visual of Malcolm X's death that opened this chapter, we could not remain unaware of the complicated history of circulating images and stories of Black suffering, ranging from Frederick Douglass's recounting of the beating of his Aunt Hester to contemporary front-page pictures of Black men's brutalization and murder at the hands of the police, as well as everything in between, through various periods of representing the repression of protest movements and the persistence of racialized poverty. The challenge, as cultural historian Saidiya Hartman has put it, is to "give expression to these outrages without exacerbating the indifference to suffering that is the consequence of the benumbing spectacle."[104] Any politics in reproducing the photo must thus contend with the weight of the demise of Black men in a nation and a world—still, always—grappling with racism, while also articulating that to other forms of racial injury, another feature of the political present in which I write this book.

Even as Kochiyama's and Malcolm X's exchange draws into alignment the imperial and colonial histories that have resulted in centuries of anti-Black and anti-Asian violence, the specificity of "not-Blackness" as a "vital property in an anti-Black world," as Claire Jean Kim puts it, must give us pause.[105] We are accustomed to treating this phenomenon vis-à-vis ethnic

AN INTRODUCTION TO HARLEM

FIGURE 0.5 "From Harlem with Love: A Mural for Yuri and Malcolm," 125th Street and Old Broadway.

Photo by Kiran Klubock-Shukla.

whiteness, given the popularity of stories that feature white flight from poor urban areas, but the identities of Asians and Latinos, even when referencing racialization, have also been constituted through anti-Blackness.[106] In majority-minority Harlem, the thickness of racism's effects and disavowals needs attending to, as does the reality that no vision of Harlem is possible without Blackness at the center. Remember that Kochiyama's intense relationship was not with Harlem in general, but with Black Harlem; Blackness was a primary modality in which politics were lived for this Japanese American activist.[107]

Those who study culture are drawn to explain possibilities that offer hope, and I am no exception, as I have looked around the edges to imagine something different in the midst of uncertainty over the very future of

AN INTRODUCTION TO HARLEM

Harlem. In reconfiguring the artifact of the photo to function as far more than a flashbulb memory, I have pressed it into service as a flashpoint—one toward which histories of exchange between two racialized figures have developed, and illuminating across the occasions of *Cross-Cultural Harlem* and the current realities of Asian American, Latino, Black, and indigenous activists coming together to resist global capitalism and racism. The promise of deep presence can be grasped in a 2016 artwork by a multiracial group of political activists at West 125th Street and Old Broadway, entitled "From Harlem with Love: A Mural Project for Yuri and Malcolm." It presents only one model for solidarities and understanding, respecting difference yet alive to connection.

Cross-Cultural Harlem makes contradictions productive. James Baldwin conjured up competing and proximate affects when he wrote about his father dying in Harlem at the same time as his youngest sibling was being born on the very same avenue, "life and death so close together."[108] The figures and texts of this book echo Baldwin's interpretive challenge. Hughes enjoined his readers to imagine freedom of mobility with a mixed-race Afro-Latino character while also asking us to carry the pessimism of Black female subjectivity in the United States. Marcantonio's ability to advocate for people utterly unlike himself far away from Italian Harlem encourages, but inspires some sadness when we think about his untimely death from a heart attack (and maybe a broken political heart) at a moment when he felt defeated by the excesses of McCarthyism, on the eve of the *Brown v. Board of Education* decision. While Piri Thomas may have reveled in expansive ideas about belonging, he also displayed frustrations about the constraints of identity when to be understood as simultaneously Black and Puerto Rican he had to scream at his interviewer.[109] Thus what will follow in these pages are reverberations of Kochiyama's reach across to a dying Malcolm X, always about opportunity and loss both.

These representations pose questions about where each of us dwells in difference and place, and may even provoke a desire to identify: Have we felt something like that before, can we imagine ourselves there, which of those experience resonate and, importantly, how is all of that shaped by who we are? To lean on Fredric Jameson's evocative term for a practice that is at once phenomenological, critical, and political, we are always engaging in "cognitive mapping."[110] And so my own writing of this book has been thoroughly emplaced. I began this project when I lived and worked in Morningside Heights in New York—a border area where the conflicts of belonging are especially tense and contain troubled relationships between poor and minority communities and the ever-expanding institution of Columbia University—and I completed it in Charlottesville, Virginia, which in 2017 gained notoriety as the site of white nationalist protests and became an international symbol of racial trouble in the United States.[111]

Harlem and Charlottesville do not pose exactly the same kinds of questions about how to inhabit difference, but they do offer some shared concerns about race and nation, about who is to live and die and where people can reside. This particular juxtaposition is not one that social theorists such as Walter Benjamin, Henri Lefebvre, or even Manuel Castells or Marshall Berman would have imagined given their foci, in the first instance on European urban modernity and in the second on major Western cities such as New York and London.[112] But taking globalization seriously means understanding that flows of all kinds have remade the urban and diversified various regions. After bringing ideas from the Caribbean to Harlem, we might consider moving them to the smaller city of Charlottesville, and after that to towns and municipalities in other areas of the United States (as well as other countries). Charlottesville has been made by a Southern history of plantation slavery and Jim Crow, but it is also now being shaped by migrants and refugees from all over the world, in various states of legality and belonging; African American, African, Asian, Latino, and Middle Eastern peoples regularly cross urban and suburban spaces to give new meanings to the region. And even when we go to the more rural eastern shore of Virginia, where former governor Ralph Northam grew up and infamously posed for a yearbook photo in blackface, we will see active discussions of anti-Black racism and concurrent struggles for cultural membership by Latino farmworkers. Interrogations of big and small places and different (and shared) pasts of race, class, and development will only enrich the inquiry into social formation and encourage us to think about where we are situated in a range of cultural geographies, anxiously and hopefully and always differentially. Accompanying that inquiry must be the very problematization of "we," to acknowledge that different voices and peoples cannot inhabit that same narrative and emplacing perspective.

In addition to theory, method, and materials, every book has values, and this one's lie in cross-culturality. *Cross-Cultural Harlem* was inspired not by an impulse for inclusiveness, but by the realization that when I faced Harlem, the choice between Blackness and whiteness was insufficient for a place that was made by so many diasporic, migrant, ethnic, and racial formations, variegated versions of whiteness included. Capturing the dense majority-minority affect seemed important as a response to divisive discourses that engulfed both scholarly and popular meanings for the place. Though cross-culturality can never operate in some abstract utopian realm—it must contain failures and disappointments, especially when whiteness or anti-Blackness or anti-Semitism has been wedged between groups—it does offer instructive models. Encounters on the pages that follow remind us that grief and hope are essential for political change, and that Harlem can be not just a past but also a future. In the midst of its potential extinction, these stories ask about life for Harlem and the project of ethical living in difference itself. This is to say that there is a great deal at stake for all of us in seeing Harlem as cross-cultural.

1

LANGSTON HUGHES'S HARLEM

"Spanish Blood" and Geographies of Blackness

Like so many Black writers before and since, Langston Hughes waxed eloquent on how important Harlem was to him. In his 1940 autobiography *The Big Sea*, he wrote, "I was in love with Harlem long before I got there,"[1] conjuring up the symbolic power of and personal (always racial) attachment to this iconic site.[2] A deep investment in place marks so much of his poetry and prose. Always dogged in his pursuit of complexity, Hughes represented how people found their footing in shifting maps of social experience, those that had been made for them and those they might be able to shape and reshape. That sort of racial geographic imagination makes Hughes—a writer synonymous with Harlem and yet so attentive to its fragile lives—a particularly helpful guide for the spaces that *Cross-Cultural Harlem* seeks to bring into presence. The current chapter explores how Harlem's cross-cultures are given depth in Hughes's 1934 "Spanish Blood." In this remarkable short story, a mixed-race (Puerto Rican and Black) protagonist and his southern-U.S. Black mother vociferously debate race and belonging in a city-space that promises all sorts of boundary-crossing freedoms, yet also polices identity. "Spanish Blood" asks what

FIGURE 1.1 Langston Hughes in Harlem.

Photo by Arnold Newman Properties/Getty Images.

Harlem means for diasporic Black subjects, and in just ten pages effectively treats the big issues of territory, difference, and modernity.

Through the vast body of scholarly work about Hughes, "Spanish Blood" has received little attention, partly because critics may not know just where to put it.³ It does not seem to provide direct access to Black experience in the way that some of his other works do, nor does it explicitly describe places outside the nation—thus it is caught between categories of "U.S." and "global" literature. That interpretive limitation has something to do with how the global and the local have been seen as distinct fields, and also with how diaspora may in some formulations seem to deemphasize dwelling, the main preoccupation of "Spanish Blood." But Blackness itself has broken down such oppositions, as Valerie Babb notes: "The world at large has always been a concern of writers of African descent. In their literary record, engagement in a world without borders was essential to their psychic and cultural survival as they addressed the experiences of a people who were coercively encouraged to see their worlds as no bigger than a field or a house."⁴ Hughes's world-making captured those apparent contradictions—expanses and strictures, freedom and oppression.[5] And his "Spanish Blood," on the canonical edges though it might be, gets to the heart of the matters of its time and place: race in late-1920s and early-1930s Harlem.

As a representative figure of Blackness as well as someone who confronted its instability, Hughes was alive to the shifting meanings of Harlem. He developed a mixed-race protagonist in "Spanish Blood" who compelled readers to work through mutually mediated and spatialized Spanishness and Blackness. The story's first line zeroes in on the complicated project: "In that amazing city of Manhattan where people are forever building things anew . . . there lived a young Negro called Valerio Gutierrez whose mother was a Harlem laundress but whose father was a Puerto Rican sailor."[6] The "but" of the sentence gives us pause, to wonder about a putative opposition between Harlem and Puerto Rico, between the emplaced work of a laundress and the continuous travels of a sailor. Less on the surface immediately, but coursing through the rest of the story is an uncertainty about whether Valerio is Black in U.S. terms (a Negro), or in other, Spanish/Latin American fashion, *negro*, and most of all where and when those possibilities meet, if at all. Hughes here offers the figure of the Afro Latino to help navigate that thicket of complex identifications, prefiguring by several decades much important critical work in Latinx and Black diasporic studies.[7] Moreover, "Spanish Blood" brings to the surface the consciousness of a mother who is a Black woman, with a historical-experiential vantage point that develops an alternative geography, what Katherine McKittrick has called "a different way of knowing and writing the social world . . . to expand how the production of space is achieved across terrains of domination."[8]

Given that Harlem comprised Black subjects and others who also felt liminal to a variety of social and class formations, it could paradoxically be a center for edginess and movement. An experience of being an outsider was what it meant to inhabit a new space, always in development, to engage with the place of Harlem. And the broader context for the writing and circulation of "Spanish Blood" in 1934 was multiplicity. Harlem was Black American, to be sure, but also populated by Jewish, Italian, and Latin

American migrants (and their children), so that ethnic crossing was central to the navigation of neighborhood blocks and community life there. With clubs and other settings in which racial mixing and gay sexuality thrived, Harlem hosted performances and explorations not altogether authorized by the dominant culture. What Amiri Baraka later called a "BangClash"[9] of racial and ethnic groups sitting side by side was a fitting approach to Harlem, certainly as compared to any social scientific model existing in Hughes's time.[10]

How did Hughes come to tell *this* story, imagine this world, titled with "Spanish Blood"? First, the author had visited Cuba and spent considerable time in Spain supporting antifascist political efforts there. He also spoke Spanish fluently, the result of (and producing, we might imagine) another kind of feeling and identification.[11] Second, a vexed attachment to the Americas percolated through moments of Hughes's early life, in one of which his father had moved to Mexico. That configuration of a father abroad with a mother at home in the United States rather resembles the one that faces the protagonist of "Spanish Blood." Indeed, a familial dynamic undergirds the fictional story, with concerns about the difficulties of globality embedded in the relationship between the characters of Valerio and his mother, Hattie, as she evinces the specter of loss of Blackness and her son to forces over which she has little control. While it is the responsibility of critics to separate the author and his literary protagonist, we cannot deny that transferences shape an imaginary, and the one between Hughes and Valerio provides fruitful analytical echoes. If masculinity provides one obvious axis of projection, Hughes's elevation of the Black woman's consciousness in Hattie may indicate a differently gendered identification.

The density of Spanishness, on which "Spanish Blood" pivots, offered perfect fodder for Hughes, always preoccupied by the ideological and social force of racialized histories and peoples. Spanish in the story doubly signifies as a global term, first and most obviously designating a space outside of the United States and second, referring to a local set of migrants and peoples from elsewhere. In early twentieth-century Harlem, cultural and political formations that could be called "Spanish" included those of

Puerto Ricans, Cubans, Mexicans, and Central and South Americans. Notably, this heterogeneous Spanishness structurally mirrored Blackness, which comprised African Americans, West Indians, and Africans. If Spanishness expanded the possibilities for identification in Harlem, it also, in a more diasporic register, opened out into the Americas, to its linguistic and racial mixtures and its histories. It also linked Harlem itself to worlds outside the boundaries of its geographic territory and, of course, to continental experience that exceeded nation. The Atlantic slave trade, the long half-life of colonial labor arrangements, and the sexualized and gendered effects of those geopolitical crossings could not be ignored in any discussion of Harlem or its migrants from the Americas. Furthermore, the invocation of Puerto Rico and Puerto Rican peoples in "Spanish Blood" highlighted yet another specific form of political connectedness: the imperial-colonial relationship to the United States.

Even when engaged with elsewhere, "Spanish Blood" is fundamentally about Blackness, and the crucial question that Hughes poses therein, and with which this chapter wrestles, is what *kind* of Blackness that is and where it lies. The first line of the story may literalize the opposition between locality and globality (the "Harlem laundress" vs the "Puerto Rican sailor"), but it serves as an opening into a deeper inquiry about subjectivity in between those poles. The limits and possibilities of Blackness could only acquire clearer shapes as they came in contact with other kinds of difference, in a majority-minority space where there were a range of negotiations on the ground between and among subjects who were racialized (or ethnicized) vis-à-vis dominant political and economic arrangements. The material and imaginative geography of Blackness was worlded, this is to say, from within and from outside.[12] Hughes's fictions of place worked through these basic ontological and epistemological dilemmas. We see that not only in "Spanish Blood" but also in his Simple stories over the course of twenty-three years,[13] and in the 1951 *Montage of a Dream Deferred* to which this chapter turns later, among many other works.[14]

Disagreements about race and place in the dialogue of "Spanish Blood" may at first seem to elevate the freedoms that the character of Valerio models as he moves through Harlem landscapes at will, but a Puerto Rican

"Spanishness" lies within Blackness, in the body that he inhabits. And the always-present Hattie represents more than U.S. Blackness: she raises the specter of embedded transatlantic histories. Thus the iconic conflict between U.S. racial minorities and immigrants is undone, reminding us that it would be much too simplistic to cast the subjective (or political) tension as one between the global and the local; nor can it be a choice between parochialism and expansiveness. Such spatial registers or affective identifications are never mutually exclusive, as this story expresses again and again in its dramatization of many different visions of Harlem and different ways of being Black in the world.

Still, the deep anxiety about crossing that runs through "Spanish Blood" testifies to the high stakes for questions of Blackness, and for Hughes himself. Critics may not have focused on this story, but we know it was important for its author, not only because it was part of the widely circulated 1952 collection *Laughing to Keep from Crying*, but also because he seemed to plan for it to be included in the first volume of his autobiography, *The Big Sea*. Both the intention and the missed appearance make an argument for seeing "Spanish Blood" as central to Hughes's thinking. Active discussions of Blackness in Harlem reached a crescendo in the years of the Harlem Renaissance and afterward, and never far from the minds of artists, cultural figures, and readers were transnational frames: African roots, diasporic solidarities such as Garveyism, and exchanges across Europe. Hughes, a master depicter of interiority, threw his hat into the ring of those public debates by turning to the intimacies of domestic and social life and the fine-grained detail of relationships therein. And so, in *The Big Sea*, a work so interested in racial subjectivity and family at home and abroad, a piece of short fiction about the depth of feeling for a mixed-race protagonist and other Black residents of Harlem could not but also reflect back on Hughes's own cosmopolitan life.

That jumble of the personal, the political, the fictional, and the social manifests in Hughes's promiscuous dabbling in forms: he wrote poetry, novels, plays, nonfiction, and more. He was very explicit about the porous border between fiction and experience, saying about the famous "everyman" character, Jesse B. Semple, that he had created: "The facts are that these tales are about a great many people . . . it is impossible to live in Harlem and not know at least a hundred Simples."[15] And Hughes's claim in the draft of *The Big Sea* that "Spanish Blood" would fill out a description of Harlem night life is misleadingly modest, given what the story in its many lives brings to the surface.[16] A quasi-ethnographic impulse is there, yes, but so is a complicated baring of personal-authorial dilemmas. And yet another epistemological imbrication can be seen in how the work approaches the meaning of race, the incommensurabilities of globalism, and other philosophical questions through competing identifications with characters such as Valerio or Hattie.

Hughes takes Harlem, a paradigmatic site of race and class formation of the United States, and reconfigures it into a contested point in the Black diaspora. To ask about the relations between Puerto Ricans and African Americans in this space is not simply to invoke competition between U.S. minority and immigrant formations: it is to contemplate how the exchanges of Harlem—a lived urban cosmopolitanism—are situated in other maps. Many scholars have explored the view to Africa from Harlem, both during the Harlem Renaissance and in 1960s decolonization and 1970s Afrocentric movements, but "Spanish Blood" has us pivot in a slightly different direction, to the Americas. It is hard to miss the significance of the fact of Hughes, an African American writer who spent so much of his imaginative energy on Black Harlem, being here, representationally, in other Harlems. And we cannot forget that from the very beginning the story telescopes an intention to shift time–space registers from a node of modernity's "newness," New York, to the domestic realm. The short story is a literary genre concerned with space, particularly in its economy. Hughes presses it into service for an exploration of more open expanses.

In all these ways, "Spanish Blood" is a particularly full expression of how sophisticated and subtle a race *and* place thinker Hughes was for his time. Because, in the end, this story is not really about blood or Spanishness: it is about a contested racial geography built by encounter. It argues against essentialisms and simplified identity politics while also attesting to the deeply gendered consequences of racism. Raising the ideal of mobility alongside a sober look at what movements across continents have meant for Black peoples, "Spanish Blood" exemplifies literature's ability to bring to the fore questions of deeply felt contradiction and also, as a Harlem story, the realization that modern urban life is always cross-cultural.

HUGHES COMES TO THE WORLD OF HARLEM

An approach to "Spanish Blood" must begin with a closer look at its author's fundamental worldliness.[17] Hughes traveled to many countries through the Spanish Americas, Haiti, Africa, Europe, the Soviet Union, and China, and developed a vast and deep knowledge of spaces of difference outside of the United States, particularly in a hemispheric setting in which Spanish figured prominently.[18] Many scholars have discussed how his literary-cultural imaginary was always working through these experiences and inclinations.[19] In addition to Spanish fluency, Hughes had a command of French. No less importantly, he had already traversed the midwestern United States well before he was an adult and moved to New York to go to school, from his birthplace in Joplin, Missouri, to Lincoln, Illinois, to Lawrence, Kansas, and then to Cleveland, Ohio. So it is not surprising that Hughes highlighted expanses, even a kind of wayfaring, in the titles of his autobiographies, *The Big Sea* and *I Wonder as I Wander*.[20] All that is entailed by movement—a familiarity with uprooting, the experience of alienation, a need to adapt, and a shifting sense of home—that constructed Hughes's cosmopolitan identity, or, as comparative literature scholar Vera Kutzinski calls it, a "translation sensibility." As she explains: "It was a matter of taking other languages and cultures into the very fiber of his being."[21] Understanding Hughes to possess a "translation sensibility" differs from treating him as a translator bridging the space between formations, precisely because it calls attention to the relationship between subjectivity and environment. Certainly, the state of continually migrating can produce a form of exile, of having no place or being out of place.[22] But another argument can be made about the movements that enable deep connections with multiple places. In that vein, we might see how an engagement with

Spain was strengthened not only by bilingualism but also by political identifications.[23] Hughes's attachments spanned the globe and took shape across regions. When he first arrived in Harlem as a student at Columbia University (after having spent a long period with his father in Mexico), he noted: "I stood there, dropped my bags, took a deep breath and felt happy again."[24] Biographer Arnold Rampersad suggests that Hughes derived pleasure and comfort from "seeing his own people," with the narrative linearity of homecoming.[25] But this insight is not necessarily incompatible with Hughes's continual comings and goings and his abiding experience of difference: visible through those layers is the dynamic between dwelling and mobility.

In a world in which the very notion of home could never be rendered simply or nostalgically for peoples on the move from slavery or lynchings or Jim Crow, settling into a place demanded a complex assessment of the terms of racial negotiations. So even if Harlem held extraordinary idealist potential, it could not but also be measured realistically. In Hughes's literary hands, that process occurred through the representation of unstable and contingent communities, wherein Blackness was a question rather than a fact. Many of his short stories express longing and irony as they elaborate the crossings of race in place. Published in 1934, the same year as "Spanish Blood," the collection *The Ways of White Folks* maps the social geography of race as both white and Black characters "pass," and as they experience multiple recognitions and misapprehensions in their encounters in Harlem and other sites.

Readers may know something of the actual Harlem on which "Spanish Blood" drew, its turf battles and its class and race content, but perhaps less popularly available, and what Hughes was really after, was a deeper experience and affect, an urban phenomenology of mixture and movement. So even if, at first, the protagonist's background conjures up regional divides, with a U.S.-American mother representing Black Harlem (central and west), and an absent Puerto Rican father standing in for "Spanish" Harlem (east), Valerio's embodied mapping guides us through a richer landscape, from exchange (and its sexual and romantic intimacies) to conflict (and division), as we learn early on in the story that the couple has separated. The "blood" of the title recalls Black–white miscegenation, a historically haunting but also narratively productive racial anxiety, especially when Hughes revises it through a new set of exchanges in and around Blackness. Because what is made use of is Blackness's fundamental heterogeneity—consonances, divergences, and tensions—built by peoples from Hispanophone, Francophone, and Anglophone island not-yet-nations such as Puerto Rico, the Dominican Republic, Cuba, Jamaica, Trinidad, Barbados, Martinique, and Guadeloupe, who settled in various neighborhoods across east and west Harlem.

Harlem in continual motion engenders the transformative potential that is one hallmark feature of modernity. As the narrator observes in that very first line of "Spanish Blood," people there were "forever building things anew." Like many writers of his time, Hughes was concerned with the questions of what a "new" society would look like and what language, or aesthetic modes, could best represent it. But his twist was to gaze at racial worlds and, further, as we see in "Spanish Blood," to consider encounters saturated by difference. The very question of change, then—of the nation, of the globe—was cast in terms of how people could not only tolerate difference, but live in it. Local conflicts over territories, between "east" or "Spanish" Harlem and "west" or "Black" Harlem, could spin out into these philosophical concerns of the modern world. To be plainer, the newness of the modern was very much about race and its negotiations.

Fittingly, Valerio seems to be a natural physical outgrowth of his setting, imbricating environment and embodiment. We see this is in the first paragraph of "Spanish Blood," a section of which reads: "Valerio grew up in the streets . . . he was swell at selling papers, pitching pennies, or shooting pool . . . he became one of the smoothest dancers in the Latin American quarter north of Central Park. Long before the rhumba became popular, he knew how to do it in the real Cuban way."[26] Here is a subject engaged in spatial practices, in continual movement: pitching pennies, selling papers (walking, perhaps running), dancing all over East Harlem. Already established as neither only Black nor only Puerto Rican, but *both*, Valerio never stands still, physically or subjectively. Interacting with many different kinds of people, on the streets, develops a localized intelligence, and as a racialized flaneur Valerio makes compatible cosmopolitanism, traveling through and across borders, and "street sense," knowing one's place.

The story's invocation of music and dance further references unbounded heterogeneous cultures. Rhumba has drawn from Cuban son and conga, referenced Afro Latino traditions from neighboring countries, combined with American big-band sounds, and developed as ballroom styles. An expansively diasporic form, never just about connectivity between homeland and migrants' places of settlement but constructed through all sorts of cultural exchanges across nations and racial-ethnic peoples, rhumba morphed into a new shape in Spanish Harlem. By the period in which Hughes wrote "Spanish Blood," the music was already circulating through dance halls such as the Park Palace Ballroom at 110th Street and Fifth Avenue, as well as midtown clubs self-marketing as "Latin."[27] A border-crossing production was matched by astonishingly multicultural consumption: musical and dance events attracted African Americans, white ethnics (Italian, Irish, and Jewish), Cubans, and Puerto Ricans of varied class backgrounds. Connecting dots across urban space were two important figures, Frank "Killer Joe" Piro and Tito Puente, both born in East Harlem and active in the midtown scene. Even as Piro and Puente seemed to hail from specific ethnic groups (Italian and Puerto Rican, respectively), they came of age through exchanges among Black, white, and Latino worlds in Harlem and throughout New York. Piro himself noted: "Negroes . . . that's where these new dances come from—I watch them and steal their stuff."[28] Those skills were learned, or appropriated, when he spent time at the Savoy Ballroom, a local space famous for racial mixing. And the Black or "Negro" subjects that Piro observed there were likely more diverse—African American, Cuban and/or Puerto Rican—than he may have been able to discern at the time.[29]

"Spanish Blood" holds these pasts, presents, and futures in the worlds through which Valerio moves. Exceptionality lies not just in proficiency but in an assimilation of the new even before it has registered as such. This future-oriented, modern, experience emerges from the streets of Harlem, in which, as readers will see as the story continues to unfold, difference is being contested, sometimes bluntly and other times more subtly. Valerio's mastery ostensibly articulates to authenticity, as he dances in "the real Cuban way," even though he is not actually Cuban. Instead, a mixed-race background, for which a single identification cannot be presumed, confers flexibility. Notably, the delicate balance needed to bring forth inventiveness and somehow own it is managed through dance. Improvisatory performance entails communication—Valerio's openness helps him connect with an audience that is itself negotiating various sensations of urban space all the time. It is a deeply physical matter: his body surfs the currents of diaspora and also settles into place, routing and rooted at the same time, both free and constrained, as cross-cultures always are.[30]

THE BLOOD OF RACE AND LANGUAGE

A complex knot of authenticity and mutability is only further tightened by the blood of the story's title. Coming from the race critic Hughes, an invocation of Spanish blood can be no less than jarring. And that is the desired effect: surely it must be more, mean more, readers might ask, than what it appears, than what the characters want blood to be? Such dilemmas take hold in the early sections of the story, which focus much more on quasi-philosophical conversations than on plot. One exchange between Valerio and his mother Hattie establishes what is at stake:

> "You'll never amount to nothin'," Hattie, his brownskin mother, said. "Why don't you get a job and work? It's that foreign blood in you, that's what it is. Just like your father."
> "*Qué va?*" Valerio replied, grinning.
> "Don't you speak Spanish to me," his mama said. "You know I don't understand it."
> "O.K. Mama," Valerio said. "*Yo voy a trabajar.*"
> "You better *trabajar*," his mama answered. "And I mean work, too!"[31]

At first glance, the mention of Hattie's preoccupation with blood seems satirical, meant to poke fun at her parochialism as well as her sore feelings about her husband's abandonment. But blood becomes a more complicated metaphor in this story for that which seems so elemental or rooted and yet circulates, renews, disperses, and even connects disparate peoples. And with that maneuver, Hughes casts a critical eye on the racial science of his time, posing a question that is no less significant today, of what makes race.

The relationship between blood and race is, of course, not just a U.S. preoccupation. Race-marked blood in the story no doubt has a wider set of reference points, through Hughes's transnational interests across Spain and Latin America and into Spanish and Black Harlems. In other words, Black–white miscegenation could not but be seen alongside Spanish and Latin American racial questions for someone like Hughes, whose literal and figurative travels led to his translating Spanish-language texts, and also to his own works being translated. Dellita Martin-Ogunsola has argued: "Anyone familiar with Spanish Peninsular culture knows that . . . the emphasis on blood manifests itself in the obsession with *limpieza de sangre*, or pure pedigree, a centuries old struggle in which 'Old' and 'New' Christians' grapple with their African/European/Jewish/Moorish legacy in Spain and, by extension, Spanish America."[32] If the organic quality of blood seems to signify something biological or natural, it is quickly put to ideological use to ensure a continuing cultural and representational life. It is no small irony that blood is often emphasized when it has a fictive and undetectable quality, particularly in discussions of racial mixture and racist hierarchies.

The blood of the story narratively flows, almost seamlessly, into language, another wellspring of embodied connection and exclusion. Valerio's first utterance, "*Qué va?*" draws a line between him and Hattie, who seems at first to play along, feigning a lack of understanding. But if her putative linguistic incompetence mimetically rehearses social segregation between Black Americans and Spanish-speaking immigrants, it also reminds us that the exchange between those two groups is undeniable. Hattie's lie is called out when she says, "You better *trabajar*, and I mean work." This relationship to Spanish, vis-à-vis Valerio and the readers of the story, serves as a source of amusement, an instance of the "bilingual games" that critic Doris Sommer, drawing on Ludwig Wittgenstein's understanding of language as a space for everyday negotiations, proposes as a way to think about the "busy borders between languages."[33] To the extent that bilingualism is useful as a model for what the character of Hattie is performing in the knowing movement between her own and her son's affiliations, it may be more a matter of illuminating difference, and "twoness," than portraying ease of exchange. As Sommer has described it, bilingualism can express "nervousness" and the need for "caution and respectful distance."[34]

In this way, the exchange between Valerio and Hattie about language compels readers to consider translation as a strategic practice to bridge the distance, to supersede more fixed differences and more biological, presumptively natural, blood-based explanations. Not merely about moving from one language to another, translation can be essential to performed communication, to addressing the hopes and dreams (as well as failures) of connection. The passage from "Spanish Blood" suggests, in the first instance, a clear divide between speakers of English and Spanish and the language communities that they represent, and in the next, a barrier to exchange. Naoki Sakai has proposed that translation can be "an essentially hybridizing instance" of porous epistemologies.[35] The family bond is a relation that exceeds the linguistic: mother and son cannot ever remain fully estranged, even if their experiences of the world seem to differ so wildly. That reminds us that any moment of language exchange is social and psychic and, in this case especially, given meaning in a context of racialization. And, importantly, while many translation theorists explain what has been left behind, what is illegible, when moving from one language to another, Sakai points to the encounter itself as productive, writing, "What is translated and transferred can be recognized as such only after translation," which rings especially true in a space of intersecting subjectivities.[36]

In fact, by the time it is revealed that Hattie understands Valerio ("you better *trabajar*"), she has already assimilated difference. Valerio is half–Puerto Rican and half–African American, which adds up to a contested

Blackness, Negro and *negro* at the same time. And Hattie and the broader Black American community often respond to this subject-formation by outwardly disciplining a wayward son, a testament to the capacious power of diasporic attachment. Consider the quoted passage where she pretends not to understand Valerio (and any others when there is a question of language) for what it says about how recognition ("you are like me," or "I know who and what you are") is managed through entanglements of the everyday. In that locality, Hughes draws on a cosmopolitanism that contemporary readers of "Spanish Blood" most likely already knew from transnational projects of Garveyism, anticolonial African and Caribbean movements, and the literary-cultural imaginaries of Négritude, and holds up comparison as a tool to reveal fractures in the field of racial formation.

Still, Hattie refuses an explicit acknowledgment of the knowledge or ease of exchange. Her resistance could be interpreted as personal, related to her failed relationship with Valerio's father. But, situated in a Black geography of linkages and fractures, Hattie bears imprints of something deeper and more structural about a historical background of subjugation, and negative experiences of hierarchies that her mixed-race son reminds her of, however innocently. It might be called racial *ressentiment*, if we position Valerio as a stand-in for that force that has been the cause of Black people's frustrations and pain all over the world. Diaspora is often cast as connection, much like that between mother and son, but however much, and especially when it is a space for heterogeneous and multilingual Blackness, the borders between experiences become visible. Hattie's movements, even those across languages, can never be entirely free, and she is ultra-aware of roadblocks that present to Blackness. So she asks again and again if Valerio can really move between Blackness and whiteness. As she reminds him later in that same exchange: "no matter . . . what language you speak, you're still colored less'n your skin is white."[37]

Race and language come together in extended discussions of Valerio's physicality. He is described as developing from a child "with olive-yellow skin and Spanish-black hair, more foreign than Negro" to a "taller and better looking" young man. The narration continues, "Most of his friends were Spanish-speaking, so he possessed their language as well as English."[38]

Placing "possessed" closely adjacent to the racial and national mixtures that Valerio represents certainly gives pause for its suggestion of something more than facility of social use: an almost bodily capability.[39] The terminology, of *possessing* Spanish, could suggest more fluid incorporation or dominant assertion, but in either case, like any mere individual experience of ancestry, it is aided by a recognition coming from less narrow conceptions of race. Complicating that picture is the fact that neither of the language communities being crossed is racially singular.

What might it mean for Hughes to represent the ability to speak Spanish? We can look to *The Big Sea*; though ultimately that published text did not include "Spanish Blood," it bears the traces of intention and the personal logic for all kinds of worldviews. Hughes recalls therein his own experience of crossing borders while traveling on the train back to Cleveland from Mexico. He explains that a fluency in Spanish aided his evasion of Jim Crow: "There, I simply went in the main dining room, as any Mexican would do, and made my sleeping-car reservations in Spanish."[40] At least in this moment, his description of language use does communicate ease ("simply") and foregrounds strategic code-switching more than it does cultural knowledge. Racial experience and racial realities, Hughes implies, necessitate bilingualism. And the double consciousness uniquely suited to the use of language establishes an awareness very much in charge of its cross-cultural performance, extending beyond the effects of translation. Moreover, in "Spanish Blood," Spanishness functions as a nonnormative, quasi-outsider language for some of the characters, possibly many of its readers, and maybe even for Hughes, but that just might be why it is important. One could speculate that Hughes conceived of Spanish as an alternative site for working through the transitions of the period, not unlike how Black dialect was put to use by white Anglophone writers.[41] If English was the dominant language for modernism and for the articulation of constitutive dilemmas of freedom, one could imagine how ambivalence would register even more profoundly through the otherness of Spanish. In this formulation, linguistic difference offers a productive distance not only for keeping things apart, but for providing a privileged opportunity for becoming.

A racial optic of brownness brings into clearer focus Hughes's language use on that train from Mexico, just as it does Valerio's and Hattie's conversations about Spanish in Harlem. No doubt Hughes could be intelligible as a Spanish-speaker because of his mixed ancestry, and the character of Valerio, too, can pass among Latin Americans and Black Americans in the story because of his complexion. Brownness compresses the distances between nations: Hughes literally and figuratively bridges Mexico and the United States with his speaking (brown) body. In Harlem, shared minoritization forms part of the background for potential encounters. The English-Spanish language exchange has, as it were, a different cast there than it would in a space of whiteness. And it is worth observing that neither at the border nor in Harlem is Spanish thoroughly foreign to any of the figures, Hughes or his fictional characters—those edge-spaces create propitious ground for translation itself. Paradoxically, the domestication of Spanish helps us conceive of globality's vicissitudes.

THE SPANISH SPACE OF HARLEM

Conversations between the characters of Valerio and Hattie about Spanishness create the narrative architecture of "Spanish Blood" for relationships of language, culture, and space. Testifying to a deeper imbrication, the argument in the story about who can and should speak which tongue quickly morphs into one about where the characters should dwell, literally and subjectively. When Hattie says, "I'm gonna move out o' this here Spanish neighborhood anyhow, way up into Harlem where some real *colored* people is, I mean American Negroes," Valerio replies by asking, "Can't we live nowhere else but way up in Harlem . . . ? Down here in 106th Street, white and colored families live in the same house—Spanish-speaking families, some white and some black. What do you want to move further up in Harlem for, where everybody's all black? Lots of my friends down here are Spanish and Italian, and we get along swell."[42]

At least at first, the lines seem to be drawn between the uptown of Black Harlem and southern and eastern Spanish Harlem and the identities associated with those regions. Michel de Certeau has suggested that the spatial story always involves "operations of marking out boundaries."[43] "Spanish Blood" exemplifies that project through representing the pulls of belonging and aspirations of transgression. Hattie's desire to go to a place where "real" Black people live hews to the racial segregation of groups she is familiar with, but the psychic aspects of internalizing those divides are consequential, so that when she more explicitly contrasts Black Harlem and the place "down here" where there are "Cubans and Puerto Ricans and things," she imagines a trench between "U.S." and "foreign" (or North and South) racial minorities into which her own son could fall. And how Valerio conceives of dwelling in Harlem does not exactly denationalize the territory in some idealist fashion despite the force of that wish. His response to Hattie's apparent desire for sameness relies on platitudes of social exchange, of multiple ethnic groups "getting along," that Hattie and Black readers might have doubts about.

Earlier versions of "Spanish Blood" manifest the complicated ideas about race that Hughes was working through as he developed these characters. In the 1934 manuscript that most likely resembles the piece published that same year in the small magazine *Metropolis*, the last line of the quote above reads, "Lots of my friends down here are Spanish and Jewish and Italian and Argentine *and not colored at all.*" And just three years later, in a revision for *Stag* magazine, Hughes removed "Jewish" from the list of ethnic groups.[44] Sometime, then, between 1937 and the 1952 *Laughing to Keep from Crying* collection, it had either become problematic to identify these ethnicities as not colored (white?) or seemed to not accord with how Hughes wanted to represent the character of Valerio in the landscape. Certainly, during the years of World War II and afterward there would have been a special sensitivity to how Jews were racialized. We can also read in Hughes's compulsion to edit the story an unease about race in Harlem and his own place there, one that percolates through other parts of "Spanish Blood."

To paint the social world as flexibly accommodating different groups coming in and out is to access a U.S. story of urban transformation within which racialization cannot be easily situated. Valerio references a familiar diversity discourse when, in response to Hattie's plea that he remember his Blackness does and will matter—"no matter where you move, or what language you speak, you're still colored less'n your skin is white"—he replies with a perhaps naïve faith in the liberal possibilities of integration, "Well, I won't be, I'm American, Latin-American."[45] If Valerio is performatively investing in a multicultural dream of the United States and its possibilities for hyphenated ethnicity, his utterance may also indicate an orientation to Latin America. Certainly there is enough ambiguity to point in both directions. Not altogether clear is whether Valerio's imaginary, just like "the United States" (or "Latin America," for that matter) can accommodate Black Americans. Hattie responds with "Huh!," vocalizing a skepticism of hyphenated ethnicity for nonwhites, which effectively undoes myths of the United States and questions, too, any singular identification with the international. The answer to Hattie's and Valerio's problems, the "Latino," a figure who is *both* racialized and transnational, is one that did not yet feature prominently in public discussions of race in 1934.

Still, Hughes makes available a *Latinidad* articulated simultaneously to a narrower conception of Spanishness and an ambivalent set of identities. Spanishness only further dramatizes the race question, as it spans two groups, because some "Spanish" peoples are white and some are Black, as Valerio himself admits. Even in a 1934 context, any discussion of Spanishness must include an awareness, even an irony, about a colonial past for both the Caribbean and Latin America, not least because a Spanish background or identity also implied an aspirational whiteness.[46] If a more Eurocentric Spanishness does not fully connect with the pan-ethnic landscape of "Spanish Blood," it still haunts the local formation by establishing a wider set of reference points: Spain, Latin America, and Latin American residents. Traces of history register in the story's represented present. Linking the multiplicities of colonial-imperial background and a contemporary minoritized landscape are the many references to Hattie's work in a Chinese laundry. Indentured and formerly indentured laborers mixed with enslaved and free Blacks throughout the Caribbean just as these groups together inhabited spaces built of racialization and economic hierarchy.[47]

Worlds outside and inside are joined through dwelling, Hughes reminds us throughout "Spanish Blood." The notion of a "Latin-American quarter," early in the story, seems to partly reference a hemispheric ethnicity, especially when we reflect on why Hughes would have changed the language from "colony" in a previous draft.[48] Both "quarter" and "colony" pointedly depart from the terminology for the neighborhood "Spanish Harlem," which was in popular use at the time before El Barrio had become widely circulated. But colony implies, generally, a containment by a dominant force—this was as evident when Hughes was writing as it has been since— and had specific geopolitical meanings with regard to those peoples from Puerto Rico, Cuba, and other places throughout the Caribbean and Latin America. Hughes had referred to the whole of Harlem as a colony in several of his writings, emphasizing the peripherality and underdevelopment of this racialized space in and within the United States and perhaps contrasting that with the more romantic connotations of Harlem as a capital of the Black diaspora.[49] Somewhat differently, the use of "quarter," for the area where migrants lived, could accent membership.

Popular debates and controversies would have provided Hughes with many resources for thinking through these questions. In just one example, a 1927 letter to the *Amsterdam News* illuminates the ambient stresses of ethnicity and race for local residents. A man named Edward Ryan writes of a search for rentals in Harlem and continually being told that vacant apartments were being held "only for Spanish." His interpretation of the experience echoes the represented divides of "Spanish Blood" when he notes: "It does not matter what the complexion of the prospective tenant is, so long as he speaks the lingo. . . . This is rank discrimination against the native Negro and which I consider dangerous, as it puts the same race of people against each other merely on the grounds of a difference in language."[50] Ryan identifies the replacement of one form of racial housing discrimination, in which color would be the primary factor, for another preferential system that he casts as language-based, but that clearly has to do with ethnicity. His own African Americanness, and all that that means, provides a standpoint for viewing how the space of Harlem is built by relations among minoritized peoples and also through the heterogeneities of Blackness. Twinned here are the disappointments of local competition between groups and a more diasporic desire for connections among African Americans ("natives") and, presumably, Puerto Ricans, which reflect an alternative, if complicated, imaginary for place, not unlike the one that Hughes contemplated in his fiction.

THE INNER TERRITORIES OF RACE

The most elemental relationship of "Spanish Blood," between Valerio and Hattie, pulls together and cleaves apart all of the narrative dynamics. Structured by an opposition, the mother–son dynamic courses through inner psychic territories and shared interests of the more public sphere. When Valerio and Hattie wrestle with globality, their disagreements about neighborhoods and visions of the United States or the Americas have everything to do with their identifications with one another (they live together in more than one way), as well as their need to separate. In this way, the intimate is an especially important spatial register of the story, pushing readers to regard the always-gendered edges and boundaries in a different way. As Geraldine Pratt and Victoria Rosner have written: "Intimacy is . . . disruptive of the geographical binaries and hierarchies that often structure our thinking."[51] The story's contestations over blood, which call to mind racial mixing and language exchange, unsurprisingly take shape in the body, a preferred vehicle for intimacy, one that mediates the material and symbolic, too.

Hattie's refrain about labor, concerning Valerio's (often absent) work and her own in the laundry, at first opens up different compartments for U.S. Blackness and diasporic ethnicity. She compulsively returns to Valerio's not having a job, at least not of the sort that she deems legitimate—"the long hours and low wages most colored fellows received during depression times never appealed to him"—and establishes a clear-eyed understanding of an everyday Black existence and her suspicion that those circumstances could be easily overcome.[52] No doubt she holds a grudge against Valerio's kind of being. She had only become Hattie Gutierrez after marrying a Puerto Rican sailor in her home town of Norfolk, Virginia, who subsequently abandoned her with their son, after she had been providing financial support. As the narration represents the experience, Hattie remained behind while her husband "just disappeared, probably missed his boat in some far-off port town, settled down with another woman, and went on dancing rhumbas and drinking rum without worry," in a classic gendered opposition of female domestic stasis vs male social mobility, or the racialized one of entrapment vs freedom, or both.[53]

But the story, as it were, is more complicated, because Hattie's objection to her son's activities may be situated in another past, one where oppositions between nation and globe cannot be maintained. Valerio begins to make money by dancing in nightclubs and hosting white tourists of the Harlem cultural scene. The sexual undertones of this arrangement occasionally rise to the surface, when "guests would get very drunk" and "sometimes one might sleep with Valerio."[54] Pointedly, a "Chilean lady" purchases neckties for him and provides him with pocket money, and a "Spanish widow" buys him clothes. That Valerio is consorting with Latin and, eventually, white women who are presumably lighter than he is means that a comparative racial subjectivity is part of the romantic-sexual dynamic. One subtext may be that even if Hattie has not engaged in these specific kinds of exchanges, they are familiar to her, not just because she is the former wife of a rhumba-dancing sailor, but because she is a Black female subject in the world. In that formulation, her own hard work has been part of the crossings and mixtures that constitute the continuing half-life of transatlantic slavery and the consequent "miscegenation" and racial segregation.

She may not have traveled outside the country, but remember that Hattie Jones from Norfolk, Virginia, is multilingual and cosmopolitan in her own way, even when it leads her to question the inequalities and unevenness of

Black diasporas. Because to cast the conflict as merely parochial or naïve is to be inattentive to the fundamental heterogeneity of Blackness itself, which both Hattie and Valerio embody, whether the rubric is the U.S. South and its continued life in Harlem (a formation born of migration) or a contemplation of Spanish blood. The question running through the story is not whether diasporic history matters for localized identities in Harlem, but which histories matter, and how. Can an alternative consciousness point the way to a more insurgent idea of place? A conception (Hattie's) of Blackness that is not too tightly tethered to U.S. discourses of diversity, as Valerio's is, may actually situate Harlem in a wider and more open network. Indeed, Katherine McKittrick has pointed to the inescapable embeddedness and challenging potential of the Black woman. She writes that "the continuities, contexts, and ruptures that contribute to the construction of black femininity shed light on how black women have situated themselves in a world that profits from their specific displacements of difference," while hastening to add that "black women's geographies push up against the seemingly natural spaces and places of subjugation, disclosing, sometimes radically, how geography is socially produced and therefore an available site through which various forms of blackness can be understood and asserted."[55]

Yet another gendered dimension finds expression in the specific anxiety related to a mother–son relationship, one explicitly felt by Hattie and perhaps repressed by Valerio, to signal how profoundly racism molds complexes of selfhood. Hattie may be trying to bring Valerio back to her, but importantly, it is to an understanding that dreams of diversity will be curbed by the real strictures of Jim Crow in the United States. Hattie says again and again to her mixed-race son that one cannot escape race. This raises larger questions: can one move about freely, without regard to barriers, can a desire for something outside overcome all that holds one in place? If Hattie subscribes to a more pessimistic vision, it is only because she has some lived experience that matters. And her despair rehearses generations of Black women's laments: can anyone win when children's life chances are based on the color of their skin?

EDGE-WORLDS OF HARLEM

The story's contemplation of freedom might be rather differently understood when we consider that the note that accompanied the intended inclusion of "Spanish Blood" in the early draft of *The Big Sea* evidenced Hughes's desire to illuminate a fluid social world. He wrote: "Fantastic days, these days of prohibition, bootleggers, gangsters, rum-runners, white sight-seers in Harlem, numbers and the New Negro Renaissance. About one aspect of those days, I wrote a story called: Spanish Blood."[56] Recounting all these details might together have been intended as an elevation of social transgression. Nightclubs were widely known for allowing for all kinds of mixing, between Black, white, Latino, and Asian and gay and straight peoples, and men and women.[57] Many of these crossings were global not just in abstract terms, but in and through explicit engagements with peoples and places in other countries, indexing both the expanse and critique of U.S. imperialism.[58] To further explain this sort of openness, Shane Vogel argues that we can read many of Hughes's works as processing concerns about queer sexuality, not in the literal terms that a debate on whether Hughes was gay or not would dictate, but through literary-poetic themes and forms. We might, then, consider that Hughes had different reasons for challenging the policing of boundaries, in particular the surveillance of nightclubs where queer life flourished, in a fiction such as "Spanish Blood."[59]

Celebrating working-class cosmopolitanism was necessary to critique capitalist productivism and the demands of social reproduction during this period. That sensibility may have diverged from some authoritative representations of Black community but was certainly in company with the portrayals of Harlem in works such as Claude McKay's 1928 *Home to Harlem* or the stories in the 1926 little-magazine collection *Fire!!*.[60] Hughes's political radicalism, like that of McKay and other writers, profoundly shaped the imagined possibilities of "Spanish Blood." In this sense, Valerio's activities, which blur the line between the categories of labor and leisure, develop a familiar socialist theme of the period: "When the Cuban music began to hit Harlem, they hired Valerio to introduce the rhumba. That was something he was really cut out to do, the rhumba. That wasn't work. Not at all, *hombre*! But it was a job."[61]

But a focus on Hattie's distrust about the freedom of this world, asking whether the sexualized labor of dancing was problematic, for example, extends the critique of capitalism in somewhat different directions. Like Valerio, she does not follow familiar visions of ascent, as a very different kind of subject than, to take one example, Nella Larsen's middle-class aspiring Black women in *Passing*, a novella that was published just three years before "Spanish Blood."[62] Hattie makes especially vivid the constraints of labor arrangements and the limited choices that are available to gendered subjects. Her identity as a working woman within a landscape of historical movements and encounters highlights Black women's classed geography, which might be understood to be a corrective to, if not a critique of masculinist visions of the proletarian solidarities of diasporic Blackness. If Hattie insists that race and work matter, it is not merely on national or class grounds, which could be cast as parochial by transnational writers (and critics) seeking to romanticize the freedom that comes from travel. Her objections concern the deeper intersectional hierarchies that structure Black female experience in global capitalism.

But mixed-race Valerio is not entirely free, either, and the arc of "Spanish Blood" makes that plain as it tracks the possibilities and eventual failure of movement. His fluencies and fluidity are first portrayed as seductive, bringing him attention in the active economies of Harlem's worlds of clubs and musical cultures, where, in the metaphor-rich narration, "His sleek-haired yellow star rose in a chocolate sky."[63] Valerio partners with an African American acquaintance to run an after-hours club that is wildly successful. Ultimately, though, a flagrant affair with the white mistress of a gangster—a transgression of many different boundaries—results in confrontations first with the gangster's colleagues and then the police who support them. These bring the club down and land Valerio in jail. The specter of containment, which has been raised in different ways throughout the story, becomes literal incarceration.[64] Especially violent punishments ("They beat his face to a pulp") remind us of the vulnerability of the nonwhite body, forever bearing the marks of injury; Valerio's famously handsome visage retains a "nightstick scar across it that would never disappear."[65] And he discovers while still in jail that the gangster (Italian, presumably local) operates a prohibition-era "champagne racket and own[s] dozens of rum-running boats," making somewhat more explicit the traffic with the Caribbean as well as Europe, yet another instance of internationalism that has not exactly liberated Valerio.

One narrative of "Spanish Blood," then, moves from contestation over racial-spatial limits through the exhilarating freedom associated with crossing social boundaries to a grand fall due to Black–white strictures. Its development could be read as a parable of the dangers of a naïve belief in conviviality, a moral lesson about remembering Blackness. Because Valerio's experience, in the end, proves Hattie right, not just on the grounds of a Black–white dichotomy, but in and through a more complex transnational network of intimacies (which have made Valerio "mixed") and exploitative economies. In that frame, rhumba continues to perform symbolic work. Valerio relates to rhumba nostalgically and transcendently: it was a dance to which his father had exposed him very early on when they were together in Norfolk, and it resonated, the story suggests, "like a gay sweet longing for something that might be had, some time, maybe, some place or other."[66] Rhumba connects psychic and geographic spaces, but it may also be sweeping away from sight the constitutive tensions and inequalities.

Harlem appears here as a character in the story, operating for some broader collective. It verbalizes contradiction and ambivalence rather than moralism, and occupies a position within but also on the edge of narrative space. Like Valerio, Harlem may initially sentimentalize racial encounter, but must ultimately acknowledge what actually happens in place. When Valerio seems to be moving with impunity, Harlem interjects: "'That boy sure don't draw no color lines, . . . No Sir!'"[67] This gaze may literally communicate judgment, with the appearance of omniscience, but what is conveyed in terms of tone is admiration, even yearning, in the irruptive "No Sir!," which is less a negation than an affirmation. If we read Harlem here in terms of Blackness, it is still an entity (or character, or subjectivity) in formation, and one that is somewhat conflicted.[68] In this voice of Harlem, too, Hughes may be questioning what a respect for cultural difference, identity, and historical investments in community would sound like on the street. By suggesting that difference may be porous, Harlem also effectively asks what is at stake in its invocation.

THE BINDS AND BOUNDS OF RACE

The ideal of the cross-cultural that the character Valerio longs for bookends "Spanish Blood," accompanied throughout by racial facts on the ground. If the conclusion of the story brings us an apparent sense of failure and powerlessness in the face of regulating bodies (the police and the underworld), other affects get us closer to a critical understanding of Hughes's hopes and dreams. Hughes slightly changed the language of the ending in successive manuscript drafts. In an early version, Valerio replies to his mother's questions about his plans for the future: "Start practicing dancing again. I got an offer to go to Paris—a big club in the rue Pigalle."[69] Paris served as an actual and imagined space of exile for many diasporic Black subjects during this period,[70] so it is unsurprising that this is the form that Valerio's verbalized desire would take for an elsewhere, for freedom from U.S. racial dichotomies. But between 1937 and 1952, Hughes changed the second line of that quote to read, in the version that appeared in *Laughing to Keep from Crying*: "I got an offer to go to Brazil—a big club in Rio."[71] The transnationalist gloss of that second articulation is differently resonant than the earlier one: like other characters in African American fiction, Valerio may be understood to be imagining Brazil as a fantasy-space where racism will not be felt, and a specific kind of place outside of the United States in which many different kinds of encounters might be possible.[72] And yet any romanticizing of "racial democracy," at the time in which Hughes was writing or since, could occlude the lived experience of discrimination and inequality that Black people *in* Brazil faced.[73] A deeper understanding of diaspora itself, then, significantly complicates the question of how to read any desire to escape anti-Black racism, for the fictional character at the end of "Spanish Blood" or for the author.

Just as Hattie's reminders that one can never be free of race reverberate through all the moments of crossing in "Spanish Blood," even through Valerio's dreams, Hughes himself could never push away a national conception of Blackness, especially when that Blackness was in question. In his landmark 1926 essay "The Negro Artist and the Racial Mountain," an exhortation for African American writers to embrace rather than deny their Blackness in the face of the pressures of literary universalism, Hughes constructs an imagined dialogue in which a fictive interlocutor says to him: "You aren't black."[74] We might consider, then, how the racial anxiety of "Spanish Blood" could also be a writing of Hughes's own and other Black intellectuals' and writers' worries about their relevance in the face of shifting urban realities after the Harlem Renaissance. There is so much in Hughes's works to remind us that he was alive to just this kind of complexity as well as necessity in the project of representing race.[75] And representing "blood" could only further illuminate personal and political debates about borders, basic to historically weighty questions of the time.

The expanded landscape of the Americas both opened up and closed down the possibilities for Hughes's dilemmas. He represented enjoyment in being a racial subject in a non-U.S., nonwhite space in his 1920 "A Diary of Mexican Adventures (If there be any)," writing that "here nothing is barred from me. I am among my own people, for . . . Mexico is a brown man's country."[76] A deeply felt comparativism between Hughes's African American brownness and a Mexican brownness is the identificatory glue of this version of continental globalism. Later, in *The Big Sea*, Hughes describes race in a way that suggests a consciousness of comparative racism. Hughes's father's attitudes toward Mexicans were clear: "He said they were ignorant and backward and lazy."[77] Just a few paragraphs earlier, as Hughes reflected on an unhappy period of spending time in Mexico, he bitterly noted: "My father hated Negroes. I think he hated himself, too, for being a Negro."[78] The adjacency of the notes about anti-Mexican and anti-Black racisms only further deepens the connection between social and psychic dimensions of these formations. As Hughes puts it here, a rejection of Blackness is a rejection of the self and perhaps, more implicitly, the rejection of one's loved ones. The elder Hughes urged his famous Black American son to leave the United States for good, which did not come to pass, for so many obvious reasons. Represented relationships to Blackness can never be politically or personally neutral. When we think about what Hughes was working through and how, then, in familial and subjective spheres, might we not read the fictional Hattie's desire to be with other African Americans a bit more sympathetically, and her son Valerio's dismissal of racial singularity a little more skeptically?

The intervening period between appearances of "Spanish Blood," in which public conversations about civil rights and internationalism took different directions, was also one in which Hughes was pondering his position in a variety of imaginaries. His fictional and nonfictional works manifested a close interest in the costs of rejecting Blackness, which of course has been so constitutive a concern in and through racial formation in the United States and elsewhere where various mixtures created the possibility of passing.[79] Engaging in passing, or not, was a decision to be made based on myriad political inclinations, understandings of ethics, and personal-familial loyalties. Where better to dramatize the parameters of race that the skin muddies than at a national border? Hughes seems to ask in an autobiographical reminiscence of crossing back into the United States from Mexico. Like all stories of passing, this one begins with misrecognition: "Several American whites on the train mistook me for a Mexican, and some of them even spoke to me in Spanish, since I am of a copper-brown complexion." The underlying dynamics of the scene are crucial: Hughes's relationship to race could not but have been especially distressing just after he has left his self-hating father in Mexico and is anticipating a return to life as a Black writer in the United States. Thus his own choice—"I made no pretense of passing for a Mexican, or anything else"—communicates the full force of agency. Hughes goes on to represent the pleasure he derived from being discovered to be Black by a white Southerner ("'You're a nigger, ain't you?' And [he] rushed out of the car as if pursued by a plague. I grinned.")[80] Ultimately Hughes does claim

Blackness in post-Plessy America; when asked by the cashier in the St. Louis station about whether he is "Mexican" or "Negro," to determine if he will be served, Hughes replies unequivocally that he is "colored," to be refused and relegated to (U.S.) Blackness. Even if he seems to portray clarity of self-presentation in a world full of ambiguities, it is hard to forget that Homer Plessy himself was mixed-race and able to pass in New Orleans, a space of mixture, on another edge of the nation.[81]

Hughes's ambivalence about the Americas may have had one point of origin in Mexico, with his father's rejection of a Black family, but settled into another space in which the large resident Latin American population of Puerto Ricans brought different forms of otherness, and its negotiations, to the surface. The 1920s and 1930s conjure up not only the Harlem Renaissance but also Harlem's close quarters, in which translations and comparisons could take hold. One flashpoint can be seen in the riots, or protests, of 1926. Most accounts of these events point to the context of unemployment in the area and general tensions between long-time Jewish merchants and newer Puerto Rican business owners. It seems likely that economic competition influenced social relations and an experience of neighborhood blocks, its intensity of feeling underpinning succession. If some reports, like those in *Jewish Daily Bulletin*, cast the conflict with Jews in the role of victims—"Jewish residents resenting invasions of [*sic*] Porto Rican tenement dwellers by the thousand and Porto Rican storekeepers" faced antagonists described as the "advance guard of the Porto Rican army . . . armed with staves"[82]—others, including those in the Spanish-language newspaper *La Prensa*, paid attention to the attacks on Puerto Rican youth in particular.[83] Conflicts spun out from 115th Street between Lenox and Park Avenues, an area with populations not easily contained in one or another neighborhood, especially before "Spanish Harlem" became known as such in the 1930s.

Articles in the Black press affirmed that these encounters, which could only be called racial, distilled the tensions of the landscape. An *Amsterdam News* account settled around familiar themes of a changing neighborhood, describing the "ill-feeling" between "young Porto Ricans and others of Spanish blood who have been moving into Harlem in large numbers recently and the older residents of the district" and left the "residents," who in other accounts were Jewish, unnamed.[84] But a piece in the *Pittsburgh Courier* centered African Americans in the same conflicts, commenting that "the well-known friction which exists in Harlem between natives of the West Indies, who have swarmed there in large numbers recently, and old American negro residents reached a climax of serious proportions when a battalion of Porto Ricans . . . invaded the section in the neighborhood of 115th street and Lennox avenue [*sic*], with the express purpose of starting a fight with residents there."[85] Interestingly, in this discourse, Puerto Ricans are folded into the category of "natives of the West Indies," producing a layered racialization that must necessarily reference other conflicts within Blackness, between African Americans and Anglophone West Indians (Jamaicans, Trinidadians, and others) who were more prominent to the west of this interstitial space. Indeed, the article ends by noting: "The friction between the two groups, which make up Harlem, has been long demonstrated. . . . The failure a few years ago of the Hart Department Store at 137th street and Seventh avenue, which was hailed more or less as a national misfortune, was caused by the failure of Americans to patronize the West Indian owned store to any great extent. There does not exist a free mixture of the two groups of the race, although most of Harlem's small Negro owned businesses belong to foreigners rather than American Negroes." In its strange ignorance of (or silence on) other local encounters, particularly involving white ethnics, this article's focus on the conflicts within a broadly conceived Blackness (including those from the Spanish and British Caribbean) opens out onto an imagined geography well beyond specific blocks of the neighborhood.

And less than three months after the first publication of "Spanish Blood," another set of political events spectacularly brought Blackness and Puerto Ricanness together. In March of 1935, Lino Rivera, a Puerto Rican teenager in Harlem, was accused of stealing by white shop owners and, though quickly released through the back door, was mistakenly thought to have been beaten and/or killed. Subsequent anger among African American residents stemmed from the perceived oppression of a Black youth and succeeded in occluding the ethnicity of Rivera in favor of his Blackness.[86]

Historian Lorrin Thomas has discussed the racial complexities of this event, noting that both African Americans and Puerto Ricans at the time participated in the disavowal of Rivera's "Puerto Ricanness," the first group seeking to emphasize the divide between Blackness and whiteness and the second wishing to maintain a distance from U.S. Blackness.[87] Almost all the ways that the Harlem Riot of 1935 is remembered have to do with the race and class conditions of Black Harlem. Strikingly, in the careful city commission report, which included so many details about the Black population in Harlem, even assessing the poverty and resentment toward the police that had led to the riot, there was no mention of the presence of Puerto Ricans in the area or the ethnicity of Rivera himself, who had been the lightning rod for the disturbances. A missed opportunity for a full description of Harlem (or the event) was especially glaring in the note that read "Except for the West Indian element, the Negro population is native-born and the West Indians themselves are an English-speaking people."[88]

But there were other perceptions, from minoritized voices, at the edges of representation. If the white press referred to Rivera as "Negro," the Spanish-language newspapers made a more careful distinction between Negro and *negro*, a Spanish term for Blackness, but one that is fluid in terms of identifications. Those pieces also emphasized that Rivera was still fluent in Spanish, as a sign of how important language was for the distinction between Puerto Rican and Black American identities. When recalling the incident later, West Indian Claude McKay referred to Rivera as a "Puerto Rican boy."[89] The keen Puerto Rican observer Bernardo Vega discussed the misapprehension of Rivera: "Several women who witnessed the event thought Rivera was a Black American, although he was of course Puerto Rican, and rushed out into the street to protest the abusive manner in which the private guards (whites, of course) made the arrest."[90] The repetition of "of course" may signal a racial common sense, an on-the-ground-understanding of how race worked in Harlem, not available within institutional views like that of the New York City commission. It may be, too, that the women who "witnessed" could not or would not see the racial complexity—just as for Hattie in "Spanish Blood," Blackness won out.

Still, with this group of examples, of *La Prensa*, McKay, and Vega, one wonders if perspectives built through Caribbean elsewheres might have opened up horizons in which to think about race in fuller ways than the United States and its "urban crisis" offered at the time.

Hughes, awash as he would have been in the political and social aftermath of the events of 1926 as well as the exchanges and conflicts that gave rise to the 1935 Lino Rivera affair, chose to create a figure of Puerto Rican–Black American mixture to ventriloquize his own hopes, dreams, and anxieties and speak to the concerns of race *and* space. The cross-culturally Black Valerio may have been a provocation to multiple racial-ethnic groups that could potentially claim him. But his situatedness within neighborhood blocks affirms that he is *of* Harlem, a kind of native. Even his linguistic fluencies and movement practices were developed there, not in Puerto Rico. He may have been with his father for a short time in Norfolk, Virginia, but clear mention is made that he "grew up in the streets" of Harlem.[91] Like Rivera's, Valerio's double minoritization—Spanish and Black *both*—questions the viability of each, and in fact all racially singular identities and spaces. In the story, such a mixture is traumatizing, not least because it cannot be pulled away from the family, primarily the protagonist's relationship with his mother. Certainly, then, the prospect of escape from the United States in the ending of "Spanish Blood" conveys something other than a clear triumph. And the powerful dream of mobility, and its affect, still hang over and outside Harlem and its Blackness.

What "Spanish Blood" proposed was that there were alternative fields in which one could be cross-cultural and racial, inside and out, even if globality could never assuage all the difficulties. It bears emphasizing that there have been profound shared experiences in dense environs between Black Americans and Puerto Ricans and other ethnic groups—that changing mix that Hughes kept updating in the story—and, as well, in similar disempowered relationships in the United States. No doubt, as a Black leftist Hughes was attentive to (and cautious about) all solidarities while also maintaining a critical relationship to internationalist conceptions of citizenship. Situating Harlem in that world of possibilities was to deemphasize its U.S.-Americanness, even as it brought to light the structuring race and class dilemmas of nationality. Hughes, then, was thinking deeply about space: neighborhoods (Spanish and Black Harlems), hemisphere (Americas that include Mexico and Puerto Rico), and a multilingual diaspora (that extends to Brazil), together.

To add to the spatial complexities via the issue of naming, to readers in 1934 as well as to those since, "Spanish" has doubly signified as a global term, first in a more conventional way by conjuring up a world outside the United States, and second, with local significance, relating to immigrants inside the nation. In the early twentieth-century Harlem at which Hughes gazed, cultural and political groups that could be called "Spanish" included Puerto Ricans, Cubans, and Spaniards. Notably, this Spanishness was heterogeneous, just as was Harlem's Blackness—composed of African Americans, West Indians, and Africans. While *Spanish* was the term of the day, we cannot help but think its use here was also nodding to the power dynamics of many of the conflicts embedded in the story: a kind of false consciousness for Latin Americans who identified with whiteness and, relatedly, a colonization of regions and peoples. Puerto Ricans made vivid a conflation of nation and race, considering that beginning in 1917 they were U.S. citizens and persistently, to this day, have been viewed as foreign. And the signified of "America" always alternates between the dominant United States and a continental formation extending through to the Southern Cone and possibly encompassing Caribbean islands. The Spanish-American War, not so distant a memory in the first decades of the twentieth century, highlighted debates on sovereignty. Those shifting regional frames captured a Harlem that was simultaneously an actual locale and a source of so many dreams for peoples caught within the bounds of others' categories.

MOODS AND FORMS OF THE STORY

Hughes was not only polyglot and effortlessly multilingual, but also a polymath, moving promiscuously across forms and genres (poetry, short stories, plays, novels, reportage, and nonfiction), seemingly without regard for their boundaries. Accordingly, his writing was deeply hybridized: literary characters stood in for real people, represented familial tensions, had autobiographical reference points. Social life and fiction were entangled. In any one of Hughes's works, knowledge—of people, of interpersonal dynamics, and of place—was simultaneously reported, performed, and interpreted, a ringing testament to interdisciplinary technique. James Weldon Johnson remarked on that imaginary: "Hughes is a cosmopolite and a rebel, and both of these attributes are reflected in his poetry. As a rebel, he will not be bound by poetic form and traditions. As a cosmopolite, he takes his subject matter from any level of life that interests him. His forms are for the most part free, and his subject matter is often from the lower strata. . . . He is more apt than [Countee] Cullen to portray life as he sees it rather than as he feels it."[92] In that discussion, Johnson advanced a notion of the cosmopolitan that had to do with an ability to engage with different class formations and transgress the confinements of forms. This representational quality carried an element of the ethnographic (seeing life) not entirely accounted for by a purely aesthetic property of the literary (producing "feeling"). We can see that inclination in how Hughes represents conversations at home and on the streets, in a way that seems to derive from fieldwork notes. In "Spanish Blood," such a style could create a rich description of what it was like to live in a place and across its boundaries. At the same time, we might challenge the opposition between the observational and invested modes that Johnson sets up, especially through their fundamental inextricability in "Spanish Blood." As Arnold Rampersad suggested, for Hughes, the short story was "a way for him to express some of his more complex moods as he faced the world."[93]

The form of this short story, in which no more than ten pages could do global work and that asks us to think about the compression of field and affect, offers a particular kind of exploration of spatiality. On one level, this could be about narrative space—Henry James argued that the short story was reliant on the anecdote, a small incident that could signify broader trends, and Hughes's representation of Valerio's and Hattie's conversations, of dancing the rhumba in the streets, of goings-on in nightclubs, have been interpreted here in just that light, as articulated to major historical experiences. As a poet, too, Hughes was especially inclined to make the detail and image do major storytelling work, and so it is not surprising that he could use those seemingly peripheral elements to express the intimacy that was so central to "Spanish Blood." Partly this literary technique concerned relation and comparison and questioned structures. Hughes's ability to take the short form and open out into broader "big" questions, produces a scalar reimagining, where what is big and what is small (or trivial or important) become less obvious, all the while that globality is instantiated in place. Paradoxically, then, the prospect of incommensurability in a minor work of a minority author opens up problematics for how we understand the world.

Without presuming any necessary correspondence between author and his subject or protagonist, we can still identify how the autobiographical impulse is palpable when the fictional story is situated in a context of personal reminiscences and experiences.[94] As this chapter has argued, Hughes's emotionally complicated encounters with the Spanish language and with Latin America and Spain more broadly can only enrich our interpretation of his writing. As is characteristic of the short story, "Spanish Blood" fails to resolve personal and political tensions, leaving the questions that emerge from deeply symbolic dialogues between Valerio and Hattie about race, nation, and freedom hanging in the air, with multiple possibilities.[95] Uncertainty is the governing affect, the reading experience of a story that connects Harlem to the rest of the world. Ambiguity inoculates against the very reductivism that "blood," as well as national Blackness, direct.[96] That Hughes left "Spanish Blood" out of his autobiography could be read as yet another sign of ambivalence, vis-à-vis questions about the constitution of his Black subjectivity. But all these points do come into sharper focus when we circle back to that original plan for "Spanish Blood" in *The Big Sea*. Though Hughes indicated that the story would illustrate the texture of Harlem nights, it seems possible, too, that it could represent something about Hughes's own life. We do not know why he chose to exclude it from the final version of the text. No less importantly, situating "Spanish Blood" in the space of the sea also worlds its complicated Harlem.

Hughes was certainly concerned with the relationship between environments and writing. In a 1929 letter to his patron Charlotte Mason, he observed: "I had a very good time in Harlem over the week-end,—or rather a very interesting time. I met so many people. . . . It seems that a new life-period is centering about me."[97] Revealing a range of responses, phases of "solitary wandering," and thoughts about the world outside, he notes, finally: "I am not, at the moment, so interested in watching myself as I used to be. Maybe that is why I enjoyed Harlem so much this time. Things seemed so fresh, alive, and new."[98] An intensity of emotion about Harlem and the contradictory appeals of interior and exterior life all seem to fire Hughes's imaginary. And Ramona Bass, the wife of Hughes's secretary, recalls that Hughes loved to go on long walks throughout Harlem.[99] Clearly the streets of Harlem provided energy as well as context for Hughes's literary works through time: he was, like his fictional character Valerio, among others, a kind of urban flaneur, acquiring sensibility and knowledge from place.

THE CONTINUING LIVES OF "SPANISH BLOOD" IN THE WORLD

The placement of "Spanish Blood" in different venues and periods points us toward other productive lines of interpretation. In the first phase of its publication history, the story appeared in three small magazines, *Metropolis*, *Modern Story*, and *Stag*, in 1934, 1935, and 1937, respectively.[100] None of these were specifically Black American publications, yet all of them were willing to include a Black voice in their offerings. Given the obvious pressures of racial representation of the time, we might imagine how "Spanish Blood" obliquely transcribed Hughes's, and other Black intellectuals' and writers', worries about their relevance in the face of shifting urban realities. Even if the openness, diversity, dialogue, and contradiction that Harlem Renaissance cultures expressed did not exactly transition over into something else on the first day of 1930, there is no doubt that the diminished economic fortunes of this particular period, the late 1920s and early 1930s, had a constraining effect on racial life in Harlem, as elsewhere.

This is to say that we cannot but be drawn to read "Spanish Blood" as an attempt to address a changing world. This included the sphere of ideas, too, in which the scientific racialism that divided society into "colored" and "white" races was being used to justify segregation *and* restrict immigration in the 1920s, while anthropologists such as Franz Boas vigorously disputed the biological explanations for inferiority.[101] And Hughes, in invoking "blood," "race," and origin in this story, as in all of his other writings, threw his hat into that ring of debates about race and inclusion. For a public intellectual, there could be no easy separation between a literary imaginary and social life: the discursive consequence can only be understood, in Mikhail Bakhtin's words, as "dialogical." As Bakhtin describes the dynamic, "The work and the world represented in it enter the real world and enrich it, and the real world enters the work and its world as part of the process of its creation, as well, as part of its subsequent life, in a continual renewing of the work through the creative perception of listeners and readers."[102]

Indeed, the multiple lives of "Spanish Blood" reflect changing perspectives and responses—the story was "continually renewed" and its meanings transformed—and Hughes had a part in the process but of course did not fully orchestrate it. When he included "Spanish Blood" in *Laughing to Keep from Crying* in 1952, it was nestled among other stories about the ironies of race, the difficulty of definition and the policing of boundaries of any particular identity. Though all the stories in the collection featured Black characters and encounters with whiteness, as well as complications around racial identity within Black American communities, three in particular foregrounded internationalism. "Little Old Spy," which had first appeared in *Esquire* in 1934, centers on a Black American narrator fluent in Spanish, who is being followed in Havana by a Cuban spy for the government of Gerardo Machado y Morales, and who makes explicit mention of a Spanish community back home as he reveals his trip's purpose: "That night, I delivered all the messages that the exiles in the Latin-American quarter of Harlem had sent by me to their revolutionary co-workers in Havana."[103] "Tragedy at the Baths," about Mexico City, must have emerged from Hughes's time in Mexico visiting his father, demonstrating as it does a close knowledge of that city and its national sensibility. A third story, entitled "Powder-White Faces," presents a protagonist named Charlie Lee who hails from "the little American possession in the Pacific" (possibly Samoa or Guam), who is not Black American but is continually referred to as brown, and is a victim of palpable racism.[104] Alongside this group of pieces about racial formation and experiences outside of the United States, the appearance of "Spanish Blood" makes a great deal of sense, as evidence of an expansive, comparative imagination.[105]

Harlem's changing cultural landscapes also developed different significatory territories for "Spanish Blood." A desire for a clear correspondence between place and literature predicated the choice to include the story in a 2005 collection entitled *Beloved Harlem: A Literary Tribute to Black America's Most Famous Neighborhood, from the Classics to the Contemporary*.[106] In the introduction, the book's editor, William H. Banks Jr., executive director of the Harlem Writers Guild, wrote in an inspiring and reverent tone of the group's founding in 1950 in an office on 125th Street, noting, of writers such as John Henrik Clarke, Langston Hughes, and James Baldwin: "They were each first drawn to the promise and sanctuary of Harlem. And once there, they fell in love with it.... It then became their beloved Harlem and ours."[107] Perhaps it was the strength of that feeling that led Banks to misdate "Spanish Blood" as written in 1959 rather than 1934.[108] But this factual error unwittingly engages a deeper sense of history, how change over time is experienced and remembered, which cannot easily be captured by periodization. Because when we think about the tensions between Black American and Puerto Rican residents in Harlem, even those related to a *post*-1940 migration, we find that in his discussion of language, territory, and crossings, Hughes actually got it right. So it is not necessarily *untrue* that the story is about 1950s East Harlem.

In expressing the longings that took shape in a late 1920s and early 1930s world, when crossings were both frequent and vexed, but less understood, Langston Hughes could give the conditions of "home" and "abroad" more openness than they had when El Barrio and Black Harlem had become more reified. He also made accessible in "Spanish Blood" a conversation about the confusing effects of modernity that formed an underlying logic of Harlem. Urban planner Kevin Lynch memorably answered his rhetorical question "what time is this place?" with a discussion of the subjective nature of time, dictated not only by material circumstances by also by experience.[109] And in the short story "Spanish Blood," in which there is a continual updating of details, we see the dynamic life-experience of Harlem, too.

Hughes's autobiographical volume *I Wonder as I Wander* approached the period of the 1930s with a characteristically keen consciousness about national boundaries. As he represented it, Hughes experienced cross-cultural affective connection in Barcelona. Hughes's brief account of a visit to a café in that city with Cuban poet Nicolás Guillén models one kind of diasporic connection, but is interrupted by another one, when he meets a Puerto Rican man from Harlem. He writes: "As Guillén and I sat at a sidewalk table on the Ramblas that afternoon, a dark young man passed, turned, looked back at me and spoke. He recognized me, he said, because he had heard me read my poems at the library in New York. He was a Puerto Rican named Roldán, who had come from Harlem to serve as an interpreter in Spain."[110] Foregrounded here is Roldán's acknowledgment of Hughes, but, reading more closely, Hughes also recognizes Roldán, if not as an individual, then perhaps as a figure, a representation of something he, too, deeply *knows*. It is striking that in a Hispanaphone setting, with a cosmopolitan writer like Guillén, Hughes is brought "home" or, at the very least, to the intimacies made in place. When Roldán says that he is en route to a club "where the Cubans and other Spanish-speaking peoples from the Caribbean gathered," he invokes a multicolored world, Spanish but also "American," that could not be unfamiliar to this writer of "Spanish Blood," so interested in Harlem's nightlife.[111]

But this anecdote also reprises the delicate dance of the "changing same" of diaspora that the short story dramatizes.[112] Yes, Hughes and Guillén were in dialogue, but they also disagreed about the proper path forward *because* of where they stood. Guillén expressed ambivalence about the enclosure and separation of Black Harlem, even for the goal of racial solidarity; his own Cuban context, he suggested, required something different.[113] His contestations about mixtures and the place of whiteness could complicate and maybe enrich Hughes's musings about the collective project of a Black consciousness that remained aware of outsides and insides. Thus an intellectual exchange with Guillén, and its physical proximity to the encounter with Roldán, may very well have provided yet another opportunity for Hughes to feel the simultaneous pull of connection and deep awareness of difficulty.[114] To return to the core insight of "Spanish Blood," the future for cross-cultural globality continually presents as vexed in its own time and place.

These textual and historical excursions abroad also suggest that Hughes's manner of being global was not necessarily easy to accommodate within canonical formations such as American literature, or even Black American literature. That may be one reason why "Spanish Blood" has not featured prominently in literary criticism on Hughes or, for that matter, in literary studies of Harlem. The urban space that he explored in that story and his autobiographical writings was variegated and variously articulated to geographic and imaginative elsewheres, essentially making both the local and the global less flat and less absolute. The coalescence of the local and the global through race, especially, complicates identity and place in the United States, where they are often conceived of as "exceptional," set apart from other national forms of belonging. Many of Hughes's works have been translated, in practices that rely on moving from one national formation to another, but we might ask if "Spanish Blood" could even *be* translated. Could its multiplicity, its bilingualism born of a particular place, be fully intelligible outside of the language and social experience of Harlem?

But the work of this chapter has been to stress that the story can and should be seen as central to Hughes's oeuvre. Hughes's interest in the cross-cultural might be most obviously and earliest revealed in the choice to have an image by the Mexican artist Miguel Covarrubias adorn the cover of his 1926 *The Weary Blues*,[115] but that travel across spatial and social boundaries persisted and marked all of his work. Yet another project that helps us assess "Spanish Blood," roughly coincident with the story's creative emergence in the 1930s, is Hughes's collaboration with Arna Bontemps on a number of children's books that made manifest his (and Bontemps's) commitment to internationalism. The 1932 *Popo and Fifina* focused on children in Haiti, the 1935 *The Pasteboard Bandit* featured an American boy (presumably white) who goes to Mexico and develops intense friendships and understandings there, and *Boy of the Border*, written sometime between 1939 and 1941, explores the experiences of a Mexican child who comes to the United States.[116] Katharine Capshaw Smith has argued that Hughes and Bontemps effectively destabilize Americanness with characters in and from unfamiliar worlds to elicit a questioning of ideas about racial hierarchy: "By unsettling biases about international cultures, the books uncover and challenge the reader's participation in a binary representational system that renders all minorities 'other'; implicitly, the rejection of the binary system would allow readers to resist stigmatizing Black Americans as 'other' as well. A world traveler fascinated by African diasporic identities and international communities, Hughes in particular shattered presumptions of Black global and cultural alienation and inferiority by rendering ethnic communities normative."[117] Bringing "the world" and "the ethnic" together, Smith suggests, was also a way to combat specifically anti-Black racism through a kind of comparison, even surrogation.

Many years after "Spanish Blood" was published, Hughes remained internationalist and committed to diversity in Harlem. He reminisced in 1963: "Harlem, like a Picasso painting in his cubistic period. Harlem—Southern Harlem—the Carolinas, Georgia, Florida—looking for the Promised Land—dressed in rhythmic words, painted in bright pictures, dancing to jazz—and ending up in the subway at morning rush time—*headed downtown*. West Indian Harlem—warm rambunctious sassy remembering Marcus Garvey. Haitian Harlem, Cuban Harlem, little pockets of tropical dreams in alien tongues. Magnet Harlem, pulling an Arthur Schomburg from Puerto Rico, pulling an Arna Bontemps all the way from California, a Nora Holt from way out West, an E. Simms Campbell from St. Louis, likewise a Josephine Baker, a Charles S. Johnson from Virginia, an A. Philip Randolph from Florida, a Roy Wilkins from Minnesota, an Alta Douglas from Kansas."[118] And in 1964, just after the

Harlem uprisings around the shooting of the Black teenager James Powell by an off-duty police officer, Hughes wrote a piece that elaborated outrage at anti-Black racism but ended, remarkably, with an anecdote about potential solidarities among peoples. It is worth quoting at some length:

> For me personally, the best thing that so far has come out of our Harlem riots is that on Tuesday night I saw a Chinese cop in Harlem. Had it not been for the riots, I can hardly believe this surprising example of integration would ever have happened. I never saw a Chinese policeman in our neighborhood before. But there he was right on 125th Street.... Ninety-three of the cops were white, one was colored, and the other one was Chinese. In my heart I welcomed him to Harlem. I hope they let him stay here after the riots are over.
>
>   To me the Chinese have always seemed a delightful people with a warm sense of humor, quiet and friendly and courteous. I am sure that this Chinese cop would not wield a nightstick so violently or shoot off his pistol so recklessly as other policemen have done in Harlem. In that long block between Seventh and Lenox Avenues his was a face that looked decent and friendly.[119]

Even at this charged moment, Hughes poses a cross-cultural ideal to overcome structural tensions, between police and Harlem residents, and between Black peoples and those whose enduring racialization had not been constructed through a history of enslavement. No doubt there was a strategic intention in the articulation, in the 1960s, when the value of "integration" had to be defended and promulgated continuously in the most public of terms. But the affective dimension of relation is also striking in its depth: Hughes welcomed the Chinese man into Harlem in his heart, and projected not only kindness but also humor onto this subject. That gesture holds a good deal more than sympathy: it communicates a kind of identification, even desire, one facilitated by the nonwhiteness of Chineseness, and one that may be perfectly appropriate for Harlem's space of comparative minoritization to which Hughes always directed his gaze.[120]

HUGHES'S HARLEM

Hughes's house from 1947 until his death in 1967 sat on the border between East and West Harlem, literally and figuratively within cultural, linguistic, and political divides. As he walked out the front door, he traced routes that would develop an imaginary attentive to but also transcending categories of identity. In a life tethered to Blackness that received a full shape and form in his literary fiction, there were outsides, too, with which, in a formative period after the writing of "Spanish Blood" (but during which the story appeared in his major collection *Laughing to Keep from Crying*) we can see Hughes to be deeply engaged. Questions about the specificity of historical experience and the meaning of freedom to which the story can be seen as a response, if not a resolution, emerge very much from those impulses to bring together mobility and dwelling. In this way, "Spanish Blood" can serve as a kind of back story for Hughes's other treatments of Blackness and urban space.

We might return to the question of how "Spanish Blood" expressed Hughes's mood, the mix of optimism and disappointment of the late 1920s and early 1930s, prefiguring what happened to successive place-based imaginaries, what gave rise to the 1951 *Montage of a Dream Deferred*.[121] Another specifically Harlem story in the form of a suite of poems, *Montage* tacked continuously between an attention to the very physical elements of space, streets, blocks, and shops and a narrative evocation of the energy of movement through Harlem. By this time, three years before *Brown v Board of Education*, Hughes was fully grappling with the complexities of minoritized space to enter into somewhat different conversations about segregation than those of the period in which he wrote "Spanish Blood."

Much has been written about how *Montage* presents an alternative modernism, an improvisational sensibility of a different, and racialized, way to approach the breaking down of all sorts of oppositions.[122] Indeed, the work is dedicated to Ralph Ellison (along with his wife Fanny), a paradigmatic Black modernist. But in closing this chapter with *Montage*, I want to focus especially on how therein Hughes contemplates the space of Harlem, traversed and given meaning by movement, in a way that connects with the cross-cultural concerns of "Spanish Blood," in part to drive home the point that conversations about the Afro Latino, the global, and encounters fill out rather than detract from the imagining of Harlem's Blackness. To begin, Hughes writes in *Montage* about Harlem as an explicitly relational space. He notes in the introductory material that his suite of poems evokes something like the time-space of music, akin to Baraka's "BangClash," with intimacies just below the surface: "like be-bop . . . marked by conflicting changes, sudden nuances, sharp and impudent interjections, broken rhythms . . . the music of a community in transition."[123]

The poems that *Montage* comprises express a self-consciousness with regard to form and content. As in "Spanish Blood," "Harlem" appears in *Montage* to be an omniscient but not disinvested narrator. The title of a one-line poem, "Comment against Lamp Post," conveys the feel of some observation from the edge. And the many poems are like bits and pieces of everyday life and conversation. Details such as "In Harlem/when his work is done/he sets in a bar with a beer" and "A woman standing in the doorway" help readers picture the place, with a sense of quotidian rhythms, tying the textual and potentially sonic possibilities together in a work that is inspired, as Hughes notes, by "Afro-American music."[124]

In critical terms, *Montage* (unlike "Spanish Blood") has a central place in the canon of Black American literature, but it is important to note that even here the represented Blackness is never just national. An attention to diaspora can be seen in the poem "Brothers," when the narrator says: "We're related—you and I,/You from the West Indies,/I from Kentucky,"[125] or especially extensively in "Good Morning:"

> Good morning, daddy!
> I was born here, he said,
> watched Harlem grow
> until colored folks spread
> from river to river
> across the middle of Manhattan
> out of Penn Station

dark tenth of a nation,
planes from Puerto Rico,
and holds of boats, chico,
up from Cuba Haiti Jamaica,
in busses marked NEW YORK
from Georgia Florida Louisiana
to Harlem Brooklyn the Bronx
but most of all to Harlem.[126]

Hughes narrates the development of Harlem with a familiar mapping of the physical and social, capturing migrants from the U.S. South and the Caribbean, and explicitly including Puerto Ricans in the category of "colored folks."

The technique of comparison that provided one logic for "Spanish Blood" is evident in the poem titled "Likewise":

The Jews:
    Groceries
    Suits
    Fruit
    Watches
    Diamond rings
    THE DAILY NEWS
Jews sell me things.
Yom Kippur, no!
Shops all over Harlem
Close up tight that night.

Some folks blame high prices on the Jews.
(Some folks blame too much on Jews.)

. . .
Sometimes I think
Jews must have heard

the music of a
dream deferred.[127]

When Hughes depicts the presence of Jewish shopkeepers in Harlem, he does not omit the resentments that come from commercial exchange. The narration of a presumably Black subject ranges from frustration ("Yom Kippur, no!") to sympathy ("Some folks blame too much on Jews"). But ultimately the thematic of a dream deferred, a kind of melancholic refrain through the poems about the disappointments of race (and economy) that structure daily life, is the source of comparative histories that Hughes may be assuming his readers are familiar with.

Tellingly, the last poem of *Montage* is titled "Island," which cannot but draw us to contemplate the spatial register of the entire work. "Island" maps Harlem, beginning:

Between two rivers,
North of the park,
Like darker rivers
The streets are dark.

And it is conscious of color and ethnicity, in its second stanza:

Black and white,
Gold and brown—
Chocolate-custard
Pie of a town.[128]

One could read a gesture toward other land masses that are more literally islands, more of the "extended Caribbean" that Hughes and other writers were aware of, one that accommodates multiplicity. Still, there can be no simple inclusion in that formation, because the dream within a dream of Black diaspora, of something else, is also deferred. And the other colloquial and figurative meanings of an island have to do with isolation, lack of integration, an aloneness. The very question of the relationship of the part to the whole or the particular to the universal and ultimately, in this text, as in all Harlem texts, the individual to a community, is open-ended and, in many respects, a challenge to triumphant stories of modernity and freedom.

In *Montage*, just as in "Spanish Blood," Hughes presents interpretive challenges to his readers that are about Harlem but that are also not bound by its geography. Poking at the relationship between place and identity, these texts open up both, making Harlem more expansive and its ethnic and racial subjectivities heterogeneous and sometimes contradictory, all the while expressing their power. If "Spanish Blood" can help us look forward to *Montage*, it might also enable a deeper consideration of all of Hughes's works, even those that do not discuss Black American–Puerto Rican encounters. Thus at issue in "Spanish Blood" are the limits and possibilities of Blackness and globality, for Hughes and Harlem both.

2

MAPPING PLACE

The Facts and Fictions of Claude McKay's Harlem Imaginary

In 1940, Black Jamaican writer Claude McKay gazed at the wide expanse of Harlem and offered an assessment that emphasized dramatic, quasi-tectonic movement: "When the Garvey movement first attracted world attention, 1918–1919, the solid Black Belt extended from 127th to 145th Street between Fifth and Eighth Avenues. From 125th Street to 110th Street, Jews dominated . . . the influx of the darker-hued Puerto Ricans and other Latin Americans speeded the change. The Puerto Ricans began penetrating lower Harlem from 110th Street up . . . as they pushed up and over from the East Side, the Aframericans surged down to meet them."[1] Already famous for his rich fictional renderings of dense spaces in the novels *Home to Harlem* (1928) and *Banjo* (1929), McKay used prose to essentially draw a map, tracing lines with central avenues and filling in the resulting blocks with social content, to convey how the place looked *and* felt.

McKay helps us understand mapping to be less a cartographic enterprise that emphasizes location and more a project of deeper illumination of shifting territories and the varieties of peoplehood that places build and are in turn built by.[2] It is no surprise that this master prose stylist decided to give a form to the sprawling and dynamic Harlem with colorful language, sentences formed by a variety of active subjects and verbs, words strung together to create rhythm. The resulting object itself was category-busting, a symbol and a material site, a set of pasts and a way forward. Just as Yuri Kochiyama's and Malcolm X's political exchange or the relationship between Langston Hughes's fictional protagonists Valerio and Hattie in the preceding chapters of this book made apparent the flux of Harlem, so too do McKay's writings offer visions of a point in the Black diaspora that challenge narrow understandings of nation and locality.

McKay's kind of map, built from a racial geography of cross-cultures, further develops the themes of *Cross-Cultural Harlem*. It exhibits a signature attention to movement. The area extends; peoples create an influx with speed, penetrating and pushing. Even when McKay indexes the presence of African Americans, Jews, and Puerto Ricans and other Latin Americans to the neighborhoods they inhabited, those minoritized spaces that I have sought to unpack, he uses especially active terms: for example, the social groups were *meeting*. Here is a more contestatory and dynamic formation than either the melting pot or ethnic enclave could conjure up, and almost presciently, McKay identifies the "breaking of boundaries," which sounds to modern ears like a critique of a social scientific approach that would understand peoples to inhabit discrete spaces. He keenly attends to a spectrum, with fine-grained detail on the colors of Puerto Ricans and distinctions among Spanish-speaking peoples, avoiding the dichotomy between Blackness and Spanishness (and places where they dwell) of popular perception.

This chapter closely considers the representation of race in *Harlem: Negro Metropolis*, a story, like the others of this book, that was constructed with passion and perspective and that exceeds the epistemological boundaries of its apparent form, the "sociological study." McKay's talents bring out especially vividly how the map is always a spatial story. He develops a thick and layered, distinctly *not* flat understanding of Harlem's social and political topographies.[3] A hermeneutic of cross-cultures operates, much as it did in in the preceding chapter's discussion of Langston Hughes and his works, to illuminate fundamental dynamics of intimacy and friction. One analytical opportunity that *Harlem: Negro Metropolis* offers for the overarching rubric of *Cross-Cultural Harlem* can be found in its commitment to multiplicity and its exchanges, *not only* in ethnic terms, but also across cultural, linguistic, political, aesthetic, and affective differences. This is not merely evidentiary material for "multicultural" or "diverse" Harlem. And in his unceasing search for formal alternatives for Blackness, McKay helps us take the racial geographic conversations of this book in somewhat different directions. It is not altogether clear if he resolves the basic predicament of whether difference and shared interest can exist together. But the possibilities for Blackness and Harlem both are still brought to the surface in a way that few literary figures or social theorists could accomplish.

Much like Hughes's "Spanish Blood," *Harlem: Negro Metropolis* is a Harlem story hidden in plain sight.[4] Originally published in 1940 and distributed again in 1968, but now out of print, it has long been understood by scholars to be part of McKay's expansive oeuvre, canonical in this sense. But it has been critically understudied for what I would argue are largely disciplinary reasons. Quite simply, literary scholars tend not to be interested in sociological works except for the purposes of background or context.[5] They reserve close reading techniques for fictions whose imaginative aspects are immediately legible—novels, short stories, plays, and sometimes extending to autobiographies. Even though almost no sophisticated cultural critic would understand there to be a strict divide between the real and the invented, reading habits as well as frank prejudices about what kinds of texts have depth put pieces such as *Harlem: Negro Metropolis* outside the purview of deeper narrative consideration. From the other side, McKay's opinionated perspectives on political figures or social formations demonstrate a lack of the objectivity often expected of works in more empirically minded fields such as sociology or even cultural history. Yet another explanation for the relative absence of this title in conversations in a range of fields might be found in the dominance of the 1920s, the Harlem Renaissance, and the particular themes of racial community (and those outside of it) that that period conjures up. Rather different preoccupations fueled the initial circulation of *Harlem: Negro Metropolis* in 1940: the decline of the Garvey movement, the Italo-Ethiopian conflict, and, necessarily, alternative visions for Blackness and Harlem.

McKay's background as a leftist and Caribbean Black revolutionary, his world travels, and the literary–place sensibility that resulted all shape the text at hand.[6] To put it in two different, related ways, because of who and what he was, McKay was able to see something in Harlem, while a life lived in Harlem (not just in its blocks, but also in its symbolic potential) shaped his subjectivity. Much of his poetry and, especially, novels such as *Home to Harlem* and *Banjo*, as well as the later *Amiable with Big Teeth* (1941), engaged with urbanity and assembled physical markers of neighborhood blocks and buildings, various social figures, political movements, aesthetic expression, and other diverse elements of that project.[7] McKay also understood that the displacements fundamental to modernity did not just characterize the city, but extended even to more rural, seemingly peripheral locales and settings, as he elaborated in the 1933 novel *Banana Bottom*.[8]

The stakes of my drawing attention to *Harlem: Negro Metropolis* also lie, in part, in how we conceive of form and its relationship to the interpretation of place. To visualize this text as a *story*, not only as a *study*, is to suggest that close investigation (the basis for any social scientific project) can only be conducted and rendered with perspective. The aim is less to self-consciously compare this nonfiction work to the novels that McKay wrote, with specific expectations around their production and anticipated consumption, and more to suggest that certain elements of fiction—narrative development and structure, character, setting—are important for understanding the imaginary of place developed therein. Like the best fiction, *Harlem: Negro Metropolis* aspires to a kind of emotional truth that exceeds facts, even when it offers them, for an agenda of its particular moment and the future it imagines.[9] Its mode and purview extend beyond what U.S. sociology of the time was able to apprehend through even careful descriptions of social relations and problems created from intensified urbanization and industrialization. Because McKay was putting Harlem onto the critical table as a space of exchange and multiplicity and approaching it with a literary sensibility, he could see the modern city in both material and affective terms. If this was an altogether different kind of work from *The Negroes in America*, a group of more straightforwardly sociological essays on Black Americans in general, which McKay had written while traveling through the Soviet Union in 1922–1923, it may be because the intervening years of novel-writing gave his imagination a richer set of resources. Also, if paradoxically, what he could engage from Harlem may have expanded and deepened the governing questions.[10]

Harlem's wild multiplicity was the first building block of McKay's vision, and in this he drew on extant understandings. Alain Locke was attuned to heterogeneous Blackness in Harlem, writing that "in Manhattan is not merely the largest Negro community in the world, but the first concentration in history of so many diverse elements of Negro life" and adding that "what began in terms of segregation becomes more and more, as its elements mix and react, the laboratory of a great race-welding."[11] Wallace Thurman had written in 1927, for a working-class readership, and in a venue that advocated "common sense," of Harlem as a place in which there were "pure-blooded Africans, British Negroes, Spanish Negroes, Portuguese Negroes, Dutch Negroes, Danish Negroes, Cubans, Porto Ricans, Arabians, East Indians and Black Abyssinian Jews in addition to the racially well-mixed American Negro ... persons of every conceivable shade and color. Persons speaking all languages, persons representative of many cultures and civilizations."[12] Throughout the period of the Harlem Renaissance, then, and the years in which McKay was developing literary treatments of urban space, multiplicity was lived, felt, and represented. We must remember, too, that McKay dedicated himself to the texture of working-class life and, often, its informal economies and spaces of leisure and sensuality. His manner and effect may have been perceived to be transgressive by many, including, notoriously, W. E. B. Du Bois, who referred to certain sections of *Home to Harlem* as "filth."[13] But they were not out of step with the sort of sensibility evoked above by Thurman. In this way, by 1940 McKay could cut a figure as a representative writer of the Harlem Renaissance and an iconoclast both.

If various Black writers and artists expressed that Harlem could not be held still as a conventional social scientific object of analysis, McKay proposed that a deeper cross-cultural investment in place, about the affect of relation and exchange, could be understood through its political possibilities. In other words, he extended, operationalized, and philosophically rendered diversity. One dominant presumption of social theory was that the city writ large was a site in which to imagine freedom. McKay shifted the view to suggest that it was in Harlem—on the margins of metropolitan New York—and its chaotic negotiations of Blackness, that broad modern predicaments could be even more productively wrestled with. As *Harlem: Negro Metropolis* elaborated a local geography, material and symbolic, built through global Blackness, it engaged the dilemma basic to cross-cultures about the investments in a kind of racial subjectivity that was shot through with difference itself. Philosophically, McKay was working out, in all his fiction and nonfiction, what peoplehood should look like, and the production of space provided a particularly fruitful venue for that exploration. So what, indeed, was Harlem *as* a "Negro metropolis"? Enclosed or open, fully overlapping with a particular group or diversely constituted, consolatory or constrained—Harlem could not be taken for granted, in McKay's account, as merely an area for groups to inhabit. Indeed, for people who have been on the move, dwelling is dynamic, and this insight marked every single piece of McKay's writing. The use of the term "metropolis" indicated, certainly, something beyond a static enclave, and raised questions of whether and how this city-formation was connected to others, or whether it was autonomous: a part or apart? In structure, this formulation mirrored the discussion of Blackness, so that "Negro metropolis" made even more sense in conceptual terms, not just material ones. And the stakes of how Harlem would understand itself had to do with its precarious economic state, having suffered deeply during the Depression.[14]

Proposing a vision of Black politics based in spatial identity entailed an especially delicate set of narrative maneuvers, prone as it was to be misread, however rooted in the world that McKay observed and knew so well. To say that the path forward for equality and freedom lay in organizations of Black community and independent development was to raise the specters of separation and segregation.[15] It would seem that McKay was aware of that danger as he so carefully moved through heterogeneity in the pages of *Harlem: Negro Metropolis*. He represented Harlem as a space of encounter, of differences coming together and internationalism coursing through group formations, but that meeting and those currents defined a point in or capital of the Black diaspora of which he was himself a product.

McKay's itinerancy bears a striking resemblance to the one outlined in the previous chapter for Hughes. With that in mind, it is worth considering again the consequences of movement more broadly for Black writers during and after the Harlem Renaissance: the rich experiences of being awash in different cultures and the attendant demands of translation. Having spent his childhood and early adult years in Jamaica, McKay immigrated to the U.S. South (Tuskegee, Alabama) and then to Kansas to continue his studies before moving to New York; he also spent time in New Hampshire and other places while working on the railroad. Moreover, he moved across continents, with sojourns in England, Russia, and Morocco, eventually returning to Harlem in the 1930s.[16] McKay may not have had Hughes's facility with languages, but we can see throughout his works an alertness to multiple grammars for experience. In more psychological terms, too, exile and opportunity shaped migration practices that crossed all sorts of borders.

McKay explicitly posed globalism against national identity.[17] As he recounted in the autobiographical *A Long Way Home* of his exchange with a local man who worked for the British consulate in Morocco: "I said I was born in the West Indies and lived in the United States and that I was an American, even though I was a British subject, but I preferred to think of myself as an internationalist. The *chaoush* said he didn't understand what was an internationalist. I laughed and said that an internationalist was a bad nationalist."[18] Colonialism's long and broad reach confounded the project of feeling national, and McKay's West Indian subjectivity, both a regional and potentially political identity, underscored that. Immigration to and settlement in the "imperial" United States could hardly resolve the uncertainties or assuage alienation for a Black revolutionary writer, especially as he moved around the world. A slyness, conveyed in the laugh, manifested an ironic distance from national categories that were being policed at hard borders of governmentality. And it is hard to miss, too, McKay's association of nationalism with colonialism, at least the British variety, and his impulse to take internationalism in a different direction, toward his own Black cosmopolitanism. In that light, it makes sense that he would look for models for cross-cultural diversity outside of the United States. As he wrote just three years before *Harlem: Negro Metropolis* was published: "I lived for over three years in Africa. And there I learned that it is possible for different groups of people to exist . . . Besides the lesser groups were three major groups, native Moors, Jews and Europeans, each group preserving its own unique identity."[19]

McKay's relationship to Harlem alternated between intimacy and distance.[20] When he arrived from Kansas, it was to a place that he saw as "a paradise of [his] own people," and his response was fittingly embodied and cathected: "I gave myself entirely up to getting deep down into . . . [the] rhythm [of Harlem life] . . . one of the most pleasurable sensations of my blood."[21] Recent origins hardly precluded membership, as most Harlemites had also moved from elsewhere, from the U.S. South, other parts of the country, the Caribbean, and more, and Blackness itself was the essential criterion for Harlem belonging. This explains how McKay could remain a central figure of Black Harlem and culture during the Harlem Renaissance even though he was not physically present in the 1920s. He pondered how these experiences had affected his creative imagination. He wrote in 1937: "I had done my best Harlem stuff when I was abroad, seeing it from a long perspective. I thought it might be better to leave Harlem to the artists who were on the spot, to give them their chance to produce something better than *Home to Harlem*. I thought that I might as well go back to Africa."[22] McKay referred to his most prominent novel, at this point at least. But other specifically Harlem works such as *Harlem: Negro Metropolis*, *Amiable with Big Teeth*, and *Harlem Glory* took shape after he had in fact returned from various international travels. These three texts dug into the sights and sounds, the phenomenology of Harlem, with knowledge born of familiarity. Which works were his "best" is not easy to determine, in a sphere of always-shifting aesthetic criteria. Still, the questions of perspective remain interesting: what could McKay see and not see close up, and how did his strong feelings and political stances from the front lines shape what he could write in a purportedly nonfictional account? Furthermore, what is objective or subjective anyway when there are such strong attachments to place, whether it is nearby or further out, in a more symbolic imaginary?

PICTURES OF A "NEGRO METROPOLIS"

McKay's interest in social space necessitated a wider array of styles than even the broadest conception of the literary could easily capture.[23] Literary nonfiction, with its attention to the craft of language (which underlay his poetic writing), does not quite appropriately categorize what Harlem's racial geography compelled at the time. But even if the material and analysis needed nonfiction's presumptions of the real, McKay could never fully abandon self-conscious formalistic questions. Nor can his critics. Eschewing the linearity of a novel, *Harlem: Negro Metropolis* ranges especially widely, across political, social, material, and psychic arrangements of group consciousness. Unlike a straightforward cultural history, it does not proceed chronologically, nor does it aim for totality. Though it has often been termed a sociological work, the text does not respect the conventional boundaries of a community. Its writing depends on multiple angles and fragments, with a remarkably open structure for a variety of historical moments and figures, cultural formations, and movements.

The frontispiece is one key to McKay's expansive vision.[24] It was the work of *Daily News* photographer Edward W. Lewis, with whom McKay closely collaborated.[25] Lewis's *Life in Harlem: A Documentary Film of America's Negro Metropolis* came out the same year as *Harlem: Negro Metropolis*, and the similarity of the titles reflects some obvious resemblance in content: in the film there were visuals of the same street life, festivals, shops, and figures that McKay described with prose.[26] But the juxtaposition also has us think about different modes and techniques of representation. If the "Bird's-eye view of Harlem" explicitly presented breadth and pointed to the desire of the photographer to gaze at the place from above, in its totality, it could also provoke questions about what existed beneath and through those streets. And the image's blurred boundaries make the object somewhat indistinct, and thus compose the space of Harlem as simultaneously partial and contained. An attention to structure in the mostly physical buildings of the photo hints at what will be important in the text: a built environment. Relative uniformity, attended to with sepia tones in the image, could only thinly mask what readers at the time even casually knew of a place filled with life and color. McKay may have relied on a convention of description, an opening photo, but the imagining here of the big place on its own and connected uncertainly to other areas on its sides, spread out as far as the camera could manage, approximates his own way of seeing. The view from above may operate as a foil, setting readers apart, only for them to be given something much closer in the pages that follow: the experience of an insider, a walker, or an ethnographer.

The actual textual configuration of *Harlem: Negro Metropolis* further reflects McKay's interest in multiplicity of approaches, even if its ostensible ambition is nonfictional. Chapters take up distinct themes: description of the social landscape, formation of the enclave, the life and influence of political leaders, and aspects of economic life. Zora Neale Hurston accentuated the near-visual effect of this arrangement when she wrote: "Claude McKay gives us a series of pictures."[27] The first few chapter titles—"Harlem Vista," "The Negro Quarter Grows Up," "God in Harlem: Father Divine, 1935 A.D.F.D.," "The Occultists"—set up somewhat different expectations for how the content of spaces, time periods and passage, and public lives will be presented. In this way, McKay departed from a conventional sociological study, which would divide up the text into segments of similar or ascending development. The structure of *Harlem: Negro Metropolis* manifests, too, McKay's unmistakable openness to epistemology, even an experimentation that could lead to understanding something new, or at least different, about Harlem itself. As a narrative strategy, the chapters assembled like a collage refuse linearity and provide various points of entry. A more lateral descriptive landscape, with soft edges, could encompass moments and events such as diasporic and global references for Blackness that are not easily accounted for by the more developmentalist enclosure of nation.

McKay establishes a definitional intervention at the very outset of the first chapter, "Harlem Vista," when he outlines the distinctiveness of

Harlem's form as a city-space. He writes that, unlike some other Black communities, Harlem is "hectic and fluid."[28] A more diasporic imagination is at play in the shift he wants to make from the "Negro Capital of the Nation," which Harlem is called by many, including leading Black newspapers, to a place he understands to be situated in the world. But the expanses lie within as well as outside, most especially in the adjoining of New York's diversity and Harlem's racial formations. McKay writes that when New York is understood as "the most glorious experiment on earth of different races and diverse groups of humanity," Harlem gives us "the most interesting sample of Black humanity marching along with white humanity."[29] So while, in the broader instance of New York, there is a more multiply constituted ethnic landscape (races and groups), in Harlem we also see a distinct divide between whiteness and Blackness, even as they proceed in tandem. Anti-Blackness deeply structures the story, even when, as in the quote that opens this chapter, McKay persistently mobilizes so many terms of movement and process—struggling, scrambling, marching. How we reconcile these many potentially overwhelming elements and affects will have a great deal to do with stepping back to assess what, after all, Harlem is as a Black place, but also acknowledging its shifts in shape and register; it does not hold quite still, just as its peoples never do.

PEOPLING THE QUARTERS OF HARLEM

With its heading "The Negro Quarter Grows Up," the second chapter of *Harlem: Negro Metropolis* ironically approaches the biography of Harlem. Playing on the idea of the slave quarters, McKay announces that this place (and its people), infantilized for so long, has come of age. But he also seems to pose a question about narration, about how we tell a story of becoming. The promise of the title lies in a developmentalist account of an enclave formation, but the subtitle of the larger work, "Negro metropolis," hangs over everything within, to shape all the material to come. And the "Negro quarter" offers yet another key to McKay's sense of the whole, an entry point as well as exemplar of the cross-cultural Harlem in which spatialization is always a project of imagination rather than an established fact.

Like many more conventional social scientists, McKay retained a special interest in the categories for spaces that particular peoples came to inhabit. Accordingly, he begins this chapter with a quasi-geographic mapping, identifying the "Southern frontier" of Central Park, the thoroughfares (including Morningside and Lexington Avenues and 141st Street), neighborhoods such as Columbia University Heights and landmarks like the College of the City of New York. A planner's eye is also revealed in the attention to buildings and other physical aspects of the area, along with the special mention of famous architect Stanford White. When he writes that Harlem is "more comparable with Chinatown" but "unlike the huddle of European minorities in New York," McKay establishes the distinction of racialized experience, even among migrants, to further complicate the ethnic enclave.[30] If the notion of the slum could not quite get at what he was seeking to bring to life (and what Harlem itself offered), it seems that McKay was not drawn, either, to use "ghetto," a term from Jewish diasporic history that was already applied to poor Jewish neighborhoods in the United States and in his time was taken up to identify poor Black and Latino areas. Even if "ghetto" were the more discursively available term, it would likely have been as problematic as "slum" for McKay.[31] He settled on "quarter," evoking a section of a whole and emphasizing physical area. In his regard for the relationship between structures and ideas, McKay echoes the insights of more contemporary urban sociologists especially attentive to spatial-racial questions, such as Michael Keith, who has usefully explained that "the configuration of the city . . . becomes a constitutive part of how we come to think of metropolitan multiculture."[32]

McKay's epistemology of Harlem extends into what we might consider a deeper theorization of space and the philosophical questions raised therein. He writes: "Harlem creates the impression of a mass of people all existing on the same plane."[33] For a poet, concerned with words and the images they generate, the language here cannot but have been carefully deliberated. A plane creates a sense of horizontality, leveling and possibly equalizing, at least in terms of perspective. And in this part of the text McKay points to the relative lack of observed hierarchy even among residents of different economic means and cultural backgrounds. But to press on the metaphor of the plane a little differently, the question of inclusion may remain in question. Flat, leveled spaces create both containment and openness; they offer alternative and even opposed possibilities for the place of Harlem, as well as for an identity of Blackness and its constituting community. The "Negro metropolis" of the subtitle, not to mention the Lewis photo that opens *Harlem: Negro Metropolis*, contrast a bit more sharply with the "Negro quarter." Metropolis evokes an expanse that is less bounded than what the locality connotes.

What was *in* Harlem, its wild complexity and dynamism, was one of the book's abiding preoccupations. McKay's descriptions showcased color and ethnicity in both the built environment and social interactions:

> African, Mongolian, European—all the types of all the races indiscriminately flung together have created a jungle of colors in which pullulate all the imaginable shades of white and black, red, brown, yellow: indigo, chestnut, slate, amber, olive, canary, mauve, orange, ruby and the indefinable. An unaware interracial and international movement dominates the thickly crowded atmosphere. Puerto Ricans and other Latin Americans have tenanted buildings whose façades are still engraved with double triangles and over five thousand years of figures which proclaim their original Jewish occupancy. "Unamerican" signs—*bodega, tienda, carneceria, dulceria, fonda,* and *imprenta* are spread across the fronts of stores. Italian Americans have pushed over from the East Side, competing with the Spanish Americans.[34]

McKay's obsession with the fine distinctions stands out. The unusual term "pullulate" conjures up mixing across lines and also a rapidity that eludes any kind of control. It is worth emphasizing that McKay's field of meaning for Harlem appeared rather differently from those built by Black–white dichotomies and national discourses on urban areas at the time. His rendering resonated with Thurman's and other Black writers' descriptions of diversity. But his understanding of Harlem also incorporated a deeper multiplicity from within and without, as well as one that existed in layers, over time, surfaces of presence to hint at other ones.

The placement of "unamerican" in quotation marks expresses a surprising awareness of anti-immigrant bias, certainly as rampant in the 1930s as in the contemporary moment, to establish McKay's stance of tolerance. Considering that the House Un-American Activities Committee had been created in 1938, by the time *Harlem: Negro Metropolis* circulated, "unamerican" multiply signified, partly as an invocation of disloyalty about which McKay would have been critical and likely sarcastic. On the streets, store signs in languages other than English have long been, and are still, a source of conflict between "natives" and newcomers, often white vs racial immigrant.[35] But how McKay represents the encounter here lends Harlem two kinds of openness. First, a linguistic otherness situates Harlem in other maps that migrations of peoples, goods and ideas, created, reiterating that meaning could not be corralled by the specifically U.S. racial or ethnic enclave. Second, McKay's attention to Spanishness did some work in softening developing divides between the communities (and areas of habitation) of different languages, namely Black Americans and Latino migrants (Puerto Rican and other, in his words). And the buildings provided yet more cultural depth: the Star of David on the façades gestures toward another time-space, to speculate on intimacies in the past, with groups of people coming into Harlem, mingling with those who were already there. In a passage so much about dynamism, those residual signs point to the present and possible futures of this place.

McKay needs the force of the detail to move from categorical definition of groups to something more relational—his "Negro metropolis" of encounter, exchange, and mixture. He begins a long subtitled section, "Racial Groups," with a case of a Barbadian migrant's assumption of the role of a Harlem local politician as a way to speak to the connections between West Indians and Black Americans: "they work together, play together, marry one another and share equally the joys and sorrows of the group."[36] Identifying narrower interest group politics, such as West Indians' advocacy simply for other West Indians, as "provincial," he proposes Black identity as more expansive, even cosmopolitan. And yet a sharp racial analysis also breaks down oppositions. McKay lingers over the linguistic formations of West Indian English, the mixtures of accent, "a colonial variant of Scotch and Irish, in Jamaica a curious hybrid Cockney," and resulting in what he so vividly renders as a "liquid dialect."[37] Notably, he does not elide the conflicts between West Indians and Black Americans, pointedly describing some desire of the former to separate from the latter, and cultural and political differences of background that develop trajectories of racial identity that do not always fully overlap.

To complicate the matter even further, McKay brings the racial ambiguities of Puerto Ricans into this mix, writing of their "relation" to Blackness, "of special and complicated interest because of the considerable numbers of Negroids within its fold."[38] Comparison in this extended discourse points to the constructedness of race itself and acknowledges that people's identities develop with reference to the self-fashioning of others. In this account, the complexity of race occasions a contemplation of race for Black Americans, and Harlem more broadly. Just as Hughes represented in "Spanish Blood" the felt divides of identity, so too McKay writes of the difficulty of translation: that "basically it is also a matter of language, that in Spanish Negro is the word for black and therefore brown cannot be black."[39] Interestingly, McKay invokes on the one hand pseudoscientific race language ("Negroid"), perhaps ironically, and on the other, the thickness of racialized life. Might the "special and complicated" racial thinking of Puerto Ricans themselves hold a degree of anti-Blackness and even denial, that is registered in and created by language? If brown cannot be black, can Puerto Ricans live in neighborhood space with Black Americans? Part of the answer to these questions lies in the fact that language difference is always racialized, so that forms of racial thinking shaped by and reflected in language collide in the lived experience of Harlem.

Those insights about identity and relation are given an even richer texture in the specific territories that *Harlem: Negro Metropolis* maps with astonishing intricacy. If conventional maps demarcate borders and offer a comparative sense of what is inside and outside, McKay's movement-infused text narrates space rather differently. The paramount consideration for him remains not just that peoples, the "racial groups," inhabit areas, but how they and their neighborhoods come together, close in, to make Harlem. And so the effect of reading "The post-war expansion of Harlem brought the considerable Puerto Rican colony to the border of the black belt" is an immediate feeling of proximity as well as the impossibility of separation.[40] The terms establish symbolic and historical depth: no one reading *Harlem: Negro Metropolis* could be unaware of how "black belt" recalled the plantation South.[41] While McKay's overall aim may be to develop an understanding of Harlem as a Black place, he cannot help returning to the diversities of that space, noting, "In Harlem there is a miniature Chinatown at the bottom of Lenox Avenue. And there are Japanese who run the neat Sandwich Shops . . . There is a small colony of Haitians and a pocket of Martinique Negroids."[42] Repudiating a melting pot-template that he and his readers were surely aware of at the time, McKay takes care to emphasize the life of ethnicity across groups, writing that "the Spanish quarter in Harlem is as definitely Spanish as the Italian quarter is Italian."[43] In this way, the text maintains a careful equilibrium between elements that could be understood as opposed for heterogeneity and ethnic-racial investment in the very life of the place. In fact, McKay writes that there are "many . . . interesting contradictions" and goes on to manage them with evocations of conviviality, the "spirit of social amenity in the life of Harlem."[44] If these representations of urban experience seem exceptional, it is also useful to recall that Thurman and Locke had described something very similar years before. This point hardly detracts from McKay's talents of observation and description, but it does ask us to think about how widely understood diversity was in life on the ground, through daily experience.

It bears emphasizing that McKay's approach to Harlem is embodied, affective as well as analytical. He conveys a more sensory enjoyment of difference, writing: "World-famed for their promenading ritual, the Spanish have given a special éclat to the tempo of the street. The Aframericans have always delighted in the strut and shuffle. And crossing and mingling steps with the Spanish, together they are making a new movement in lower Harlem."[45] Performance, evinced by the display and "ritual," not only makes use of the street but also becomes part of the street in both visual and sound. McKay represents the encounter between Spanish peoples and Black peoples as quasi-organic, with words such as "special" and "delight" closely adjacent. The practices of crossing and mingling afford resources for the newness that this modernist writer cannot but be concerned with in the site of Harlem. Strikingly, these themes and this particular Black–Spanish mixture remind us of "Spanish Blood" and its protagonist Valerio, who was its practitioner not just in demographic terms, but in tone and language. But whereas a Black perspective in the short story leads to ambivalence, the encounter here in *Harlem: Negro Metropolis* could leave readers a good deal less troubled.

One way to understand diverging narrative trajectories of Blackness is in terms of specific relationships to the histories, the facts, and the possibilities of racial mixture in sites of the diaspora. We cannot ascribe the difference between Hughes's and McKay's cross-cultural imaginaries fully to background in Black America vs Jamaica (both complex and heterogeneous fields), but something of what each figure sees in Harlem does relate to elsewheres. Both Hughes and McKay were deeply cosmopolitan, like so many Black writers at the time. Hurston recognized that advantage of perception for McKay and *Harlem: Negro Metropolis*, complimenting his "world travelled eye."[46] McKay's cross-cultural hermeneutic for Harlem evokes and is structured by the Caribbean, where majority-minority exchanges among closely adjacent racialized and ethnicized communities are haunted by the politics of race. Even a somewhat matter-of-fact approach to the map changing that opened this chapter recalls societies like those of Jamaica and the rest of the West Indies, built through the continuous movements of peoples and goods through slavery, indenture, and colonialism. As he had earlier set the island scene of his novel *Banana Bottom*: "demarcations were not as real as they seemed. East Indian and Chinese blood were mingled in the dark-brown group and obviously there were thousands who were drawn in from European stock . . . a strong transfusion of black African blood had determined their pigmentation . . . the social life of the colony was finely balanced by the divisions."[47] But McKay's points of reference, we know, ranged even more widely, and his comparativism becomes especially explicit when he notes that what he sees in the area below 116th Street "has something of the quality of the Vieux Port of Marseille."[48] Further, McKay had long lived in minoritized difference, with that deep experience of proximity, not just in colonial Jamaica, but in imperial England after the First World War, with Africans, Middle Easterners, and East and West Indians.[49]

Yet even diversity, McKay reminds readers of *Harlem: Negro Metropolis*, must be carefully situated and contextualized. If in the passages quoted above he celebrates the widest spectrum of ethnicities and backgrounds, encompassing peoples from all over the world, he quickly adds a cautionary note about the potential to romanticize that existence: "This patchwork of humanity was planned by no expert mind. It did not evolve from any blue print of interracial and international adjustment. . . . It is a crude, bold offspring of necessity."[50] Dramatizing the realities of racial life, McKay follows with a description of crime in the area, one that might seem to resemble dominant discourses of urban life and that also speaks to economic and social impoverishment. But just how this depiction of the more difficult features of Harlem functions in the narrative has to do not just with its appearance but also its proportion; quite simply, it occupies less space than it might in other kinds of sociological accounts of crime-ridden racialized communities at the time. The tone of the passages, too, creates a picture of realism without the judgment or anxiety that accompanies those often-negative portrayals.

McKay's compositional interest in space mirrors his approach to the question of color throughout the work, what he calls "that common yet strange and elusive chemical of nature."[51] Indeed, a quasi-physical logic, with the liberal use of spatial metaphors, sets this discussion of race apart from many others. Words such as "composite," "mass," "conglomerate," and "frame" mark the description. In one respect, there is an attention to the heterogeneity of Blackness—"within it are the . . . remnants of other groups, the nondescripts of miscegenation. From the Caribbean islands . . . brown North Africans, swarthy East Africans . . . ebon-black West Africans . . . have been forced into the ranks of the original Aframerican group"—and in another an acknowledgment of the fundamental difficulties of coalescence.[52] Posing the process of formation as problematic gets to the very heart of the question that McKay most wants to answer: not just what Blackness is, as an identity, but how it can function politically.

Philosophically, can Blackness's parts become a whole, or does the unpatterned diversity lead to a very different end point? Can Blackness be expansive enough to accommodate the Chineseness, Japaneseness, Italianness, Jewishness, and other possibilities that live in Harlem? Or is it an "unwieldy, inert and invertebrate mass"?[53] When McKay argues forcefully that "the group is a group nevertheless," he pivots from apparent cultural questions of constitution to political possibility. He suggests that because there is no common (in his words, "separate") religion or language as there would be for ethnic populations, generational divides could be transcended and a kind of shared Americanness formulated for the children of foreign-born Black migrants and Black people in the United States. If the invocation of nationality (and integration) seems somewhat reflexive, a concession to the social scientific discourse of the day—*Harlem: Negro Metropolis* as well as McKay's other works remain on the whole uninterested in those questions—the notion of the group, and a constituting peoplehood, surely drew the attention of many readers and critics. McKay's formulation was challenging, effectively distinguishing between ethnicity and race but accommodating the constructed nature of both.

The very ending of "The Negro Quarter Grows Up" fulsomely manifests an insurgent intellectual agenda to bring Harlem and heterogeneous Blackness together. He writes that "an examination of the mass movements of Harlem may yield an indication of the trend and direction of the group as a whole."[54] In other words, Black politics is possible in a Harlem that has already been even more multiply peopled, in the vein of thoroughgoing cross-cultures. The place-itinerary is a road map for subjectivity, and vice-versa. This twinned narrative strategy and analytical method emerge as much from McKay's straightforward political agenda as from any scholarly impetus. Nothing here is completely "objective" or "descriptive." An impassioned perspective drives the work back and forth across the lines of something like sociology and a polemical essay, by a writer who is also a poet and novelist and is always alive to the power of words and images.

MAPPING PLACE

HARLEM FIGURES, MOVEMENTS, AND TOPOGRAPHIES

The chapters of *Harlem: Negro Metropolis* that follow "The Negro Quarter Grows Up" further manifest McKay's openness to formal alternatives to both fiction and sociology. None of them are quite what their titles would have readers anticipate, coursing among popular political figures, cultural practices, neighborhood institutions, and social groups. A faint, if unstated, structure might be seen in three sections about quasi-religious formations, economic activities, and politics, each headed in a general way by prominent figures but deconstructed from the ground up.[55] As readers skate across the shapes and surfaces of the public worlds of Harlem, the stopping points, be they Father Divine or the Negro Division of the New York Public Library (which became the Schomburg Center for Research in Black Culture), serve as common places, enabling the retrieval of associations, solidarities, and memories.[56] But as critic Svetlana Boym reminds us: "The common place is not as transparent as it might seem; it is a barricade, a battleground of warring definitions and disparate discourses."[57] Indeed, McKay's stories about these common places engender identification and disidentification, projection and resistance, what we might think of as a kind of "reader response" to literary works, just as they raise social questions about what in Harlem is shared (generically common) and what is not (uncommon). Though the text overall concerns major male political figures, every single chapter elaborates formations and movements that give the production of Harlem's space temporal, cultural, and social depth.[58]

In "God in Harlem: Father Divine, 1935 A.D.F.D.," the chapter that immediately follows McKay's advocacy for the group-ness of Blackness in Harlem, he examines the especially controversial Father Divine. It is, no doubt, a jarring shift for those readers who may have been trained in relating to Black community through more mainstream leaders such as W. E. B. DuBois or Alain Locke, at least in popular writing and intellectual debate. The son of freed slaves, the man once called George Baker developed the widely influential interracial religious Peace Mission

Movement and came to Harlem in 1932 to build a local branch of the organization. By the time McKay would have returned to Harlem from his own travels to begin thinking about researching *Harlem: Negro Metropolis*, Father Divine and members of the Peace Mission Movement owned property and businesses there and had already attracted many Black residents to a program that touted economic autonomy with a Civil Rights inflection.[59] Among Black intellectuals of the time, who but McKay could best understand (and take seriously) this complicated and unusual person whose appeal seemed to be based in an ostensibly paradoxical disavowal of racial identity and respect for Black politics?[60] McKay's description of "the followers" in *Harlem: Negro Metropolis* was laced with a familiar interest in diversity: "brown and black Americans with a leaven of Negroid Spanish-Americans and West Indians . . . flecked with whites."[61] The cultural hybridity he describes in congregants' dancing practices—"rampant individual steps punctuate the rhythm. Fragments of every conceivable dance measure whirl about: a rare huddle of Guinea fetishers, an ecstatic Senegalese plunging to the call of the tom-tom, a patter of Moroccan flamenco, an Irish jig, a briefly oblique schottische, the one-step, the rhumba"— recalls the atmosphere of working-class Black Harlem depicted in *Home to Harlem*.[62] Effectively McKay makes this multiracial group and its aesthetics and sonics of performance like Harlem itself: a formation very much inside and of the place rather than other to it. It is a way of saying that the movement inspired by Father Divine made sense there. We cannot hasten to add that McKay, for all of the reasons elaborated above, was able to see the resemblances of people and place and thus the situatedness of Father Divine.

A commitment to getting closer to Harlem in order to explain support for a figure like Father Divine undergirded McKay's "method" as he engaged in what felt to him, at least at times, like a project of truth-telling. Quotes from interviews with followers develop an ethnographic-type texture in this part of the text.[63] By 1940, only two years before formally converting to Catholicism, McKay might already have been in the sway of religious possibility, so that when he writes that Father Divine "fulfilled a strangely complex and profoundly universal need" there may be more than cool observation at work.[64] McKay alights upon the unquantifiable effects of racial feeling, suggesting that though Father Divine professed no consciousness of color and his movement was broadly inclusive, his Blackness mattered. When he is directly questioned about race, McKay writes, Father Divine invokes universalism and betrays an unmistakable self-aggrandizement. He reports drily about Father Divine that "he does not say I AM GOD. But he does not ask his followers not to call him God."[65] Notably, in this section, McKay relies on documentary-type description rather than an analytical approach that many Black social scientists might have assumed.

In fact, the narrative tone of these passages is downright sympathetic. McKay casts Father Divine's legal troubles as the product of misunderstanding, not unlike what inspired the 1935 riots when false reports circulated of a Black youth being killed by a white shop owner. Even the critique of Father Divine's fundamentally capitalist values is surprisingly gentle. The repetitive observation of inclusiveness—"his kingdoms are wide open to the world"; he is "enormously adaptable and receptive"—creates a strikingly positive portrait.[66] On one level, it is hard to interpret McKay's reluctance to condemn Father Divine outside of an inclination to Black solidarity. On another, the capturing of the breadth of Harlem would certainly have resonated with this writer's cross-cultural way of seeing and being, even when the content of his and Father's Divine's ideal social movements differed so dramatically.

In the many stories that make up *Harlem: Negro Metropolis*, figures, movements, and sites that might be seen as marginal in dominant accounts are similarly brought to the center of this place. Just as highlighting Father Divine's power in the spiritual landscape of Harlem is to call attention to real affects and people therein, so too is McKay's exploration of the world of "occultists" and "cultists" self-conscious about its revelation of an understudied set of formations. And this perspective, too, enables an alternative material geography, visible to so many who live there but often absent from authorized accounts. McKay situates the life of Harlem in global maps of ideas and places, writing that "the innumerable cults, mystic chapels and occult shops which abound in Harlem are explainable only by tracing back to the original African roots. For Africa remains the continent of magic. From the northernmost tip of Tangier all the way down to the Cape ... Whether they are West Indian or southern practitioners of the occult science in Harlem, their ritual is basically similar in form and style to the performance of the Guinea fetichers.... In Harlem they have refined their work and enlarged their scope."⁶⁷ He underscores the omnipresence of these formations: "It is not so strange that these occult establishments should exist in Harlem. Like gypsies, they may be found in every place. But it is significant that such an increasingly large number should flourish there."⁶⁸ This is Harlem's Blackness, too, McKay reminds us.

In these articulations, we might see both the failures and the potential of McKay's broad international imagination, tracing currents through Africa, the Caribbean, the U.S. South, and into Harlem, the stuff of Black diaspora and its histories. As a whole "continent of magic" from top to bottom, Africa is rather essentialized, and yet there is a strategic quality to the representation, which draws on the presence of different African diasporic religious formations to bind together the varied groups of Harlem despite felt differences. This narrative of the expansion of the "increasingly large number" of magical-spiritual currents sounds two kind of predictive notes: one, that an alternative to mainstream Black church-based social life may be building, and, two, relatedly, that the antipathy of orthodox Marxists to religious experience and thought may destine them to failure in a place like Harlem, which will never eschew communities based on them. McKay's religious conversion, perhaps by then underway in some respects, could not but be part of this formulation.

While McKay's challenge to the Black middle-class establishment was already evident in novels such as *Home to Harlem* or *Banjo*, that impulse acquires a special charge through first-hand observations in *Harlem: Negro Metropolis*. He describes visiting a chapel "narcotic with the heavy aromas of burning oils and incense" and proceeds to recount details of the religious rituals, quoting the ceremony and the comments of participants.⁶⁹ Unquestionably, McKay relates to various elements as strange and exotic, but still communicates his attraction to the ritual spaces of the occult. He devotes considerable space to the mystic Madame Fu Futtam, the widow of Sufi Abdul Hamid, in the last chapter of *Harlem: Negro Metropolis*. The extended description of Futtam's mixed-race appearance ("born in Panama . . . oriental blood of some sort") manifests McKay's own inclinations, which he makes no attempt to conceal.[70] Never, that is to say, is McKay fully detached or clinical as an observer. Ultimately, his objective, to get close to the lives of those on many kinds of edges, gains the force of opinion when he ends the chapter by noting: "To those who find spiritual comfort in dim-lit rainbow colors and the opiate odors of incense, the intimate atmosphere of the occult chapel may offer as much solace as the shrine of a great cathedral does to others."[71] Tolerance here is not only about ethnic diversity: it also accommodates differences of affect and proclivity. In more formalistic terms, too, the nonfictional is open; it can hold more than the merely objective.

In the middle chapters of *Harlem: Negro Metropolis*, McKay takes "business" as a point of entry into philosophical questions having to do with Harlem's future. Economic activity, its dependency and autonomy, has long been central to questions of racial uplift as well as place. White-owned Blumstein's Department Store and the Apollo Theater were important, if different, kinds of sites for somewhat messy negotiations of race and influence.[72] Interestingly, here, McKay's overarching agenda to think through Black grouphood with an eye to multiplicity leads him to approach business through its constitutive dynamic interaction. In "Harlem Businessman," he takes readers through the problem of non-Harlemites owning and running shops in the area somewhat counterintuitively, by gazing closely at the exchange of different peoples and identifying meeting points of conflict and intimacy in the locality that is always connected to other worlds. He thus treats the enduring "outsider–insider" question by effectively theorizing this space, its internal and external boundaries and constitution, through various interests in dialogue. The possibility of "community enterprise" becomes a way for McKay to engage the energy of Black nationalist projects like those of Marcus Garvey, Father Divine, and Sufi Abdul Hamid, remaining alive to comparison. He carefully locates Spanish restaurants and white-owned cafeterias on the central arteries of 116th and 125th Streets that are patronized by Black customers, then points to Puerto

Rican, Italian, and West Indian ethnic entrepreneurship as a model for Black Americans, in a familiar discourse of stratification and competition. But there are two important distinctions. First, McKay's descriptions of all the groups attend, especially, to heterogeneity—the thick class and ethnic analysis of West Indians, whose Blackness developed against but also alongside Chinese and East Indian migrants in the Caribbean, presents identity as a story of process rather than one of fixity or naturalness. Second, he raises as an ideal the neighborhood pushcart businesses that began, again at a very precise location in Harlem, on Eighth and Lenox Avenues, and continued to evolve, together with the carts of Black and other merchants. McKay writes: "It is no longer unusual to see colored and white vendors with pushcarts offering their wares ... there is no friction."[73] Whether or not the absence of tension bore out in the everyday matters less than McKay's rhetoric, because his desire to see that harmonious multiplicity impresses.

The racial geography of commerce in the chapter "The Business of Numbers" encompasses myriad details of transnational histories and stories of underworld figures and forms of exchange. McKay's keen eye for alternative forms of sociality and economic life finds the perfect subject in the illegal lottery "playing numbers," a practice familiar in many working-class neighborhoods but one that surely rankled middle-class racial subjects anxious for respectability. McKay employs Casper Holstein, an important player in various numbers rackets in Harlem and also a community philanthropist, to help tell a story of the moral complexity of Harlem. Holstein's background, mixed-race, from the Danish West Indies, taps into the ever-deepening concerns of hybridity and migrancy in *Harlem: Negro Metropolis* as a whole. And focusing on Holstein raises the question of who a representative Harlemite is, anyway, especially when there is nary a mention in the text of other prominent personalities. The back story of the numbers game recounted here, with a range of purveyors and participants, including Puerto Ricans and Cubans who had come into Harlem and British West Indians, some who McKay notes "had worked in Cuba and Central and South America, before coming to the United States, and thus were familiar with Latin-American customs," fills out and makes even more international the broader history of Black people elaborated along the way.⁷⁴ The field for playing numbers becomes its own dynamic time-space: the "Spanish-American" neighborhood originally in the East 90s morphs into a "considerable Puerto Rican colony" at the "border of the black belt" through the postwar development of Harlem.⁷⁵

A very brief chapter, "The Business of Amusements," turns to cabarets and theaters and, like the preceding one on playing numbers, draws attention to social interactions that percolate under and at the edges of middle-class Black and ethnic communities. Resonating loudly with McKay's fictional representations, the nonfictional account again presents readers with the question of what the real substance of "mainstream" Harlem life is. The agenda here has a specific edge: a critique of the absence of Black ownership amid racial and ethnic hierarchies *and* cross-cultural intimacies. When discussing the Italian assumption of Irish speakeasies, with a nod to "rum-running," which instantiates Harlem in the Caribbean, McKay notes that Italians "were more engaging, freer and more intimate in their relationship with the Negroes." Following that is a reminder that the Savoy Ballroom is not Black-owned, despite widespread perception that it is, and observations about the ironies of Communist "interracial fiestas" there while the theater is open shop.⁷⁶ Cultural belonging and economic autonomy exist unharmoniously, this is to say, across a racial topography.

McKay's dogged commitment to the complexities of race, politics, and diaspora is perhaps nowhere more vivid than in his explorations of Marcus Garvey and Sufi Abdul Hamid in Harlem. His criticisms of Garvey were widely reported at the time and have been amply referenced in the scholarship. But it is worth further pursuing how McKay writes about Garvey and Hamid in *Harlem: Negro Metropolis* especially subtly, carefully distinguishing his own politics from those of the two figures but also painting the landscape of Black possibility as one that can manage a fairly wide range of contradictions. An opening discussion of Garvey is quite lyrical, manifesting authorial emotion and sympathies: "A weaver of dreams, he translated into a fantastic pattern of reality the gaudy strands of the vicarious desires of the submerged members of the Negro race."⁷⁷ Even as

McKay attended to the illusions that Garvey embodied "in gaudy paraphernalia and with a symbolic sword ... words ... apparently of great value even than the little action which resulted from them," he remained alive to the widespread power of that sort of address.[78] Likewise, he praised Hamid's ability to stir mass discontent in the Black Harlem population on the basis of jobs even when the project of labor organization fell short in that telling. No less importantly, Garvey's community desire for Black autonomy, acknowledged by McKay to motivate so many, could of course mirror his own polemical mission.

Pairing dreams and realities reiterated the logic of diaspora, and indeed, McKay identified, especially, how Garvey was a *cosmopolitan* Black nationalist. The Garveyist project worlded the "Negro metropolis," making Harlem a "Mecca" as a pan-African "empire" took shape in this particular city-space.[79]. McKay signaled the spatial intervention of globality in locality with the "wild invasion of Harlem by Negroes from every black quarter of America."[80] In that formulation of Garvey's routes, Harlem could be both centered and a point to be aligned with others, through France, Canada, and Jamaica. The politics of Ethiopia, too, pressed on diaspora from abroad but also from closer in, through prominent aid efforts in Harlem. McKay explicitly linked Garvey's pan-Africanism to the Harlem expressions of the New Negro, writing of simultaneity—"the flowering of Harlem's creative life came in the Garvey era"—and influence.[81] He noted that Jessie Fauset, Walter White, Rudolph Fisher, Wallace Thurman, Countee Cullen, and Langston Hughes all published writings during this period. And this chapter on Garvey ends with a complimentary, if ambivalent, assessment by James Weldon Johnson. McKay cites Johnson's observation about the extraordinary impact of Garvey, that he "stirred the imagination of the Negro masses as no Negro ever had" despite failing to fully contend with specific forms of U.S. Black resistance to racism.[82] In quoting this famous Black American intellectual so extensively and directly, McKay would seem to propose a contemplation of the difficulty of particularity and connection within diaspora from Harlem itself.

If at first it seems curious that *Harlem: Negro Metropolis* would be concluded with a chapter on the shape-shifting figure of Sufi Abdul Hamid, by this point readers have also become familiar with McKay's narrative strategy of using material from ostensible edges of representation to interrogate important social formations. Like Garvey, Hamid was an expressly populist figure who did not come from the recognized channels of Black middle-class political leadership. But his public cosmopolitan presentation was even more unusual, cobbled together from migrations less through particular places (such as Jamaica) and more through ideas and styles with which he somewhat unpredictably identified. Named at birth Eugene Brown, and born in Massachusetts, he became Bishop Conshankin in Chicago and dabbled in mystical Buddhism and Hinduism. When he moved to Harlem he refashioned himself as His Holiness Bishop Amiru Al-Mu-Minin, a Black Muslim. McKay's description of the Sufi's flamboyant attire—dressed "in a bright-colored cape, Russian long boots and Hindu-type turban"—carried a tinge of fascination.[83] The writer seemed to be enjoying himself when he observed: "Little idea had he of the hornets he was drawing to buzz around his head when he put on that Oriental turban!"[84]

But Hamid's subjectivity concerned a good deal more than style: it created an opportunity to ponder who and what this place was for and, consequently, mobilize on its behalf. To start, McKay explains that Hamid's somewhat incoherent identity touched on different points of cross-cultural diasporas, religious and cultural. And yet his Blackness animated a relationship to political and community questions, just as, surely, it greased the identificatory wheels of agitation for Black jobs in Harlem. (McKay himself had presented the likelihood that it made a difference that Father Divine was Black.) Hamid, thus, could elevate Blackness without establishing its boundaries too narrowly, effectively delinking racial representation and essentialism for a working-class population that was immiserated, in need of employment, and yet with many backgrounds in other countries and across the rest of the nation. If Hamid's outsider status mattered, it might very well have been in the service of shared interests across differences, a formation McKay deeply understood. Hamid could reframe what it meant to be an insider, not only in terms of identity but through other forms of (often aspirational) belonging.

And so McKay posed the enormously popular Negro Industrial and Clerical Alliance, which Hamid developed to militate for jobs in a wide range of white-owned establishments across Harlem in the 1930s, against left-wing organizations of "white Communists" and Socialists, which he had already widely critiqued as being unresponsive to Black worker interests.[85] A class, generational, and even cultural divide opened up within Black communities. A group called the Harlem Citizens' League for Fair Play originally overlapped with the Sufists, with a member of the latter formation attending meetings for coordinated negotiations with shop owners and even agreement on picketing those establishments that continued to hire only white workers. But McKay closely interpreted somewhat different ideas about race, class, and gender, wherein white salesgirls were understood to be workers ready to submit to trade union membership and Black salesgirls would have come from a more professional class that was less open to labor organization, especially as a source of identification. Thus when the Sufists proposed that the Black salesgirls be required to join the Negro Industrial and Clerical Alliance it became clearer that employment itself could not provide the glue for divergent conceptions even of Black workers. Nor could the distinction be simplistically rendered as pro- or anti-working-class, because the Sufists also diverged from those on the left. At least in McKay's view, the space that Sufi Abdul Hamid and his followers rushed in to fill, between Black community aspirations to join the establishment and interracial militancy, was a wide one, which could accommodate masses of Black working peoples. Although important to many people, this movement had not appeared in dominant accounts of Harlem at the time, nor has it since.

The political alternatives that McKay offers in the substantive last chapter of *Harlem: Negro Metropolis* gain heft through both structure and content. He begins with an extended argument, almost an opinion piece, on Black autonomy as distinct from separation, but often misunderstood to be the same thing. The detailing of Hamid's activities and massive support provides evidentiary material, remaking notions of what a community wants and can be, in Harlem. Partly because Hamid is so unusual, a little like a conjure man, yet studiously tied to material realities, he does not elicit the familiar modes of evaluation, indexed to either nation or globe, like segregation vs integration, and instead can bring readers to an intensely local sensibility, to ask what could, should work *in Harlem* and vis-à-vis its Blackness. That discussion of the distinctiveness of the Black enclave concerns race vs ethnicity and the very spatialization of difference. And yet, the represented desire for jobs and resources for Black residents and the need to militate for that goal all shape a vision of an independent but hardly segregated Harlem that could not but reflect back on broader philosophical concerns.[86]

When McKay turned to a defense of Hamid against charges of anti-Semitism in the pages of *Harlem: Negro Metropolis*, he spoke from and to a complicated field of relations between adjacent forms of otherness in Harlem.[87] There was a long history, dating back to the 1920s, of Black people in the area sorting through what ownership of place meant alongside other ethnic populations, and Black–Jewish tensions loomed large within that landscape. Relationships between these peoples who were suffering racial discrimination extended far beyond Harlem, too, into national and global discussions. In 1923 the *Amsterdam News* had run an editorial that touted Black–Jewish cooperation in the face of the well-publicized anti-Semitic sentiments of Henry Ford, which noted: "It is very pleasing to us to note that the colored press in particular and colored public in general has not joined Henry Ford and others in his denunciation of Jews. Much may be gained by the existence of friendly relations between these two races."[88] The ethical principle seemed also to have a strategic dimension: the piece went on to praise Jews for being the most "liberal-minded element" of Americans, and activists for better working conditions and educational opportunities, holding them up as a kind of model for success, with the "ability to think and to do things," and resented for that reason. Alain Locke gave a speech entitled "The Negro and the Jew—A Comparison" in 1927 at the 135th Street YMCA.[89] A keen awareness of these dynamics continued through the 1930s, and at the 1939 convention of the Negro Improved Benevolent Protective Order of Elks, attended by two thousand delegates from all over the country (and some from abroad), a Jewish lawyer, Samuel Leibowitz, made an impassioned and apparently newsworthy appeal for a "truce between Negro and Jew to end a growing anti-Semitism in Harlem," as the *New York Times* headline read.[90]

As someone who was extremely interested in Black–Jewish solidarity, McKay was inclined to resist anti-Semitism,[91] but in his discussion of Communists, who were threatened by Hamid's growing influence, he was also tapping into an experience of not being properly seen, for Harlemites and Black people everywhere at once. Whether the Sufi was anti-Semitic or not is less the question. More to the point is that McKay was committed to seeing him as the victim of "unfair and unjust" accusations, and that this facilitated a broader political vision in *Harlem: Negro Metropolis* of Black autonomy as well as a critique of specific white leftist projects for interracial solidarity.[92] McKay invokes the 1935 riots as an instance of misrecognition, and as the specter of a kind of colonization, when white police came in large numbers to Harlem, so that it "appeared like an occupied territory."[93] McKay believed that, in the absence of anti-Semitic sentiment, even when people were protesting, they were targeting shops in general, not specifically Jewish-owned stores. To drive the point home, he observes: "Nowhere have I seen Jews doing business more peaceably than among Negroes in Harlem. . . . The Negroes certainly draw no line between the Jews and other whites."[94]

It is in this chapter on Hamid that McKay's willingness to approach the difficulties of tangled cross-cultures for Black people and for Harlem is brought to fruition. On the one hand, he dutifully observes the heterogeneous makeup of the ethnic landscape, comprising Italians, Greeks, and Jews, and on the other, maintains how the Black–white opposition structures the conditions of social life, political movements, and economic reality. As he notes about attacks on Hamid: "The Sufi could not escape his race, whether he wore a Hindu turban, or British officer's belt, or Russian high boots."[95] A solution to the problem of anti-Black racism, for McKay, could be found in just the sort of group organizing in which other ethnic populations, especially Jews, had engaged.[96] Even a keen attention to the exchanges among a wide variety of peoples that had traveled, an awareness of the discrimination that non-Black populations faced, and a special admiration for Jews did not neutralize the power of anti-Black racism, in work or in political participation (unions, parties) that were the means of inhabiting Harlem. This was the context and the logic for an expansive conception of Blackness, drawing together U.S.-born and other populations of African descent, which McKay had outlined. While critics may remember *Harlem: Negro Metropolis* and this final chapter, especially, as a forceful critique of the Communists, a closer reading reveals deeper questions about race and place and dueling constraints and possibilities inherent in their constitution. The last pages offer a conclusion to the text as a whole, reiterating the criticism of Soviet Union–influenced Communists but also presenting an argument about how Booker T. Washington's ideas about Black autonomy might have been simplified through the model of segregation, but were reappraised by none other than the advocate for integration, DuBois. The point of this Harlem story may be, then, to acknowledge both the necessity of aspiring to cross-cultural solidarity while also laying bare the fact that white leftist projects for interracialism too often came at the expense of Black autonomy. Never a stranger to complexity, McKay left this contradiction at the door of his readership.

FRAMES FOR STORYTELLING

An important reference point for *Harlem: Negro Metropolis* would be James Weldon Johnson's 1930 book *Black Manhattan*. Indeed, McKay dedicated his own text to Johnson, "Friend and Wise Counsellor," and accorded him a distinctive degree of authority, as "the most diplomatic and distinguished representative of the Negro élite and also endowed with the shrewdest mind among contemporary Negroes."[97] With the notion of a "Black Manhattan," Johnson, like McKay, had approached Harlem phenomenologically, in terms of its major symbolic importance, its bigness for Black people everywhere, its imaginative centrality.[98] And, using language that would provide a template for McKay's vision, Johnson wrote: "Harlem is today the Negro metropolis and as such is everywhere known . . . it is Mecca . . . not merely a colony or a community or a settlement—not at all a 'quarter' or a slum or a fringe—but a black city."⁹⁹ Absent from this account is any profession of detachment or sense of proportion; Johnson's project denotes passion, even urgency, of the sort that characterizes *Harlem: Negro Metropolis*. Moreover, Johnson and McKay both expressed Black life in and out of modernist idioms, especially attentive to how newness could be explored with particular depth in Harlem's spaces of encounter.¹⁰⁰ Johnson's own racial background developed through crossings. This Southern migrant from Jacksonville, Florida to the urban north of Harlem had a Bahamian mother, was fluent in Spanish, was widely traveled, and had resided in Central America. He manifested a cosmopolitan consciousness that made him a kindred spirit for McKay. A mix of accounts of the early period of Black presence in New York, descriptions of Black artistic production, and careful consideration of social and political movements created an open narrative structure for *Black Manhattan* not unlike that of *Harlem: Negro Metropolis*.

Another frame for McKay's book is the social scientific work of the period, directed at the effects of modern industrialization and urbanization. By 1924, Australian geographer Marcel Aurousseau was surveying the field of urban geography, pointing to aerial views and other descriptive techniques that found echoes in McKay's approach.¹⁰¹ And a seminal work of the University of Chicago school of urban sociology, *The City* by Robert E. Park, Ernest W. Burgess, and Roderick D. McKenzie (1925), presented a quasi-ecological organism with symbolic and imaginative potential, "more than a congeries of individual men and of social conveniences—streets, buildings, electric lights, tramways ... a state of mind."¹⁰² But these authors' vision for interpretation was predicated on objectivity; they wrote "We are mainly indebted to writers of fiction for our more intimate knowledge of contemporary urban life. But the life of our cities demands a more searching and disinterested study than even Émile Zola has given us."¹⁰³ *Harlem: Negro Metropolis* may be considered to be "searching," but it was hardly "disinterested." How could a Black author at this, or any, time write without investment? While Park, Burgess, and McKenzie and others sought to conceptualize cities in general, McKay developed a theory for the particular Black space of Harlem, with the consequence of different answers to fundamental questions of social formation and habitation.[104] Not least of these were divergent understandings of mobility: "subversive and disorganizing"[105] for Burgess, but, as we have seen in *Harlem: Negro Metropolis*, utterly constitutive of meaning and possibility for McKay. An emphasis on Harlem's structuring globality provided another kind of departure from sociology's canonical texts that might have critiqued simplistic assimilationist understandings of pluralist America but still retained a thrust toward and belief in the bounds of nation.[106] Even *Black Metropolis: A Study of Negro Life in a Northern City*, written by St. Clair Drake and Horace R. Cayton about Chicago, endowed the term "metropolis" with considerably less breadth, its influences never quite extending beyond the United States, and scant attention to diasporas.[107]

Harlem: Negro Metropolis grew, too, out of the responses to the Depression and its intensified effects on poor and racialized communities like those in Harlem. On the one hand, it reflects a broader national set of cultural-political efforts that included the Federal Writers' Project (FWP), and on the other, it evinces a localized sense that the Harlem Renaissance had ended. A documentary impulse of the former could not but be paired with the representational responsibilities of the latter, and in this vein, Richard Wright and McKay produced the essay "A Portrait of Harlem" for the FWP to be included in the 1938 essay collection *New York Panorama: A Comprehensive View of the Metropolis*.[108] Wright and McKay committed to a full and multifaceted exploration of Harlem, and they did indeed cover political, social, and cultural aspects of life there. The scattered categories that created a broad "panoramic" vision of New York included "A Portrait of Harlem" as a chapter to illustrate the life of "Negroes." The charge to describe Black people through Harlem undoubtedly shaped what Wright and McKay would write: an almost exclusive work on those subjects, but with nary a mention of either the heterogeneity within Blackness or the other migrant groups peopling the comprising areas at the time. The essay seems unusually silent on issues that were central to McKay's perspective on the world, and also Harlem. But that feature of the negotiated writing may say something, too, about the limits of the Communist-sympathetic project, for what McKay and Wright (who were both ambivalent about the party, we know) could imagine and express within that framework.[109] They took their collaborative research and writing to arrive at different individual 1940 endpoints, with *Native Son* and *Harlem: Negro Metropolis*. If Wright's novel and McKay's collection of essays seem to manifest a distinction between fiction and nonfiction, the literary naturalist and almost social scientific discourse in the first and the creativity of the second lead us into a deeper questioning of the boundaries of forms.

In turn, it is impossible not to read the responses among some reviewers of *Harlem: Negro Metropolis* regarding accuracy and objectivity as reflecting expectations about categories of expression. To be sure, the swells of passion and opinion that ran through the book's pages and the turning up of unusual, even flamboyant, detail about life and politics in Harlem understandably gave pause to readers and critics accustomed to a more clinical language associated with community portraits. Black journalist Ted Poston accused McKay of being "intrigued by the spectacular, bizarre and exotic side of Harlem" en route to the conclusion that "McKay the poet is still superior to McKay the new and questionable social scientist."[110] If Poston cast the relationship of the poet to other pursuits negatively, philosopher and social reformer John Dewey was a good deal more generous, writing that *Harlem: Negro Metropolis* was a "model for all studies of its kind . . . written with the eye of a poet & the equipment of a scholar."[111] The antiracist John LaFarge appreciated the writerly touch, too, noting in a review in the Jesuit magazine *America*: "This is a novelist's, a poet's, a journalist's description of Harlem."[112]

A work such as *Harlem: Negro Metropolis* inevitably raised the question of representativeness for several reviewers. Poston referred to McKay's subject matter as "popular leaders," with quotation marks to cast skepticism. And historian Carter G. Woodson took his evaluation "not a great production" in a different direction, by asking whether Harlem itself was, in his words, even "typical" of Black experience.[113] When Woodson wrote that "to the Negroes in most parts of the country Harlem is not a place where one goes to do things, but where one goes when he has the ambition to do nothing—'to cut a shine' for a hand out, to find a way of escape with one's wits . . . the striking evidences of the progress of the race are not to be found in Harlem," he evinced a fairly transparent anxiety about Black working-class life or leisure activities, of the very sort that McKay was keen to express.[114] It is almost impossible to imagine McKay, a creative writer, being interested in representativeness, not least because of the inherently flawed logic of representation of the real. But Woodson's insinuations about McKay's inclination to sensationalize—suggesting about *Harlem: Negro Metropolis* that "almost any student of social conditions there knows [this] already" or that it "is not intended for the promotion of truth"[115]—might actually lay down some fruitful avenues into McKay's intentions not just to impart information but to tell a particular politically motivated story. More than a matter of the practices of a historian conflicting with those of a poet and public intellectual, this is a difference in the content of these Black intellectuals' politics.

Another piece in the esteemed *Journal of Negro Education*, by English teacher Hilda Hill, a less famous Black intellectual than Woodson, was especially attentive to the aspects of both narrative construction and multiplicity of *Harlem: Negro Metropolis*. That review begins with a description of McKay's text as "an interesting presentation of various elements that go to make up this, the largest Negro settlement in the world," without "the coldly scientific approach of the trained sociologist nor the professional detachment of the historian."[116] Hill praises McKay's poetic sensibility, his attention to color and drama, and underscores the discussion of diverse Black peoples in Harlem. Drawing attention to creative flashes, she suggests that McKay "chooses to sketch" and at times "lets himself go" while analyzing figures and features of community life.[117] This assessment is remarkable for the way in which it approaches *Harlem: Negro Metropolis* as a story, told with various emphases and in a style that reflects the perspective of the author. Hill deeply understands McKay's aims, writing of the last section of the text that it "ceases to be Harlem and the Negro and becomes all Claude McKay, his political views and philosophy."[118]

Fundamentally, McKay was a boundary-crosser: geographically, socially, and intellectually. He had a role in mind for the fiction writer in representing the world of racialization. In an unpublished essay, undated but likely from the 1930s, he makes the case forthrightly: "I think our group has need of a great novelist in the historical field." That general statement becomes rather more specific as McKay continues and suggests that such a novelist could portray "towering figures of the colored world such as Antar, the Arabian poet, Ahmed Baba, the savant of Timboucto . . . Toussaint L'Ouverture, Dessalines and Christophe of Haiti . . . Frederick Douglass, Booker Washington, Matthew Henson," and others throughout the Black diaspora.[119] It would be impossible to miss a kind of psychic projection: might not these comments provide a rationalization for his own approach to Harlem, covering formations therein not unlike those he indicates for a hypothetical work? Part of the project, surely, had to do with the variegated aspects of an ideal representation of a Black cultural world, ranging from a poet to a slave revolt leader to an explorer, which squared with the wild diversity of Harlem's space. And, of course, this description matched the eventual content, even organizational structure, of *Harlem: Negro Metropolis*.

In that same essay, McKay evoked different modes of thought with classically spatial language, saying: "the sociological field is contiguous to the psychological and sometimes they merge into each other."[120] If the move from empiricism to more multidimensional understandings of urban life was important for professional sociologists like Park, Burgess, and McKenzie to draw explicit attention from colleagues in their field, we might consider how and why McKay could effect a more fluid accommodation to that perspective from within *Harlem: Negro Metropolis* given his own interlocutors. Despite Woodson's caution about representativeness, Harlem's power lay in the symbolic of global Blackness. Another possibility has to do with the proliferation of literary and aesthetic imaginings of place in Black cultural production. Black Harlem needed this kind of range of stories, McKay seems to say by telling them with such force and specificity. Departing from prevalent understandings that ethnic neighborhoods were transitional, McKay suggests that even if the form of Harlem shifted, its contents were changing and its meanings seemed contingent, Harlem could be a focus for politicized community. None other than the international president of the Brotherhood of Sleeping Car Porters, A. Philip Randolph, intuitively understood the goal of McKay's analysis when he wrote to him that his "description of the Suffi [*sic*] movement and other currents in Negro Harlem is brilliant, penetrating and constructive" and agreed that Black autonomy was not tantamount to segregation.[121]

How to hold all of it together—another fundamentally spatial question that underlay the project—resonated through *Harlem: Negro Metropolis*. The nested structure of the text, with events, sites, social formations, and figures serving as openings to other kinds of stories, develops an inquiry into the relationship between the particular and the general and also creates a layered, sometimes uneven topography. The takeaway of the storytelling is that space is produced through people, events, and locations in not altogether linear or, for that matter, literal fashion. McKay's preoccupation with working-class cosmopolitanism also structures the intervention in debates about Blackness in geographic terms. The internationalist, cross-cultural Blackness of Harlem, seen in the projects of Garvey, the Sufi, or Father Divine, or commercial enterprises, or, more figuratively, through the openness of neighborhoods and group formations, implodes narrower understandings of how place is experienced.

It is important to remember that McKay was animating Black geographies already in formation as Harlem became a focal point of diasporas and widely understood and experienced as multiply constituted. We might recall that in her novels, Nella Larsen had represented the yearnings and inclinations for an outside and that Langston Hughes's imaginary, as the previous chapter of this book showed, drew out tensions of Blackness across the Americas.[122] With the Harlem Renaissance in the rearview mirror and the effects of the Depression still being felt deeply, diversity lived domestically and globally provided one cultural grammar for representing Harlem and posed the question of just what kind of touchstone this place could be. How, in other words, could Blackness's distinction and internal difference be part of a political future? Again, McKay's kind of Blackness was central to this project. As a prominent author of the Harlem Renaissance, he commanded authority; with Wright, he was clearly perceived by the WPA as able to say something about Harlem. And his globalism coming in and out of the United States and his exile in worlds outside, not to mention his origins in and attachment to other diasporic reference points, all complicate a stable writer's subjectivity, which could not be decoupled from his dream of an autonomous Black place and Black grouphood. A review of *Harlem: Negro Metropolis* in the *New York Amsterdam News* suggested that McKay's "deep love for his people" and "profound understanding of their problems" gave the text its weight with an insider perspective.[123] Additionally, and certainly not parenthetically, we know that this creative writer prized individualism, which, to his mind, underlay true democracy. McKay's life trajectory, based in an embrace of controversy and a willingness to go against the grain, as well as an allergy to movements that would squash difference (as he believed certain variants of Communist politics did) shaped any particular visions of community he would develop.[124] If there are no easy or critically clear avenues out of the murkiness of race and identification and their texts, we might read McKay's expressiveness about the twists and turns as a kind of consciousness of the literary, political, and philosophical conventions he was flouting.

NON-FICTION VERSUS FICTION, REDUX

Given that we remember Claude McKay as a poet and a novelist, we cannot fail to reflect on how some of his more famous literary works, particularly those about Harlem, relate to what some would consider his "lesser" *Harlem: Negro Metropolis*. To begin, because of subject matter it would be impossible to read the 1928 *Home to Harlem*, the late 1930s *Harlem Glory: A Fragment of Aframerican Life*, or the 1941 *Amiable with Big Teeth* in isolation from it.[125] An imbrication of the local and the international ran through all his novels, just as that dynamic marked the nonfictional essays. It was not just that McKay's imagination was transnational, but that the site of Harlem was effectively rendered as global in so many ways. In the case of *Home to Harlem*, Jake, the Black protagonist, crisscrosses the streets of local neighborhoods, comes in and out freely and frequently, dwelling in a male (and masculinist) working-class community and debating American and diasporic racial formation. The particularly open space is subjective, social, and political at once, and can also be seen formalistically, in the novelistic ending that resists resolution as Jake leaves Harlem, but not for good, as readers are meant to infer.

By the period in which McKay was writing *Harlem Glory* (and *Harlem: Negro Metropolis*), popular social and political movements had made their mark on the place and the hot-button issues of autonomy and integration acquired a different edge from the 1920s influences on earlier works. McKay's literary agent, Carl Cowl, has argued that *Harlem Glory* both gave fictional form to the world portrayed in *Harlem: Negro Metropolis*, with thinly veiled representations of actual figures (e.g., Sufi Abdul Hamid, as the character "Omar"), and hewed close to autobiographical influence, with the protagonist, Buster South, like McKay himself, returning to Harlem after some years away.[126] Notably, the characters of *Harlem Glory* comprise regular local residents and famous political leaders, with a nod to the public significance of this place and what was occurring within its bounds. The social space that it develops is no less open than that of *Home to Harlem*, especially if we think about its diversity and dynamism. It also depends on a sensibility of Harlem's political importance for Blackness. *Harlem Glory* would not see publication during McKay's lifetime. The 1940s was a complicated period to try to assess the relationship between labor and left-wing organizing and social movements for racial justice, and this might be one way to understand the unfinished nature of the novel,[127] with the author not having had the opportunity to edit and refine the narrative arc. But another reading could follow Cowl's more general argument that McKay was uninterested in conventional resolution, that he "simply did not share the concerns of those who believe that every loose narrative thread must be neatly tied up," and in this way was a "truer realist."[128] In this discussion of his client's writerly inclinations, Cowl, perhaps unwittingly, may also have been attesting to the boundaries of fiction that McKay would not strictly observe. If fiction could wander into the "true," might not nonfiction encompass some aspects of the fictional associated with the imagination?

In this vein, it is fascinating to trace the perceived correspondences between *Harlem: Negro Metropolis* and *Amiable with Big Teeth*. Scholars Jean-Christophe Cloutier and Brent Edwards, in fact, utilized the published

Harlem: Negro Metropolis to authenticate the latter manuscript, which Cloutier discovered in a minor archive. This serves as yet another acknowledgment of the imbrication of forms of McKay's expression.[129] The explicit subject matter of *Amiable with Big Teeth*, concerning the relationship that Communists have to Harlem, the importance of the Italian-Ethiopian conflict, and the issues of colonialism and autonomy that struggles in another point of the Black diaspora raise for Harlem, makes especially literal McKay's transnational interests and reference points. Given the sequence of these texts, with *Harlem: Negro Metropolis* published in 1940 (written before that) and *Amiable with Big Teeth* completed in 1941, it would make sense to understand the latter as a literary working through of what was raised in the former text's sociological work. But if the goal of this chapter has been to suggest both that there might not be such a clear distinction between the nonfictional and the fictional and that embracing that sensibility means looking at *Harlem: Negro Metropolis* and, indeed, a wide range of studies with different eyes, we necessarily jumble the lines of influence, too, among McKay's many works. This is less a question of dating and much more a matter of understanding the imaginative dimensions of all of these works a bit differently. The details of *Harlem Glory* being written in 1937–1938 (alongside *Harlem: Negro Metropolis* and after the novels of the late 1920s, *Home to Harlem* and *Banjo*) should reveal yet another trajectory.

With *Harlem: Negro Metropolis*, McKay foregrounded the analytical object as well as the subjective experience of Harlem. There could be no confusing the careful mapping here of territory with the aims of providing context, background, or setting for another story. Harlem *was* the story. If in a conventional approach the scale of locality would have conveyed narrowness, McKay projected bigness for Harlem. Partly this was evidenced in an articulation to global currents. Additionally, his narrative showed how Harlem demanded to be known through multiple modes, tapping simultaneously imaginative and descriptive impulses. It narrated specific qualities of dynamism and cosmopolitanism with the special charge of representativeness in a Black geography, never far from lived experience. We return to McKay's sensibility about the merging of the sociological and the psychological as a way to understand his desire to understand Harlem's *felt* territory, what geographer Nigel Thrift has called the "spatial politics of affect."[130]

Ultimately, the fully realized imaginary of *Harlem: Negro Metropolis* assumes a form in the impassioned geography of Harlem, to serve multiple aims.[131] First, McKay's most intentional gesture is to the politics of the period bookended by World War I and the Harlem Renaissance on one side and World War II and *Brown v Board of Education* on the other, for an argument about autonomy, though not segregation. Such a delicate project needed an iconic (and material) example, and Harlem fit the bill. Effectively this text maintains that we cannot fully understand Black political possibility without a Harlem geography made of many kinds of elements. Second, McKay was always theorizing diaspora, processing connections and divergences, finding relations among peoples with different histories, and constituting landscapes of movement and settlement. Harlem, a particularly famous but also complex point, in New York but of the globe, could bring to the surface developing conversations about Black worldliness after Garvey. As sociologist Paul Gilroy and so many others have detailed, diaspora raises fundamentally spatial and modern concerns: the philosophical relationship of parts to the whole and the continuing half-life of slavery for understandings of the free human subject as well as nation-state formation.[132] At heart, and through all of his creative practices, McKay was, indeed, a modernist, who brought the materiality and poetics of Blackness to that conversation, with an intuitive understanding of Katherine McKittrick's resounding premise that "black matters *are* spatial matters."[133]

Here, then, is a Harlem story bound up with other stories and cast across a range of spaces in formalistic, historical, social, and geographic terms. This place, McKay offers, can yield different answers to vital questions in 1940 and over time. In this way, the out-of-print *Harlem: Negro Metropolis* is part of that alternative archive that *Cross-Cultural Harlem* strives to build. As McKay puts Harlem under a close gaze, he breaks down and intensifies all the associations of racialized space. He can be said to deterritorialize and reterritorialize at once; building a Black geography registers displacement and exile and enables hope.[134] But just as the landscape of ideas, social formations, and politics is uneven, the differences may not be easily reconciled, nor the questions raised by Harlem fully resolved. McKay held two sets of values close—those of the cosmopolitan on the one hand and of Black autonomy on the other. In his truest expression, he would have readers uphold these ways of thinking and feeling and have Black Harlemites in particular appreciate both. Suggesting that the cross-cultural need not contradict Blackness in political terms could be seen as challenging for his time, as well as for ours.

Still, it is worth remembering the way that Blackness was central to Claude McKay and his oeuvre. If all of his works theorized race and class, they did so in a manner that made vivid Stuart Hall's formulation that "race is ... the modality in which class is 'lived,' the medium through which class relations are experienced, the form in which it is appropriated and 'fought through.'"[135] McKay's dispute with the Communist Party was really not in how it prioritized class over race, nor in its being insufficiently inclusive (both familiar critiques of leftist projects), but in the basic inability of that political formation to understand Blackness as a *modality*. Unsurprisingly, McKay was clear-eyed about the abiding presence of anti-Blackness across cultures, not excepting U.S. Black culture—even his earlier *Home to Harlem* evoked that painful tendency—and thus about the fact that the richness of cross-culturality could not, in and of itself, preclude the persistence of racism. When we raise our eyes to Harlem's gentrifying present, we cannot but think about the fact that diversity often comes in forms that threaten Black autonomy. McKay refused to gloss over that unease in 1940, even while offering encounter and exchange to be observed, studied, and enjoyed. Another, simpler way to point to the dilemma is to ask what results in this historically minority-majority locale, global capital of the Black diaspora, and space of possible extinction when Jews, Puerto Ricans of differing skin tones, Italians, African practitioners of mysticism, and other identities come into contact. McKay could not fully resolve that question, and in *Harlem: Negro Metropolis* tensions between political visions, and thus peoples, remain at the edges even as generic boundaries are rather more easily crossed.

3

CROSSINGS AT HOME AND IN THE WORLD

Vito Marcantonio's Working-Class Cosmopolitanism

I f the centers of Blackness have historically been found in western and central regions of Harlem, an eastward move renders an iconic and spatialized Italianness. This Italian Harlem, like all neighborhoods defined by some kind of identity, is both its own enclosure and also a node in other territories. One of its especially famous figures, the left-wing congressman Vito Marcantonio, helps us see the rich texture of an "ethnic enclave," of what communities can and cannot contain. Vastly different perspectives on Marcantonio have laid the groundwork for deeper critical thinking about locality and globality, class formation, difference, and urban belonging, among other concerns related to the constitution of Harlem. When asked about the historical importance of this famous representative of Italian Harlem, a longtime Catholic priest replied with noticeable vitriol, so many years later, that Marcantonio was a "traitor."[1] When leftists of a certain age remember him, they speak with a tone of awe, affectionately using his nickname, "Marc." For many New Yorkers, those in Harlem or whose families had once lived uptown, the mention of Marcantonio conjures up the spectacle of a 1954 funeral procession through East Harlem streets that attracted thousands of onlookers from a variety of racial and ethnic backgrounds.[2] Furthermore, Puerto Ricans have evoked an astonishingly sympathetic relation to someone who cannot be fully separated from the U.S. nation-state or, for that matter, white ethnic Italianness. In not altogether simple terms, Marcantonio was a man of his place and time.

Stories of Marcantonio have served various projects of political recovery and social formation. The one that will be elaborated here builds on those to fill out a representation of Harlem as a space for all sorts of crossings. Marcantonio, I argue, is an interesting flashpoint for Harlem's globality, in both the latter term's senses: the structure for relations across internal boundaries of the space and the many exchanges that stray across borders with an outside, a world. We might see him as a kindred spirit of Valerio, the fictional protagonist of Langston Hughes's "Spanish Blood," who centered these kinds of discussions of globality in locality in chapter 1. How Marcantonio embodies political–cultural edges may also remind us of what Father Divine or Sufi Abdul Hamid did for Claude McKay's understanding of politicized space. Like all the points of the developing constellation of stories of this book, Marcantonio enlivens a Harlem that is a little different from conventional renderings, to ask how geography might be reconceived, what a neighborhood is, and where boundaries lie. Cracking open enclave models for identity while also remaining attentive to racialization over time is one way to address these questions. The irony of a deeply U.S.-Americanist figure (a congressman, after all) embodying worldist trends, literal and interpretive both, cannot but further develop the complicated relationship of Harlem, a U.S. place, to ideas of nation and globe. No less importantly, Marcantonio, the Italian American subject whose whiteness was complicated but evident and whose performance of solidarity operated through politics and language, makes vivid the uneven processes of translation that are so essential to an understanding of the representation and social life of the multiply conceived place in which he stood. What follows in these pages is less a kind of political biography and more a story of territories, even as it radiates from an individual.

Marcantonio represented East Harlem from 1936 to 1950 as a member of the Republican, Democratic, and American Labor parties and explicitly addressed civil rights, economic and social class, and imperialism. Both a hometown hero and an icon for the U.S. left, he emblematized otherness for a nation coming to terms with its diversity. Marcantonio continually advocated for the interests of Italians and other minority groups in Harlem at a time of intense racism and hardening politics of white ethnicity. His steadfast support for Puerto Ricans within Harlem extended across its borders when he backed independence efforts in Puerto Rico. Such expansiveness points to the limits of thinking about even "local" politics in terms of strict correspondences such as the responsibility of elected officials to their districts or the demands of representation. Indeed, when Marcantonio argued for the naturalization of Filipinos beginning in 1939, there were no referent populations in the area that had sent him to Congress. This shape of politics had everything to do with a less bounded and unpredictable cross-culturality, a sensibility, and a critique. Marcantonio's work laid bare a deep identification with struggles of belonging and a connection between, on the one hand, leftist and anti-imperial analysis developed in Harlem and, on the other, racially subjectified peoples located elsewhere.

Crossings from an Italian American enclave into Puerto Rican communities at home and abroad through Black formations shaped by civil rights, always navigating a landscape of conflicts and intimacies, challenge static conceptions of community on a number of different levels. First and most obviously, Marcantonio's insertion of Harlem's ethnic and racial minorities into a broader story of capitalism's effects contests ideas of space that stress enclosure, like Michel Laguerre's "minoritized space," a "social construction of the space of the 'other' (ghetto, barrio, Chinatown, or heritage space) . . . the process by which we recognize and maintain difference, reproduce ourselves as dominant and the 'other' as subaltern."[3] Marcantonio's dogged advocacy for Harlem residents of all kinds through a leftist critique of their immiseration and subordination (with which he himself identified) rather than a more paternalistic discussion of service de-ghettoized the social formations. Second, engagements with African American, Puerto Rican, Italian, Jewish, and other inhabitants and activists across Harlem, not only those in East Harlem, his political district, transgressed social divides like "Italian Harlem," "Black Harlem," and "El

Barrio," which had become spatially bordered as well. In public speeches and interviews, Marcantonio often related to Harlem as a total, integrated whole, resisting the political distances among regions of "east," "west," and "central" Harlems while remaining attentive to cultural particularity. Finally, his commitment to Puerto Rican independence, shaped by Harlem experience, eroded familiar oppositions between the United States and the world. Marcantonio's locality was always and already imaginatively globalized. Left-wing, anti-imperial, working-class, and white ethnic, he could be perceived subjectively to be on the edge of dominant formations, just as Harlem itself was on the edge of the nation. Yet astonishingly he also articulated an Americanism that points to the porousness of nation in these years and afterward. If nothing else, the case of Marcantonio clearly establishes that "America" was being understood in diverse, even incompatible, terms.

In his movement beyond registers of the local, the national, and the global from the 1930s to the early 1950s, and in a broader historical arc into the present, Marcantonio personifies a specifically working-class cosmopolitanism. As Junot Díaz, whose current-day fiction portrays the diverse New Jersey suburbs, has very suggestively remarked: "when you live in a community where nobody has too much power, it opens up space."[4] Marcantonio came of age as an Italian American subject from a community that existed alongside peoples who were all othered, often differentially. His whiteness was never in question, but at the time, it carried the affective and ideological effects of minoritization, diverging from Northern European or Irish whiteness and inflected and especially influenced by the labor movement. In Harlem's close quarters and dense race and class experience, Marcantonio developed the resources for multilingualism, too, a way of being cosmopolitan that was hardly elite.

The crossings of this chapter's title are simultaneously geographic, linguistic, cultural, interpretive, and canonical. Crossing surely conjures up the spatial. As Marcantonio engaged in politics across Harlem's enclaves, he reformulated territorial belonging and the boundaries of identification. And in the way that he simultaneously articulated cosmopolitanism and Americanism (however anti-imperial) alongside the chaotic and veritably globalized structure of localized ethnic and racial exchanges based in class formations, we can see an intervention in different histories: "American," "U.S. ethnic," "global," and, for that matter, political and social. The stakes lie less in understanding how Marcantonio himself crosses, but in how Harlem's meaning is made through the movement. One way of reading cross-culturality has to do with inhabiting a particularized identity and remaining open to being changed in interactions with otherness. This practice can find its form in various experiences and discourses. Both versions of politics, with a small "p" and a capital one, need affinity; only then do they constitute a useful vehicle for exchange. It is in just that sort of politics that we see the coming together of ideological perspectives, almost always relying on racial and ethnic diversity. Moreover, if Marcantonio seems surprising or unusual, it is because scholars and critics interested in cultures of hybridity have tended to view a commitment to interethnic exchange from the ground up, but less identifiable on the stage of politics more institutionally rendered; another opposition that Marcantonio finessed was the one between the grassroots and the electoral in the very conception of the political itself.

This chapter brings to the surface how leftist politics in Harlem have been explicitly a stage for cross-cultural engagements. There were many occasions of leftist political organizing in Harlem at the time, in groups such as the Harlem Legislative Conference, antiwelfare projects, and more.[5] If those associations could be exploited for the goal of being elected to (and maintaining) office, Marcantonio's ideological work cannot be fully accounted for by pragmatism. It is difficult to prove authenticity for a historical or contemporary figure: the supporting materials that mediate access to interior life must always be read critically, and even such analysis seldom reveals intentionality. Still, we can discern from the patterns of Marcantonio's self-presentation—his speeches across different venues—and from how he was received by constituents and others vis-à-vis the network of issues he engaged, the substance if not the truth of a commitment to exchange. Recall that Langston Hughes and Claude McKay had ambivalent relationships with the Communist Party and other left-wing political groups, because for Black subjects Blackness necessarily refracted other positionalities as the central modality of experience, representation, and analysis. Marcantonio's whiteness, however "ethnic" and even undefensive, no doubt facilitated a different path of identification with majority white leftist activists. In other words, there is no question that his whiteness mattered, but more interesting is *how* it did and what the resulting affects and effects were, not only for himself, but also for others and the constitutive space(s) of Harlem.

The choice of stories to tell has been absolutely shaped by the sorts of sources available and how and by whom that archive has been constructed.[6] To begin, Marcantonio appears either to have been either an extremely private person or one whose personal life was dwarfed by activities of the public sphere. The primary substantial collection of his papers contains very little personal material.[7] But one can certainly glean engagement, commitment, longing, and frustration from a variety of discourses and practices. And there is a wealth of material of that kind to read that has been organized not only by scholars, but also admirers of Marcantonio, many of whom were former Harlem residents or their offspring.[8] Those collector-activists invested in racial and international solidarity and multicultural communities have undoubtedly created access to the crossings I analyze here. The guiding principle of recovery in that sort of curation might also be understood as a recursive relationship to the past, predicated on a presentist desire for lessons about our messy and diverse futures. This is not a desire that is absent from the pages that follow, in a book on cross-cultures. Indeed, Vito Marcantonio, I suggest, brings to these conversations an underemphasized history in narratives that cast Harlem as a multicultural place of racial–ethnic enclaves or a racial community faced with the diversification wrought by gentrification.

The Harlem of the 1930s, 1940s, and 1950s that the focus of this chapter makes visible is diverse and full of entangled conflicts and intimacies, even as there are sustained projects for ethnic consolidation. Unquestionably this view from the direction of what became constituted as East Harlem and a left whiteness differs greatly from Hughes's and McKay's Black perspectives on the politics and cultures of post-1920s Harlem that the preceding chapters of *Cross-Cultures* elaborated. And yet a juxtaposition does a great deal more than fill out different areas of uptown Manhattan; it makes for a richer dialogue between varying historical (and racial) conditions of possibility. Marcantonio helps us to understand how the form and content of radical politics furthered the social experience of multiplicity at the time. If radicalism constituted a larger proportion of the political currents of the 1930s and 1940s, it still challenged a status quo and thus conferred otherness on its agents and associated places. Furthermore, although Marcantonio has become a sign for Italian Harlem, he is an unstable and complicated one, as the priest's "traitor" comment illustrates, because he must also be understood to exceed correspondences of space and ethnicity that popular perception might dictate. Thus, this chapter continues *Cross-Cultural Harlem*'s conversation about the contours of neighborhood identities, with

FIGURE 3.1 Vito Marcantonio in front of his office at 1484 First Avenue, 1948.

Photo courtesy of the Manuscripts and Archives Division, the New York Public Library.

specific attention to often-unpredictable affective attachments and their challenge to an ethnic enclave model for social experience.

ITALIANNESS IN HARLEM

Most accounts of Vito Marcantonio begin with a statement of his being Italian, quickly followed by the explanation that he was from Italian Harlem. But what all of that means is a relatively open question, one that turns partly on how both definitional points only provide nodes of entry into the complexity of how people relate to territories to which they feel they belong. Marcantonio's background bridged generations: his father's parents immigrated from Italy, and his mother herself moved to the United States, making her a first-generation Italian American. But notably, what might be cast in terms of distance from Italy could also be understood as the substance of a more fulsome Italianness. This was accentuated by a deep locatedness, in ideas of "Italian Harlem" and its geographically specific multigenerational community. And although throughout his life Marcantonio developed a wide range of solidarities with other peoples, as we will see, it is certainly the case that an "Italianness" built one continuous arc of attachment. In just one example, barber Luigi Albarelli, who had performed the most intimate of services, grooming, remained Marcantonio's friend until his death, delivering a eulogy in Italian at the funeral.

Considering Italian Harlem, and Marcantonio's relationship to it, opens up a historical geography for questions of identity vis-à-vis cross-cultural *and* political encounter. The area of Manhattan between 96th and 125th Streets, from Lexington Avenue east, was a destination for peoples from Italy beginning in the 1890s and reaching a climax of concentration in about 1930.[9] During this period, Italians migrated to both the eastern part of Harlem and the area of lower Manhattan around Mulberry Street, though the first population was greater for many years.[10] Popular observers referred to the uptown area as an Italian colony, then quarter, and, by 1886, "Little Italy." In her careful tracking of the newspaper coverage of "Little

Italy," historian Donna Gabaccia points out that the *New York Times*, in particular, enclosed the term in quotation marks, setting it off from other purportedly factual representations. This might have indicated skepticism about the category or even acknowledged the constructedness of this space.[11] Either "colony" or "quarter" could imply enclosure, but "Little Italy," we might consider, as a country within a country, like "Chinatown," could certainly inspire the exoticism and othering that racialized (and classed) ethnicity at that time and after generated. In fact, Jacob Riis, famous chronicler of the poor, described Harlem's Little Italy in language that contained the Italian community, possessing cultures that gave rise to spectacle.[12] Over the first few decades of the twentieth century, Little Italy came to be used for the lower Manhattan community. Gabaccia speculates that "slumming" and other practices of urban tourism facilitated this shift, as visitors coming into New York City might have found it easier to see immigrant ethnic communities side by side, Italians next to Chinatown and the Jewish ghetto. Possibly, too, the two Italian communities differently related to their spaces, the uptown one settling more deeply into rapidly minoritizing Harlem and becoming associated with it, ultimately taking it on and in as part of its identity.

Indeed, early Italian residents referred to their area of dwelling as Harlem, but as the social referent for the place increasingly became Black, many of these ethnics who were already fragilely white sought geographic distance and distinction from that race–space association and found it in the latitudinal category of East Harlem. Though East Harlem may have been announced as a destination for international immigrants, in contrast to the internal migrants from the U.S. South that Central and West Harlem received, this construction, of course, elided the fact of Black Harlem being constituted as much by West Indian immigrants as by African Americans, not to mention that there were all kinds of peoples in all of the regional spaces of Harlem. A 1916 *New York Times* article describes a "race riot" involving two hundred people in the area of 126th Street and Third Avenue, an area "thickly populated by negroes and Italians, between whom there had long been ill-feeling."[13] But the perspective predicated on ideas of communities being more bounded and less mixed than demographic data would render activated in turn memories and experiences of ethnic group competition for a number of residents, though certainly not all of them.

By the time of Marcantonio's rise, Italian Harlem contained immigrants and children of immigrants in a variety of economic positions, shop owners and lawyers among them. If the area where Italians settled was relatively well-defined—as attested to by so many works in their discussions of turf battles[14]—its boundaries, like those of all enclaves, were porous. Benjamin Looker has explored how the "neighborhood" is an imaginary that emerges from responses to urban development, and argues that its invocation serves political interests, depending on whether and how it is constituted by sameness or diversity.[15] Italian Harlem, to be sure, was in and of a space that had been occupied by Irish Americans and Jewish Americans, many of whom stayed on when Italians arrived, just as most Italians may have left en masse by the 1950s; it was also the destination for Puerto Ricans beginning well before the 1940s saw migration on a larger scale. And African American populations could be found all over Harlem, East Harlem included.[16]

By and large, Italian Harlem and East Harlem more generally comprised poor and working peoples. Class was the building block of solidarities, political organizations, and identity for all within, as well as for Marcantonio himself. The politics of class gave meaning to the landscape. In the form of organized labor, as Italians became large contingents of unions in New York City and beyond, or in the everyday negotiations of life and community in dense quarters and neighborhood blocks, ethnicity and economic position were intertwined. By the time Marcantonio came of age, that sort of class-specific Italianness was long in development as well as popularly recognized. So he could tap into that idea and image, which we can see in a 1939 speech in Congress that responded to a recently passed housing bill: "Mr. Speaker, as one who was born in the slums, who was raised in the slums, and who still lives in the slums, I take this opportunity to voice the gratitude of the slum dwellers . . . go into the slum districts of the big cities. Go into my district on a hot summer night and see American babies sleeping on the fire escapes, gasping for air."[17] Marcantonio used his origin story for a political rhetoric that addressed a broader urban, even national phenomenon, with a not-so-subtle appeal to a contemporary liberal Americanism that was establishing and maintaining public works for peoples like those back home whom he represented.

In identifying himself as someone from the "slums," Marcantonio constructed a public identity with regard to place; and given how Harlem functioned in the popular imagination, he also effectively established his own otherness. The negative construction of "the slum" was one element in the discrimination or even racism toward Italians from the late nineteenth to the middle twentieth century. Poor urban America—cast in this period as a "ghetto" and inhabited by African Americans, racialized immigrants like Puerto Ricans, and Italian and other white ethnic Americans whose process of whitening was hardly full or complete—was in many ways not only liminal to the national body, which projected international dominance and domestic integrity, but also, especially given the constitutive populations, openly contradicted claims of equality. It is hardly a revelation that class and racial division complicate the American dream, but here what is also important is how that disconnect between social reality and ideology was spatialized. Marcantonio's politics relied partly on the power of the feelings of otherness for a range of peoples across the class and ethnic spectrum and in specific places; the actual and imaginary nature of East Harlem as an enclave—enclosed, separated out—intensified the experience of alienation from other integrated bodies, of the city (New York) and the nation.

In this map of subjectivity, the relationship of Italianness to whiteness assumed uneven shapes not entirely accounted for by stories of white ethnic racism or white flight from diversifying urban centers. To begin, class fractures racial formation.[18] Italians' whiteness had been in question ever since they first arrived in the United States, and their impoverishment and/or status as workers was established as they became part of reified community-spaces such as East Harlem. Thus it is difficult to read their developing identities outside of place. Marcantonio's discourses seemed to take account of that as he critiqued, simultaneously, representations of East Harlem and of Italians in the public sphere. Early in his political career, in 1938, he spent almost the entirety of a talk to a left-wing group, the Harlem

Legislative Committee, on the discrimination to which Italians had been subjected and the problematic stereotypes that popular journalist Westbrook Pegler was promulgating in the pages of the New York *World-Telegram*. He opined: "True, there are some of our boys who have been forced into crime. I just wonder if Mr. Pegler is able to discover for himself the reason. Any good sociologist will tell it to him: sleeping in slums and living on a subsistence diet would force even some of the boys and girls of the so-called 'best families' into the rackets of Chicago and New York. No, Mr. Pegler, you cannot blame a race which has done so much for our country for its few criminals. Blame does not rest on the Italian people but on the conditions under which our people have had to live. The Italians of New York are Americans. They love our country and have fought and will fight to preserve its democracy."[19] Marcantonio critiqued an anxiety that shaped how he was received, too, about organized crime or "rackets" involving Italians, and in so doing at once pointed to but cannily undid the socio-spatial containment of Italians, on the one hand providing class-based explanations for crime ("sleeping in slums") and on the other developing an identity that could move from the locality of New York to the nation, as "Americans." That emphasizing of Americanness challenged stereotypes of immigrants as overly tied to their homelands just as it legitimized his own status.

To emphasize otherness, as so many accounts of Italians in Harlem did, is not, however, to deny Italians' steady, defensive march toward whiteness, in their Harlem neighborhood as well as elsewhere.[20] At Our Lady of Mount Carmel, on 115th Street between First and Pleasant Avenues, once the symbolic heart of Italian Harlem, Peter Rofrano, that priest who was troubled by Marcantonio, outlined the regional dimensions of race: "This is not Harlem. Harlem begins at 125th Street, that is Negro or black; this is East Harlem. East Harlem is about immigrants."[21] Rofrano's discussion relied on oppositions—between "immigrant" and "black" and between "East Harlem" and "Harlem"—which do not hold up to historical scrutiny: African Americans had lived in East Harlem, and immigrants in Central and West Harlem, and the dividing line itself was shifting all the time. Testifying to the ideological nature of that map, another Italian resident, Peter Pascale, noted: "Harlem was never East Harlem, Harlem was Harlem, this was called Harlem. When the blacks started to come toward this area . . . we said we live in East Harlem. The people who were in East Harlem were the Italians, and the other Harlem, they didn't say West Harlem, then Harlem itself, that's where the blacks were."[22] As these two Italian men looked back and thought of the history of Italians in Harlem they used contrast to defend territory in terms of race. Surely influencing these responses to local tensions was the national background of contestation over classification and arguments about cultural citizenship. Conflicts between Italians and African Americans and other racialized minorities, especially Puerto Ricans, as we shall see, were rampant in Harlem, as they were all over the country.[23]

Given this background, it is intriguing that Marcantonio never accentuated his whiteness, nor seemed invested in that comparative ethnic-racial identity. As a second- and third-generation Italian American, he could be understood as an "ethnic" rather than "immigrant," with reference to the categories that signal stages in the assimilation and integration into the national body, and, especially, for the case of those from southern and eastern Europe, whitening.[24] But somehow his identification with outsiderness, in terms of space (east Harlem) and class (working people) effected a maneuver around a simplistic identity of whiteness. Rofrano's memory of Marcantonio as a "traitor" likely carried a racial connotation, given the intense (and racialized) competition between the Italian and Puerto Rican populations during the period when the men both lived and worked in East Harlem.[25] But if Rofrano's whiteness cannot be read outside of the locale to which he understands himself to belong, neither can Marcantonio's reluctance to self-present as white be understood without processing affiliation to a deeply cross-cultural space.

There is no question that Italian Harlem was densely constituted and could be a complicated source for solidarities and disavowals. So was the very quality of "Italianness." To begin, the former was composed of sub-enclaves, with concentrations of peoples from Bari, Santiago, Sicily, Calabria, and Sarno living in particular blocks.[26] Garibaldi M. Lapolla, whose fiction about Italian Harlem unfurled a kind of informal community ethnography, begins his 1935 novel *The Grand Gennaro* with a description of a typical multifamily house in the area: "In it three Italian families, all from different sections of Italy, were to meet, mingle, and separate, each bearing in charred burdens of memory the shock of their encounter."[27] Their "encounter" could doubly signify, to refer to each migrant family's interactions with the United States and to point to exchanges among families as a result of residential contiguity. America's national discourse for ethnicity, in turn, depended on constitutive nationality, so that for immigrants from various parts of Italy, as well as for Marcantonio, to be Italian was to belong in the United States; the spatialization of that identity meant, too, that Italian Americanness was seen to correspond to an enclave, as occupying territory was tantamount to belonging. National cultural ideology and Harlem massaged Italianness and Americanness together. As Salvatore Mondello wrote about growing up in East Harlem in the 1930s and 1940s: "I had learned to write and read in Italian and well as English. . . . As an Italian I could influence and enjoy the world outside East Harlem. As a Sicilian I could not."[28] It is clear that Mondello saw an Italian identity as essential to membership not only in Harlem, but also in the broader multicultural rubric of, presumably, the nation, as well as the nation in the world.

Yet even the building of a national ethnic identity, Italianness, could not paper over other forms of heterogeneity, of class, politics, even affect. Being "Italian in Harlem" signified something collective, to be sure, but this ethnic prospect disassembled with regard to various interests and needs and at particular historical flashpoints. Marcantonio noted about Italians, "They are a progressive people"[29]—though what "progressive" was at the time (or since) could be open to debate. A more colloquial understanding of progressive as something like forward-looking, while not signifying the political in quite the same way as it does in more recent history, could nonetheless encompass this people's active participation in the United States and, in fact, a wide network of organizations in Italian Harlem at the time testified to that meaning. Many accounts of Marcantonio's rise point to inheritance, wherein liberal, half-Italian Fiorello La Guardia heard De Witt Clinton High School student Marcantonio speak about social security and pensions and immediately apprenticed him, supporting his legal and then political career. Indeed, Marcantonio ran for and won La Guardia's former Congressional seat in East Harlem, originally also as a Republican and through the same strategies of appealing to constituencies across ethnic and racial lines.

But a broader view, one more attentive to complicated and even contradictory political currents, illuminates subjectivity and place more deeply than a story of individual figures can. The world of left-wing politics is one context for Marcantonio. In high school (1917–1921), he was awash in conversations about and activism around trade unionism, housing rights (Marcantonio organized the East Harlem Tenants League), and anticolonialism (against the British occupation of Ireland), and was especially influenced, as Christopher Bell writes, by a socialist teacher.[30] It was in high school, too, that Marcantonio first became associated with reformer and activist Leonard Covello, whose social justice initiatives in East Harlem assumed the same cross-cultural shape that his own politics would come to take. Even by the time he worked for La Guardia at his firm and La Guardia had arranged for him to become Attorney General of the southern district of New York, Marcantonio's political inclinations reflected localized activist investments in East Harlem, with distinctly internationalist strains. Constructing a tight relationship between electoral representation and service to local communities, the La Guardia Political Club featured Marcantonio as one of its prominent members and administrators. While this club, formed in 1930, maintained an "ethnic" component as a hospitable space for Italian progressive causes, it was also organized more broadly around service, education, and immigration issues.

Politics of the homeland cut through place in a variety of ways that were politically conservative and more radical. It is worth remembering that Italy in the early-to-middle twentieth century was experiencing both the rise of fascism, with the founding of Mussolini's Fascist Revolutionary Party in 1915, and the increased activity of socialist parties intersecting with the politics of syndicalism. All these currents could be felt in Italian Harlem. It seems that the Fascist organization Circolo Mario Morgantini, with about one thousand members, had an office on East 116th Street, near Marcantonio's residence.[31] The Casa del Popolo or "Peoples' House," formed in 1920, was connected to a local Protestant church, but its worker-oriented services evoked the socialist settlement houses of pre-Fascist Italy. Marcantonio, educator and reformer Leonard Covello, and La Guardia worked for, in, and through this kind of organization, just as they did in the La Guardia Political Club. And if these groups finessed the divide between "political" and "social" activity, they also provided the conditions of possibility for Marcantonio.

No vector of that space (understood in local, regional, or national terms) was more generative than that of labor politics. For instance, by the 1930s, Italian Harlem's working-class people constituted large proportions of the locals of important unions: the Amalgamated Clothing Workers Union, the building trades unions, the longshoremen's union, even the musicians' union. Other groups specifically organized under the rubric of ethnicity, such as the Italian Unemployed Association and the Italian Welfare Association. In fact, in 1940, the latter organization wrote to Marcantonio suggesting that his speech on a bill for the unemployed be translated into Italian.[32] When Marcantonio advocated for workers' rights and poverty relief, he did so in his community as an engaged social activist and on the national level as a representative of this community. These were politics of class and also ethnicity, not least because the cultural membership of Italians in America was not yet complete. The specific and localized instantiation of class organization and advocacy could thus be indexed to national trends. If La Guardia had moved on to city and state politics by the time Marcantonio was elected, he could nonetheless claim political origins in, not to mention support from, that formation. Developments in Harlem, which could be thematized as labor organization with a left-wing touch, were similar to those in cities and regions all over the United States. Still, the depth and the embeddedness of Marcantonio's leftist labor participation (and identification) illuminate locality, too.

Organized labor's relationship to leftist/socialist political parties and ideologies constructs another lens for understanding Marcantonio. As the politician moved through Republican, then Democratic and, finally, American Labor Party affiliations, we see less a change in his own ideological inclinations and more a shifting sense of accommodation, an ability to see himself under the rubric of one or another party and as the parties changed over time to encompass different kinds of issues. Workers' interests, as well as antidiscrimination, always resonated for East Harlem residents. When Marcantonio became head of the American Labor Party in the late 1930s, he foregrounded the importance of those inclinations, but even earlier on, he had proudly worn the label of socialist. While he did not admit to being a member of the Communist Party, Marcantonio never repudiated the political organization that was so active throughout East and West Harlems, and that in turn influenced other groups in which he participated.[33] The years of his political career, 1934–1954, of course, captured the efflorescence of left-wing politics during the Popular Front, as well as an anti-Communist backlash.[34]

So it came to be that Vito Marcantonio could be associated with this rendition of *left-wing* Italianness, as an outsider to the body politic rather than a symbol of assimilation. The fact that Marcantonio was different from other congressional representatives in terms of subjectivity and politics was not lost on his constituents. The Red-baiting that they read about and saw him facing may have felt, even to many people who were not on the left, like an assault against Italian Harlem. The difference of Marcantonio could be grasped as analogous to the difference of Harlem. This did not work in exactly the same way for La Guardia, who was also left-wing, attentive to community politics, and at least half-Italian. (His father was Italian and his Jewish mother from Trieste, then part of the Austro-Hungarian empire; his maternal grandmother was from a prominent Italian-Jewish family.) But La Guardia could not construct himself as an Italian Harlemite quite as Marcantonio could. Marcantonio's public identity conveyed an organicity that was received as understanding. In this vein, literary critic and political activist Annette Rubinstein noted: "He was born on 112th Street between First and Second Avenues and was living on 116th Street between Second and Third Avenues when he died. He lived and died within four blocks. I think that's part of why the people of East Harlem loved him."[35] When Puerto Rican historian Félix Ojeda

Reyes wrote in 1978, "Marc conoció el Este de Harlem como la palma de su mano" (Marc knew East Harlem like the palm of his hand)[36] he echoed Rubinstein's sentiments about embodied dwelling.

Many scholarly discussions of identity have stressed routes instead of roots, suggesting the latter to be facile or simplistic. Stuart Hall famously decried identity based in a hardened sensibility of where one is from or seems to belong, and Gilles Deleuze and Félix Guattari employed the metaphor of the rhizome to accentuate the practice of moving across and through a space laterally, rather than sprouting up from the ground.[37] But a deep situatedness, of an Italianness in place, was the stuff of Marcantonio's "roots," and enabled the crossings that would define his life. At the time, this particular kind of Harlem Italianness no doubt found a model in Harlem's other and most prominent racial (and political, cultural, social, and geographic) imaginary. Blackness, an always heterogeneous formation, was constituted early on by African American migrants from the U.S. South, immigrants from the West Indies and Africa, Anglophone, Hispanophone, and Francophone peoples, all continually processing slavery's aftermaths. This is to say that present-day negative connotations of "identity politics" may fail to deal with the very fullness of connection and awareness of difference that race and ethnicity themselves have historically produced.

An alternative and more open sense of identity helps us to think, too, more expansively about this place. To begin with, Italian Harlem and East Harlem could not but have a relationship to Black Harlem. Their correspondences lived partly in the sphere of political affect. Even if the trajectory of Marcantonio's politics seemed to be autonomous (related to left-wing Italianness and the influence of the Communist Party), might we not think about his progressivism as having had some more inspirational and/or aspirational relationship to the insurgent Blackness of the time? Generations of white leftist activists have expressed alliance with Black politics. Such efforts have been critiqued for their inability to truly connect with racial experience or, even more negatively, for perceived fetishizing of Blackness. This offers the lesson that affiliation cannot be easily mastered through individual will, nor can it be received without qualification or hesitation. From the other side, Black leftists also forged their own paths in Harlem and elsewhere.[38] Above all, the specifically political nature of Marcantonio's mode of identity shifts—in theorist Wendy Brown's expression, from "I am" to "I want"—helped him to develop an orientation toward work to obtain resources as well as freedoms for the multiple communities with which he was engaged.[39]

Here we might consider the wide-ranging meanings and practices of solidarity.[40] One enduringly productive vision has been group solidarity and the political articulations that flow from it, those that previous chapters of *Cross-Cultural Harlem* explained with regard to race-thinkers such as Hughes and McKay and that were established throughout African American intellectual history.[41] Philosophers Jean-Jacques Rousseau and Émile Durkheim have differently reflected on solidarity as a moral or a civic responsibility.[42] But cross-cultural solidarity *in place*, and in a place *like Harlem*, I want to argue, functioned less in abstract or idealist terms, and not only through race or ethnic consciousness, but also as a form of political identification in which there was a shifting sense of similarity and difference in the experience of class and racialization/ethnicization and othering. This is to recognize the political possibilities of Marcantonio being engaged with Black people's movements for civil and economic rights and their building of an autonomous and resourced Black Harlem, even when he was a political representative of Italian Harlem. And if this cross-cultural solidarity was a signature element of Marcantonio's public life, it can best be understood in proximate geographies.

While that formulation emphasizes the possibilities of shared aims, it is important to also keep in mind the limits imposed by Black–white divides and also, surely, the gendered effects of a figure such as Marcantonio. It is to state the obvious that his self-presentation of a working-class identity open to all sorts of engagements was enabled by white masculine privilege. And the body—a vehicle for gendered operations—bears some further comment. Famous images of Marcantonio show him shaking his fist or gesticulating with his arms, radiating physicalized energy. Even his represented verbal facility, his sharpness and irony, registers as gendered. Several accounts suggest a contradiction between Marcantonio's forcefulness and his short stature. No less significant is how movement itself, across physical space certainly, but also social boundaries, is often possible for men but not for women. Evoking classically gendered divisions between the public and the private, materials from Marcantonio's papers and published sources stress civic aspects and include very little meditation on his personal life: he was married and did not have children, and although his Italian upbringing was centrally important in his construction of a political identity, his family members did not play an especially prominent role when he appeared before constituents or participated in organizational work. Marcantonio's male subjectivity enabled his moves. If that is a familiar story about gender, race, and ethnicity, it also, here, puts a soft brake on any tendency to overvalorize the inclusivity of cross-cultural politics.

MARCANTONIO IN THE WINDS OF CHANGE

Marcantonio's lifespan, from 1904 to 1954, made him a historical witness to many important domestic and international events: the Depression, the Popular Front, the strictures and openings of immigration to the United States, World Wars I and II, the development of the Soviet Union, the Korean War, and various phases of the Civil Rights movement. During his time as a politician in the 1930s and 1940s, Marcantonio was caught in various winds of political and social change. Most simply: the boundaries (within and without) of the neighborhood and the world became increasingly blurred, if they had ever felt solid. What gave Marcantonio's space meaning—the one that he affected and that affected him—was, indeed, the sense of flux. Important frames for that dynamic energy were, first, the mix of peoples in East, Central, and West Harlems and, second, the relationship of the United States to the world. Neither of these phenomena were new, but they had specific forms in the period of Marcantonio's political activity. During those years, in Harlem and the nation writ large, different peoples came together and apart, languages were situated in relation to one another, visions of place clashed. And one abiding question throughout was how encounters in the United States, at home, shaped encounters abroad.

Though the descriptive terms East Harlem and Italian Harlem were associated with one another, they were isomorphic, never meaning the same thing, never having fully overlapping content. From the late nineteenth century on, East Harlem had contained many peoples: Irish, Jewish, African American, Cuban, Puerto Rican, and even Bengali. Even when critical masses of groups had receded, small residual populations and their cultural institutions remained to become part of the mix. By at least the 1930s the constitutive ethnic tension of East Harlem was between Italians and Puerto Ricans. If there are memories that rely on urban ecological explanations, of one group being pushed out by another through racialized oppositions, other stories reveal an experience of shared territory. A 1967 memoir about East Harlem during the 1930s to 1950s by Puerto Rican writer Piri Thomas, *Down These Mean Streets*, which will be treated more fully in the next chapter, describes conflicts between Puerto Ricans and Italians in vivid detail.[43] Thomas remembered Marcantonio, noting in an interview: "The Puerto Ricans and Italians were always fighting and he was helping everybody out." Preceding that statement of apparent blindness to cultural division is Thomas's admission of complicated identification and misrecognition: "I thought he was Puerto Rican because he helped everybody, all nationalities," suggesting that the affective dynamic between these two figures was somehow still shaped by the pull of different ethnic Harlems.[44]

If the lines of causality are not altogether clear—whether Marcantonio's politics were shaped by a diverse East Harlem or he responded to increasing diversification—the centrality of a cross-cultural imagination is obvious. When Thomas emphasized "helping," he spoke to the importance of service in how Marcantonio acted and was received, alongside the obvious but still remarkable ability to relate to different peoples. In fact, a range of organizations fostered the joining of service and social equality during this fertile political period. Groups such as the Harlem Center Civic Association, whose board of directors and governing council seemed to consist entirely of Italians, strove to address the "conditions of poor families without distinction of class, creed or race."[45] Harlem was still a space of various kinds of minoritization, and that produced a vexed relationship to the state, one that Marcantonio could, too, mirror for these peoples. The left-wing Harlem Legislative Conference, whose chairman he became in 1941, described its own founding "by a group of social minded citizens representing the entire community of Harlem."[46] The "East Harlem Organizers Manifesto" stated clearly that Marcantonio was simpatico: "[T]his public expression of understanding culminated in the making of the most progressive community in the American Nation. This have [sic] been shown with the election of the most progressive congressman, Vito Marcantonio, fearless fighter for the Latin-american and specially [sic] for the Porto Ricans."[47] The sensibility of inclusion was no doubt formed through the grim reality of shared deprivation. In 1947 Marcantonio joined with local politicians via the Harlem Legislative Conference to demand that the New York City administration address basic economic and political issues of the "Negro and Puerto Rican citizens of Harlem" regarding public welfare and the "full citizenship rights and equality for the Negro and Puerto Rican people and other minorities."[48] And Marcantonio's support for Social Security explicitly addressed the resources available to Italians as well as older Jewish residents who lived inside and also just across the borders of East Harlem.

Civil rights struggles of the 1940s affected African Americans and others in Harlem as a whole, and Marcantonio sustained deep affinities to these peoples and issues. He worked with Leonard Covello, principal of the multiethnic Benjamin Franklin High School in East Harlem, which enrolled students from many backgrounds.[49] Both known for cross-cultural understanding, Marcantonio and Covello together helped to defuse racial tensions in 1945 between African Americans and Italians that had been misrepresented as a "race riot." Marcantonio's pursuit of integration and racial justice could be seen in the camaraderie he built with African American intellectuals, particularly on the left, and support of projects all over Harlem.[50] He worked on many issues with another Harlem congressman, Adam Clayton Powell, Jr., including an effort to desegregate public schools and other public facilities in Washington, DC.[51] These issues became part of Marcantonio's political profile on a national level: He argued for repealing the poll tax, for providing sufficient funding to the fair employment practices commission, and for an inquiry into discrimination against African American players in national baseball years before Jackie Robinson integrated the Major League. Marcantonio's outspokenness about the latter issue inspired particularly virulent responses from some local constituents, testifying to the continued strength of anti-Blackness vis-à-vis cultures imagined as representing "America."[52]

Surely we might ask whether Marcantonio's embrace of issues having to do with race and civil rights was standard operating procedure for the left, or if his moves out of and across ethnic–racial communities reveal ideals that were emplaced in Harlem, at least for some. Both questions essentially ask about political sincerity, a quality that is so difficult to confidently establish. But Marcantonio does give us a way to think about the relationship of the experience of place to political subjectivity in patterns of activity that reveal connections. When Italian American Salvatore Mondello reflected on the milieu of 1940s East Harlem, one shaped by the educational projects of Covello, in his memoir, he noted: "Franklin [High School] had prepared me for a cosmopolitan world.... I had met and befriended kids of different cultures."[53] Mondello's invocation of cosmopolitanism generated from locality instructs us in the personal, institutional and political effects that Marcantonio lived, too.

There can be no question that discussions of the rights of working people and immigrants, of discrimination against Puerto Ricans, Italians, and African Americans, and of questions of racial justice in the United States and the world were happening at the same time and, moreover, that Marcantonio saw them as connected. This could not have been more evident than when he intoned in 1943 that "the effects of anti-poll-tax legislation extend beyond our own borders. Not only will the abolition of the poll tax lift the morale of the 13,000,000 loyal Negro Americans in this country, and thereby forge that national unity which is so essential to victory, but it will be living evidence and reaffirmation to our United Nations Allies and to the colonial peoples in India, Africa, Latin America, and the Caribbean, of our earnest and high resolve to win the battle for a free and democratic world."⁵⁴ Marcantonio attached domestic questions to a familiar Americanist global project, the "battle for a free world," but also referenced another kind of internationalism, one that saw anticolonial struggle as a matter of racial justice.

In no sphere were these questions more vivid than in Marcantonio's work on behalf of Puerto Rico. His working-class cosmopolitanism becomes even more complex when we think about the intensity of this advocacy. The only time Marcantonio traveled outside of the continental United States was to Puerto Rico. One way to approach the structuring solidarity is with the understanding that Marcantonio's cosmopolitanism was rich, unconventional, left-wing, and patterned by negotiations "at home." In arguing for the social welfare of Puerto Rican residents or the political independence of Puerto Rico, Marcantonio could still somehow manage to be the congressman from Italian Harlem, to inhabit the subjectivity shaped by those neighborhood blocks, which, as I have argued, gave rise to broadly Harlem crossings. Territorial tensions of the time might have generated a question of whether it was possible to be Italian and pro–Puerto Rican at the same time—the notion that Italians were "pushed" out by the newer Puerto Rican populations is predicated on a vision of hardened spatial compartments—and Marcantonio's emphatic "yes" was locally relevant, but also attached to a broader geography beyond the limits of nationality. With a position against U.S. occupation or annexation of Puerto Rico, he wielded not only an expanded notion of a United States of America, but also something more akin to an "Americas" sensibility that could simultaneously emphasize connectedness and autonomy, much like the cross-cultures in Harlem. And, of course, the world beyond Harlem was a manifestation of Marcantonio's leftist internationalism, as he made explicit in a public speech before the House of Representatives in 1939: "My interest in Puerto Rico is due not only to the fact that I represent the largest Puerto Rican constituency . . . but also to my desire as a progressive to defend the most exploited victims of a most devastating imperialism."⁵⁵

Marcantonio served Puerto Ricans *in* Puerto Rico just as he served his formal constituents at home. Those on the island asked him for help in making claims to the U.S. government regarding back pay for military service, or in obtaining Works Progress Administration jobs, or even about more personal issues regarding impoverishment and displacement.[56] The intensity of effort bears further comment. In one case, Marcantonio intervened with Harold Ickes, the secretary of the interior, on behalf of an eighty-year-old man who was unable to pay the taxes on his land in Puerto Rico.[57] In another, a poor painter named Guadalupe Ruiz wrote from the island first to the mayor of New York and then, after receiving no response, to Marcantonio to explain that his son had been imprisoned in New York City and that he could not visit him from such a distance. Marcantonio responded by contacting the New York Department of Corrections and then the Parole Commission, with positive consequences. The mother of that prisoner wrote, about contacting Marcantonio, that "un rayo de luz iluminó mi cerebro, y el nombre del valeroso y ferviente defensor de los puertorriqueños el Hon. Vito Marcantonio resplandecio en mi mente como un astro" (a ray of light illuminated my brain, and the name of the brave and fervent defender of Puerto Ricans, the honorable Vito Marcantonio, gleamed in my mind like a heavenly body). This is my translation of her letter; Marcantonio's translator put it more economically and certainly less poetically, as "I know that you are very good to all the Puerto Ricans and that is the reason why I appeal to you." If the Spanish version of the sentiment communicates an understanding of Marcantonio's elevated and heroic status, the English translation (and the one that he probably read) establishes inclusion for "all" Puerto Ricans across and beyond the continental United States.[58]

The needs that residents of Puerto Rico expressed were significant to their lives. They had an everyday quality of economic or political disadvantage, very much like those of Harlem's inhabitants who were Marcantonio's constituents in a more literal sense. How, then, can we understand the relationship between Marcantonio's formal congressional district and a zone that was also established as a space of representation? That question has a particular charge when we think about the anxieties in the United States at that time about that which lay outside its borders, alongside carefully managed and contradictory ideologies of colonial annexation and effective inclusion.[59] Puerto Rico was apart from and a part of the

United States, in varied ways; this dilemma mirrored Marcantonio's own status as a national figure. In and through that knot of spatial issues, Harlem and Puerto Rico could be seen as in a geographic region of an extended Caribbean opening up the Americas, an always contested formation.[60] This continuum can also be understood through diasporic space: Puerto Rican Harlem was bound to the place of origin of many of its peoples, migrants maintained connections with those back home, and there were deep identifications that, surely, were shaped by the powerful U.S. nation-state, but not fully articulated to that formation.

Marcantonio's working-class cosmopolitanism decisively framed solidarities across boundaries of the nation-state, while still allowing for local investments and attentions in Puerto Rico. Structurally, this was similar to the sensibility that processed racial and ethnic exchanges and maintained roots in Italian communities. In Marcantonio's relationship to Puerto Rico, too, the disempowerment of working peoples created the foundation of a political vision: Puerto Rican unions formally supported Marcantonio and he supported them. He appeared before the Wage and Hour Division of the U.S. Department of Labor on behalf of the United Railroad Workers Union, and he also argued for increasing the wages of WPA workers in Puerto Rico.[61] That worker-centric political vision was inextricable from a critique of colonial power; thus Marcantonio moved from supporting Puerto Rican statehood to supporting its independence. When he went to Puerto Rico in 1936 to defend independence leader Pedro Albizu Campos, he was met by huge, supportive crowds; he returned to Harlem to find large rallies there, too, populated by advocates for independence.[62] Through the 1930s and 1940s, Marcantonio maintained close relationships with a number of Puerto Rican independence leaders and intellectuals. There is no question that his frank socialism found a congenial home in a space that experienced and protested the continuing exploitation of capital (big sugar companies), and that many, though not all Puerto Rican migrants who settled in Harlem shared that political sensibility, just as many people in Italian Harlem had been shaped by leftist currents back home. The cosmopolitanism of attachment thus had a distinctly political nature—conjuring up the global anticolonialism of the day across Asia, Africa, and Latin America—even if it was not only indexed to electoral interests.

Citizenship cases involving Puerto Ricans were particularly interesting in this regard. These were predicated on narrow conceptions of nationality, yet inevitably raised the complications of more global belonging. And the status of those in and from a place that was continually colonized and only semiautonomous at the best of times could not be anything but vexatious.[63] Many people wrote to Marcantonio about difficulties in obtaining citizenship rights, not least because of the ambiguities of the rules surrounding the distinctive situation of Puerto Rico, which was neither state nor nation. Not surprisingly, there were mixtures that reflected other historical encounters and did not fit neatly into the already-fragile boxes of identity imagined by the U.S. nation-state. Many Corsicans had migrated to Puerto Rico in the late 1800s to work in the coffee industry and intermixed with populations already existing there. Some of Marcantonio's correspondents wrote about being denied U.S. citizenship despite having been born in Puerto Rico, because of having Italian rather than Spanish fathers.

The ripples of these social formations were felt across Puerto Rico's boundaries, wherever migrants came to settle, in East Harlem and other sites, thus making all of these places more complexly worlded. As Jesús Cariel, whose father was Italian, explained it to Marcantonio, "if I am not a citizen, there must be about a half million of Porto Ricans who are voting and using the rights of an American Citizen although they are still aliens without knowing it. In the Spanish colony in Harlem in New York, half of the population are the same way, as I know quite a few people from my home town and others."[64] Marcantonio argued for and helped to pass a bill in 1940 that granted citizenship to all those who had been born in Puerto Rico, extending birthright nationality across the borders of the continental United States and its annexations to provide another continuous zone of identification for those in Harlem and Puerto Rico, while also incorporating all sorts of mixtures in diasporic subjectivity. The two sites of Puerto Rican diaspora were linked, obviously, in many ways, but

Marcantonio certainly was a part of the glue, through his political work mapping a transnational space and, in that way, remaking the territories of both El Barrio and Puerto Rico.

A central cause with which Marcantonio was identified, positively and negatively, was Puerto Rican independence. But not every Puerto Rican in New York or, for that matter, in Puerto Rico, supported independence.[65] One could argue, however, that Marcantonio's relational approach was deeper, more subjective and transformative, than an interest in any single issue or even set of issues would reveal. This can be seen in feeling as much as advocacy: Marcantonio took on Puerto Rico and its citizens from outside his zone of operation and brought them inside a political body (of constituents, of the working class, of racialized minorities), and into his own subjective experience of those formations, all while respecting the constitutive integrity and difference of Puerto Rico. Knowledge was key to this relationship; he built attachments to Puerto Rican activists and political figures consistently throughout his life, and it is clear that he read Puerto Rican newspapers and other materials regularly. He was also recognized as a kind of authority on the subject in the United States; in one case, a Princeton University professor even sought Marcantonio's expertise on the issue of Puerto Rican independence.[66] A great deal of archival material testifies to reciprocal affect: Puerto Ricans wrote letters that evoked not only the need for services, but the fact that Marcantonio *cared* about people who were unlike him. This feeling echoed the one that Piri Thomas had observed Marcantonio practicing in Harlem.

When a man named Pedro Biaggi contacted Marcantonio in 1936, after his one Congressional election defeat, to request an interview for an article on Puerto Rico for Latin American newspapers, he initially appealed to felt connections across the usual parameters of time and space, offering to treat him to "some Spanish or Italian lunch."[67] He wrote: "Puerto Rico fully realizes that you have made a supreme sacrifice for our sacred cause of independence" and, later, referred to the understanding of the adversity that Marcantonio faced in "our homeland." The use of the pronoun "our" is not altogether legible or certain as indicating only Biaggi's ownership. Does it capture Marcantonio? The represented affective bond across boundaries between the continental United States and Puerto Rico only became deeper and more complicated as Biaggi went on to remark that when he had first learned of Marcantonio "in connection with the Harlem political and social struggles," he had assumed that the politician was Puerto Rican, because he had known in Puerto Rico a Corsican family named Marcantonio with members living in Harlem, "rather blond or blue blood." Less important than the accuracy of this perception was Biaggi's inclination to read Marcantonio through a more personal experience. His own family had come to Puerto Rico from Corsica, and he wrote that recalling struggles there "makes me think if there is not some spiritual bond tying you to our beloved and so ignominiously treated homeland." In this discourse, "homeland" doubly signified for a Corsican writer raised in Puerto Rico (and who seemed recently to have spent time in Buenos Aires), who was ever-conscious of diasporic space reaching across to Harlem, as he seemed to identify with Marcantonio. Different, dynamic, and comparative accounts of disempowerment come to settle on this moment in the late 1930s, and in and through three spaces, Corsica, Puerto Rico, and Harlem, each of which might be understood as colonial.

For both Biaggi and Marcantonio, Puerto Rico was a key site in which to work through important questions of nationality and globality. Marcantonio's leftist inclinations certainly seamlessly assimilated Puerto Rican nationalism, but one cannot rule out the possibility that the experience of relation also wrought something less predictable. In the 1930s and 1940s, as through all periods of history, the United States was "under construction" and its relationship to other places and regions changing. If Marcantonio was articulating a different vision of what place could look like at home, he was also ever-conscious of the world and the shifting allegiances of the regions that made it up. When he spoke Spanish in public broadcasts, he suggested that his audience was not only Puerto Rican, but that people from other Latin American countries were listening, too. Puerto Rico could, in this way, be seen as articulated to the Spanish-speaking Americas, not only to the United States. Centers and peripheries were redrawn, just as the limits of the frame of the nation-state for thinking about place and difference were laid bare.

RHETORICS FOR UNDERSTANDING

Solidarity requires boundary-crossing and also, to work fully, profound relation; language conveys and receives understanding of that project. As a means of expression, an essential set of practices of the everyday, and a sign of cultural knowledge, one can think of language, too, as an exceptional vehicle for cross-culturality—and it was one that Marcantonio worked on and through with great commitment. There was, first, an electoral aspect to his legendary ability to speak Italian, Yiddish, and Spanish in a district that had significant populations who primarily spoke those languages. Like his predecessor La Guardia, Marcantonio made political speeches in multiple languages to appeal to a diverse East Harlem and, one can presume, to adequately represent area peoples locally and nationally. Language difference can impede inclusion of all kinds, especially for migrants from other countries, and so Marcantonio's multilingualism aided his advocacy for those peoples. No less importantly, understanding that this practice emerged from East Harlem helps a modern-day scholar to understand the working-class cosmopolitanism that he was staging in many other realms.

Marcantonio's relationship to Spanish is especially striking for how multifaceted it was, expressed in a range of political and even more personal spheres. In 1941, Angelita Santaella, who shared a godchild with Marcantonio, wrote from Puerto Rico: "Yo le escribo en español, porque he sabido por Ada y Gilberto que usted sabe nuestro idioma, y aunque sé un poco de inglés, suficiente para expresarme, lógicamente, lo hago mejor en mi idioma." My translation of this sentence is "I write to you in Spanish because I know from Ada and Gilberto that you know our language, and although I do know a little English, enough to clearly express myself, I do better in my own language."[68] But when the original letter was translated at the time for Marcantonio's review, it read slightly differently: "I have been informed . . . that you master our language pretty well." We might consider what the deeper sentiment around knowledge is: what it might mean for Santaella to think that Marcantonio knows *her* language?

She intimated that she felt more comfortable communicating with him in Spanish, with the expectation that she would be understood. She ended another letter to Marcantonio with a more direct statement about his role in Puerto Rico: "con los deseos de que sea usted siempre nuestro querido REPRESENTANTE, y que tiene los votos de los puertoriqueños, que le han elegido y reelegido, por sus grandes méritos. Los de aquí y de allá tenemos los mismos gustos" (with the hope that you will always be our beloved REPRESENTATIVE, who has the votes of the Puerto Ricans, who have elected and reelected you for your substantial merits. Those of us from here and there have the same desires).[69] It was in Spanish that Santaella could close a number of gaps between herself and a U.S. congressman—she emphasizes identification by using all upper-case letters to announce that Marcantonio is her representative—as well between East Harlem Puerto Ricans who have formally voted for him and those like herself, on the island, who have not been able to.

Marcantonio frequently utilized Spanish to connect to a broad audience of constituents and others. In a radio program during his 1949 mayoral campaign, he began by saying that he was pleased to be speaking to listeners in the "language of Cervantes," gesturing toward high literary Spanish, possibly European, traditions. But he quickly undid any potential elitism when he followed up with: "Yo no estudié español en Salamanca, España. . . . Mi español es del hombre común que trabaja y supere" (I did not study Spanish in Salamanca, Spain. . . . My Spanish is that of the common man who works and prevails).[70] Identifying his kind of Spanish as imperfect because not formally studied and pointedly not that of the colonizer could only be in service of working-class Puerto Ricans (and possibly other Spanish-speaking inhabitants) of New York City. Connecting with the daily lived experience of Puerto Ricans who might have felt like second-class citizens, Marcantonio mentioned that he was aware they had been targeted by law enforcement—"víctimas de los más horrendos ataques de la polizia" (victims of the most horrendous attacks by the police)—and been subject to prejudice from the Relief Office. When Piri Thomas referred in his 1967 memoir to the similar position that Puerto Ricans, Italians, and others found themselves in with regard to the Relief Office during the period of Marcantonio's political representation, writing, after a particularly fraught encounter between local residents and an administrator, that all the mothers needed their children to interpret for them, he raised questions about intelligibility that were about both language and class.[71] And Marcantonio tapped into those concerns for his own solidarity with Puerto Ricans.[72]

Mikhail Bakhtin's discussion of discourse as built through the diversity of social phenomena (dialects, voices, worldviews) and unbound by expectations of a singular literary language presents an especially important way to understand Marcantonio's verbal utterances. While on the one hand he drew on the authority of Spanish itself, in that moment and to that audience, with even a particular kind of Spanish (that of Cervantes), on the other he undid the authority of the literary and the colonial as he marked his preference for the language of the common man. Both rhetorics, and still others, appear and can even be seen to compete in what he says in that moment. As Bakhtin vividly puts it: "the centripetal forces of the life of language, embodied in a 'unitary language,' operate in the midst of heteroglossia. At any given moment . . . language is stratified not only into linguistic dialects . . . but also . . . into languages that are socio-ideological: languages of social groups, 'professional' and 'generic' languages, languages of generations and so forth."[73] The wild multiplicity's heteroglossia, it should be added, hardly discounts the profound importance of using one language or another at any point in time.

A sense of language's openness interestingly shifts questions related to translation, such as cultural trace, comparison, and legibility. Marcantonio's style of Spanish was Italian-inflected in terms of both vocabulary and accent. Throughout his time in Congress, he clearly employed someone who translated constituent letters and other materials, but Marcantonio also himself read and communicated in Spanish.[74] In audio recordings one can hear the difference between Spanish speeches that were written for him, more grammatically correct, with more precise word choice, and interviews in which he spoke Spanish on the fly, using many Italian words, such as "polizia." Yet what also rings true, from one radio program in particular, is his expression "Ustedes me conocen, yo lo conozco" (You know me, I know it). With this awkwardly worded (in both languages) but still compelling statement, Marcantonio appeals to reciprocal understanding, to *knowing*—it may take shape in Spanish but cannot but supersede narrow expectations, articulated as it is in such a heavy Italian accent. The sonic and the more formally textual aspects are components of what Bakhtin has referred to as "dialogized heteroglossia."[75] This linguistic-social practice also challenges any clear divide between monolingualism and multilingualism.[76]

To read Marcantonio's language use as an instance of translation is to consider cross-culturality in another way. Here, as in other elements of his politics, we do not see a completed move across borders, but instead a dynamic exchange in which he is both himself and porous enough to accommodate otherness. Just as Bakhtin directs us to pay attention to the "authentic environment of an utterance," how could we not understand Marcantonio's choices for communication vis-à-vis his campaign in the early 1940s to reverse policies in Puerto Rico that mandated English as the main language of instruction? The perspective that Marcantonio pragmatically used Spanish to connect to those who would vote for him can be complicated with the possibility of an authentic recognition of difference and respect for the experience of place. If recent work in translation studies has explained the limits of moving from one language or culture into another, we might see Marcantonio's crossings as aware of boundaries, too, and deeply ethical in that sense.[77]

The difficulties of translation, in terms of an incommensurability of experience or worldview, might be seen a little differently in the case of Marcantonio. His linguistic translations, imperfect and registering multiplicity, were nonetheless intelligible, and remind us that the intimacy of communicating in the same language need not always entail mastery. Marcantonio here is translating, and he is also being actively translated. Language itself, and its use, can build a space for identification that incorporates all kinds of differences, rather than simply be used as a tool of authority. These translations raise, then, the question of comparison. Moving across languages and cultures is to interrogate what is shared and what is different therein. Marcantonio's ability to communicate in Spanish may indeed have been aided by his fluency in Italian, precisely because of certain exchanges among southern European–derived linguistic practices. To put it more simply, Italian was sort of like Spanish. And if spoken Italian in the United States was already a mix of dialects (from the melting pot of Italy itself), its competency may have had an intrinsic linguistic flexibility. In this way it was structurally similar to Spanish in former colonies, not practiced necessarily as it was in the land of Cervantes, but undergoing change and hybridization and, in the world of Marcantonio's time, also shaped by diasporic movements. A vernacular cosmopolitanism was both born of place and not reducible to place's material (or national) limits. More difficult to determine is whether the language parallels and exchanges were matched by other kinds of cultural compatibility, controversial as "culture" itself is.

We cannot overstate how Marcantonio's translational practices were also deeply transnational, stretching across the boundaries of the nation and the constitution of belonging for a range of peoples and ultraconscious of differences. The inclusiveness of that geopolitical field he was navigating and symbolically constructing was astonishing. In 1916 public intellectual Randolph Bourne had famously argued for a "transnational America," to acknowledge the potential contributions of European immigrants whose nationality might be conceived in nonsingular terms.[78] But Marcantonio, awash in the lived local realities of discrimination against immigrants *alongside* racism against African Americans and others, expanded the conception of American democracy even further than Bourne was able to in his time. When Marcantonio argued in a public radio address against the proposed registration of foreign-born people, he remarked: "The noncitizen resident is an integral part of America . . . when the founding fathers said in that everlasting document, the Declaration of Independence, that all men are created equal, they did not say that all men are created equal except Italians, they did not say that all men are created equal except Jews, they did not say that all men are created equal except Negroes, nor did they say that all men are created equal except noncitizens. They said that *all* men are created equal. By this they meant no discrimination, no segregation, and no persecution of the foreign-born."[79] Even in a period of anxiety about the "foreign," Marcantonio held out the "noncitizen" as entitled to U.S. rights, capturing those migrants not yet eligible for citizenship but also extending, one might imagine, to Puerto Ricans on the island, which was an ambivalent and liminal part of the United States. This especially flexible understanding of nation and its limits rationalized the project on which Marcantonio was working in many ways throughout his lifetime. Its central theme was connectedness, among African Americans, Jews, Italians, and others perhaps not even in the nation proper, as a way to reimagine the space of community.

Marcantonio's experience in Harlem helped him conceive of a different kind of nation, but that imagination was not tethered to locality. It operated and took shape through other spatial registers, the global and the national, which seemed rarely to be in conflict. Central to the discursive toolkit of his politics were the ideals of human rights and national openness, which could be put to use for many purposes. In 1939, Marcantonio supported the Wagner-Rogers Bill, which would have allowed the entry of twenty thousand German Jewish children (and which ignominiously failed in the Congress). In that same year he also protested the practice by the Bureau of Immigration and Naturalization to remove Puerto Ricans from boats arriving at mainland U.S. ports and ask them to prove the citizenship of their parents.[80] These interventions at borders sought to establish central meaning-making of the nation-state at the same time. The possibilities of America rippled through Marcantonio's alliances during the war years. Like many on the left, he supported U.S. efforts during World War II, with his own angle from cross-cultural and working-class formations within the broader space of Harlem. He worked with Adam Clayton Powell and African American, Puerto Rican, Jewish, and Italian political activists in groups such as the Harlem Victory Council, the Harlem Defense Committee, the Jewish Peoples Committee, the National Negro Congress, and the Italian Club, not to mention the American Labor Party and Communist Party and Youth Communist League, to argue in favor of the rights of the "foreign born," of full participation in the armed forces and industries, and of economic and social justice, while also supporting the war.[81] All of these engagements had some Harlem content while also being articulated to political projects such as the Popular Front, which espoused not only a wartime vision, but also a future-looking, antiracist, and economically equitable United States.

Marcantonio's humanistic and progressive ideological orientation is one frame for his work in another cause, on behalf of Filipino naturalization. Another is his attention to the edges of citizenship and nationality.[82] Neither, it should be noted, can be merely about electoral interests, most obviously because of the absence of a substantial Filipino population in Marcantonio's congressional or, later, potential mayoral district. He used the lofty language of principle, noting at the time that prohibiting Filipinos from becoming citizens "creates certain social, economic and political conditions which sap the strength and vitality of the democracy in which we live."[83] Because they were from a U.S. "territory" (1898–1946), those Filipinos who had come to the United States were "nationals" but not citizens. Many of them had fought for the United States, and though their entry was not restricted the way other Asian peoples' was, particularly after the 1917 Immigration Act, they were often lumped together with other immigrant groups in terms of naturalization strictures as well as general public response, shaped by class-inflected anti-Asian racism. Marcantonio began advocating for the naturalization of Filipinos who were permanent residents of the United States in 1939, which was not granted until the 1946 Luce-Celler Act. The Filipino War Workers Committee celebrated Marcantonio, writing: "In our record, you are still the champion of the working and minority people in Congress."[84] None of the groups with which he worked on this issue, nor a single one of the numerous signers of petitions, was from outside of California.[85] At the very least, this gives some credence to Marcantonio's insistence that this issue was a matter of principle, not electoral interest for him.

The relationship of democratic principles to Americanism has historically been a thorny and at times contradictory prospect. Marcantonio's politics, too, registered those complexities, especially in the middle of the war. He made an impassioned speech to Congress about the loyalty of Italian Americans,[86] and though rigorously antifascist, he may have been concerned about the response of pro-Fascist Italians in his district when declining to attend a protest against the Italian invasion of Ethiopia.[87] Throughout the 1930s and 1940s, Marcantonio fought continuously for the rights of peoples from many racial and ethnic groups, even, as we have seen, for those not in his district, yet he did not oppose Japanese internment during wartime. One could speculate only that he, as did so many Americans, even progressives, perceived that opposition to the intensely discriminatory program would weaken the war effort.[88] And yet many Japanese Americans seemed not to hold a grudge, especially in light of Marcantonio's advocacy of the rights of naturalization for those of Asian descent, beginning in 1943. As Paul Susumu Seto noted, in the familiar language of antiracist social justice: "We regard this as involving values of more than political significance; and as such commendable to the attention of others, to the attention of others who, like ourselves, are concerned about human issues and human values."[89] Even Japanese internees expressed support of Marcantonio's efforts, individually and through internment camp newspapers.[90] One can speculate that a certain kind of accommodation and tolerance on the part of both the Japanese Americans and Marcantonio paved the path forward. The 1946 Luce-Celler Act addressed the naturalization of Filipinos and other Asians but left unresolved other efforts around civil rights that were so central to Marcantonio's politics. Disappointment, even grief about the pace of progress on that front, as well as about the increasingly anticommunist climate, was evident in his correspondence, as in a letter he sent to constituent Clarence Reid in 1948: "I regret to inform you that this Congress has failed to provide any civil rights legislation. I fought for this legislation from the very first day of this Congress to the very bitter end.... The failure to provide civil rights legislation was due to the bi-partisan reactionary character of the Congress."[91] As Langston Hughes wrote about Harlem, too, just a few years later, his was a "dream deferred."[92]

The arc of Marcantonio's political career as an outsider, from Harlem, a place that has always stood in ambiguous relation to the nation, could be seen with one end point in his defense of W. E. B. Du Bois in 1951. By this time, Marcantonio had left Congress as well as failed in his bid to become mayor, but was continuing his work advocating for neighborhood residents. He also took on legal cases, many, notably, for civil rights leaders. Marcantonio's relationship to Du Bois was another example of his cross-racial (and cross-Harlem) alliances. The two men were different figures, one having worked inside the electoral political system and the other consistently outside of it. Their working socialism, too, took varied forms. Their constituencies, of course, were distinct, having emerged from multiple organizations and parties and, often, separated regions of Harlem and the world. Yet their lives as political figures came together—Marcantonio had run for mayor of New York in 1950 and Du Bois for U.S. senator, both on the American Labor Party ticket. They failed despite garnering support among many working-class and minority residents across color lines. Neither man ceased fighting for peace and anti-imperialism, even at a time of deepening anticommunist feeling. So when DuBois was brought up on charges by the U.S. government for failing to register as a foreign agent while circulating the Stockholm Peace Appeal in 1951,[93] it made a great deal of sense that Marcantonio would defend him, which he did, successfully. This moment crystallizes the cross-cultural politics of both men, with reference to Harlem, too: solidaristic, idealistic, critical of narrow conceptions of the nation, and on all sorts of edges. It offers yet another opportunity to think about the relationship between Americanism and globalism and the limits of both possibilities, as well as the trajectories of different forms of otherness, ethnic whiteness, Blackness, leftism, and more.

THE AFFECT/EFFECT OF BOUNDARY-CROSSING

When Vito Marcantonio died in 1954—a symbolically significant year, given the *Brown v Board of Education* decision—the procession closed down large swaths of East Harlem as residents came out of their dwellings and workplaces to publicly grieve his passing, moving toward a memorial service that was an exemplary multicultural affair. Both aspects of the spectacle, the mark of Marcantonio on the place and the performance of

FIGURE 3.2 Funeral passes the Marcantonio Club at 247 East 116th Street, 1954.

Photo courtesy of the Manuscripts and Archives Division, the New York Public Library.

interethnic solidarity, are crucial to an understanding of the affect and effect of his crossings. Thousands stood on the streets to observe the body being transported, and more filed in and out of the funeral parlor the whole of that day and the next. Scholar-activist Gerald Meyer wrote of the funeral's "enormous scope and extravagant expression of loss," as indexed to the central, wide-ranging importance of Marcantonio to the Italian American community in Harlem.[94] It was an outpouring of emotion that conveyed a great deal about ownership and belonging. Marcantonio was an outgrowth of Italian Harlem in political, social and personal terms, and that was deeply felt, not always with regard to specific affiliations or identities.

The correspondence between notions of community and political figures does not necessarily fully overlap. Memorials to Marcantonio represented an extraordinary breadth of solidarities that included that Italian world from which Marcantonio emerged and other identities as well. On the tribute list at his service were Marcantonio's barber, Luigi Albarelli, his longtime associate Leonard Covello, his Puerto Rican assistant Manuel Medina, and W. E. B. DuBois.[95] Paul Robeson penned an essay in memoriam: "Negro Americans Have Lost a Tried and True Friend"[96] and Gilberto Gerena Valentín, a Puerto Rican community organizer who also worked with the American Labor Party, wrote "La comunidad se quedó huerfana" (The community has been orphaned).[97] And, of course, people from these and other communities were devastated by the death of a figure who, deeply embedded in locality, had in equal measure become a national hero for the left.

The religious ground of attachment was inevitably gnarled for Marcantonio, especially as his body came to rest in it. When he died, police found a metal crucifix and a rosary in his pocket, testament to a private relationship to Catholicism, at least. Yet the Archdiocese refused him a Roman Catholic burial: the spokesperson of the chancery indicated that Marcantonio "had not practiced his religion in a great many years and was not reconciled with the church before his death."[98] Many supporters protested the decision and circulated petitions, sensing perhaps that there was a more problematic political logic at work, as Cardinal Francis Spellman was notoriously anti-Communist and supported Senator Joseph McCarthy. By 1954, the political climate had shifted a great deal. Although Marcantonio had managed his support for the Communist Party in a careful and sincere way, he had been attacked by those on the right and was kept under surveillance by the FBI. It became harder than ever to express his views as the Cold War intensified and complex positions about the Soviet Union were reduced by critics to "anti-Americanism."

Meyer has suggested that Spellman's decision was interpreted locally not only as influenced by nationalist ideologies but also by ethnic resentments in New York, between Italian American Catholics and Irish American control of the church.[99] It is important to remember that Catholicism was itself politically diverse. Dorothy Day, founder of the Catholic Worker movement, who inveighed against anti-Communism, wrote "the thing that we will remember Vito Marcantonio for was 'he understood concerning the needy and the poor.' The Psalmist said 'Blessed is he who understands concerning the needy and the poor.'"[100]

The sight of thousands lamenting Marcantonio's death impresses and even confounds. Not everyone in Italian Harlem nor, certainly, everyone in Harlem as a whole could have been sympathetic to his politics, which critiqued economic inequality and argued for tenants' rights, greater social services for the poor, racial equality, and Puerto Rican independence. So how might we explain the loyalty that so many neighborhood residents felt toward him? At work in many responses to Marcantonio was affect—contradictory, complicated, not always explained by political ideology, and often experienced almost viscerally. There is a good deal of scholarly discussion on the meaning of affect and the related terms of emotion and feeling, and how we might distinguish between that which is experienced individually and that which has social consequences.[101] Jonathan Flatley explains his interpretation of the difference as: "Where *emotion* suggests something that happens inside and tends toward outward expression, *affect* indicates something relational and transformative. One *has* emotions; one is affected *by* people or things."[102] Affection—its intensity, particularly—has also been associated with affect (the words bear a similarity) in the work of seminal philosophers such as Baruch Spinoza and Henri Bergson.[103]

One way to view Harlem residents' loyalty to Marcantonio is to recognize that he created an affect for people, just as social formations created something for him. A letter to the editor of the *New York Times* on just this topic lays bare the pull of place. Joseph H. Louchheim wrote: "Despite his unsavory foreign policy voting record . . . he consistently knew and served the local needs of his constituents. Because he made himself always available to the people in his district he built up a host of faithful supporters. Contrary to common practice, he never had to return home 'to mend his fences' . . . few, if any, could match his knowledge of his district and his loyal, whole-hearted conscientious effort on its behalf."[104] This New York resident, at least, could decouple one kind of politics from another, elevating personal contact and intimacy. Furthermore, Louchheim ascribed faithfulness and loyalty not only to Marcantonio's supporters, but to the man himself, undoing the familiar (one-way) direction of service to suggest the fundamental reciprocity of affect. Dorothy Day described Marcantonio's relationship to his constituents, unsurprisingly, with the language of ministration—"the poor of East Harlem felt that Vito loved them and was interested in them. 'It was like the confessional or the clinic,' someone said of his office"[105]—even as she conveyed intense attachment and abiding contact.

How, if at all, can we reconcile affect and ideology, especially when their forms and contents could take us in very different directions? How might we describe, without overreach, the deeply felt radical potential of social formations? The frame of "militant particularism," associated with political-cultural critic Raymond Williams, helps to illuminate the specific contours of the 1930s–1950s Harlem that made and was made by Marcantonio. Williams writes that "place has been shown to be a crucial element in the bonding process."[106] Geographer David Harvey, in turn, critically reads Williams's representative example of a Welsh general strike in 1926 as suggesting that even a focus on place-based politics could not remain purely within the sphere of the "local," that the inspiring possibility of an alternative in the here and now is inextricable from ideas and realities that circulate outside of the community. As Harvey puts it: "How these external impulses were transformed and internalized as a very local 'structure of feeling' is a crucial part of the story."[107] These formulations for connecting local material experience to abstract ideas of socialism may have been resources for a very different context, but the question of the relationship of "lived experience" to "ideas" pertains to how we think about the constitution of both East Harlem specifically and Harlem more generally, including ideals generated from within and from outside.

The paradox of Marcantonio settles around how he managed to be both local and extra-local, just as the place that he was from and remained embedded in registered that complexity. As much as a quality of movement and citizenship of the world dictates crossing of the sort in which he continually engaged, it can also reveal the intricacies of positionality, often in terms of political consciousness or economic disempowerment. Marcantonio practiced and represented thoroughgoing engagement with others, with one consequence in cross-racial social movements and another in more individual terms of experience such as care, interest, and affiliation. The constellated moments of this chapter address and revise the classic wisdom of deep antagonisms between ethnic and racial groups in a place like Harlem while at the same time never abandoning the pulls of specific forms of identity.

Marcantonio was often pictured shaking his fist, a sign of energetic resistance that is essential to understanding his relationship to Harlem. When he died, the *New York Times* obituary describing his life began by noting that though he consistently denied being a Communist, "his record showed a constant espousal of communist causes." Yet this reflexively anticommunist piece ended with both an evocation of Marcantonio's combative spirit (it quoted him as saying "I believe in the capitalistic system but not in Red-baiting. And just because I often agree with the Russians, that does not mean I'm a Communist. If the Communists advocate wearing clothes, I'm not going to start a nudist colony just to be different.") and acknowledgment of his power to move constituents ("he won the fanatic loyalty of thousands of many races in Harlem who mourned him.").[108] There were so many ways in which he was embattled, politically and culturally, and part of his appeal, which the *New York Times* unwittingly opens up, is that to many people, Marcantonio stood in contestation to dominant stories. His position of liminality enabled a more careful thinking about central spaces, of "America," of urban space, of ethnic and racial division. Marcantonio's crossings may have had unpredictable effects. It is very possible that one sort of movement out of received wisdom may have enabled other kinds of unconventional thinking.

The story of Vito Marcantonio in and of Harlem can only be made richer by considering the social, political, and economic forces that press on affect in seemingly polarized ways, through longing and disavowal. Father Rofrano's comment about Marcantonio as a "traitor" and the cardinal's refusal to grant him a Catholic burial manifest (and create) energy from betrayal. The very evocation of betrayal highlights the complicated nature of identity precisely because it relies on the sensibility that someone or something is like you, and different, in terms of interests and possibilities.[109] Robert Orsi has pointed out that Marcantonio came to prominence at a time when the status of Italians in Harlem was already changing, and that regarding him as disloyal could be a screen for middle-class Italian Americans who were working through their own feelings of guilt about class aspirations that left parents and older relatives behind as they moved to other areas of the city. Such are the complications of family, community, and identity in the context of urban reorganization.[110] Indeed, the constitution of Italianness in Harlem, particularly as it refracted the figure of Marcantonio, might best be seen in terms of its decline.

REVERBERATIONS OF A LIFE AND THE MEANING OF PLACE

Tensions—between pasts and presents, insides and outsides—appropriately thematize the politics and life of Marcantonio. Dominant narratives of ethnicity and race and their relationship to places dictate how identities are indexed tightly to neighborhood blocks, to enclaves or ghettoes. But Marcantonio's crossings in majority-minority space burst open those enclosures, making minoritization itself more open and dialogic and space more porous and fluid, to create a different cultural geography of Harlem. Italian Harlem, from which Marcantonio came and to which he remained affiliated, was full of all sorts of rich political contradictions and possibilities. Poverty brought lots of people together, and when Marcantonio and others politically mobilized it, it made difference empowering rather than disenfranchising.

Marcantonio's embodiment of the cross-cultural cannot be easily incorporated into winning stories about diversity in the nation. His effects can be understood through the lens of internationalist left-wing politics, as well as the complexities and contradictions of "Americanism" in the immediate postwar period. But the work of this chapter is also to cast this influential man's life and discourses more locally, as comprising a "Harlem story." I have intentionally identified the category of "Harlem" rather than "East Harlem" to emphasize that the way that Marcantonio's performed globality was not only about bridging a divide between Italian American and Puerto Rican ethnic communities: it was also about a deeply felt relationship to Harlem, symbol and city-space. His working-class cosmopolitanism spilled across neighborhood blocks and articulated itself to worlds inside and outside. In many ways, Marcantonio, not Black, could still be seen as a powerful metonym for Harlem: for its exclusion, its difference, and its uneasy relationship to the nation, at once seeking representative power but also resisting assimilation. Anti-imperialism, and anti-anti-Communism, found fertile ground in many different regional spaces of Harlem, east and west. And might we take something from Marcantonio's moving across different regions of Harlem, east, west, and central; might this reconceived, more holistic Harlem be mobilized to address the defensive whiteness that is central to some stories of East Harlem, or the anxieties about immigration, about "new people" coming in? This move would not substitute "multiethnicity" for Blackness as an essential meaning of Harlem—in fact, its Blackness is one occasion of that more cosmopolitan formation—but it does suggest that the perils and possibilities of multiplicity are at the heart of any imagining of Harlem.

In much of the scholarship on cities, we are offered the familiar story of ethnic competition—of, for example, Italians resenting Puerto Ricans and African Americans, shored up by ideas of white ethnicity as a racial and racist phenomenon. This approach converges with some sociological models about community shifts, too, the quasi-ecological idea that there is a natural movement of one group moving in and another moving out, and that in that organic flow there is both competition and repudiation. But the reality on the ground, as evidenced by Marcantonio's work and life, is that there are connections and intimacies and many different kinds of people learning to live together, without denying, at the same time, other forms of more singular identity: retrenchment, say, in Italianness, or whiteness. Negotiations between different impulses occur all the time.

We can see some of the fruits of his vision in 1959, five years after his death, when the Good Neighbor Italian–Puerto Rican committee sponsored a trip to Puerto Rico for Italian high school youth from East Harlem. Termed a "goodwill tour," the trip was a transformative experience for the boys; as one article noted: "Though five of the seven admitted they were prejudiced before the trip, they said it helped change their attitudes from anti–Puerto Rican to pro."[111] It seemed, for this group of Italians, that contact with Puerto Ricans at home was experienced in terms of the hardened identities and conflicts of intergroup competition, but travel to Puerto Rico, facilitated by a progressive political formation fired by the possibilities of cooperation and exchange, and the hard work of figures such as Marcantonio and Leonard Covello, had made a difference. Whether this moment of crossing, of relating to and being changed by otherness, outside of the boundaries of East Harlem, no less, was more than an outlier—more than peripheral to the central experiences of the space—matters less than its flashing up at a moment of movements that reconceived of identity and difference. And the high schoolers' testament to the power of place would resonate. One of them, Joe Proto, remarked to the newspaper reporter: "When we say Puerto Rico is beautiful, don't think we are trying to knock East Harlem—we love East Harlem."

By the 1960s, when the Italian population in Harlem had declined to not more than twelve thousand, lines of race were drawn and crossed in myriad ways. Groups of African Americans and Puerto Ricans supported welfare and antipoverty projects, and many Italians opposed them, not least because they perceived that the building of low-income housing projects would encroach upon their residences and institutions.[112] A 1968 *New York Times* article on Italian Harlem seized on the tensions in the area, beginning with a strangely problematic description of a "tight Mediterranean island . . . a 'fortress,' surrounded by a rising Negro and Puerto Rican sea," but ending by observing that a cross-cultural formation was afoot in the iconic Our Lady of Mount Carmel Church, where "all five priests" were able to speak Spanish.[113] Since then, the annual festival of that church has accommodated a wide range of middle-class Italians and their descendants, who have left the area but still perform identities based in some notion of belonging. In recent years both a candlelight procession and daytime march proceeds with those Italians in front holding a statue that represents the patron saint, with Haitian women from areas in Brooklyn and elsewhere, who also worship her, following behind.[114]

CROSSINGS AT HOME AND IN THE WORLD

Today, when areas of Harlem are so deeply mixed and diverse, large concentrations of Italians and Puerto Ricans no longer define the area and its encounters. Community claims, nostalgic memories, political assertions, and economic development all play a role in the answers to the question of who owns this place. But how we think about Harlem in the past offers lessons for a future that hangs over the concerns of this chapter. A discussion of a political figure might at first glance present as biography or political history, but, as I have stressed throughout, Vito Marcantonio is inextricable from his place. To read the important moments of his life is to understand how Italian Harlem, East Harlem, Harlem as a whole have been and continue to be constructed. Also informing that inquiry are the insights of social history, which explain the role of movements and community formations in making such historical agents. Marcantonio was of his time, the 1930s, 1940s and 1950s, and of various communities, but the explanatory frames, cross-culturality, and working-class cosmopolitanism given depth by the flashpoints examined here, have explanatory power for different moments. Can we understand white ethnicity as enabling exchange rather than only giving rise to a defensive politics of place even amid tensions of another set of political moments? Marcantonio offers glimpses of that possibility, however idealistically.

4

SELFHOOD AND DIFFERENCE

Piri Thomas and Aladdin on the Streets of Harlem

When Piri Thomas began his 1967 autobiography *Down These Mean Streets* with "This is a bright *mundo*, my streets, my *barrio de noche*,"[1] he evoked a deeply felt connection to a city-world, to a Harlem that was both expansive and intimate. An expressed bravado of ownership—*his* streets, *his* neighborhood—only thinly conceals the vexed nature of belonging that unfolds through the pages of this coming-of-age tale by a Puerto Rican and Black writer from El Barrio that moves across regions of Harlem with volition and uncertainty both. The question of what it means to be part of something as well as yourself is central to all autobiographies, but has a special charge in the abundant stories of people finding themselves in the legendary place of Harlem. Harlem has been a home, a refuge, and a respite from difficulties elsewhere, and as such it is a place with which many people dearly want to identify. As a space of difference, it also stokes intense attachments, not just with the kind of difference articulated, but with the very fact of difference itself. Even as there is a push to say "I am part of this place," there is a pullback, an undercurrent of otherness, to almost all autobiographical narratives of Harlem. And Harlem's edginess, on the edge and cutting-edge, is apparent everywhere.

SELFHOOD AND DIFFERENCE

An implication for everyone feeling they are other to Harlem is that Harlem might itself be constituted by otherness. Can anyone or everyone belong, or is it that no one really, fully does? Underlying anxiety about that question yields important insights about the limits of a multicultural racial ideal that "minoritization" paradoxically offers.

Like Thomas, Alaudin Ullah dwells in peripheries. Ullah, the actor who assumes the stage name "Aladdin" in comic performances and narrates his life in public and private, may seem to be the most liminal figure yet of all those that *Cross-Cultural Harlem* has discussed. He is not African American, nor Puerto Rican, nor even Italian or Jewish, all identifications that would gesture at significant population presence in Harlem over the years. He often refers to himself the "Bangladeshi comedian from Spanish Harlem," simultaneously correlating and contrasting ethnic identity and ethnic space. The apparent disconnect between those two registers constructs Aladdin as an outsider—part of what is perceived to be funny—and an insider at the same time. But having been raised in East Harlem and shaped by the deep cross-cultures across Harlem, which include Blackness and Islam, and shared (if differential) minoritization, Ullah embodies the histories of numerically smaller local groups. His stories of self-invention draw energy from the mobility of dwelling, disrupting familiar associations and creating newness. He also provides a fast track to and through Harlem's globality, continually conjuring up the imaginary of an elsewhere in Bangladesh and staying attentive to the internal cosmopolitanism of locality.

Thomas's Blackness *and* Puerto Ricanness and Ullah's Bangladeshi *and* Muslim racialization bring the critical problematic of otherness to this book's discussions of Harlem's cross-culturality in an especially direct manner. At and from many sorts of edges, these author-performer-residents prompt deeper questions about which renderings of a place matter. What is at the center of Harlem, and why, after all? Is centrality rendered through a large referent population? What happens when that changes? How do we consider professions of cultural ownership? Recall that Claude McKay came from Jamaica, via Kansas, to "a paradise of [his] own people,"[2] and that Langston Hughes grew up in the Midwest, but said he finally "felt at home" in Harlem.[3] Those extravagant utterances betray the depth of a wish related to the kind of Blackness that they sought and ultimately embodied as outsiders who became insiders, both when they were adults. And Thomas and Ullah, born and bred in East Harlem, but living always in reference to the imaginary of Black Harlem that exceeds central or western areas, make plain just how central desire is to identity and place.

Life stories, with their explicit announcements of developing selfhood and belonging, thus provide an important resource for thinking about the meaning of Harlem. The story of a life here is flexibly understood, at times coming into shape as a literary genre, as in the text read in multicultural literature courses (where *Down These Mean Streets* may seem to correspond to an ethnic experience), at others through looser narrations of developing individuality, as manifested in Ullah's plays and personal recollections.[4] In the spirit of the preceding chapters, I am concerned with discourses that gain meaning from production, consumption, and circulation, with an eye to their internal and external multiplicity—something akin to Mikhail Bakhtin's notion of the literary language as "stratified and heteroglot in its aspect as an expressive system, that is, in the forms that carry its meanings"[5]—but in the pages that follow I focus especially on self-referential works. These accounts chronicle and express selves that have lived, worked, and dreamt Harlem. As such, they are more about identification than identity, at least inasmuch as contemporary invocations of the latter have been formulated. To put it more plainly: Thomas and Ullah engage in worldmaking to render not just who they are but where they are and have been, with a special awareness of the constructed and performative nature of the tales told.

Inquiries into the formation of self are always, at root, nostalgic projects, but racialization certainly thwarts easy longings for a place or time: belonging is just too vexed for those who have been pushed to the edges of dominant arrangements of citizenship based on the color of their skin. And so the nostalgia of *these* Harlem stories, told by racially, ethnically, economically, and religiously minoritized peoples, will have us think more critically about the frictions and intimacies intrinsic to transformation. Svetlana Boym has referred to a nostalgia that emerges from "a new understanding of time and space that made the division into 'local' and 'universal' possible."⁶ Loss may be ever-present in Thomas's and Ullah's accounts, but remarkably does not lead irretrievably to sadness; instead, it operates as a thematic, an opportunity for revisiting moments of encounter with multiple peoples and histories. In this sense, nostalgia is "reflective," as Boym describes it, concerned with "the relationship between individual biography and the biography of groups and nations, between personal and collective memory" on the one hand and processing "shattered fragments of memory and temporaliz[ing] space" on the other.⁷ As nostalgia appears through the reflections and constructions here, it reminds us that investing in Harlem is more than a matter of recovery: it is also a project bound up with reconstruction and repair, of a racial sort, with political implications.

Presenting in particularly open forms, Thomas's and Ullah's life stories exploit the dueling significations of "the streets," a vehicle for movement, a stable site of activity, and a marker of territorial divides. Thomas's representation of who and what he is grows from navigations within blocks and various routes of travel beyond them. The conventional teleology of a journey away from family and community gets a different spin through his continual departures and arrivals within imagined Harlems across actual regional territories. If in the end the subject of *Down These Mean Streets* finds personal redemption, the story as a whole still refuses resolution. Ullah's irreverent plays and personal reminiscences highlight the ironies of minoritized life as a Bangladeshi Muslim existing between local and diasporic formations of Islam and showcase formative experiences in the public world of the neighborhood. Always evident for both Thomas and Ullah as they conceive of spatial mobility are the possibilities of transgression and the enduring realities of limits.

Developing selves from the 1960s through the 1990s could not but be engaged with Civil Rights and Black Arts movements and discourses of racial struggle and self-actualization, as well as developing Latino political and cultural communities. Just three years before the publication of *Down These Mean Streets*, the shooting of a Black teenager by police in Harlem inspired days of protests across the city and beyond.⁸ The urban crisis of that period compelled many responses, and if popular discussions of impoverishment and pathology created a narrow conception of how race

SELFHOOD AND DIFFERENCE

was lived in city-space—Daniel Patrick Moynihan's controversial *The Negro Family: The Case for National Action* appeared in 1965[9]—stories written by minoritized subjects themselves expanded and complicated the representational field.[10] Ralph Ellison registered his objections to the dominant discourse, writing: "I don't deny that these sociological formulas are drawn from life, but I do deny that they define the complexity of Harlem. They only abstract it and reduce it to proportions which the sociologists can manage. I simply don't recognize Harlem in them."[11] The radical activist organization the Young Lords sought their own definitional autonomy by setting some terms for a Latino-ness articulated to Black Power and its critiques, with an autonomous identity, in that classic cross-cultural formation.[12] Over the course of several decades the Nuyorican movement and other artistic communities provided another space to think through the cultural consequences of significant migrations of Puerto Ricans to New York and the ensuing dilemmas of identification and expression.[13] Growing up in the 1970s, Ullah likewise worked through the predicaments and possibilities of political and cultural milieux articulated to social movements. For both Thomas and Ullah, as for so many subjects living in Harlem, Blackness outlined a political grammar and an urban aesthetic.[14]

If *Down These Mean Streets* swam in all these currents, its purposefully autobiographical mode operated to address questions about the internalization of the world outside. This text registers insurgent ethnic influences and also reads as a piece in which an unstable sense of "community" remains on the edges. Not quite undoing urban crisis, Thomas presents movement along the (mean) streets as culturally, psychically, and socially rich. His book title nods not to the crime and poverty of Martin Scorsese's 1973 film, with which contemporary readers will be more familiar, but to Raymond Chandler's emphasis on the character-building born of experience, recounted in a 1944 essay on his detective stories, where "down these mean streets a man must go who is not himself mean, who is neither tarnished nor afraid . . . He is the hero; he is everything. He must be a complete man and a common man and yet an unusual man."[15] In a familiar masculine move, the public sphere is counterposed to the domestic one and the urban subject assumes the position of the flaneur, stimulated and fortified by his traversal of all sorts of social spaces. European models for *flânerie* have emphasized the ability to move on without deep attachment, but the practices and attendant subjectivity in Harlem have the quality of cathexis, investments and attachments based in racialization. Thomas's story pours out of an imagination of the possibilities and limits of a place that has been built through heterogeneity and contingency and, in this case, the dense mutual constitution of Blackness and Latino identity. Like other figures in this book, Langston Hughes and Vito Marcantonio especially, Thomas breaks through the divides of ethnic–racial neighborhoods. As he writes a story of the Puerto Rican self that increasingly identifies with Blackness and feels at home in Black Harlem, he challenges the foundational logic of compartmentalized spaces.

Lifelong experiments with identity, this is to say, are made vivid in porous cultural forms rooted in urbanity. *Down These Mean Streets* may hew to some basic guidelines of what literary theorist Philippe Lejeune describes as a characteristic correspondence between author, narrator, and protagonist in the autobiography,[16] but in its discussion of rather specific and storied histories and community formations, which the author assumes alternating intimacy with and distance from, it also resembles the memoir. As a story of a life, it delicately balances the compulsions of truth-telling and description with fictionalization fueled by fantasy and a political unconscious, like both a sociological study and a novel. And Ullah's comic one-man plays produce identifications with the writer–urban observer that are predicated on understandings of experience that may veil the formative nature of performance. If the discussions in the following pages seem less interested in the distinctiveness of the genres of autobiography or drama or, for that matter, of the relative accuracy of sources, of the interview or personal letter, they nonetheless pay attention to the varied kinds of expressions of the self that constitute life stories.

While chapter 1 of this book refers to the challenge of maintaining a separation between Langston Hughes and his fictional protagonist Valerio vis-à-vis the literary short story "Spanish Blood," it is even harder to pull apart the authorial and represented subjects in the works considered here. Piri Thomas in *Down These Mean Streets* provides a narrator character in

Piri, who alternates between omniscience and implicated perspective. The issue of separation is as complex when Ullah performs selves of the present and the past, making explicit construction and production (as well as, in audience response, consumption) and divides between creator and character especially murky. These occasions have us think productively about transferences fired by the desire of and for place, something more than a literary or dramatic environment that can be held still. Individual fragmentation and mixture—with investments and experiences that remain unresolved—are structurally reflected in the territory of Harlem that is insurgently Black, but also multiply constituted, cross-cultural.

Another frame for these stories of self, then, may be "spatial practice." Harlem has offered particular kinds of opportunities for experimentation, projection, and possibility that take shape across a range of autobiographies, memoirs, personal histories, and auto-fiction.[17] This last chapter of *Cross-Cultural Harlem* explicitly brings the conversation about represented pasts into the presents of Harlem, through population and economic shifts and a changing national political landscape that moves through a post-9/11 period and its intensified discrimination against Muslims. Living and thinking in shared space with a deep awareness of history produces a kind of intertextuality somewhat different from the incidence of literary references. Ullah's rich evocations of place recall those that Thomas has elaborated. In an interview, Ullah in fact installed himself in this particular trajectory of Harlem writing with mention of a visit to Thomas's house, during which he was encouraged to "keep writing," the expression of which emphasizes the continuing nature of the exercise, the unfinished quality of the project pointing to the openness of this space.[18] Stepping back to see Thomas and Ullah together, then, may bring into shape connections and overlaps, more of an extant dialogue across times and spaces than any proposal of inheritance can convey. And to further explore influence, Ullah discovers resources in his parents' immigrant stories that go even further back, while mirroring and diverging from the traces we see in *Down These Mean Streets*. In putting these two sets of occasions together, of different canonical scale, for sure—Thomas is widely known in scholarly circles, Ullah significantly less so—I do not mean to imply comparison in the formal analytical sense or even the more neutral strategy of juxtaposition. Instead, I wish to illuminate a continuum, based in the idea that if we start with Thomas's kind of mixtures and negotiations, it can open us up to seeing what Ullah's performances offer for the project of rethinking spatiality. From there, we might be able to develop a deeper understanding of the presents and futures of cross-cultural Harlem.

PASTS AS PROLOGUE

Piri Thomas was born in 1928 to a dark-skinned Cuban father and a lighter Puerto Rican mother, into the complicated racial landscape of East Harlem, with a range of unstable identifications based in a familial racial past that continually processed ambivalences about Blackness. And so *Down These Mean Streets* turns over possibilities of identity and newness—concerns of any story of a life—vis-à-vis the structuring power of Black Harlem. The broad narrative arc begins with a young Piri walking in East Harlem after an argument with his father in 1941, still a grim economic period for many poor people of color, and extends through his life in various other regions, lingering on self-conscious moments of racial–ethnic and gender formation. The worlds into which Thomas literally and figuratively stepped were diversely peopled. Migrants from various parts of Latin America had lived in Harlem since the late 1800s, well before larger waves of Puerto Ricans came to East Harlem in the 1940s. Cubans and Puerto Ricans built anticolonial organizations and found hospitable spaces of political engagement there.[19] Puerto Ricans were U.S. citizens, but their complex relationships to locality and nation had everything to do with a racialized colonial-imperial relationship of United States to Puerto Rico. And thorny questions of belonging faced African Americans, West Indians, and other Black peoples in Harlem: migrations from the U.S. South imprinted experiences of Jim Crow onto urban memory and immigration from colonies that were not independent made being "national" anywhere a shaky prospect.

SELFHOOD AND DIFFERENCE

Comparative and contrastive racialization thematized popular representations of Harlem neighborhoods. As Puerto Ricans came to dominate East Harlem from the Great Depression through the postwar period's economic crises of urban life, El Barrio became the counterpart to Black Harlem. Tales of Puerto Ricans in El Barrio focused on the conjuncture of race and class, just as the poverty of African Americans had long been central to how Black Harlem was received and experienced. A 1950 *Amsterdam News* series of articles entitled "The Inside Story of Harlem's Puerto Ricans" explicitly drew out parallels between adjacent African American and Puerto Rican communities, with the working assumption that systemic problems had spatial dimensions: "low wages, low standard of living, overcrowding, high incidence of illness and disease, police brutality, and a not too sympathetic public opinion."[20] Communities responded with all kinds of solidarities based in class as well as, at times, careful delineation of groups and self-definition.[21]

Down These Mean Streets emerged against this charged backdrop, deliberately speaking from a particular place to multiple elsewheres but dispensing any expectations for a purely social-realist account. Thomas's prologue begins: "Hey, World—here I am. Hallo, World—this is Piri." That world could mean many things: the global geopolitical sphere and its breadth, something outside of where the character Piri stands, or Harlem itself. Spatial work can be tracked through perspective, when Thomas writes: "How many times have I stood on the rooftop of my broken-down building at night and watched the bulb-lit world below . . . this my Harlem."[22] A bird's-eye view, much contemplated by geographers and cultural theorists, as stressing the "big picture," takes in more than the immediate neighborhood of one's daily life.[23] Rather than subscribe to a vision of place in which regions and peoplehood are bound up with one another (Puerto Rican or Italian in East Harlem, African American in Central and West Harlems), this vantage point helps to illumine a more dynamic sociality from the very outset:

> This is a bright *mundo*, my streets, my *barrio de noche*,
> With its thousands of lights, hundreds of millions of colors
> Mingling with noises, swinging street sounds of cars and curses.[24]

SELFHOOD AND DIFFERENCE

All these sights and sounds (lights, colors, noises) create a sensation very different from one tightly associated with one or another ethnicity.

With that multiply constituted world of the very first pages, Thomas poses a diversity to be filled out textually socially, and affectively. The prologue is written in poetic verse rather than prose, unlike the rest of the text, which hews more closely to the style of narrative autobiography. Like a poem, too, the prologue directly addresses the reader. In this way it is performative, stagey even, rather than informational, in a more nonfictional manner. This entry point thus presents a generic layering within which race, subjectivity, and place will develop. And the story of *Down These Mean Streets* will become even more complex through the representation of self, the autobiographical-fictional "I" of the character of Piri, a young boy with complicated parentage who experiences, in turn, the turf conflicts of life in East Harlem, a subsequent family move to Long Island, a return to the world of Harlem streets and its crime and poverty, and a stint in prison and ultimate return to Harlem. Textual multivocality lies not just in who Piri is or becomes (the standard thrust of autobiography), but also in how he is fictionalized with regard to the Harlems made vivid in the setting.

The book's structuring dialectic between selfhood and spatiality takes shape across divides. In an early chapter entitled "Alien Turf," Thomas expresses territorial binds in which a mixed subject might find himself, through the protagonist Piri's consciousness of boundaries: "Sometimes you don't fit in, like if you're a Puerto Rican on an Italian block."[25] Writing before multicultural diversity became the dominant expressive mode of ethnic autobiography, Thomas is explicit about a crude classification system and conveys alternating forms of intimacy and distance in a tense turf-controlling exchange:

> Someone called: "Hey you dirty fuckin spic." . . .
> I turned around real slow and found my face pushing in the finger of an Italian kid about my age. He had five or six of his friends with him.
> "Hey you," he said "What nationality are ya?"
> I looked at him and wondered which nationality to pick. And one of his friends said: "Ah, Rocky, he's black enuff to be a nigger. Ain't that what you is, kid?"

SELFHOOD AND DIFFERENCE

> My voice was almost shy in its anger. "I'm Puerto Rican," I said. "I was born here." I wanted to shout it, but it came out like a whisper. . . .
>
> I looked around for some friendly faces belonging to grown-up people, but the elders were all busy yakking away in Italian. I couldn't help thinking how much like Spanish it sounded. Shit, that should make us something like relatives.[26]

Rocky and his boys and young Piri eventually come to an understanding, through a developing narrative about Blackness (and consciousness). And Thomas's deeper understanding and construction of self, readers will see, cannot be outside of those exchanges.

In relaying this and other moments of a developing imaginary, seeing both his own likeness and an image of otherness in a way that cannot but recall a basic psychoanalytic structure, Thomas engages with preexisting stories about Harlem but sets up the possibility of a different experience.[27] The storytelling mode blends easily with the work of careful quasi-sociological description. Piri, in other words, reads and represents the field. But as Thomas narrates Piri's inability to fully understand the context of this dramatic incident, he also casts him in a nonomniscient role. His innocence is both a product of youth and a feature of complicated ethnicity on the streets. We see this in a gap between author and character, as Thomas narrates how Piri looks around for support in his confrontation: "I dug three Italian elders looking at us from across the street, and I felt saved. But that went out the window when they just smiled and went on talking. I couldn't decide whether they had smiled because this new whatever-he-was was gonna get his ass kicked or because they were pleased that their kids were welcoming."[28] It may well be that the codes and practices of the famous "street sense," a mark of membership, vary in ways that those who are especially invested in authenticity are simply unable to process.

An internal dialogue continues to work through different visions of relation and opposition. When one of the Italian kids asks Piri about nationality, he is of course conflating whiteness and Americanness; Piri's response about being Puerto Rican but born "here" could be a nod toward either hyphenated ethnicity or a Harlem racial belonging that supersedes nationality. In this way Thomas recasts the storied Italian–Puerto Rican conflict that had been central to the experience of many in East Harlem to be about more than the ethnic competition resulting from these two groups living side by side.[29] Language becomes a sign not just of difference or foreignness but of the comparisons of something that cannot quite be explained by national diversity. Thus, when Piri remarks on how Italian sounded like Spanish, and the potential for translation, we may recall Vito Marcantonio's Italian-accented Spanish of the previous chapter or the intimate linguistic understanding between the fictional characters Valerio and Hattie in "Spanish Blood." Ultimately, Piri finds consolation in Blackness, in a racial performance that straddles worlds. He notes about being in enemy territory, "deep in Italian country," that he "went, walking in the style which I had copped from the colored cats I had seen, a swinging and stepping down hard at every step. Those cats were so down and cool that just walking made a way-out sound."[30]

Piri's mimetic assumption of Black style in the chapter on turf conflicts with Italians is followed by another kind of exchange in the local welfare office that makes the differences and connections (and their authenticity) even more ambiguous. In the represented 1940s, young Piri and his mother experience humiliation with other residents of various backgrounds from all over Harlem. Piri observes: "Most of the people were Puerto Rican and Negroes; a few were Italians. It seemed that every mother had brought a kid to interpret for her."[31] In this moment, African Americans, Puerto Ricans, and Italians—at odds in the streets and on the borders of different regions of Harlem—are all incapable of reading the state and being understood and need another generation to translate. One cannot underestimate the effect of impoverishment as a shared experience: Harlem has not only been the site for racial otherness, it has also been a place for *poor* people. Italians who came to East Harlem, African Americans who migrated from the U.S. South, and Puerto Ricans all landed in a substratum of U.S. society, in manual labor, in domestic service, and often without jobs at all. And the administration as well as experience of social programs highlighted the comparative and felt possibilities of racialization and ethnicization.

But reciprocity can be difficult to take in, Thomas's story reminds us, especially because poverty has long been a source of shame. When the investigator formulaically responds to the Italian woman seeking help, she says: "'Aghh' . . . disgustedly . . .'No-o, I didn't mean that, Mr. King. Yes, please— try to do the best you can. Try to . . .'" In narrative voice, Piri remarks: "I turned my attention elsewhere. Her pleading was too close to my people's: taking with outstretched hands and resenting it in the same breath."[32] Piri's awareness of the intimacy of relation does not necessarily bring him closeness. When we think about Thomas writing about this past incident in the politicized late 1960s, it is hard to miss both the promise of something, even someone new, as well as the difficulty of solidarity. That people can share hostilities and needs and may even understand that, while also turning away from connection, puts a brake on any idealization of the cross-cultural.

Promises and failures spring up all over the broad field of Harlem as Piri moves from the welfare office on a trolley across neighborhood streets. He arrives at the ethnically heterogeneous La Marketa (usually spelled *la marqueta*), recognizing it as a public space for exchange, at least structurally like the one he has just left. But here, acts of consumption give vexed relations between different peoples a bit more agency, if not freedom. An observation of the chaotic multiplicity of La Marqueta echoes earlier sections of *Down These Mean Streets*: "there wasn't anything you couldn't buy there. It was always packed with a mess of people selling or buying, and talking different languages." Instead of Italian sounding like Spanish, a kind of linguistic proximity that does not always lead to understanding, Jewish vendors here translate, perfectly, it seems: "they spoke Spanish like Puerto Ricans."[33] Piri's mother functions as a straightforward consumer, one kind of participant in a multiethnic exchange economy, but his father is both more alive to the ambience of the place—enjoying haggling with the vendors—and more skeptical, too. The resemblance between the father and son, inhabiting the cross-cultural world of Harlem, is unmistakable. Piri notes, "Poppa discounted the vendors' friendly '*Cómo estás?*' He said that 'How are you?' were the first Spanish words the vendors learned so they could win the people's confidence and gyp them in their own language. I wondered if Poppa didn't like Jews the way I didn't like Italians."[34]

SELFHOOD AND DIFFERENCE

Piri's father, then, exhibits a commitment to a more protective, even defensive identity. His resistance to crossing is an important part of this story and the masculinity of an attachment to narrower forms of identity or street sense is palpable.

Language's importance can be seen not only in presence but also in the contours of absence, when the possibility of communication is raised and then painfully extinguished. As Piri moves with his family from city to suburb, in a familiar immigrant trajectory, the resulting misrecognitions of race and place take shape in a pointed lack of social understanding that must be verbalized. At a high-school dance, Piri is asked by a white girl: "Are you Spanish? I didn't know. I mean, you don't look like what I thought a Spaniard looks like." Piri replied: "I ain't a Spaniard from Spain.... I'm a Puerto Rican from Harlem." "Oh—you talk English very well," is the response. "I told you I was born in Harlem. That's why I ain't got no Spanish accent."[35] When the girl then goes on to compare Piri's accent to another African American boy's, Piri is able to comprehend not only what is going on with his own subjectivity (and its reception) but also the cross-cultural processes of life in Harlem. Piri says: "Yeah, I know Jerry.... I know Jerry is colored and I know I got his accent. Most of us in Harlem steal from each other's language or style or stick of living."[36] Comparisons of race and language thus register through something more elusive: voice. The discovery of that kind of affective connection in the text is frequently marked by a kind of recession or slipping into the background: shyness with anger, turning away, speaking softly, as Piri does above. There is no easy expression for those moments, either for the character of Piri or the authorial self that is Thomas.

JOURNEYS INTO BLACKNESS

Explorations of Blackness cannot but start with the familial, and that is vividly rendered in *Down These Mean Streets*. Like many Puerto Ricans and other immigrants, those in Thomas's family see themselves as different from African Americans. When confronted with Piri's developing racial consciousness, his brother José reacts with a familiar sentiment using a slang term from the Spanish-speaking Caribbean: "We're Puerto Ricans, and that's different from being *moyetos*."[37] And so the intense domestic fault line between Piri and his father runs through a frank and widespread anti-Blackness even among those who might themselves be its victims and who live alongside racial minorities. Piri suspects that his dark-skinned Cuban father desired his mother because she is light-skinned. It is not surprising when the hypermasculine competition between the adolescent son and his increasingly less powerful father erupts over race. As Thomas writes on the page that precedes the very first chapter of the book: "Pops, how come me and you is always on the outs? Is it something we don't know nothing about? I wonder if it's something I done, or something I am."[38] The "outs" and the "ins," intimate entanglements and distantiating desires, are certainly at issue in the Blackness that extends beyond the local here and now. Is Blackness inherited, is it reconstructed, can it be renewed or worn away in the space of a generation? And what does that question mean for peoples scattered by African slavery?[39] While *Down These Mean Streets* implicitly may determine one potential family (and source of family tensions) to extend across seas, we must also read Thomas as putting onto the table the Afro-Latino, who diverges from national ethnic and racial possibilities. Perhaps the strains between Piri and his parents result in estrangement and alienation precisely because that subject is not fully available, in the 1940s and 1950s of Thomas's childhood or even the 1960s of his retrospective. But much later, in a 1980 interview, when asked whether he felt Black or Puerto Rican, Thomas irrupted with, "I felt both Puerto Rican and Black, you understand?"[40]

Thomas and his autobiographical text echo many Harlem pasts that shape community logics. Dilemmas about competing identifications of race and ethnicity have long confronted African American, West Indian, and African peoples in the United States and elsewhere. If African Americans' or Caribbean Americans' expressions of that have been more public throughout Harlem's history, other Black diasporic migrants' uncertainties have been no less constant. The difference between the case of Harlem residents from the British Caribbean (Jamaica especially, but also Trinidad and other smaller islands) and Puerto Ricans, whose region had a specifically colonial relationship to the United States, is partly chronological—West Indians first arrived in the early part of the twentieth century, at a time of intense Black nationalism, and Puerto Ricans came in larger numbers in the 1940s—with obvious linguistic components. And geographic settlement affected the differences: West Indians settled in Central and West Harlem (already conceived of as "Black") and Puerto Ricans in East Harlem, a historically white ethnic immigrant world. Also important were the specific valences of Black consciousness from the homelands.

One especially famous antecedent for a relationship between Blackness and Puerto Ricanness is Arturo Schomburg, a collector and public intellectual who migrated to New York in 1891, well before larger numbers of Puerto Ricans would come. Most people remember Schomburg as Black but his mother's family was from St Croix and his father was German and Puerto Rican, to complicate the picture even more. Significantly, his navigation of multiple racial (and national) registers took shape in the mix of Harlem.[41] That Schomburg could be both Puerto Rican and Black somehow seems less remarkable than his continual movement through domestic and transnational articulations of racial subjectivity and, as well, his nestling into an identity that could be more publicly, if not seamlessly, articulated to African American political and cultural life. In some ways, Schomburg may have been a kindred spirit for Piri Thomas the writer, though perhaps not Piri in *Down These Mean Streets*.

What does Blackness mean for Thomas? A partial answer lies in the development of consciousness for Piri, represented ego of and vehicle for the author. However episodic, Piri's represented pull toward Blackness is unmistakable. A certain restlessness associated with shifts in identity has a geographic component: Thomas's imaginative leaps entail physical movement into the "heart" of Harlem, into central and western regions of the place, and then ultimately to the U.S. South, as many African Americans and whites had gone before him. Another pressure comes from the outside world, in which some people, at least, consider Piri to be nonwhite. Illustrating that is the incident when a young Piri has a conflict with a school principal and an African American woman, Miss Washington, rises to his defense, saying "Now hol' on, white man."[42] Effectively building a dichotomized vision of racial community (whiteness v. nonwhiteness) and authority (minority students against a white school administration), this scene also recalls the earlier one in the welfare office; together, they reflect the context of the 1940s, in which many groups in Harlem organized African American and Puerto Rican residents to pressure the city to administer social programs more justly and expansively.[43]

But it bears special attention that *Down These Mean Streets* traces Piri's development of racial consciousness without the language of contemporary identity politics. Notably there is no "Eureka!" moment, where the protagonist in a story discovers some kind of confirmation of who he really was all the time; instead, it is the hard-won knowledge about his self in the world that results from multiple interactions over time. For Piri, Blackness is characterized by becoming rather than being. After not getting an interview for a job while his white friend did, Piri responds to "a colored cat" who tells him that this discrimination is commonly experienced by African Americans, reflecting: "I know that . . . but I wasn't a Negro then, I was still only a Puerto Rican."[44] This is a transformation in the works, one that cannot only be relegated to the writer Piri Thomas's past, but is also of the present of 1967. And being "only" Puerto Rican in any moment calls attention to insufficiency. The sense of being both himself and changing through an exchange with otherness, that deep cross-cultural affect that explains so much of the experience of Harlem, is elevated as Thomas processes those traumas associated with the pressures of singularity. In this regard, descriptions of the sound of the place in *Down These Mean Streets* communicate a great deal: "The noise of the block began to break through to me. I listened for real. I heard the roar of multicolored kids, a street blend of Spanish and English with a strong tone of Negro American."[45] Piri commits to interpreting the multiplicity that gives meaning to this space by truly "listening." By this point in the text, multiplicity has become a refrain, but here it is rendered a little differently, on the one hand dichotomized in Spanish and English, the latter's "strong tone" evoking the U.S. national formation of Blackness, "Negro American," and on the other the mixture or blend, in which it is not always easy to delineate origins.

All this is to say that race always, narratively, demands conversation. On the eve of a visit to Norfolk, Virginia for the explicit purpose of exploring Blackness with his friend Brew, whom Piri has earlier called one of his "tightest *amigos*" and also "as black as God is supposed to be white," Brew's girlfriend Alayce puts on the table a more restricted vision of race.[46] She says of Piri: "He's a Porto Rican and that's whar he is. We's Negroes and that's whar we're at."[47] It cannot be unintentional that the strict divide here between the two is reminiscent of the tensions that Piri has felt with his family, particularly with his father and brother, who have wanted to claim whiteness as a form of distinction from African Americans, in Black Harlem especially. The subsequent journey into the soul, a presumed source of Blackness in the U.S. South, strongly echoes that of so many "race writers" before Thomas, to function as a literary convention.[48] The territory of his identity map expands as Piri finds complexity and uncertainty alongside experiences of discrimination that resemble those he had had in Harlem. In Virginia, Piri meets Gerald West, a light-skinned Black social researcher from Philadelphia who had moved to Norfolk to research African American life, and who exposes him to perspectives on race that resonate on a number of different levels.

Comparison and commensurability are modes that *Down These Mean Streets* employs as Piri refers to Gerald's family history as "multicolored," like his own, but with a wider palette of white, Malay, Black, Indian (from India), and Spanish "blood." But the racial palimpsest acquires a different charge when Gerald notes: "Of course, I feel that the racial instincts that are the strongest in a person enjoying this rich mixture are the ones that—uh—should be followed."[49] At the outset, the privileging of instinct here suggests that race may be phenomenological rather than material. But even the sphere of racial feeling that seems so very much to be about the present cannot be disentangled from a deeply embedded global history. The interface, and competition between Blackness and something called Spanishness looms large for the characters of *Down These Mean Streets*, just as it has for generations of Spanish-speaking peoples around the world, in

Spain and Latin America and, in the United States, among Latino Americans. That social fact is tapped into by the ensuing dialogue, when Gerald expresses, with an obvious stutter: "I—rather—feel—sort of Spanish-ish, if I may use that term. I have always had great admiration for Spanish culture and traditions. I—er—yes—feel rather impulsed toward things Spanish. I guess that's why I have this inclination to learn Castilian. Of course I don't disregard the other blends."[50] An apparent flexibility and posing of "Spanish" as cultural and linguistic are taken to task by Brew, who remains the voice of insistent Black identity as well as the conscience that reminds everyone about the power of racism. He asks Gerald, first, if he has ever been mistaken for "Caucasian" (he has, probably) or for "Negro," the reply to which speaks volumes about anti-Blackness among immigrants, mixed peoples, and light-skinned subjects: "I feel white. . . . I look white; I think white; therefore I *am* white."[51]

Brew's skepticism, voiced in code that many readers would understand because it denotes such widespread mythologies about blood—"Don' yuh-all feel a leetle bit more Negro than that?"—thrusts utopian racial thinking into the lived political landscape of the time. Those ideas are certainly accessible to Piri when he sees his own dilemmas mirrored in Gerald: "I was thinking that Gerald had problems something like mine. Except that he was a Negro trying to make Puerto Rican and I was a Puerto Rican trying to make Negro."[52] Indeed, Gerald's way of thinking about racial identity flusters Piri, who observes, "What he had said about choice had shattered my own ideas."[53] It certainly must have unsettled readers in 1967, when political protests against racism in Harlem and the rest of the United States might have been less focused on identity than on resources. And if antiessentialism has become a standard approach to questions of race, there is no question that introducing *choice* into the debate remains a deeply contested move.[54] Brew's importance as a character in this text is not just as a foil; he represents another kind of pushback meant to, if not quite close in racialization, then certainly say that it matters, deeply, in place and time. He implicitly reminds Piri in the text and the readers outside of it that generations of even racialized migrants have gained privilege from *not* being Black or claiming Blackness. That sentiment resonates, even if

SELFHOOD AND DIFFERENCE

Thomas's questionable transcriptions of Black dialect might suggest a certain authorial distance from Black peoples.

Two encounters make vivid for Piri the enduring power of race and his instantiation in arrangements built through racism. When he and Brew are in Mobile, Alabama, Piri insists on going into an all-white restaurant, while Brew remains outside. Thomas's description of the physical divide interestingly, perhaps unwittingly, recalls philosopher Frantz Fanon's discussion of Jacques Lacan, where looking into the mirror of whiteness can initiate deep racial trauma, but here it is inverted: "Brew had warned me about going in, and I could see him through the plate-glass window, standing outside, waiting, with no expression on his black face, the only black face around. I was the alonest."[55] In this formulation, Piri's ego-information relies on Blackness. When Piri, read as Black, is predictably refused service, he describes an eruption in racialized and ethnic terms, hitting his fist against the counter "with all [his] Puerto Rican black man's strength" and swearing in Spanish. But instead of being overwhelmed by or disidentified with Blackness (as Fanon might have described his Black subject's relationship to whiteness), Piri establishes a solidarity and kinship with Brew ("he dug what I was thinking"), who has by this time become a figure of national Blackness in this story.[56] A second example of Piri's relayed racial consciousness carries more gendered and also diasporic effects, not least because it takes shape at the United States–Mexico border. In a way that is reminiscent of the actions of the character Bigger Thomas in *Native Son* or that evokes the sentiments of the autobiographical figure that Eldridge Cleaver cuts in *Soul on Ice*,[57] Piri imagines sex with a white woman as a response to the degradations of racism, crudely putting it: "I wanted to break out against this two-tone South; I wanted to fuck a white woman in Texas."[58] The "two-tone" quality of the place would seem to refer to the very limited Black–white racial dichotomies that the segregated South presented to Piri, but it also recalls the racial world of Harlem in which he has struggled to find his place.[59] Thomas's working through the shared hemispheric identifications of Latino-ness (though unstated as such in *Down These Mean Streets*, because the term was not in popular usage in 1967) occurs in relation to Mexicans, certainly a large population concentration at the border though not yet present in East Harlem, and also, importantly, part of a developing minoritized imaginary of nationality and transnationality.[60]

Piri's felt solidarities are, as always, one window onto his character's, and Thomas's, affiliations and identifications. Just as a close friendship with Brew inflames and makes more urgent Piri's explorations of Blackness, a kinship with a local Mexican is key to what might be cast as a "Latino" reading of the ensuing scene. When Piri gets off the ship at Galveston, he immediately approaches a group pitching pennies, and is cheered on by a Mexican man who presumes that Spanish will be understood and says: "*Bueno, hombre, bueno!*" It is an axis of identification that allows for divergence, for specific cultural traces, and Piri accordingly notes: "We went to a *cantina* and had some drinks—he, tequila, and me, to be true to all *puertoriqueños*, rum." The man then instructs Piri on how to utilize transnationality to sidestep the specifically U.S. institution of racial segregation: "If you do not speak a word of English, you may pass for Puerto Rican."[61] He obediently pretends he does not speak English in the hotel that the two men go to, and interestingly the clerk, and procurer of prostitutes, asks "Dónde tu eres?" The grammatical mistake, omitting "de" before "dónde," and switching the placement of subject and verb, are of course minor enough not to impede translation, and in fact, to Spanish-speaking readers it might function as another reminder of the seams in all sorts of presumed connection, another example of which is the felt falsity of Piri replying "Puerto Rico."[62] When the clerk asks if Piri is a "nigger," the Mexican replies unequivocally that he is not. And Piri reciprocates in kind, extending masculinized protection by telling the Mexican man to leave the scene before any trouble begins.

The expressed unveiling of Piri to the prostitute says a great deal about both the revelations of race in the United States and diasporic currents. At the end of his sexual encounter, Piri says: "I just want you to know . . . that you got fucked by a nigger, *by a black man!*"[63] While the epithet "nigger" may exist within a narrower racist lexicon, "black man" signifies more broadly, globally, across the Americas. Blackness, in this moment of the text, so close to the Blackness that undergirds Jim Crow, as well as to the articulations of the character Brew, is U.S.-American as well as relatable to the Caribbean and Latin America. And Piri tellingly inhabits both possibilities. To escape, Piri mentions, he must return to what he calls "his turf," which is a ship, an exemplary vehicle for cross-cultural contact through hemispheric spaces, and pan-African histories, too. He leaves one kind of Blackness, it is true, but embraces another, as this ship is going to the West Indies, and he pointedly signs "this time . . . on a black gang," a deliberate play on words, using the term for laborers who stoke the coal engines, that would bring color and class together.[64] It is also worth remembering that the Caribbean is itself a heterogeneously racial space. When Piri and his brother have a debate about race in chapter 15, tellingly entitled "Brothers Under the Skin," the history of Indian coolies and indigenous peoples bubbles up in reference to their father's background.[65] The racial story unfurled in *Down These Mean Streets* again and again refuses the coherence for identity that the nation would compel: it divides continually between Black Caribbean and Black-Latin formations, Mexico and Puerto Rico, and their racial landscapes, without finding glue in diasporic space, which is also itself fractured and differentiated.

After becoming Black in a new way in the U.S. South, Piri returns to Harlem, literally and figuratively, to that world of minoritized peoples negotiating space, its divides and its adjacencies, and its social–economic difficulties. The homecoming initiates a criminal descent that becomes in turn an object lesson for the book's essentially redemptive trajectory. Surely that kind of plot needs prison, not just for the character development for which "reform" can be a shorthand, but also for its isolation from other areas of activity in the autobiography, a different site for the emergence of new individuality. But even if Thomas adheres to that basic narrative structure, the penultimate section, entitled "Prison," about the aftermath of a prosecution for a shooting, actually challenges the configurations of selfhood and space. For Piri, the meaning and experience of prison has been made by translational Harlem. He is compelled by his encounters with Black Muslims, their opposition to stimulants, and, as well, their pointedly political perspectives on the state of America, much like Malcolm X had written about three years before *Down These Mean*

SELFHOOD AND DIFFERENCE

Streets.⁶⁶ But Piri also apprehends this group through what he knows: "I heard . . . what sounded like 'Asalam-aleecum.' . . . I thought of the Jews in Harlem and how close this sounded to the 'Sholom' I'd heard them greet each other with once in a while."⁶⁷ The exchanges between Italian and Spanish of earlier sections of the text about childhood reverberate through his developing adulthood. Piri notes that he had seen Black Muslims before in Harlem, but that he can now engage with them because by this point he fully understands that minoritized peoples can sound like one another, not to mention that there are also many ways to be Black.

These revelations bring Piri, and Thomas, to a Harlem ending. Harlem can embrace Piri with that "warm *amigo* darkness" of the prologue that echoes Langston Hughes's image of safety and acknowledgment in his poem "Dream Variation:"

> To fling my arms wide
> In some place of the sun,
> To whirl and to dance
> Till the bright day is done.
> Then rest at cool evening
> Beneath a tall tree
> While night comes gently
> Dark like me⁶⁸

A deep attachment evoked in the title of the concluding chapter, "Hey, Barrio—I'm Home," processes the exchanges and new possibilities for collectivities in the preceding pages, but also settles into what had been a touchstone throughout.

LIVES FOR A HARLEM STORY

The manuscript that Thomas put together in prison was titled "Home, Sweet Harlem," but he notes that when it was "reborn" as *Down These*

Mean Streets "it was even better."⁶⁹ Perhaps breaking from the familiar language of home freed Thomas to explore different questions from those that writers had discussed in the past. Indeed, at the very outset of the published autobiography, when Piri attempts to get his father's attention by leaving his house, he notes, pointedly: "I had run away from home but not from Harlem."⁷⁰ We might consider how separating the character of Piri from Harlem-as-home enables the mobilization of other places, not just for dislocation, but as satellite sites for character building and the procession of plot. The narrative space thus can be made less linear, structured as much by continual departures and arrivals, not any developmental move away from older forms of identity. Diaspora, too, and its jumbling of points of origin and settlement becomes accessible as a cross-cultural scaffolding for Thomas's story, focusing on locality, globally rendered.

When Thomas reacted emotionally in interviews to the question of whether he was Puerto Rican *or* Black, one could hardly blame him for resenting the pressure of singular identities, which would shrink the field that he had so carefully enlarged in *Down These Mean Streets*. Even if multiculturalism had taken hold, the translation of racial arrangements from other countries into U.S. templates for difference was still vexatious, and many racialized or mixed peoples settled into Blackness. Pressure certainly mounts when and where Blackness has represented an insurgent identity and being "something else" inspires pathos and alienation in a dominant minoritized and politicized space like Harlem. If Schomburg chose Blackness at the turn of the twentieth century, we might ask what paths would have been open to Piri in 1940s and 1950s Harlem. And by the 1960s, the lines of race were drawn around welfare and antipoverty projects, which African Americans and Puerto Ricans supported and the dwindling population of Italians opposed, not least because they perceived that the building of low-income housing projects would encroach upon their residences and institutions.⁷¹

With the press of all of these identificatory forces, Thomas forged a path of individuality, one that returns us to the relationship between the writer and subject ("I") of autobiographical discourse. There is a good deal of ambiguity surrounding the status of *Down These Mean Streets* as autobiography, but Philippe Lejeune's basic definition, of a "retrospective prose narrative written by a real person concerning his own existence," remains descriptive: the writer Piri Thomas bears a striking resemblance to the character of Piri who is processing selfhood and coming out on the side of the individual. Writing is a solitary aesthetic pursuit based in individual creativity, and Thomas's writing of his self into the text as Piri evidences psychic projection and invention. Still, I would suggest that liberal individualism is not quite the proper category for the end point of the process that Piri describes undergoing. What *Down These Mean Streets* makes vivid is less the result of the individual prevailing over the collective and more the practice of a subject continually, inconclusively contemplating his relationship to broader social formations.

We can apprehend the subtle dialogue between those often-opposed spheres by more fully paying attention to how Thomas's subjectivity, via his protagonist Piri, develops through the practice of performance. To begin with, performance not only rethinks the relationships among author, narrator, and publics, but also draws attention to the different elements that aid and abet description and structure the space of storytelling. For Thomas, this fundamentally concerns creativity: he relished the license to mold characterization and plot to produce certain effects, sidestepping the question of accuracy without dismissing the authenticity that is basic to his own writerly authority. Second, to conceive of the autobiographical project, and the genre, of *Down These Mean Streets* in this fashion is to engage its origins in and expression of social life with its literary effects. Performance, as many scholars have elaborated, is a form of *making*, constructing the self, and, here, also producing the space.[72] To say that the self is in question, unstable, is to constitute the performance as elaborating an edge of conventional representation, a periphery of which author and reader are always ultra-conscious.

A good deal of the work of the performance of this text occurs in the space of language.[73] Language in general, and specific languages, have charged values, operating in and through dominance and resistance. Thus from the prologue, with its Spanish expressions for ideas that have special meaning, the space a *mundo*, a *barrio de noche*, through the rest of the text in which there are a variety of other terms that cannot be given precise English translations, Thomas displays an intense interest in words and how they can be arranged and rearranged unconventionally. When asked about a particular phrasing, Thomas replied: "That was my personal idiom, my personal style of writing, as a majority of one."[74] But commenting on the form of the text and in response to a question about whether some of the "memoir" was fictional, Thomas averred that it was "real," that he "utilized prose and poetry and made it all a common language."[75] It seems that Thomas can make his way out of an apparent contradiction or, at least, very different ways of thinking about the fictions or nonfictions of autobiography, with a self-conscious literary logic of writer as artist, playing with possibilities, too, performatively.

Another important effect of seeing Thomas's work in terms of performance has to do with the very meaning of ethnicity. Being alive to the newness that forms through creativity and circulation is to move away from the stability and consensus of group identity toward a densely constituted, continually interrogated relationship to social formations. Perhaps this is why recognition is posed as a problematic so early in *Down These Mean Streets*, left open as a possibility, having to do with the family and a variety of racial groups, lovers, and friends. Throughout that web of associations and affects, the common language assumes unpredictable forms. So, too, can Thomas give a different spin to the complicated relationship between Spanish and English in the spaces that Piri inhabits. We may recall how in the previous chapter Vito Marcantonio's intelligibility rested on more than absolute linguistic mastery: it was a *lived* bilingualism that created understanding. Here, the shared language between Italians and Puerto Ricans or among peoples in the welfare office, at least in places such as Harlem where different cultures share territory, is expansive, often even unspoken.

Not surprisingly, some of the performative aspects of Thomas's writing, and the text, take shape in and through the body, its affects and effects. Piri's hypermasculinized body is, indeed, the central site, agent, and repository for a set of negotiations that produce him as a subject in place. His encounters on the geographic edges of a territory, his sexual activity with a prostitute in Texas or with transvestites in Harlem, all perform an aggressive (and pointedly heterosexual) masculinity. In so many of those moments when Piri's body is at the center of representation, we see violence, a failure of translation (and remaining on the periphery), or an emphasis on gendering, for which there is surely some expense. Violence, in this way, is also a way to work out and work through experiences of proximity and distance, those that are central to any individual's relationship to a set of social possibilities. This is especially vivid when Piri describes his last major interaction with his father and the climax of that intensely troubled relationship. The scene unfolds midway through *Down These Mean Streets*, after his mother has died and he discovers a picture that he views (from the description) as a white or very light-skinned woman with whom his father was having an affair. The father and son's altercation is dramatically physical, with hitting and slapping, and it escalates when Piri speaks in a Southern Black drawl and incenses his father. Piri wields a knife and his father a baseball bat.[76] If the father is most obviously expressing authority, Piri does more than respond with filial disobedience (and Oedipal protection of/attraction to the mother); he performs racially, to establish his self in contrast to his father's, as well as, at this point in the text, to suggest that he can, fluidly and with intention, construct himself as Black.

To observe that Piri wants to express independence and his freedom to move among and across different categories is hardly to suggest that he is individualistic or eschewing of the social. On the one hand, through his lifetime Thomas felt deeply affiliated to Black organizations such as the Harlem Writers Guild (and had a special relationship with its founder, John Oliver Killens), but on the other, Thomas declared his autonomy from those formations, a stance we might explain through his investment in the multiplicity of racial affiliations, being Puerto Rican vis-à-vis African American groups and Black-identified vis-à-vis Puerto Rican and Latino formations. Quite unlike Schomburg's acceptance of U.S. Blackness, Thomas's refusals maintained less singular identifications and foregrounded the movement itself. When he was once asked about how he understood himself, he replied with an evocation of planetarity: "I'm not just a geographic location, a color—or sex—or preference. I always thought

I was an earthling. . . . Where my feet are, that's my turf, earth."[77] The obvious contradiction, in disavowing geographic location and standing on a turf, can be made a bit less sharp by thinking again about the sort of global space that I have emphasized throughout this book, in and through which any "geographic" territory is imagined and symbolic, never only about physical coordinates.

Importantly, in Thomas's hands, the spatial notion of the "planetary," understood by critics as a way to overcome the constraining form of nationality and emphasize egalitarian humanism, stops well short of a universalism that erases difference. If his use of the planetary reminds us of many scholars' discussions and critiques of globalism, it functions a little differently when it opens out into a representational space shaped by negotiations among varied forms of minoritization and the effects of anti-Blackness.[78] To be plainer, Thomas may not wish to be perceived as part of a category ("geographic location . . . color . . . sex . . . preference"), but inasmuch as he stands by his writings, he fully embraces racialization, however complicated. Still, in his 2001 statement, Thomas's recourse to the wider spatiality of the planet has a rhetorical effect, surely to draw attention to the gap between his own sensibility about race and culture and a post-1990s multiculturalist identity politics. And this cannot but complicate our reading of *Down These Mean Streets*, produced *pre*-identity politics and continuing to be circulated and consumed over time.

CIRCULATING STORIES OF PLACE AND IDENTITY

Down These Mean Streets came out in 1967 to a positive reception from readers and critics who were hungry for first-hand experiences of the "inner" city and accounts by Latinos, an increasingly visible population in U.S. urban spaces, to fill out those pictures. Knopf, the original publisher, announced the book's address rather sensationalistically, labeling it "A Stunning Autobiography of Corruption and Innocence." The Signet paperback edition of 1968 explained under the title and author on the front cover, "A man from Spanish Harlem makes you live with him in hell."[79] To the extent that there was already a public discourse elevating the individual struggling to resist the negative influences of drugs and crime in poor neighborhoods, Thomas's text could offer a story that reaffirmed popular stereotypes—reviews in the *Christian Science Monitor* and *New York Times* referred to the "gutter world" depicted—even as it developed the reader's unmistakable sympathy for the author/protagonist.[80] But that construction of physical or psychic escape from the ghetto is not exactly held up by the text itself;[81] that frame cannot account for the pull of Harlem that Thomas never disavows. And the overriding love of place even through the deeply located problems of poverty in *Down These Mean Streets* hardly communicated the "hell" of popular scrutiny.

Still, Piri Thomas allowed his text and his authorship to accommodate all sorts of projections of the period from immediately after publication until well into the 1970s. Readers who had grown up in or lived in El Barrio, Puerto Ricans from all over New York and other urban centers, and Latinos more generally, described flashes of recognition and the satisfaction of visibility when they read *Down These Mean Streets*, at a crucial time when urban problems were mostly portrayed in Black and white terms.[82] If lectures and symposia provided income for a self-sufficient writer—and we can see from some of Thomas's correspondence that he diligently followed up on honoraria and other payments—his frequent visits to area middle and high schools, in particular, developed a slightly different trajectory of involvement. In many cases, his appearances were meant to fill out encounters with the text of *Down These Mean Streets*, and teachers asked students to write to Thomas afterward; the letters he received were filled with extraordinary expressions of identification and appreciation.[83] The complications of racial identity for Puerto Ricans had, ever since the time of publication, become a topic of great interest and widespread cathexis, though not all readers embraced the manner in which Thomas saw it. In one letter, a man who appears to be a teacher evinces mostly appreciation for *Down These Mean Streets*, but also writes: "Mr. Thomas . . . I want you to realize that you are a descendant of Puerto Ricans and that we are not regarded as black."[84] Thomas spoke at a range of college campuses, elite and nonelite, emphasizing the need for more Latino writers and cultural producers in publishing and literature and in all sorts of institutions, including those of the state; he was arguing for Latino representation, a goal that aligned with efforts for affirmative action and other kinds of projects in the complicated aftermath of the Civil Rights movement.[85] Thomas maintained a close exchange with a member of the New York Police Department as its administration developed a manual to teach officers on the street about Puerto Rican peoples and their culture and behavior to improve police–civilian relations.[86] In all these ways, Thomas was a public intellectual, too, actively involved in producing knowledge about Puerto Ricans and urban life, a representative figure and a translator, despite the way his major text problematized categories of identity and left open-ended many possibilities about who and what people in Harlem were. Like Hughes and McKay and other prominent Harlem writers, Thomas was a kind of polymath, producing a play and television specials and painting, and this body of varied work deliberately captured a variety of audiences.

But *Down These Mean Streets* became a rather different kind of political flashpoint in the late 1960s and 1970s, when school systems in Salinas, California and Teaneck, New Jersey and Flushing, College Point, and Whitestone in Queens, New York moved to take the book off their library shelves and out of their developing multicultural curricula. Those leading the charge against the book opposed its "deviance" and "obscenity," using staple terms of urban crisis, and couched their campaigns as the protection of youth. Many cited the use of profanity in the text, which raised the issue of language in such a way that it could only rouse the passions of those invested in literary freedom. And so Thomas himself, along with librarians, parents, political officials, and fellow writers, took up the mantle of aesthetic liberty and successfully framed the issue to be one primarily about censorship.[87]

Different ideas about who could write and what they could write bore down on this debate, but the battles being waged during the period (and well afterward) also distilled other sorts of conflicts, over race and territory and the content and form of relation. (Not to be missed is the irony of

SELFHOOD AND DIFFERENCE

Down These Mean Streets addressing the shifting identity and location that undergirded these conflicts.) Many of the areas in which objections caught fire were majority white, middle-class, and suburban, but also beginning to experience demographic and cultural changes that were, for many, unwelcome signs of urbanity. Whiteness in these spaces, just as in the nation writ large, in the post–Civil Rights era and during Black Power uprisings in cities across the country, was embattled, policing its bounds and unsure of its authority. And *ethnic* whiteness could not but be deeply saturated with anxiety, not only because of its status vis-à-vis more dominant (Protestant) whiteness, but also because those who claimed it were themselves, in generational terms, not long out of central urban areas that they had once defined, through Italian, Irish, or Jewish enclaves. When Flushing's Community School District 25 board voted to ban the book in 1971, for example, the five-member voting majority included four people whose candidacy had been endorsed by the Home School Association, an organization of Roman Catholic schools, and one Orthodox former rabbi.[88] That the efforts at banning the book took shape in institutional formations of school or community boards unwittingly filled out another sensibility of the autobiography, namely the pull of locality and the situated maps of race, ethnicity, and class. When the rabbi on Flushing's board, Karl Applbaum, was asked about his reaction to the text, he noted that he doubted the veracity of the description of Puerto Ricans in New York.[89] He may simply have been suggesting that the evocation of life in East Harlem was fantastical. But another reading would have us situate the articulation of this Jewish American subject in a deeper urban history. One could speculate that Applbaum was conscious of the background of Jews in Harlem and other areas, and might be laying claim to those kinds of spaces while also expressing some dissatisfaction with Piri's shape-shifting identity.

The meaning of the cultural event that was and is *Down These Mean Streets* certainly shifts over time, shaped by consumption and circulation, framing and interpretation, pressed on, too, by forces and interests from outside. What is the book's status as a literary artifact when it has a continuing history and is subject to readings, misreadings, and projections? Thomas contested narrow conceptions of identity, particularly any that posited a strict divide between Puerto Ricanness and Blackness, like the one that had had a deep impact on his own life, but at publication there was already a developing conversation, extending beyond those who were interested in Puerto Rican or Latino literature, about the porous boundaries between different kinds of affiliation. Nuyorican and Young Lords place-based aesthetics and understandings of the world posed additional complexities as they addressed the thick and layered diasporic attachments that were lived socially and politically. By the time of the thirtieth anniversary edition of the text in 1997, a different group of readers and critics deeply shaped by institutionalized multiculturalism and ethnic studies and ethnic politics could consume the text as a staple of particular canons. Whether that categorization can truly do justice to the category-busting experiments that *Down These Mean Streets* makes available remains unclear.

ALADDIN—BANGLADESHI FROM SPANISH HARLEM

We can enter into these concerns about context and interpretation from a different kind of edge with writer, dramatist, and comedian Alaudin Ullah. Although Ullah is South Asian, in his comic performances he uses the stage name Aladdin to allude, ironically, to the ethnic-racial otherness of a Middle Eastern subject in a shifting setting, some area of the East, as in *One Thousand and One Nights*, a work that itself announces storytelling. Ullah was born in 1968, the year after *Down These Mean Streets* was first published, and picks up the baton from that text and its considerations of selfhood in place. He moves in and through rather different formations of race, ethnicity, and region from the ones Thomas inhabited and represented, but he utilizes imaginative resources developed by those earlier histories. Like Thomas's, Ullah's subjectivity represents something fundamental about cross-cultural Harlem while also challenging conventional understandings of who and what that is. As such, his life story is especially useful to end this book with.

SELFHOOD AND DIFFERENCE

Like all of the figures and occasions of *Cross-Cultural Harlem*, Ullah represents a working-class cosmopolitanism. Whether he narrates the self on stage or in person, he begins by noting that he grew up "in the projects," the George Washington Carver Houses, a public housing development in East Harlem, and quickly adds that his floor of the building was wildly diverse, "the United Nations of Spanish Harlem."[90] Class position, for Ullah, is tightly bound up with multiplicity: the "projects" have often signified poor urban life and speak to the ghettoization of minority groups, but not always the ethnic diversity with which he insists he grew up. He dramatizes the anomaly of his Bangladeshi family when he situates it alongside West Indian, Puerto Rican, African American, and other residents from larger Harlem populations. Using different accents on the stage, Ullah as Aladdin comically performs ethnicity and embodies translation, a desire for and identification with otherness, and taps into that long history of circulation and flexibility with the name of a character whose story was added by a French orientalist to an already loose collection of folk tales and has become the basis for countless adaptations in popular culture.

If there is obvious insufficiency as the Bangladeshi comedian voices another kind of person, there may also be some gloss on that translation limit, when Aladdin's oft-stated and physicalized brownness constructs potential racial ambiguity. The choice to discuss multiplicity in internationalist terms, such as "the United Nations," also significantly strains U.S. compartments for ethnicity—South Asians were, after all, in Caribbean countries, and part of third worldist political formations that included Africans and African Americans. Other writers and scholars have discussed the experience of being part of a small minority among larger minoritized populations in Harlem, white in Black and Latino East Harlem, Jewish in Black Harlem.[91] But Ullah's story is distinguished by its assured belonging, one that stems from shared class experience. One way to cast that feature would be in terms of deprivation trumping race or ethnicity; another is through the necessary and natural tolerance, even conviviality, of cramped quarters. Ullah's working-class identity also derives from his father's occupation. Indeed, a 2018 work about his father's life (and by extension, his own) is entitled *Dishwasher Dreams*.[92]

Ullah's life story could be interpreted through alternative rubrics to the ones that organize *Cross-Cultural Harlem*, South Asian/Asian American drama most obviously, but its departure from the conventions of those canons bears further exploration. An emphasis on cross-cultures cannot be overstated: the imaginary, Ullah himself says again and again, comes from locality *and* from the deep diversity therein. Like other important Harlem figures who have taken on the challenge of self- and community representation, Ullah stays true to particularized racialized identities, his own especially; so much of the discourse hinges on the origin of Bangladesh, from which his father came to the United States in the historic year of 1947, and where his mother experienced domestic abuse and essentially fled from much later. Generational conflict, an archetype of immigrant and ethnic writing, appears, to be sure, but a divergent "second generation" identity is not quite what Ullah seeks to evoke. Instead of representing himself and his parents as having utterly different concerns and interests, he explains much more subtly how they are bound up with one another. Another thematic of the ethnic story told from the perspective of the United States often revolves around the American dream, and the title *Dishwasher Dreams* announces that structuring grammar of nationalization. But here, too, the pull of locality is felt, drawing viewers away from class ascent and racial assimilation (vis-à-vis whiteness), stock elements of that narrative of "becoming American," and into a more complicated concern with place-based identity.

The distinctiveness of Ullah's constructions of self has a great deal to do with the specific wave of Bangladeshi immigration from which he emerges. As historian Vivek Bald has carefully explored, beginning in the 1920s, Bengali men left British ships to settle near port cities in the United States, in communities where they could avoid the gaze of authorities and where they often intermixed with other minoritized peoples, thus lending some credence to the perception that white people could not tell those of color apart.[93] Though Ullah's father came a couple of decades later, he was part of an early population of Bengalis in Harlem and markedly not a member of the much larger post-1965 wave of migration that has shaped more middle-class South Asian American cultural formations in the

SELFHOOD AND DIFFERENCE

United States. So when Ullah identifies his father's American aspiration as "dishwasher dreams," it is a differently classed imaginary than the one often associated with the Indian immigrant doctors and engineers of the 1960s and 1970s or, certainly, the high-tech workers of recent years. He opens up another trajectory of migrants and their children, with beginnings in the working-class space of Harlem. Furthermore, the relationship of poorer and smaller Bangladesh to the much bigger and more powerful nation of India points to yet another axis of peripherality, even outsiderness, geopolitical, imaginative, and symbolic.[94]

Ullah's accounts all feature a protagonist constituted with consistency as a Bangladeshi subject. It is important to note that although he may situate himself in other networks of identification, in terms of place or culture Ullah never self-presents as *other* than Bangladeshi Muslim; that identity is utterly central to who he believes himself to be, but also how he is seen, interpreted, and circulated, both inside and outside of Harlem. We might recall here Yuri Kochiyama's expressed respect for Malcolm X's acknowledgment of "heritage and history" and her Japanese Americanness underlying all moments of self-construction.[95] Every performance and personal narrative by Ullah begins with the discussion of an experience auditioning for a part in a Hollywood film, describing the director's expectation for a reinforcement of racist stereotypes of Muslims as religious terrorists opposed to the United States. The portrayed realization, yet another announcement that he will be telling a story, functions to telegraph the centrality of this specific form of ethnic religious identity to the representation. This provides continuity with the father–son dynamic that we have seen in many Harlem stories of this book, between Langston Hughes and his father and Piri Thomas and his.

Despite the stability of the self (his own and his father's), Ullah's stories derive meaning and humor from misrecognitions of place and race. Here, he certainly instantiates himself in a long tradition of Black comedy (Richard Pryor, Chris Rock, and more) as well as within recent works that ironize ethnicity, such as the *Harold and Kumar* films and television show and stand-up comedy by South Asians Aziz Ansari or Hasan Minhaj.[96] But the source of humor regarding being out of place actually comes from place, and here a particularly relevant point of reference is the 1984 film *Brother from Another Planet*.[97] Famous and much-circulated scenes of that film feature a Black man from outer space finding himself in Harlem, amid crime and poverty and racial minority subjects who both are perplexed by the character's strange and unusual Blackness (his outsider-ness) and instinctively solidaristic, most especially when he is being pursued by white villains from his world, who have effectively enslaved Black people. Ullah's story of arrival is structured by a similar misrecognition, with the twist of religious identification. As he tells it, when his father landed at 110th Street and Lexington Avenue and was approached on the street by young neighborhood men aggressively policing their territory, Ullah Sr. said, "Please don't shoot. I'm from Noakhali." And his response to the question of why he was there, in that particular location, "for freedom," inspired hilarity *and* irony.[98] But the national gap (ideological, cultural) is closed through religious-diasporic attachment, and so when Ullah's father mentions to the toughs that he is Muslim, their attitude changes: not only do they help him up and dust him off, but they even give him twenty dollars to help him settle in.

Islam—its affiliations, and most of all its diasporic solidarities—is a primary source of identification for Ullah's represented selves and, especially, for the family's cross-cultural exchanges in Harlem. What the quality of being Muslim conjures up at the various moments over time that Ullah represents, and into the future, *in Harlem* is important for understanding the entanglements that cannot be contained in strict neighborhood blocks. For example, there are different ethnic effects of Ullah saying that he is from Spanish Harlem and that his father revered Muhammad Ali. Spanish Harlem, of course, means the Puerto Rican population concentrations in East Harlem, and Ali points to Blackness writ large, if not specifically in Central and West Harlem, then certainly gesturing in that direction. Ullah's production of identity crosses regions, not just through race or its affect but also, here, through religion. One cannot miss the reference to Blackness, however unstated, not least because there is a structural similarity, as Islam itself is a diasporic, quasi-racial identification. In his play *Indio*, Aladdin states in his mother's voice: "I tell you to pick up our Quran, I tell you to read and study Mohammed and all you can tell me is that he floats like a butterfly, he stings like a bee. This is the wrong Mohammed!"[99] This represented utterance may fracture the field of projection, but also, in another way, engages the very dilemmas of diaspora's changing same.[100] What, indeed, does it mean for Muhammad Ali to consciously take on the name of a religious prophet, and how is that set of possibilities read and experienced in a Bangladeshi Muslim household in Spanish Harlem? Recall, too, that the Black Muslims in prison, and their language, reminded Piri Thomas of home.[101]

This phenomenology of comparative racialization can be seen in Habibi Ullah's origin story (and thus his son's). Aladdin in *Indio* describes his father's racial naïveté, saying that even years after having first watched *I Love Lucy* and living in Spanish Harlem, he still believed Lucy to be Puerto Rican, saying, "Lucy is a very beautiful Spanish girl!" A young Alaudin replies: "Pop, she's white!" only to be answered with "She looked brown on my TV!"[102] This sets the scene for the elder Ullah's encounter with local residents. Here, unlike in the other narrative about sympathetic Black Muslims, Ullah is described as coming in contact with Italians in East Harlem, just as turf-controlling, but figured as white vis-à-vis other racial minorities in the space. One Italian, identified in the script as "Dumb Guy," says to "Pops," "Lookit we got another spic fresh off the boat. So where in Porto Rico you from palooka?" After Ullah Sr. goes into a lengthy discussion of his homeland, expounding on the complexity of even that origin, having left a place that was once India, that has become East Pakistan, the response is "Hey, Shut up Tonto! I don't care where in Porto Rico ya from ya ain't welcome here! . . . this here block is for full-blooded eye-talians not no spics you's!" Ullah's color overwhelms, and this Italian Harlemite, at least, cannot see him outside of the racial maps that are locally produced. And when the elder Ullah despairs to himself in Bengali, "Dumb Guy" elaborates on spatialized ethnicity, saying, "That don't sound like no Spanish! Maybe he's from Jamaica! . . . Remember this is eye talian country. Stay on the side wit the spics where you's belong."[103] This Italian American's evocation of East Harlem aligns closely to that notion of a restricted "minoritized space," one not only about minoritization in terms of dominant whiteness, but also a clear sense of bounded enclaves for those who are alternately ethnic or racial.

All of this need not suggest that misrecognition is only a negative experience. In fact, Ullah represents many moments of being known a bit differently as generative. The title of his play derives from the name a friend from Harlem, José, had assigned to Ullah Sr. When José calls Ullah Sr. "Indio," it might be interpreted as bringing him into the fold. We know that "Indio" in a Spanish-speaking context can be a very matter-of-fact nickname, an endearment for someone in a Latin American country who has more indigenous background or is a little darker than those who have more apparent Spanish ancestry, an acknowledgment but not necessarily a cordoning off of difference. In the section of *Indio* just following the encounter with the Italian neighborhood toughs, José, indeed, seeks to shift Aladdin's father from the trauma of one kind of spatialized interethnic competition to the geographic life of class difference:

> What's the problem Indio? Don't worry I'm going to show you something. You can go all over the world but you no gonna believe this porque you no going to see anything like this in the whole wide world! This is where the rich meet the poor and everything begins and everything ends.... Look downtown what do you see? Penthouses, nice cars, blancitos—white people. Look uptown what do you see? Broken down buildings, old cars, black and Latino people. Only one block separates them. This is the meaning of life my friend.[104]

There are multiple acts of translation here: one informed by language, in which Spanish bridges the gap of ethnic–racial difference, and another shaped by class formation. Ullah Sr. is the translated subject and might in fact experience the process not just through a deficit, of how he is not seen (something left behind), but through an acquired belonging, one that preserves rather than erases difference. A small but telling biographical detail is that Ullah Sr's first wife was Puerto Rican, which intimates a deeper, personal cross-cultural exchange.

SELFHOOD AND DIFFERENCE

The character of Mohima Ullah, Alaudin's mother, also lives cross-culturally, but in clearly gendered terms. Importantly, Ullah constructs in Mohima a subject whose two stories of becoming emphasize female strength. Mohima marries Habibi, a much older man, as a means of escaping an untenable social and familial situation in Bangladesh, demonstrating unusual agency. And when she returns to visit her homeland after many years in the United States and is told to veil herself, she challenges the villagers, a fact that Ullah conveys with genuine admiration. The second story of Mohima's settlement in the United States reflects an experience of East Harlem that diverges from that of her husband. Ullah pointedly remarks: "Living in Spanish Harlem she learned to speak Spanish before English. Como está? Grácias."[105] And he exalts mixture, referring to the legendary marketplace La Marqueta, in which he remembers Mohima wearing a sari, physically manifesting difference yet existing in the flow of East Harlem, noting: "La Marqueta was jumping, everyone was there."[106] At La Marqueta, this Bangladeshi woman could obtain produce and spices that could "pass" as ingredients for her ethnic cooking, an experience that resembles those of many early migrants who may not have had access to their "own" foods nearby but shopped at other ethnic markets, South Asian, East Asian, West Indian, Latino, or African.[107]

But even with the colorful image of dynamic and entangled cultures, we know that the day-to-day life betwixt and between is not easy. The represented character of Mohima registers the difficulties of multiplicity. To begin with, she is deeply hampered in her ability to translate, and also to be a translated subject (as her husband is), by her lack of English proficiency. Ullah does not actually comment on his father's English skills, but his mobility, literal (on the street) and cultural (with a friend named José) must be possible because of either some linguistic competency or the fact of masculinity, and likely both. And it is not Habibi who eventually facilitates Mohima's learning English (he is in fact obstructionist), but her son Alaudin, who watches *Sesame Street* with his mother for the purpose of acquiring basic language skills. Mohima in this account is a gendered subject who cannot live in difference fluidly, without cost. If she is amid multiplicity, she is also isolated as a woman, poignantly saying to her husband:

SELFHOOD AND DIFFERENCE

"Look Habib! I don't know anyone here. All I do is cook, clean and when I am sad and alone who can I talk to? NO one. We live in Spanish Harlem! I have no friends here. Who can I speak to in Bangla?"[108]

As Ullah brings Mohima to life through a combination of representing her, as he speaks in her voice, and describing her through more straightforward narration as Aladdin, he constructs a complicated subject that both draws on a tradition of negative portrayals of ethnic women patrolling the boundaries of group identity and pushes past them to something more sympathetic, more attentive to gendered difference.[109] Here, as we have throughout *Cross-Cultural Harlem*, we see familial and domestic intimacy as a crucial space for working through the pain and possibility of cross-cultures. In one anecdote, Mohima scoffs at expensive sneakers, but once she learns that they are named for Kareem Abdul-Jabbar, a Muslim, she relents and purchases them for her sons, to serve as a means of at least partial assimilation, and we might suspect, a way of connecting to her children while saving face.

A central and dramatic story of racial anxiety and recognition that Ullah tells not only in his public performances through Aladdin, but also personally, in interviews, concerns the consequences of his brother's dating a "Black" (assumed to be African American) girl while in high school. All accounts begin with a discussion of how "hot" the girl is, and, one assumes because of that, from a contemporary (and multicultural) perspective, how unreasonable a concern about this pairing would be. But the real humor of the anecdote derives from the absurdity of race. Is it about color, or is it about something else? For those who are themselves racialized, *colored*, in fact? Ullah/Aladdin describes his mother calling the girl a "'kaloowa,' or Bengali for nigger," and the extended family assembling for a "stop dating a black girl intervention."[110] From that comic point, he moves into some challenging questions about comparative racialization, when he asks his uncle: "aren't you a ka loo wa?" Aladdin quickly adds, in a nod to a history of Black comedy style: "my uncle was so black he could leave footprints on tar," but the seriousness of the moment cannot be easily swept away.[111] Ullah further relies on humor when he recounts a visit to Bangladesh, remarking about his grandmother: "She looked just like Cicely Tyson. I said aloud without really thinking, wow, she's ka loo wa!"[112] In each of those cases, Aladdin represents his mother slapping him, to direct him to clearly distinguish among color, race, and culture, in a way that may illustrate more broadly for the audience, too, the racial (and racist) perspectives of immigrants, and the divides among generations about race, which is another way of understanding Piri's conflict with his father in *Down These Mean Streets*.[113] What remains unstated in Ullah's anecdote is the very irony that Tyson herself was the daughter of immigrants from Nevis, and had grown up in East Harlem, yet one more reminder that place and context are important.

In another discussion about the incident, Ullah offers a crucial detail about his father, the later omission of which in public performance might signal an interesting ambivalence about his parents, as well as a developing consciousness about gender, ethnicity, and representation. Ullah notes that his father rose from his sick bed to say, "you boys date whoever you want."[114] This recounting counterposes a liberal father to a conservative mother who imagines the boundaries of identity more narrowly. In that same conversation, Ullah reminded me that his father married a Puerto Rican, a testament, if anything, to Ullah Sr.'s ability to cross. But in the public presentation of this story in the 2018 *Dishwasher Dreams*, there is a much more sympathetic portrayal overall of Mohima Ullah, which does not include her husband contradicting her concerns. If that feature of the discourse signals a rather more feminist inclination, produced in contemporary conditions of representation, it is also an explicit acknowledgment of the difficulties, as well as pressures, of cross-cultural experience for all the Ullahs. Translation, this is to say—cultural, linguistic, racial—for Mohima, for Habibi, and for Alaudin, is slow and complicated. Misrecognition and resistance mark the contradictory and decidedly nonlinear process.

When Ullah opens his extended self-presentation with the evocation that he is a "Bangladeshi comedian" from Spanish Harlem, he traffics in the surprise, irony, and deep symbolism that accompany urban knowledge.

Moreover, the imaginary here, of Spanish Harlem, illuminates a great deal more than what the term literally refers to, in terms of neighborhood blocks. An urban consciousness delicately but deftly navigates the construction of Harlem's complicated spatiality. When Ullah notes: "Spanish Harlem is partitioned just like India," he employs comparison and identification, other powerful modes of translation that are about the ability to imagine oneself as like the other. He is so attentive to the ethnic compartments of place, representing them, as in the anecdote about his father meeting up with Italians, but also transgressing them as he himself and his father and his mother, from the outside, manage somehow to lay claim to the place, however it may be constituted. This is to say that Ullah at once reaffirms the power of the specificity of Spanish Harlem—that locale and idea reverberate through self-definition—and shows how porous and contingent space can be, much as *Cross-Cultural Harlem* has demonstrated, again and again. Ullah explicitly conjoins movement and transition when he notes: "I grew up walking ... every five blocks something would change."[115] Like many who have long lived in all parts of Harlem, he laments the rising rents and displacements of the most recent phase of gentrification. Ullah no longer resides in Harlem proper, but does still remain on the area's geographic edge, some blocks from the (shifting) southern boundary. At the same time, his representational comings and goings, unlike those, say, of Thomas, do not end within the physical confines of the place.

The Bangladeshi comedian from Spanish Harlem may produce origin in specific regional terms, but like other minoritized cultural and political subjects, he has found something deeply powerful in Harlem's Blackness writ large, and this, too, has become a central mode of identification. Aladdin's lived and performed language gestures continually at storytelling traditions of African American humor that comment on the absurdist realities of race and class in America, as when he says about his parents' hometown: "Noakhali was so bad, it made the South Bronx look like the Hamptons" or in the comments referenced above, on the Blackness of his relatives, that they were "so black. . . ."[116] When asked about formative artistic influences, Ullah refers mostly to Black comedians, especially Chris Rock. Even the notion of being street-wise taps a history of Black literary and cultural representations of urban life after the 1960s.

Especially striking is how, to Ullah, Harlem signifies Blackness *and* multiplicity. That space is one of consolation for him precisely because it is open to difference. He identifies the childhood experience of going to the Boys Club after school with "all sorts of people" as deeply formative. And it is worth pausing to imagine how, in a sea of racial differences, African American, West Indian, Latino, and others, a working-class Bangladeshi child might blend in and feel acknowledged. Undoubtedly, that is facilitated by heterogeneous (and diasporic) Blackness and Latino-ness, in and through which an ambiguous brownness could be misrecognized in even liberatory ways. Ullah continually describes his devotion to the New York Yankees and his special admiration for Reggie Jackson, noting in a 2018 performance that "being half-black and half-Puerto Rican, people from the projects loved him, because he was like them."[117] The example of Reggie Jackson, technically one-quarter Puerto Rican (his father, Martinez Jackson, who played baseball in the Negro League, was half Puerto Rican and half African American), may appeal to Aladdin as much because of its simultaneous presentation of racial mixing and Blackness as its sporting appeal.

A story that Ullah tells in public and private venues doubles Reggie Jackson and his father, through a discourse that intersperses a play-by-play of an important World Series game featuring Jackson, "Mr. October," and eulogies during his father's funeral, at which pictures of Malcolm X's colleagues were displayed alongside those of his father and uncles.[118] What results is a kind of multiplicity, of Black and brown Muslims together, that recalls what Mikhail Bakhtin has memorably discussed as "a plurality of independent and unmerged voices and consciousnesses, a genuine polyphony of fully valid voices."[119] Though Bakhtin referred to the novel form, that invocation of voices and its implication of the sonic vividly describe in interpretive terms the polyphony of Aladdin's performance. But the deeper textual implications resonate here, too, as the construction of the self does not merely rely on a single narrative voice and instead remains committed to multiplicity. For the representation of racialized and emplaced experience, Ullah may intertwine, on the one hand, a hybrid Americanism, and on the other, a set of diasporic-migrant attachments, but each track is easy to hear and thus never fully integrated:

> *Eulogizer:* Asala Walakum. My name is brother Malik. I met brother Habib a long time ago.
> *Scooter:* Well folks, it doesn't look good. The Yankees are down 6 to 3 in the bottom of the 9th and nobody on. WE gotta get a rally going, Willie Randolph at bat.
> *Eulogizer:* He was a man with dreams but no gameplan.
> *Scooter* (excited): Base hit up the middle. Randolph on 1st base.
> *Eulogizer:* He came here with nothing! He couldn't speak the language, had no education . . .
> *Scooter:* Holy Cow! Randolph steals second. Runner is in scoring position.[120]

Ullah's father's corpse lies in the middle of the mise-en-scène. This part of Aladdin's many bodily performances betrays a keen awareness of the particular ironies and extremities that physical presence negotiates. But the body does not pull all of that together. Indeed, the fragmented narrative of the account only lays bare a fragmented self that even death cannot quite resolve within the divides of a lived Harlem. And as it recalls, perhaps unwittingly, James Baldwin's famous discussion of his father dying just as the 1943 riots broke out, it may tug on other racial histories of conflict.[121]

Through every utterance and scripted performance, Ullah remains extremely self-conscious about the fact that he is telling a Harlem story. Both aspects of that term are important—Ullah's attachments to all that is Harlem and to the story-ness of his self- and public presentations. Thus it is not surprising that he employs literary conventions of U.S. cultural history: for example, the Northern racial subject traveling south to experience discrimination in its rawest form. Just as Thomas represented that sort of trip as an occasion to understand specifically American arrangements of segregation, Ullah narrates his father expressing shock at not being served at a lunch counter. When the waitress says, "I'm sorry but we don't serve your kind. You gonna have to take this to go. I'm sorry we don't serve ya'll on account of Jim Crow," Ullah's father's response registers innocence: "What do you mean you don't serve my kind? Who is Jim Crow? Let me speak to this Crow. Tell him I am very hungry. I have money. I'm sure this Jim Crow fellow will understand."[122] Later, during the predictable revelation of racism in the United States, which contradicts national mythologies, it rings hollow when Ullah Sr. concludes, "I will not leave until you serve me! If a man is hungry he should have the right to eat. This is America!"[123] This is yet another moment in the delicate and longstanding back-and-forth of racial recognition; if there have been instances in Ullah's stories where shared minoritization was the governing affect, here he emphasizes the crucial distinction of the racialization of a Bangladeshi migrant, who falls under the strictures of Jim Crow but has not fully experienced the (African American) life of racial codes and segregation.

History is perhaps the most important horizon of both attachment and separation for Ullah's life story. An autobiographical impulse can never be decoupled from history: to tell a story of the self is to range widely across time, with an acute sense of how the past has influenced the present. And there is no question that the past provides an obvious vehicle for nostalgia, a central affect of the form. Ullah's narratives of becoming rely on excavation, of family dynamics and social relations in place. But origin, as we have seen, is complicated for a child of Bangladeshi migrants, and the back story that he provides in his public self-presentations has been filled out more recently by a trip he took to Bangladesh in connection with a larger project on early Bengali migrants.[124]

Ullah's evocation of Bangladesh could be said to be deeply translational, but also departing from some conventions of a more linear immigrant autobiographical trajectory from one fixed place to another. Rather, in this discourse Bangladesh and Harlem exist in a horizontal relationship, in a zone of comparative possibility. When Ullah discusses the appeal of Islamic fundamentalism in Bangladesh, he notes about certain Muslims that "they are full of shit," but that the men there did not intimidate him, because he is "from Harlem," and "Harlem gave me a brilliant radar for bullshit." Here, Harlem can be a source of a tough ghetto self, imparting a kind of street sense to facilitate relation. That background enables him to see through purist constructions of identity and culture. Comparative possibilities built from cross-cultural experience direct a subtle racial analysis, as when Ullah notes that South Asians are complicated about race, "just as Puerto Ricans, Jamaicans, etc., are."[125] Insights about race and place are bound together in this production of self. This is dramatically announced in *Dishwasher Dreams* when Aladdin says, about his father arriving in the United States in 1947: "India became free, Jackie Robinson integrated the MLB, and my father got his first apartment in Spanish Harlem."

Borders of the past and present are porous in all memory projects, including the (personal and public) performances of Ullah. It is worth pursuing just *how* his discourse and presentation construct the relationships among place, time, and identity. Joseph Roach has written, about performances in general, that "they make publicly visible through symbolic action both the tangible existence of social boundaries and, at the same time, the contingency of those boundaries on fictions of identity, their shoddy construction out of inchoate otherness, and consequently, their anxiety-inducing instability."[126] Ullah's delicate dance between expressing the fact of boundaries and describing the continual crossings acquires clearer focus through that idea of "contingency," which might refer to time and place, in particular the time *of* place.

There can be no overemphasizing that a particular place, in this formation, illuminates the productive contradictions of subjectivity. Harlem is utterly essential for the selves of Ullah. It provides an explanation for the remarkable consistency of his discourses, across public performances and in interviews. There is no question that there is sincerity, a genuine impulse toward truth-telling, but more than that, Ullah continually evokes a kind of referentiality or materiality, a deep lived connection to a Harlem that exists in the world. This life history of a son of Bangladeshi migrants is simultaneously a story about routes and rootedness, a dynamic text that illuminates at once a place, a time, and an experience.

FORMS OF NARRATING THE SELF

Ullah and Thomas have offered another set of answers (and dilemmas) for the question of how we tell a story of Harlem in formalistic and affective terms. In the assumption of modes such as the literary autobiography, the oral historical meditation, and the comic performance, these occasions provoke a rethinking of the real. As opposed to a story that is "told to" a writer, which would garner skepticism about its truth claims, *Down These Mean Streets* is self-presented as the outgrowth of its author and is, as Lejeune's theorization of autobiography has explained, "referential," illuminating a "reality" outside, unlike a novel, which does not generically self-present in that way. Lejeune wrote in the early 1980s when poststructuralism was widely influential and was in no way blind to the complexity of how reality is represented; indeed, he was careful to distinguish between strict accuracy, a "resemblance to the truth," and a looser intention of the author. Still, he would not abandon the world outside the text.[127] Thomas mirrored such trends. When asked many years after writing *Down These Mean Streets* whether he engaged in "poetic license," he replied: "Not much. It was so—so real. I utilized prose and poetry and made it all a common language."[128] This expression mediates the demands of authorship and readership, insisting on the truth of perception and the necessity of different styles of language for communication. But Thomas remained attached to the *creative* act of writing, saying that though "there is nothing in *Down These Mean Streets* that didn't happen," he built the composite character of Brew from two people he knew. He may very well have understood his own autobiographical impulse and product through frames that were less about the hard edges of specificity and more about the irresolution of honestly working through complicated engagements.

Paul John Eakin describes his interpretation of Lejeune's "autobiographical pact" as a "contract between author and reader in which autobiographers explicitly commit themselves not to some impossible historical exactitude but rather to the sincere effort to come to terms with and understand their own lives."[129] The processual nature of that aspect of the writing finds its companion in the represented slow revelation of the personal narrative.

Thomas and Ullah never disavowed experience, even as they asked about its place and time. Both were interested in nonlinearity, the representation of selfhood that required that "common language" but also a mashup of forms, a kind of literary or dramatic experiment. How striking that Raymond Williams, when elaborating on the genealogy of "experience" in his famous work on keywords of culture and society, actually indicated early links to the concept of experiment.[130] If Williams's discussion of the experiment was more concerned with its sense of a test, in invoking it in relation to experience he furnished both terms with the quality of openness and provisionality, which contemporary ideas about experience may have shed but by which Thomas and Ullah can be seen to be shaped. A sensibility about how Thomas might understand experience as the basis for his literary work or Ullah relate to it in his creation, Aladdin, illuminates, too, how they approach forms, following the trajectory of a life story, detailing social life in Harlem, and exploring the psychic complexities of the self relating to community and collective formations through deeply contemplated prose and poetic language, a back-and-forth through time. Resistance to the prescriptions of identity, in many respects, finds an analogue in implicit but evident debates on the prescriptions of form.

Wilson Harris's cross-cultural imagination provides another way to think about the genesis and effect of these writers' experiments. Harris suggests deep links between the creative process and the landscape. Although his own example, of novels especially, comes from the natural world of Guyana, it is not a far stretch at all for us to think about the stories of self-exploration here (all fictions even while autobiographical) as being created in and through the urban landscape of Harlem. Ullah and Thomas resist categorizations based solely in ethnicity or identity—Black or Puerto Rican or South Asian writing—and instead are brought into being by the deep interconnectedness among peoples and histories of the space, what Harris has called "true-diversity-within-intimate-yet-ungraspable universality."[131] Furthermore, when the cross-cultural Harlem imagination takes shape in the evocation of relationships throughout Black, Caribbean, and South Asian diasporas, extending to Texas and Bangladesh and ultimately into New York, it accesses, not always consciously, traumatic histories of displacement born of slavery, indenture, colonialism, and empire, very much in the way that Harris had described the worlds he himself took into consideration. This brings into clear view all these stories' hemispheric and emplaced articulations.

Down These Mean Streets, *Dishwasher Dreams*, *El Indio*, and the self-presentations of Ullah and Thomas themselves are all noticeably unpreoccupied with the process of Americanization and in this way are what I would call sideways stories.[132] They depart from the verticality of primary and sustained reference to the nation or, for that matter, to the dominant racial identity of whiteness. And as such, they intervene in how we imagine the social in spatial terms, wherein the majority-minority space, often considered an edge of the central formation, has an internal logic and is a world unto itself. Somehow, Ullah and Thomas's stories avoid a foreign vs domestic opposition, even as they lock into a globality for the future. In part that is achieved through their abiding racialized flânerie.[133] As geographer David Harvey has put it, an urban subject maps "the city's terrain and evokes its living qualities" and makes the geography his or her own.[134] Piri's traversal and critical reading of Harlem territories, which questions belonging and presents Puerto Ricanness and Blackness as both internally differentiated and diasporic, embodies resistance. Ullah's emphasis on misrecognition evokes a walking through and out of categories. Something is at stake in the continual movement of flânerie, as well as in its cosmopolitan engagements.[135] It is from the tension between insider and outsider that these texts derive energy, challenging generic forms of the autobiography, novel, or play, as well as the expectations of a racial or ethnic story, directed as they are to illuminating the mutual implicatedness of Blackness, Puerto Ricanness, and even Bangladeshiness.

However irreverent about conventional bounds of genres they may be, these stories do ask us to consider how the representation of selfhood might provide a special window onto the phenomenology of space. Their obvious constructedness or fictionality effectively dispenses with empirical pressures to determine whether everything is accurate: the working truths necessary for performance are more interesting and ultimately more important. This opens readers and critics to the texts' planetarity that Thomas touted. Here, the formalistic crossings do not profess to be only about the aesthetic or the social, but assume the imbrication of those epistemological modes. Recall that all the inhabitants have been migrants in some way, and that home cannot be a stable referent. Dwelling must be, at least partially, disentangled from being *at* home. We are reminded of this chapter's opening: that the very constitution of Harlem as a racial place generates tremendous desire for belonging and identification, as well as anxiety. No one ever says "well, I'm not really part of Harlem." To the contrary: most Harlem cultural figures try very hard to elaborate their relationship to the place, however vexatious or complicated they maintain it is. So much of Harlem autobiography (and fiction and even ethnography) works through the difficulties of that project.

What Karl Weintraub has called the "historical mindedness" of autobiography bears closer attention in the context of this discussion.[136] It can be hard to argue with that notion of history producing the modern individual, and certainly Thomas's and Ullah's deeply masculinist stories, full of agency, support what can become teleological. But as always, racialization has us think differently about forms and affects and, especially, history's primary actors and plots.[137] Moreover, an ethnic or racial consciousness is one of fragmentation rather than integration. Writers and performers elaborate lives necessarily engaged in processes of representation that may mediate between general humanist-individual values of the modern, antiracism among them, and postmodern knowledges born of multiple perspectives. In that field of possibility, what remains observable is the inextricability of the self from social life over time.[138]

SELFHOOD AND DIFFERENCE

HARLEM'S PASTS AND FUTURES

At the heart of Ullah's and Thomas's stories is a deep relationality, one that is linguistic, cultural, political, and racial, as well as continually performed. Roach refers to a long history of cultural performances, in which we can locate those of this chapter, as a "custom of self-definition by staging contrasts with other races, cultures, and ethnicity."[139] Though he may prefer the overriding rubric of the intercultural, I want to suggest that performance is quintessentially a mode of the cross-cultural of the sort that has been explored throughout *Cross-Cultural Harlem*. In this vein, both Thomas and Ullah—representatives of "Puerto Ricans" or "South Asians"—grapple with Blackness as central to a Harlem selfhood. In Ullah's narrative that Thomas inspired and encouraged his work—when he was ten or eleven, he went to Thomas's house for dinner, he says—he may be drawing on shared background in East Harlem *and* a deep interest in Blackness.[140] One explanation for this certainly lies in the way that Blackness is a reference point for both racialization and disempowerment. In the end, most of what we see of the "cross-cultural" comes out of a desire to affiliate for everyone involved, and the subjectivity of the outsider makes that even more apparent. Harlem means something to Thomas and Ullah, just as it has to every figure in this book: Yuri Kochiyama, Langston Hughes, Vito Marcantonio, Piri Thomas, and more. The fact that these figures had their own, and oft-expressed, experience of racialization does not make the projection or desire any more real, but it is crucial to the dynamic of exchange.

If the constructed nature of stories of the self limits the field in one sense, it also, paradoxically, as it puts onto the critical table the very fact of borders, asks "should they contain, or be transgressed?" Ullah's tightly constructed performances and more casual observations, in the present but about the past, are fictional inasmuch as they are attentive to their "story-ness" and also gesture to his own real-life experiences; Thomas's changing relationship to the representation of self and place bring us into the present, as *Down These Mean Streets* becomes canonical. In life and word, these cultural producers pull off the trick of deep commitment to race and ambivalence about its constitution. Still, as open as it all might seem, these maneuvers unquestionably are enabled by the entitlement of masculinity, the ability to move through space, across boundaries that might otherwise close in people and identities. Even the working-class solidarities forged on the ground, in the everyday, tell an alternative story, but they harken back to the gendered negotiations of other male figures in Harlem. The question that all these works ask is how expansive any creative imagination, any performance or genre, can be.

Thomas's evocation of his own/Piri's prison experience in *Down These Mean Streets* raises the question of freedom more vividly. It situates past autobiographical remembrances into a temporality of the readers' political present and new futures. Carlo Rotella has powerfully argued that racialized urban crisis of the 1960s produced representational conventions for the outside world looking at "the ghetto," its poverty and drug problems and racial conflicts, but that many writers such as Claude Brown and Warren Miller sought to portray another perspective, from inside neighborhoods of Harlem and other places.[141] Like other intellectuals writing during this period, Thomas first presented a story of delinquency and an emergence from difficulty into possibility. Redemption is a theme that he takes up in later works.[142] *Down These Mean Streets* deeply resembles African American–authored texts that vigorously critique the state and its imprisonment of racial others—*The Autobiography of Malcolm X* comes to mind—but this particular remapping of Harlem space through questioning categories and stability does not offer closure. As the text reinstantiates a changing Harlem—when Piri returns there after prison, he notes, "My Harlem had a somewhat different face."[143]—it may frustrate readers' desires for a stable touchstone for community or a clear target for public policy. A little differently, Ullah's inability to find a reasonable rent in Harlem surely has us think more critically about the displacements that continue to make this place. Harlem's present is one shaped by the prospect of extinction. It needs and, in Thomas's and Ullah's stories, receives longings that foreground encounter. But, as this chapter has elucidated, such longings are always complex negotiations of time and space. Svetlana Boym has written about "retrospective but also prospective" nostalgia,[144] which can hardly propose a simple return to the past or even idealize the future. It is, instead, "ironic, inconclusive and fragmentary . . . aware of the gap between identity and resemblance."[145] The gap is a productive space for the definitional freedoms of individuals and communities and their forms, which Thomas and Ullah seize for their creative expression.

A CODA FOR THE STORIES

Futures for Harlem

In the chapters of this book, I have drilled down into cross-cultural encounters, across regions and communities, and through the varied forms that give them presence for a new way of thinking about Harlem. I have sought to illuminate the relationality that defines this extraordinarily important site while also understanding the force of Blackness in particular as well as other identities that energize political and social life. If that seems a difficult needle to thread in the fraught contemporary moment of displacements and reshaping of Harlem—an assault on its continued importance and very existence that occasions defensive discourses about just what this place means—it is one that moves fluidly across many lived experiences and imaginings over time, as seen here. And the political present of Harlem itself presents opportunities for contributing to rich scholarly and popular conversations on intersections, on differential and connected racializations, and on the gendered and sexual oppressions within. In a context of social and cultural ferment, works such as "Spanish Blood," *Harlem: Negro Metropolis*, and *Down These Mean Streets* and figures such as Vito Marcantonio and Aladdin offer possibilities: of navigating difference, struggling against racism, building class and other solidarities, and performing autonomous and creative selves. These stories usher us into the thick intimacies and frictions of alternative geographies.

It bears emphasizing that my goal in *Cross-Cultural Harlem* has not merely been to advocate for an additive or recuperative model that includes groups of people who have been unseen, but to argue for the importance of encounters. The preceding pages have encouraged a wider, more inclusive view, yes, but they also remind us that difference is not just about race or ethnicity or identity. Cross-cultures rethink the class divides and divergent political inclinations that have made Harlem. And affirming the practices of living *in* difference, not just with it, has stakes that extend well beyond the borders of northern Manhattan. The frame of cross-cultures may derive from Caribbean critical thought but also helps us understand a fundamentally modern experience of the world, accessible across cities and suburbs, in the United States and other countries as well, of people and their histories coming together and sorting through the consequences.

If living in difference is a social fact, it is also a measure of longing for connection and even comparison, though, we must hasten to add, never sameness. How else to describe Roi Ottley's evocation in the 1943 work *New World A-Coming: Inside Black America*, after a meticulously detailed discussion of the varieties of Blackness, the different groups of Puerto Rican peoples, and various Asian groups that lived in Harlem, of what he called "pleasant incidents."[1] He wrote about the funeral of a Chinese businessman in Harlem being widely attended by Black residents, and a local African American musical quartet refusing to play "Minnie the Moocher" because of Chinese objections to its representations that sensationalized Chinatowns as filled with opium dens—all to evoke sympathetic exchange among peoples that suffered discrimination and also shared space. If the figure of Chineseness has been utilized throughout history to signify extreme otherness to culture and nation, Ottley brings that imaginary inside, repurposing it, at the end of a chapter entitled "How Colored is Harlem?" to open up minoritization within. Here, we might recall Langston Hughes engaging in a similar kind of gesture, surprisingly identifying the presence of a Chinese policeman in Harlem as a sign of possibility. Both the reports of cross-culturality itself and the impulses to offer it speak of an affect that transcends tolerance. It is something deeper, more reflective, and consequential. The discovery and narrating of crossing boundaries bring a kind of pleasure, but also process difficulty, including, in Ottley's work, ethnic stereotyping and death. In the occasion that opened *Cross-Cultural Harlem*, we might hold together the promises of Asian–Black activist collaboration in Yuri Kochiyama's relationship to Malcolm X alongside the dangers of romanticizing solidarity and flattening different racial experiences.

Key to unlocking the embedded and sometimes repressed psychic-social complex that contradicts multiculturalism's assumption of groups sitting side by side is the basic heterogeneity of all forms of peoplehood. So many writers and cultural and political figures who have seen themselves as members of ethnic-racial groups have exhibited an awareness that connections need not amount to sameness: Hughes always poked at Black Americanness; in "Spanish Blood," it was via Puerto Rican mixtures. Claude McKay developed a Black geography characterized by many shades and perspectives. Vito Marcantonio's Italian left-wing subjectivity confronted all sorts of definitional conflicts. Piri Thomas's Puerto Ricanness deviated sharply from his father's particular anxiety about race. Differences have come together, densely constituting place. Ottley, who was the child of Grenadian and Danish West Indian immigrants (Caribbean like McKay, but with U.S. upbringing), wrote of the consolidation of Harlem that "nearly every type of person that inhabits the earth is seen on the sidewalks of the Black Metropolis. Here live hundreds of different peoples, subdivided into a bewildering array of clans, tribes, races, cultures, and colors—of red, brown, yellow, white, and black, and unimaginable shades in between. But if one is mystified by the whirl of colors, he is likely to be staggered by the march of diverse types."[2]

It is not merely the observation of wild multiplicity that I want to point to here: it is the question of what we do with that fact, analytically. Ottley gives us one narrative road map. After those comments on multiplicity within Blackness and descriptions of the complicated color makeup of Puerto Rican populations and the presence in Harlem of "Asiatic" groups of Chinese, East Indians, Japanese, and Filipinos, he moves on to discuss Black–Jewish relations, a topic as charged in his time as it has been through the twentieth and twenty-first centuries.[2] Ottley argues that blanket statements about anti-Semitism among African Americans or anti-Black racism among Jews would miss the mark *because* those groups are internally diverse, holding a wide range of political and other inclinations, a way, I would suggest, for him to show that something is at stake in how he understands difference, not simply through the available paradigm of cultural pluralism or inclusion. And in that way big questions about "America," how we think about its very constitution and life, are engaged.

Cross-cultural affinity, we know, is neither seamless nor inevitable. While pointing to divergences within peoplehood to problematize solidarity may sometimes feel destabilizing, this book maintains that it is ultimately productive. The presence of Black middle-class peoples in gentrifying Harlem raises questions about the limits and possibilities of group sympathies. In particular, what does Blackness mean? What does it do in and for Harlem? If McKay's *Harlem: Negro Metropolis* posed those dilemmas many years ago, they have acquired an even more forceful charge today as race and class so powerfully divide peoples and places. Similarly, it is not easy to square the activist work of a group such as the Vito Marcantonio Forum, which describes itself as "an educational organization dedicated to perpetuating the historic memory and significance of the most electorally successful progressive Congressman in American history . . . the Thaddeus Stevens of the 20th Century"[4] with the gauzy, politics-free recollections that populate the webpage of "italianharlem.com," carrying the subtitle "Embracing the memory of when East Harlem was Italian!" That latter formulation consciously or unconsciously, but unmistakably, occludes other ethnic content for the area, with an echo, perhaps, of the Catholic priest's narrative of Puerto Ricans pushing Italians out as discussed in chapter 3 of this book. How else to read that exclamation point?[5] And the separation from African Americans by other groups that some Black and non-Black characters of *Down These Mean Streets* sought and others decried provides an important back story for the ever-increasing diversity, of race, class, language, and citizenship uneasily brought together under the rubric of "Latino" in a "barrio" that is fading fast.

A CODA FOR THE STORIES

When we attend to the intersections, we fundamentally reimagine Harlem space. If the structure of space has been understood through centers and peripheries that expressed arrangements of world capitalism, much important scholarship has critiqued the translation of hierarchies of influence into the discourses undergirding colonialism and imperialism.[6] We are thus critically primed for a different apprehension of what is important, where, and why, even if that understanding has not necessarily resulted in a wholesale disruption of place-histories. I have suggested here that stories from edges, those that might be conceived of as minor, will tell us something essential about Harlem, but not because Harlem itself is marginal. To think of Harlem as a "minority" space is a misreading twice over: because Blackness is central, providing a political grammar that reaches beyond locality, and, more implicitly, because whiteness is destabilized by class and migration histories. We shift the "center" from a conventional rendering of Black–white domestic opposition to Blackness as dynamic and edgy, global, colonial, postcolonial, and cosmopolitan. Each chapter of this book correspondingly offers a different model for spatial thinking, for locality and globality both. One contribution to this discussion is an abiding dynamism—Hughes, McKay, Marcantonio, Thomas, or Aladdin never stand still in any one site or any one vector of meaning, in a show of masculine agency, it needs to be added. But neither can Kochiyama, the character of Hattie in "Spanish Blood," or Ullah's mother in his family's stories of Spanish Harlem be consigned to the periphery, especially when they offer critiques of dominant stories of attachment through their own gendered negotiations. Consolation and inspiration can be found in transgressions of boundaries and implosion of the customary dichotomization of movement and dwelling, in physical and symbolic terms at once. Another way to put this is that *Cross-Cultural Harlem* has shed light on people mapping place and moving through authorized and resistant accounts to develop new meanings for themselves and others.

Undoubtedly, we cannot think about the depth of Harlem without history. Accordingly, the chapters of this book roll out multiple historicities. First, in turning to flashpoints of convergence, these stories have developed a past of Harlem that renders possibilities and concerns of the present. Those have been moments of limits being reached, grievances nursed, solidarities thickened. Both the symptomatic quality and prescience of the encounters remind us that threats of extinction are hardly new, precisely because racialized space is always precarious. If one sign of modernity is newness, another is an anxiety about the change that brings, never not related to how peoples and experiences will come together. Will mixtures and exchanges mean the end of a place and what we value about it? While this book's throughline may reorder some temporalities (of past, present and future) as it illuminates a simultaneity built from intertextuality, it still hurtles toward questions about what Harlem can be like in years to come.

Second, this book's occasions fall into a frame, from the 1930s to the first decades of the twenty-first century. To start after the Harlem Renaissance is not to diminish its importance, but instead to highlight its symbolically and experientially formative role. Even in its ending, which converged with the Depression (and its attendant economic immiseration) and made vivid a disappointing disconnect between U.S. efforts to critique tyrannies of race abroad and maintenance of racist hierarchies at home, the Harlem Renaissance defined Harlem and its complex Blackness. Likewise, the winds of change that I argue thematize Vito Marcantonio's politics can be raised to the level of a general rubric, blowing across and also destabilizing every moment of racial-spatial expression of this book. To look toward the other end, in 1986, Richard Schaffer and Neil Smith published a seminal article about Harlem that indicated that "reports of gentrification are emerging,"[7] and by the 1990s these developments had surely taken hold. This paved a path to twenty-first-century Harlem, one that accommodates the stresses of displacement and myriad political and cultural responses of often creative opposition to how Harlem is "planned" by developers. When we step back to contemplate this book's span of years as a historical period, it is one in which Harlem has come into being as an icon, with local, national, and international significance—culturally. as capital of the Black diaspora, the ethnically resonant El Barrio or surround for Italian or Jewish Harlems (in formation and aftermath), politically, as source for insurgencies based in race and class arrangements, and economically, as symbol of urban restructuring and displacement.

Third, one can detect through the readings of Yuri Kochiyama's and Malcolm X's represented relationship, the racial mixtures of "Spanish Blood," the formalistic transgressions of *Harlem: Negro Metropolis*, Vito Marcantonio's politics, and Piri Thomas's and Aladdin's autobiographical-place fictions, the same delicate negotiation of time referred to above—moments evincing something of the past, illuminating a present we know, providing instructions for the future—and, with that, an unmistakable desire to excavate the lost histories of cross-cultural encounters and communities. Such a project rests on an assumption that particular exchanges, not to mention the kinds of insights they bring to the surface, have not figured as prominently in other accounts of Harlem, and that when they are foregrounded, they open up different meanings for how space therein has been produced. The methodological intervention into what kinds of materials to consider and how to interpret them is part of the answer to the theoretical question of the constitution of peoplehood itself. Beyond the obvious point that any subject understands and expresses him- or herself multiply, the formations that we call "social," groupings or categories, and their assembly in space, are porous as well as contingent. It has been particularly important to be attentive to boundaries, not simply for their separating role, but as sites themselves, that contain and produce meaning for people and for Harlem as a whole. Another sort of shifting edge is temporal, the difficulty of identifying the precise force of particular organizations of experience at any given moment, or even within a historical period. Many of the occasions of this book suggest that to declare the presence of a social formation, somehow, is already to signal decline. We can think about trace, even absence, as we seek to understand deep and textured habitation, and engage in readings that are simultaneously reparative and recuperative.[8]

No doubt there is a polemic here, but one, I hope, that has a soft touch, laced with the understanding that the originating problematic dynamic is anti-Blackness and racist, colonial, and classist perceptions of Puerto Ricans and Italians, and anti-Semitism as well, and the overwhelming influence of these discriminatory and disempowering ideologies on institutions that govern the distribution of resources. Still, it is essential to emphasize that what we see in the examples that these chapters have offered are also choices, my own and others': this vision of Harlem, not that one, this form of identity as opposed to something else. No doubt, any rejection brings with it loss, and that, too, will need processing in the difficult realities of the present.

Cross-Cultural Harlem offers a theory, not a policy. It develops an imaginary, a place to think in and from, out into urban and other spaces of the modern world. As I have detailed in all the chapters, the materials and moments in which we access exchange, relationality, mixture, and race itself are open: the short fiction incorporates personal history, the sociological study is fired by literary passion, a cosmopolitan political consciousness travels imaginatively, autobiographical reminiscence processes history. These are Harlem stories, above all, exceeding the limits of their forms. And, as stories, they present resources that are not finite, but that circulate, gaining energy and possibility from being disagreed with or attached to. I have encouraged a different kind of reading, at the edges of conventional representation, for submerged histories, and with an alertness to shifting dynamics, to bring a city-space into view that disrupts simplistic associations of race and neighborhood, and discourses of identity, too. But because Harlem is always changing, as it struggles for its very survival it will give rise to other experiences and representations that draw on those of a long history of presence. With that energy, surely, we can believe in Harlem's future.

ACKNOWLEDGMENTS

Through the long period that I have been working on this book, so many individuals and institutions have provided support, and it is a pleasure to be able to acknowledge them here. As I mentioned in the introduction, *Cross-Cultural Harlem* began when I lived in New York, but really came to life in Charlottesville, where I have been on the faculty at the University of Virginia. And so the first tier of my gratitude has been built by UVA. I would like to thank the intellectually capacious and always impressive scholars in an august English department who hired me even though my literary studies training was not *exactly* in evidence—chairs Alison Booth and Jahan Ramazani didn't blink an eye—and then have, to a one, patiently supported my work at every turn. Mrinalini Chakravorty, Rita Felski, and Susan Fraiman gave me helpful feedback on sections of the book. American Studies is more than my other departmental home: it has been a shared project over the years. Thanks to Maurie McInnis for bringing me into the fold, and to my colleagues and friends Sylvia Chong, Lisa Goff, Jack Hamilton, Matthew Hedstrom, Carmen Lamas, and Penny Von Eschen for their enduring camaraderie; I also appreciate Lisa Cacho offering to read my work without even being asked. Kevin Gaines generously spent time

ACKNOWLEDGMENTS

with the introduction and grasped the project immediately. Lawrie Balfour, Jennifer Greeson, and Grace Hale have provided invaluable reinforcement with their helpful readings and excellent company. Anna Brickhouse has gone the extra mile in all ways, over so many years, in close conversation with this book and me. I am grateful to Camilla Fojas and Debjani Ganguly for organizing and participating in a workshop under the aegis of the Global South Lab of the Institute of the Humanities and Global Cultures, which provided the final push toward completion. My former UVA colleague and forever interlocutor Eric Lott engaged my work before, during, and after that workshop.

I can recognize now a continuum of orientation and interest across projects that in their time seemed so different, and in the people who have helped me track that with their long presence in my scholarly and personal lives. Lok Siu has seen this book through its various iterations, with always perceptive reading. I have been fortunate to benefit from Carol Greenhouse's extraordinary support; her intellectualism spills over disciplinary boundaries, and this is also a far better book for being read by just the kind of anthropologist that she is. Jean-Christophe Agnew, yet again, helped sharpen my ideas and prose. My dear and brilliant friends Vilashini Coopan, Miranda Massie, and Heidi Tinsman patiently discussed, read parts of, and made their marks on what appears in the preceding pages. Also with this project over the long haul have been: Emily Bernard, Faulkner Fox, Cindi Katz, Kathy Leichter, and Rebecca Weston.

I am grateful for fellowships at the Schomburg Center for Research in Black Culture, the Society for Humanities at Cornell University, and the Virginia Foundation for the Humanities; the College of Arts and Sciences at the University of Virginia also provided support for summer research for a number of years. I first worked through some ideas for this project at the Re-Imagining Community conference at the University of Lancaster; thanks to Anne-Marie Fortier for inviting me. Other institutions at which I have presented (and the scholars creating those opportunities) include: Mount Holyoke College (Michelle Stephens), Cornell University's Department of Anthropology (Viranjini Munasinghe), Princeton University (Carol Greenhouse), Northwestern University (Nitasha Sharma), University of

ACKNOWLEDGMENTS

Vermont (John Gennari), the University of Chicago Center for Race and Culture (Michael Dawson), and American University (Núria Vilanova and Max Paul Friedman); I also thank my fellow panelists and audience members at conferences at the University of Dublin, University of Hong Kong, American Anthropological Association, American Studies Association, Latin American Studies Association, and Association for Asian American Studies. Vera Kutzinski gave me extensive feedback on an early version of chapter 1; and her comments and Anthony Reed's on another piece I wrote for their edited collection helped my thinking on Langston Hughes. Gerald Meyer, the foremost authority on Vito Marcantonio, closely engaged with my analysis. I want also to thank those who let me know in conference and other spaces that they were anticipating this book. In that "shot in the arm at crucial moments" category I would include: Hazel Carby, Martin Manalansan, David Eng, Fiona Ngo, Jeffrey Melnick, and Vivek Bald, as well as the members of committees for American Studies Association prizes who expressed appreciation for some of the discussions of *Cross-Cultural Harlem*: Neda Atanasoski, Magdalena Zaborowska, Miriam Petty, and Deborah Paredez. For over two decades I have deeply valued working alongside my comrades on the editorial collective of the *Radical History Review*.

I hope that all those people who took the time to sit down and talk to me about Harlem will see here some reflection of their rich perspectives. Thanks, especially, to Alaudin Ullah, for sharing his thoughts and his works with me on multiple occasions. The staff at the Manuscripts Division of the New York Public Library, the Beinecke Library at Yale University, and the Chicago Public Library Vivian G. Harsh Research Collection of Afro-American History have my gratitude and admiration for the important work they do. And thanks to Eric Brandt and Mark Mones at UVA Press, who led me to the excellent mapmaker Nat Case.

I am grateful for the opportunities I have had to share ideas with undergraduate and graduate students. For bibliographical and other kinds of assistance over the years, I thank: Vanessa Agard-Jones, Haegi Kwon, Andrew Kaplan, Morten Hansen, Brandon Walsh, Lily Beauvilliers, Eli Dunn, M Stiffler, Darya Tahan, and Tom Berenato. Sophie Abramowitz's

ACKNOWLEDGMENTS

fine work at the New York Public Library was especially helpful for chapter 3. Katie Campbell kept me organized when I initially submitted the manuscript for review. Anran Wang's research intelligence for the last stages of this book was utterly essential.

The two anonymous readers for the manuscript at Columbia University Press gave me feedback that immeasurably improved its contents. One reviewer stayed in my mind throughout the revisions—he or she didn't tell me to change anything in particular, and yet somehow, in the course of a complimentary but challenging reflection, created the freedom for me to reconceptualize key frameworks and materials. Philip Leventhal expressed early interest in the book and with great patience and perceptiveness brought it to fruition. Production editor Marisa Lastres was wonderfully supportive. I am extremely grateful for copyeditor Katherine Harper's carefulness and erudition.

Finally, I want to thank those closer in for their love and support. The knowingness of my sister Sobha and my mother Ranjana sustains me. Tom Klubock is still my ideal reader. With him, and our amazing sons Kiran and Ishan, I share full days of laughter and debate about politics, literature, sports, music, and so much more, which creates the very best perch for thinking and writing about the world.

NOTES

AN INTRODUCTION TO HARLEM

1. Photo by Earl Grant depicting Malcolm X's assassination. Accompanies Gordon Parks, "The Violent End of the Man Called Malcolm," *Life*, March 5, 1965, 26–31, photo on 26–27.
2. The front cover of the *Life* issue containing the photo featured a destroyed Black Muslim mosque in Harlem—not the result of neoliberal economic "development," but instead a bombing in retaliation for Malcolm X's murder. The photo was titled "A Monument to Negro Upheaval."
3. Two plays have utilized the relationship between Malcolm X and Yuri Kochiyama as a central conceit: Timothy Toyama's *Yuri and Malcolm X* (2013) and *When Yuri Met Malcolm*, written by Rosie Narasaki and directed by John Miyasaki (2022). The art installation *Raise Your Voice* by Amanda Phingbodhipakkiya, presented at the Museum of the City of New York in 2023, featured an image of the two activists in an opening panel.
4. Another argument can be made here about how each figure was drawn to Islam. For Malcolm X, it was obviously a sustained pursuit, and Kochiyama converted quietly and even discreetly, for a much shorter period. Diane Carol Fujino, *Heartbeat of Struggle: The Revolutionary Life of Yuri Kochiyama* (Minneapolis: University of Minnesota Press, 2005), 206.
5. In keeping with contemporary usage, I have capitalized "Black," but when I distinguish different groups comprising that racial category and identity, I specify: "African American," "Caribbean" or "West Indian," "African," and more. The distinction between identity and background, to be sure, is often murky, but through the course of

AN INTRODUCTION TO HARLEM

Cross-Cultural Harlem, I try to identify specific inflections and identifications within that broader category of race.

6. For a synthetic popular history of Harlem, see Jonathan Gill, *Harlem: The Four Hundred Year History from Dutch Village to Capital of Black America* (New York: Grove Press, 2011), as well as the classic text by Jervis Anderson, *This Was Harlem: A Cultural Portrait, 1900–1950* (New York: Farrar Straus Giroux, 1982).
7. Michael Henry Adams, "The End of Black Harlem," *New York Times*, May 27, 2016.
8. Andy A. Beveridge, in "An Affluent, White Harlem?" *Gotham Gazette*, August 27, 2008, provides some useful comparative numbers over time. On Italian populations: Gerald Meyer, "Italian East Harlem: America's Largest and Most Italian Little Italy," *Marcantonio: Defender of Human Rights* (blog), August 26, 2012, http://vitomarcantonio.com/east-harlem/italian-east-harlem/. Numbers by neighborhood can be found at: https://communityprofiles.planning.nyc.gov/ and http://www.harlemcdc.org/departments/neighborhoods/central_harlem.html.
9. Monique M. Taylor considers intra-class issues in *Harlem Between Heaven and Hell* (Minneapolis: University of Minnesota Press, 2002), as does Derek S. Hyra in *The New Urban Renewal: The Economic Transformation of Harlem and Bronzeville* (Chicago: University of Chicago Press, 2008).
10. Kirk Semple, "Immigrants Who Speak Indigenous Languages Encounter Isolation," *New York Times*, July 10, 2014. Remnants of the Wecquaesgeek's presence can still be found in present-day Harlem—a village that was settled by approximately sixty tribe members is now buried beneath the pavement at Park Avenue and 98th Street. See "Wecksquaesgeek Indians in Harlem 1626," *Harlem World Magazine*, February 21, 2019.
11. Sarah England, *Afro Central Americans in New York City: Garifuna Tales of Transnational Movements in Racialized Space* (Gainesville: University Press of Florida, 2006). England notes about early 1970s Garifuna migrants that they chose Harlem instead of other places in New York not only because it had cheaper housing, but because there they could "camouflage themselves" to elude immigration authorities (p. 51), and that into the present Garifuna populations have lived in both Central and East Harlem.
12. The paradigmatic case of encounter, the conquest of the Americas, has been discussed by Tzvetan Todorov in *The Conquest of America: The Question of the Other*, trans. Richard Howard (New York: Harper and Row, 1984). And scholars have paid closer attention to the continuing ramifications of encounters that have masked dispossession and extraction; for an overview, see Lorenzo Veracini, *Settler Colonialism: A Theoretical Overview* (New York: Palgrave Macmillan, 2010). Mary Louise Pratt, in *Imperial Eyes: Travel Writing and Transculturation* (London: Routledge, 2008), also problematizes encounter. Louis Althusser's discussion of encounter relies on basic economic relations that give rise to proletarianization, in *Philosophy of the Encounter: Later Writings, 1978–87*, ed. François Matheron and Oliver Corpet, trans. and introduction by G. M. Goshgarian (London: Verso, 2006). Also see Fred R. Dallmayr, *Beyond Orientalism: Essays on Cross-Cultural Encounter* (Albany: SUNY Press, 1996); and Robert Holton, "Cosmopolitan Borders, Strangeness, and Inter-Cultural Encounters," in *Political Sociologies of the Cultural*

AN INTRODUCTION TO HARLEM

Encounter: Essays on Borders, Cosmopolitanism, and Globalisation, ed. Barrie Axford et al. (London: Routledge, 2021), 139–52. Lastly, Lisa Lowe offers a nuanced study of a variety of encounters across the Americas in *The Intimacies of Four Continents* (Durham, NC: Duke University Press, 2015).

13. Scholars of the various Harlems I am bringing together in this book have been attentive to diversities, not only because of interpretive inclination, but also because it is impossible to fully engage with any formation in singular terms. The resulting works have opened up different modes that destabilize race and ethnicity. John Jackson Jr. has emphasized racial performances of place with the term "Harlemworld" (also the name of a 1997 album on Arista Records by the rapper Mase), and both Monique Taylor and Robert Orsi used the spatially resonant word "between" to connote imperfect inclusion within any one category of identity or experience for Black middle-class Harlemites and Harlem Italians, respectively. Arlene Dávila understood the expansiveness (and limits) of "Latinoness" for psychic-social aspirations with her book title *Barrio Dreams*. Jeffrey Gurock rejected models for singularity by explaining the existence of Jewish Harlems, in the plural, and an understanding of the complicated relationship between Jewishness and Blackness. Zain Abdullah's title *Black Mecca* alludes to a racial-religious imaginary that captures multiple groups. Vivek Bald may have focused his lens on Bengalis, but the "lost histories" he uncovers reveal the exchanges essential to understanding how and where these migrants settled. What I mean to suggest with these examples of prominent works organized under what might seem at first to be one or another group identity or region of Harlem is that much of the most important and recent scholarship on Harlem has been careful to point out the instability of race and ethnicity. See John L. Jackson, Jr., *Harlemworld: Doing Race and Class in Contemporary Black America* (Chicago: University of Chicago Press, 2001); Taylor, *Harlem Between Heaven and Hell*; Robert Orsi, "The Religious Boundaries of an Inbetween People: Street *Feste* and the Problem of the Dark-Skinned Other in Italian Harlem, 1920–1990," *American Quarterly* 44, no. 3 (September 1992): 313–47; Jeffrey S. Gurock, *The Jews of Harlem: The Rise, Decline and Revival of a Jewish Community* (New York: New York University Press, 2016); Arlene Dávila, *Barrio Dreams: Puerto Ricans, Latinos, and the Neoliberal City* (Berkeley: University of California Press, 2004); Zain Abdullah, *Black Mecca: The African Muslims of Harlem* (Oxford: Oxford University Press, 2010); and Vivek Bald, *Bengali Harlem and the Lost Histories of South Asian America* (Cambridge, MA: Harvard University Press, 2013).

14. There is a voluminous body of works on Chinatowns in North America and all over the world, but two texts that are especially attentive to critical geographic questions are: Kay J. Anderson, *Vancouver's Chinatown: Racial Discourse in Canada, 1896–1980* (Montreal: McGill–Queen's University Press, 1991); and Anthony Lee, *Picturing Chinatown: Art and Orientalism in San Francisco* (Berkeley: University of California Press, 2001). One helpful way to think about how race and place are bound up with one another is through Michel Laguerre's notion of a "minoritized space," in which the political-social separation and devaluation of racial groups, in ghettoes, Chinatowns and other kinds of enclaves produces in turn ideological and physical confinements. *Minoritized Space: An*

AN INTRODUCTION TO HARLEM

   Inquiry into the Spatial Order of Things (Berkeley, CA: Institute of Governmental Studies Press, 1999).
15. My discussion of racial geography builds on the rich discussions in the field of Black geographies. See Camilla Hawthorne's useful guide "Black Matters Are Spatial Matters," *Geography Compass* 13, no. 11 (November 2019): 1–13; Katherine McKittrick and Clyde Woods, eds., *Black Geographies and the Politics of Place* (Toronto: Between the Lines, 2007); Adam Bledsoe and William Jamaal Wright, "The Pluralities of Black Geographies," *Antipode* 51, no. 2 (2019): 419–37.
16. McKittrick and Woods, "No One Knows the Mysteries at the Bottom of the Ocean," in *Black Geographies and Politics of Place*, 5. I also want to point to another mapping project, "Digital Harlem: Everyday Life 1915–1930," developed by Shane White, Stephen Garton, Graham White, and Stephen Robertson, which seeks to elaborate the texture of social space through "everyday" stories for the period between 1915 and 1930: http://digitalharlem.org.
17. Kevin Lynch, *The Image of the City* (Cambridge, MA: MIT Press, 1960), 46.
18. Lynch, *Image of the City*, 47.
19. Ted Fox, *Showtime at the Apollo* (New York: Holt, Rinehart, and Winston, 1983); Richard Carlin and Kinshasha Holman Conwill, *Ain't Nothing Like the Real Thing: How the Apollo Theater Shaped American Entertainment* (Washington, DC: Smithsonian Books, 2010); and Garrett Felber, "Apollo Theater," in *The Encyclopedia of New York City*, ed. Kenneth Jackson (New Haven, CT: Yale University Press, 2010), 46–47.
20. George Barner, "Santa Claus Greets Kids at Blumstein's," *New York Amsterdam News*, December 6, 1958. A much later article by Christopher Gray, "Streetscapes/Blumstein's Department Store: How a Black Boycott Opened the Employment Door," *New York Times*, November 20, 1994, states that Blumstein's had the first Black Santa in 1943, not too long after protests about discriminatory hiring, to suggest that it was a political response, but there is no documentation of that in either the *New York Times* or *Amsterdam News*. One could speculate that this urban legend serves the self-presentation of Blumstein's as antiracist or inclusive, but the source of its emergence is not clear.
21. Robert Orsi, *The Madonna of 115th Street: Faith and Community in Italian Harlem, 1880–1930* (New Haven, CT: Yale University Press, 1985)
22. Over the years, as middle-class Italians began to leave East Harlem for suburban New Jersey, the Bronx, and Long Island, and as Puerto Ricans began to arrive en masse in the area, the proportions in the ethnic mix shifted, and the dominance of Italians decreased considerably through the 1930s and 1940s. Some, though certainly not all, Italians registered these demographic changes through resentment toward these people they perceived as nonwhite. The absence of Puerto Ricans from the largest and most public Catholic church in the area, as well as from its spectacle of the parade, was notable. See Orsi, "Religious Boundaries of an Inbetween People."
23. Paul Stoller, *Money Has No Smell: The Africanization of New York City* (Chicago: University of Chicago Press, 2002); Boukary Sawadogo, *Africans in Harlem: An Untold New York Story* (New York: Fordham University Press, 2022).

24. The works of local historian Christopher Bell have detailed the diversity of East Harlem over time and have especially addressed the tendency to ignore the African American presence in the area in the ethnic-racial dividing up of Harlem's regions. See his *East Harlem Revisited* (Charleston, SC: Arcadia, 2010); and *East Harlem Remembered: Oral Histories of Community and Diversity* (Jefferson, NC: McFarland: 2013). For his 1904 dissertation "The Sociology of a New York City Block" (Department of Sociology, Columbia University), Thomas Jesse Jones considered fourteen multifamily dwellings on an unnamed block in East Harlem, in which families of various ethnicities lived, largely Irish, Italian, Jewish, German, and African American, but also Cuban, Danish, and mixed groups. Note, too, that the actual marketing of "diversity" on 116th Street can be seen as early as 1969 in a document submitted by architect-artist (and advocate of participatory community-based democracy) Roger Katan to New York City's community planning board 11 for multifaceted development of housing and commercial spaces. In the first subtitled section, "116th Street in the total community," Katan wrote of a history of diversification, from early Germans and Jews to Italian migrants and then Puerto Rican, Caribbean, and African American peoples, noting that "116th Street is not only a part of East Harlem but is in many ways a microcosm of the total community." Roger Katan Planning Consultants, "116th Street Renewal Plan: from East River Drive West to 5th Avenue," prepared for the City of New York and the Borough President's Community Planning Board No. 11 and the Council of Advisors, May 15, 1969, 3. (Located in "Neighborhood File" of the City of New York archives.)
25. In his fine study *The Jews of Harlem*, Jeffrey S. Gurock makes the point that the Old Broadway synagogue has existed beyond the boundaries of the western Jewish Harlem, but I indicate its presence because it has become a kind of sign for longer-lasting ethnic and religious formations in the area writ large. Any understanding of "Jewish Harlem" is indeed complicated. For the period beginning in the late 1800s until before World War II, Gurock explains, there were two Jewish Harlems: in the west, one that was largely German and middle-class, and the other, in the east, more Eastern European working-class. The latter group had been displaced due to the urban "development" of the lower east side, an interesting prefiguring of economic transformations that would affect all Harlem residents in later decades. And these histories of migration and settlement, like many, contain multiple temporalities, with peoples coming in successive but not always overlapping waves, with a variety of political inclinations and quite different visions of how to relate to the city and the nation. Somewhat early in this history, an article entitled "The New Jewish Quarter of Harlem" in the *American Israelite* quoted a Jewish observer who identified differences in east and west Jewish Harlems through a changing relationship to Americanization: "On the East Side . . . my people have gained that which they sought first from America, freedom; but in the newer colonies they have gained more than freedom—they have gained their right to be Americans." February 10, 1904, 8, 10.
26. Harlem Heritage walking tour, September 2012.
27. Cheryl Lynn Greenberg, *Troubling the Waters: Black-Jewish Relations in the American Century* (Princeton: Princeton University Press, 2006).

AN INTRODUCTION TO HARLEM

28. Toni Morrison, *Jazz* (New York: Alfred A. Knopf, 1992), 8. See also: Roberta S. Gold, "The Black Jews of Harlem: Representation, Identity, and Race, 1920–1939," *American Quarterly* 55, no. 2 (June 2003): 179–225.
29. To take just a few examples: Langston Hughes mentions Lenox Avenue in "Juke Box Love Song" (1950), "Lenox Avenue: Midnight" (1926), "The Weary Blues" (1928), and "Consider Me" (1951); James Baldwin features Lenox Avenue in his book of essays *The Fire Next Time* (New York: Dial Press, 1963); and Gil Scott-Heron's 1970 album is entitled *Small Talk at 125th and Lenox*.
30. See George Chauncey, chap. 9 in *Gay New York: Gender, Urban Culture and the Making of the Gay Male World, 1890–1940* (New York: Basic Books, 1994) for a detailed cultural geography of this space. Other important studies include: Eric Garber, "A Spectacle in Color: the Lesbian and Gay Subculture of Jazz Age Harlem," in *Hidden from History: Reclaiming the Gay and Lesbian Past*, ed. Martin B. Duberman, Martha Vicinus, and George Chauncey (New York: Penguin, 1989), 318–31; Shane Vogel, *The Scene of Harlem Cabaret: Race, Sexuality, Performance* (Chicago: University of Chicago Press, 2009). While those works deal with earlier histories of Harlem, William G. Hawkeswood's posthumously published study is based on ethnographic work he did with African American men in Harlem during the late 1980s and early 1990s: *One of the Children: Gay Black Men in Harlem* (Berkeley: University of California Press, 1997). John Henrik Clarke describes the scene and the effects of La Guardia's visit to the Rockland Palace to seek the support of Father Divine's followers in the preface to the 1971 reprint of Sara Harris's *Father Divine* (New York: Collier Books, 1971, xiii; book originally published in 1953 by Doubleday).
31. Melanie Grayce West, "Pathmark Closure Jars East Harlem," *Wall Street Journal*, November 17, 2015; Juan Gonzalez, "Retail Ripoff Stung in Stealth Deal to Sell Off Store Site for Luxe Apts.," *New York Daily News*, October 7, 2015; and, for some details about the urban zoning issues involved in development, see Alessandro Busa, "After the 125th Street Rezoning: The Gentrification of Harlem's Main Street During the Bloomberg Years," *Urbanities* 14, no. 2 (November 2014): 51–68. For broader discussions of these issues, see Richard Schaffer and Neil Smith, "The Gentrification of Harlem," *Annals of the Association of American Geographers* 76, no. 3 (September 1986): 347–65; Lisa W. Foderaro, "Harlem's Hedge Against Gentrification," *New York Times*, August 16, 1987; and Sabiyah Robin Prince, "Changing Places: Race, Class and Belonging in the 'New' Harlem," *Urban Anthropology and Studies of Cultural Systems and World Economic Development* 31, no. 1 (Spring 2002): 5–35.
32. For details about the range of city-owned housing in Harlem, see the Manhattan link at https://www.nyc.gov/site/nycha/about/developments.page. For discussions of the early history of race and property, see: Gilbert Osofsky, *Harlem: The Making of a Ghetto, 1890–1930* (New York: Harper and Row, 1966), 92–104; and Kevin McGruder, *Race and Real Estate: Conflict and Cooperation in Harlem, 1890–1920* (New York: Columbia University Press, 2015).
33. More elegant row houses in the upmarket Sugar Hill area, once the homes of wealthy European immigrants and then middle- and upper-class African Americans in the

1920s, and spacious apartment buildings on Seventh Avenue and particular blocks in central Harlem reflect a rather different setting.

34. As David Maurrasse has written of gentrification: "Visually, Harlem's overall landscape smacks of transition—a convergence of the neighborhood's past and future." *Listening to Harlem: Gentrification, Community and Business* (New York: Routledge, 2006), 7. See also Jerome Krase, *Seeing Cities Change: Local Culture and Class* (Farnham: Ashgate, 2012). And in fieldwork conversations dating back to 2008 and continuing to the present, African Americans, Puerto Ricans, Mexicans, and West Indians have articulated being unable to afford living in Harlem.

35. This kind of conflict has a long history. See Thomas Bender, ed., *The University and the City: From Medieval Origins to the Present* (Oxford: Oxford University Press, 1991).

36. Stefan M. Bradley, *Harlem vs Columbia University: Black Student Power in the Late 1960s* (Urbana-Champaign: University of Illinois Press, 2009).

37. Two pieces from the 1960s lay out those competing impulses: James Ridgeway, "Columbia's Real Estate Ventures," *New Republic*, May 18, 1963; and Peter Kihss, "Columbia Spurs Massive Renewal North of 125th Street," *New York Times*, May 19, 1968. Brian D. Goldstein, in *The Roots of Urban Renaissance: Gentrification and the Struggle Over Harlem* (Cambridge, MA: Harvard University Press, 2017), has explained that Black power was one logic for arguments about local economic control over the space, with anticolonial influences of the moment and pragmatic needs for economic transformation.

38. Carter B. Horsley, "Softening the Edge of East Harlem," *New York Times*, July 30, 1978.

39. Studies of Dominicans in New York include: Sherri Grasmuck and Patricia R. Pessar, *Between Two Islands: Dominican International Migration* (Berkeley: University of California Press, 1991); Ana Aparicio, *Dominican-Americans and the Politics of Empowerment* (Gainesville: University of Florida Press, 2006); and Jesse Hofnung-Garskof, *A Tale of Two Cities: Santo Domingo and New York After 1950* (Princeton: Princeton University Press, 2008).

40. Ned Kaufman, "Heritage and the Cultural Politics of Preservation," *Places* 11, no. 3 (1998): 58–65.

41. George J. Sánchez, "'What's Good for Boyle Heights Is Good for the Jews': Creating Multiculturalism on the Eastside During the 1950s," *American Quarterly* 56, no. 3 (September 2004): 633–61; Avery Gordon and Christopher Newfield, eds., *Mapping Multiculturalism* (Minneapolis: University of Minnesota Press, 1996); and Bhikhu C. Parekh, *Rethinking Multiculturalism: Cultural Diversity and Political Theory* (Basingstoke, UK: Palgrave Macmillan, 2006).

42. Fred D'Aguiar, "Wilson Harris by Fred D'Aguiar," *Bomb*, January 1, 2003. Some of Wilson Harris's works include: *Palace of the Peacock* (1960), *The Far Journey of Oudin* (1961), *The Whole Armour* (1962), and *The Secret Ladder* (1963)—which collectively make up *The Guyana Quartet* (London: Faber and Faber, 1985)—*Black Marsden: A Tabula Rasa Comedy* (London: Faber and Faber, 1972); and *Companions of the Day and Night* (London: Faber and Faber, 1975). He has also published several collections of essays, including *The Womb of Space: The Cross-Cultural Imagination* (Westport, CT: Greenwood Press, 1983).

43. Wilson Harris, *The Radical Imagination: Lectures and Talks*, ed. Alan Riach and Mark Williams (Liège, Belgium: Department of English, University of Liège, 1992), 141.
44. It is worth noting here that Harris's, and this book's, use of cross-culturality diverges dramatically from an earlier invocation, in the Human Relations Area Files project, "to promote understanding of cultural diversity and commonality in the past and present," for a technique of comparison based on formal behavioral characteristics. See https://hraf.yale.edu/cross-cultural-research/. That earlier usage implied that the normal condition of culture is homogeneous and singular, whereas cross-cultural here goes the other way, to explain crossings as deeply embedded in subjective and historical experience.
45. In *Cities of the Dead: Circum-Atlantic Performance* (New York: Columbia University Press, 1996), Joseph Roach has utilized "intercultural" to describe cultures of deep exchange; other scholars have also found that frame to be helpful, the "inter" pointing to phenomena that are in between, among, or reciprocal through others. See, for example, Ming Xie, *Conditions of Comparison: Reflections on Comparative Intercultural Inquiry* (New York: Continuum, 2011). While I can imagine the intercultural to be potentially illuminating of what I describe in this book, my own choice of (primary) terms has to do with wanting to bring readers' attention to the movement, the crossing, in particular.
46. Édouard Glissant, *Poetics of Relation*, trans. Betsy Wing (Ann Arbor: University of Michigan Press, 1997).
47. Fernando Ortíz, *Cuban Counterpoint: Tobacco and Sugar* (New York: Alfred A. Knopf, 1947), 98. Note that Ortíz was also clearing ground for a more dynamic understanding of cultural exchange, what he called its "intermeshed" history—he was setting up transculturation against acculturation.
48. Glissant, *Poetics of Relation*, 11.
49. Immanuel Wallerstein, "Feudalism, Capitalism, and the World-System in the Perspective of Latin America and the Caribbean: Comments on Stern's Critical Tests," *American Historical Review* 93, no. 4 (October 1988): 873–85, 879, 880. See also Irma Watkins-Owens, *Blood Relations: Caribbean Immigrants and the Harlem Community, 1900–1930* (Bloomington: Indiana University Press, 1996).
50. Stuart Hall, "Pluralism, Race and Class in Caribbean Society," in *Race and Class in Post-Colonial Society: A Study of Ethnic Group Relations in the English-Speaking Caribbean, Bolivia, Chile and Mexico*, ed. John Rex (Paris: Unesco, 1977), 150–84; Stuart Hall, "Cultural Identity and Diaspora," in *Identity: Community, Culture, Difference*, ed. Jonathan Rutherford (London: Lawrence & Wishart, 1990), 222–37.
51. Winston James, *Holding Aloft the Banner of Ethiopia: Caribbean Radicalism in Early Twentieth-Century America* (London: Verso, 1998). Charles V. Carnegie has also discussed the different kinds of spatiality that Caribbean cultures and politics offer in: *Postnationalism Prefigured: Caribbean Borderlands* (New Brunswick, NJ: Rutgers University Press, 2002).
52. In discussing political formations of the early 1900s, Winston James contrasts Caribbean and African American populations, writing that "the United States was the only society in the Americas, from the days of slavery onward, within which 'race' was articulated in

a binary manner, with no intermediary position recognized or privileged to any notable degree by the white ruling class." *Holding Aloft*, 110. See also Watkins-Owens, *Blood Relations*; Philip Kasinitz, *Caribbean New York: Black Immigrants and the Politics of Race* (Ithaca, NY: Cornell University Press, 1992); Louis Parascandola, ed., *"Look for Me All Around You": Anglophone Caribbean Immigrants in the Harlem Renaissance* (Detroit: Wayne State University Press, 2005); and Joyce Moore Turner, *Caribbean Crusaders and the Harlem Renaissance* (Urbana: University of Illinois Press, 2005).

53. These questions have a long history in Harlem. See: "West Indian and American Negroes: Relationship Discussed by Chandler Owen of 'Messenger,'" *New York Amsterdam News*, February 28, 1923; "'No West Indian Problem': Domingo: Immigration of West Indians Should Not Be Restricted," *New York Amsterdam News*, April 4, 1923; and W. A. Domingo, "Gift of the Black Tropics," in Alain Locke, ed., *The New Negro: An Interpretation* (New York: Albert and Charles Boni, 1925), 341–49.

54. Janice Morgan, "Re-Imagining Diversity and Connection in the Chaos World: An Interview with Patrick Chamoiseau," *Callaloo* 31, no. 2 (Spring 2008): 443–53, 449.

55. As Ralph Ellison put it, the residents are "not quite citizens, yet Americans." "Harlem Is Nowhere," *Harper's Magazine*, August 1, 1964, 53–57.

56. Immanuel Kant, *Anthropology from a Pragmatic Point of View* (The Hague: Martinus Nijhoff, 1974), 4.

57. Doreen Massey, "A Global Sense of Place," *Marxism Today*, June 1991, 29. Attempts to put a name to the nexus of migration, settlement, and marginalization, like the afterlives and discontents of multiculturalism, the affinities of city life, the hope of conviviality, or the futures of a radical multiracialism, processes the imbrication of the local and the global. This is an abbreviated discussion of many important works of urban social and cultural theory, which include: Iris Marion Young's *Inclusion and Democracy* (Oxford: Oxford University Press, 2000); Ash Amin and Nigel Thrift's *Seeing Like a City* (Cambridge, MA: Polity Press, 2017); Kenan Malik's *Multiculturalism and Its Discontents: Rethinking Diversity After 9/11* (Calcutta: Seagull Books, 2013); Paul Gilroy's *After Empire: Melancholia or Convivial Culture?* (London: Routledge, 2004); and George Sanchez's *Boyle Heights: How a Los Angeles Neighborhood Became the Future of American Democracy* (Berkeley: University of California Press, 2021).

58. If I prefer "global" to "worldliness" or "planetarity," it is not to deny the critiques that a number of scholars have offered, but to suggest that I still (optimistically) see possibilities in the widely discursive availability of globality. On productive uses of "the world," particular vis-à-vis cosmopolitan literature, see Edward W. Said, *The World, the Text, and the Critic* (Cambridge, MA: University Press, 1983); and Pheng Cheah, *What Is a World? On Postcolonial Literature as World Literature* (Durham, NC: Duke University Press, 2016). Gayatri Chakravorty Spivak discusses possibilities for thinking in terms of the planet in *An Aesthetic Education in the Era of Globalization* (Cambridge, MA: Harvard University Press, 2012), especially chapter 16, as does Dipesh Chakrabarty in "The Planet: An Emergent Humanist Category," *Critical Inquiry* 46, no. 1 (2019): 1–31.

59. Yuri Kochiyama, *Passing It On: A Memoir*, ed. Marjorie Lee, Akemi Kochiyama-Sardinha, and Audee Kochiyama-Holman (Los Angeles: UCLA Asian American Studies Center Press, 2004).
60. Kochiyama, *Passing It On*, 40.
61. Kochiyama, *Passing It On*, 47.
62. Kochiyama, *Passing It On*, 65. In addition to being a musical artist, actor, and activist, Paul Robeson also played professional football.
63. Yuri Kochiyama, interview by Amy Goodman, *Democracy Now!*, February 20, 2008.
64. Kochiyama, *Passing It On*, xxiii.
65. Kochiyama, *Passing It On*, xxiii.
66. For further discussion of this topic, see Timothy Brennan, *At Home in the World: Cosmopolitanism Now* (Cambridge, MA: Harvard University Press, 1997); Bruce Robbins and Paulo Lemos Horta, *Cosmopolitanism* (New York: New York University Press, 2017); and Elijah Anderson, *The Cosmopolitan Canopy: Race and Civility in Everyday Life* (New York: W. W. Norton, 2011).
67. Fujino, *Heartbeat of Struggle*.
68. Kochiyama, *Passing It On*, 7.
69. Yuri Kochiyama, "The Impact of Malcolm X on Asian-American Politics and Activism," in *Blacks, Latinos and Asians in Urban America: Status and Prospects for Politics and Activism*, ed. James Jennings (London: Praeger, 1994), 128–41. Quote is in the sidebar on page 132, in a reprinted interview with Miya Iwataki for KPFK radio, May 19, 1972.
70. Kochiyama, *Passing It On*, 70.
71. See Karl Evanzz, *The Judas Factor: The Plot to Kill Malcolm X* (New York: Thunder's Mouth, 1992), 11–12; and Manning Marable, *Malcolm X: A Life of Reinvention* (New York: Viking Penguin, 2011), 95.
72. In one of many examples, DuBois writes in *Dusk of Dawn: An Essay Toward an Autobiography of a Race Concept* (New York: Oxford University Press, 2007 [1940], 48): "The total result was the history of our day. That history may be epitomized in one word—Empire; the domination of white Europe over black Africa and yellow Asia, through political power built on the economic control of labor, income and ideas." For a long history of Black–Asian solidarities, see Bill Mullen, *Afro-Orientalism* (Minneapolis: University of Minnesota Press, 2004).
73. An alternative political geography of Malcolm X and many Black nationalists extended beyond Harlem. See James Tyner, *The Geography of Malcolm X: Black Radicalism and the Remaking of American Space* (New York: Routledge, 2013).
74. Kochiyama, "Impact of Malcolm X," 135.
75. Yuri Kochiyama, "Redemption Song," interview by Maya Jaggi, *Guardian*, December 16, 2006.
76. James Clifford, *Routes: Travel and Translation in the Late Twentieth Century* (Cambridge, MA: Harvard University Press, 1997).
77. Gilles Deleuze and Felix Guattari, "What Is a Minor Literature?" *Mississippi Review* 1, no. 3 (Winter/Spring 1983): 13–33; Françoise Lionnet and Shu-mei Shih, eds., *Minor Transnationalism* (Durham, NC: Duke University Press, 2005).

78. Lionnet and Shih propose "cultural transversalism," connected to Glissant's discussion of relationality, and in which they stress multilingualism. The later work of these important thinkers on creolization is also, I believe, similar to what I am seeking to illuminate in Harlem, though I prefer the term "cross-cultural." And Susan Koshy has argued for "minority cosmopolitanism," which I see as illuminating my earlier insights about globality in locality with the potential of thinking in terms of minoritization. See Susan Koshy, "Minority Cosmopolitanism," *PMLA* 126, no. 3 (May 2011): 592–609. Rather than comment on the relative precision of all of these rich approaches to advance an argument that cross-culturality is *more* useful than the other terms, which are also so attentive to depth, mixture, and exchange, I shall simply identify my own choice as one that I believe helps us productively gaze into Harlem.

79. Paul Gilroy, *Black Atlantic: Modernity and Double Consciousness* (Cambridge, MA: Harvard University Press, 1993). It is also helpful to think about white ethnic populations' diasporic understandings of themselves and racial and ethnic identity; see Matthew Frye Jacobson, *Special Sorrows: The Diasporic Imagination of Irish, Polish, and Jewish Identity in the United States* (Cambridge, MA: Harvard University Press, 1995).

80. In this discussion, I am condensing debates in spatial theory across a number of fields. Classic works include: Henri Lefevebre's *Production of Space*, trans. Donald Nicholson-Smith (Oxford: Blackwell, 1991); Yi Fu Tuan's *Space and Place: The Perspective of Experience* (Minneapolis: University of Minnesota Press, 1977); Michel de Certeau's *The Practice of Everyday Life* (Berkeley: University of California Press, 1980); Edward Soja's *Postmodern Geographies* (London: Verso, 1989); and Doreen Massey's *For Space* (London: SAGE, 2004). Two very helpful reviews are: John A. Agnew, "Space and Place," in *The SAGE Handbook of Geographical Knowledge*, ed. John Agnew and David N. Livingstone (London: SAGE, 2011), 316–30; and Charles W. J. Withers, "Place and the 'Spatial Turn' in Geography and in History," *Journal of the History of Ideas* 70, no. 4 (October 2009): 637–58. Massey's formulation of space as "simultaneity of stories-so-far" and places as "collections of those stories, articulated with the wider power-geometries of space" (130) is helpful for the project at hand. It will become clear that I hope to disrupt any dichotomy between space as general and place as particular, as do most of the works I have just cited, as well as associations of the prior with movement and the latter with stillness. The distinction of the terms will evolve through usage and description as I develop an understanding of the place, of Harlem, through specific configurations of investments over time, and its space as ways of organizing the meanings of social, material, political, and psychic relations.

81. Dilip Parameshwar Gaonkar, ed., *Alternative Modernities* (Durham, NC: Duke University Press, 2001).

82. Wilson Harris, *The Guyana Quartet* (London: Faber and Faber, 1985); Wilson Harris, *Four Banks of the River of Space* (London: Faber and Faber, 1990).

83. In describing Harlem as method, I am influenced by Isabel Hofmeyr's discussion in "The Complicating Sea: The Indian Ocean as Method," *Comparative Studies of South Asia, Africa and the Middle East* 32, no. 3 (2012): 584–90.

84. Caroline Levine has proposed a similar approach in *Forms: Whole, Rhythm, Hierarchy, Network* (Princeton: Princeton University Press, 2015).

85. Fredric Jameson, "Third World Literature in an Era of Multinational Capitalism," *Social Text* 15 (Autumn 1986): 65–88; and more recent discussions, Jonathan Arac, "Getting to World Literature," *NOVEL: A Forum on Fiction* 50, no. 3 (November 2017): 329–37; and Neil Lazarus, *The Postcolonial Unconscious* (Cambridge, UK: Cambridge University Press, 2011).
86. Philip Brian Harper, *Abstractionist Aesthetics: Artistic Form and Social Critique in African American Literature* (New York: New York University Press, 2015).
87. Wilson Harris, *Selected Essays of Wilson Harris: The Unfinished Genesis of the Imagination*, ed. Andrew Bundy (London: Routledge, 1999).
88. For a discussion of the dilemmas that face scholars in literary and cultural studies who seek to incorporate fieldwork, see the introduction and essays in Shalini Puri and Debra Castillo, eds., *Theorizing Fieldwork in the Humanities: Methods, Reflections, and Approaches to the Global South* (London: Palgrave Macmillan, 2016).
89. It is worth explaining that the project here is not to discuss the literary nature of ethnographic writing—as anthropologists have become concerned with, beginning with a landmark collection of essays, James Clifford and George Marcus, eds., *Writing Culture: the Poetics and Politics of Ethnography* (Berkeley: University of California Press, 1986)—nor to bring a geographic perspective to literature as has been done in Franco Moretti, *Atlas of the European Novel: 1800–1900* (London: Verso, 1999) and Robert T. Tally Jr., *Topophrenia: Place, Narrative and the Spatial Imagination* (Bloomington: Indiana University Press, 2019). I hope, instead, to see the twinned foci of literature (broadly considered) and anthropology, in the space of culture, as more deeply structuring of one another than associated disciplines have truly contended with.
90. "Historic Harlem," Big Onion Walking Tour, New York, May 19, 2012.
91. An extremely compelling example of auto-ethnography can be found in Sharifa Rhodes-Pitts's meditation *Harlem Is Nowhere: A Journey to the Mecca of Black America* (New York: Little, Brown, 2011). Also see John Jackson's reflections in *Harlemworld* on how his own background and experiences enrich an ethnographic project.
92. Robin Kelley, introduction to *Harlem on the Verge* by Alice Attie (New York: Quantuck Lane Press, 2003). The question that Kelley cites originally appeared in James Weldon Johnson's essay "Harlem: The Culture Capital" in Alain Locke's *The New Negro: An Interpretation* (New York: Albert and Charles Boni, 1925), 308.
93. Nella Larsen, *Passing* (New York: Alfred A. Knopf, 1929), 70.
94. See George Hutchinson, *The Cambridge Companion to the Harlem Renaissance* (New York: Cambridge University Press, 2007); David Levering Lewis, *When Harlem Was in Vogue* (New York: Alfred A. Knopf, 1981); Rachel Farebrother and Miriam Thaggert, eds., *A History of the Harlem Renaissance* (Cambridge, UK: Cambridge University Press, 2021); Cary D. Wintz, *The Harlem Renaissance, 1920–1940*, 7 vols. (New York: Garland, 1996); and Cheryl A. Wall, *Women of the Harlem Renaissance* (Bloomington: Indiana University Press, 1995).
95. George Hutchinson, *The Harlem Renaissance in Black and White* (Cambridge, MA: Harvard University Press, 1995); Emily Bernard, ed., *Remember Me to Harlem: The Collected Letters of Langston Hughes and Carl van Vechten* (New York: Vintage, 2002).

96. Mikhail Bakhtin, "Discourse in the Novel" (1934–1935), in *The Dialogical Imagination: Four Essays*, ed. Michael Holquist, trans. Caryl Emerson and Michael Holquist (Austin: University of Texas Press, 1981), 259–422.
97. Doris Sommer's proposal of "bilingual games" offers a bit of insight into this process, on which I will elaborate in greater detail in chapter 3. See Doris Sommer, *Bilingual Games: Some Literary Investigations* (New York: Palgrave Macmillan, 2003).
98. Sandhya Shukla, "Harlem's Pasts in Its Present," in *Ethnographies of Neoliberalism*, ed. Carol J. Greenhouse (Philadelphia: University of Pennsylvania Press, 2010), 177–91.
99. De Certeau, *Practice of Everyday Life*, 129.
100. The preponderance of walking and bus tours organized around the Harlem Renaissance and its history testifies to this fact.
101. Raymond Williams writes that culture has two equally important definitions: "to mean a whole way of life—the common meanings [and] to mean the arts and learning—the special processes of discovery and creative effort." "Culture is Ordinary," *Raymond Williams on Culture & Society: Essential Writings*, ed. Jim McGuigan (Los Angeles: SAGE, 2014), 3.
102. See Sara Blair's *Harlem Crossroads: Black Writers and the Photograph in the Twentieth Century* (Princeton: Princeton University Press, 2007) for an important discussion of the porousness of the literary (influenced in many cases by deep engagements with documentary and other photographic projects), and the encounters that made exchange possible.
103. De Certeau, *Practice of Everyday Life*, 115. He uses the idea of "spatial practice" in more generic terms than Henri Lefebvre does in *The Production of Space*.
104. When Kochiyama told a story of the self, she was drawn to include in the resulting text a number of letters, reflections on social events, and political essays for Japanese American publications about Black struggles, suggesting that her intense feeling for Malcolm X and for Harlem needed a hybrid form of writing. Malcolm X's engagements with Kochiyama started with a quick meeting but deepened with the postcards he wrote, which could hardly hold extended description.
105. Walter Benjamin's language for constellations has inspired my use of the concept. In *The Origin of German Tragic Drama*, trans. John Osborne (London: NLB, 1977), he writes: "Ideas are timeless constellations, and by the virtue of the elements' being seen as points in such constellations, phenomena are subdivided and at the same time redeemed" (34). Graeme Gilloch's rather more operational definition is: "The constellation involves a fleeting but irrevocable shift in the perception of phenomena which preserves their individual integrity and their mutuality." *Walter Benjamin: Critical Constellations* (Malden, MA: Blackwell, 2002), 71.
106. Gilles Deleuze and Félix Guattari, *Anti-Oedipus: Capitalism and Schizophrenia* (New York: Penguin, 1977 [1972]).
107. There are other cultural forms, in music, art, and new media, for different stories of mixture, crossing, and flux. John Reddick, a local historian, is currently working on Black and Jewish musical cultures and giving lectures on the topic; one example is "Ragtime to Jazz Time: Harlem's Black and Jewish Music, 1890–1930," Columbia University,

AN INTRODUCTION TO HARLEM

New York, NY, November 4, 2016. https://sps.columbia.edu/events/columbia-community-scholars-lecture-ragtime-jazz-time-harlems-black-and-jewish-music-1890.

108. Saidiya Hartman, *Scenes of Subjection: Terror, Slavery and Self-Making in Nineteenth Century America* (Oxford: Oxford University Press, 1997), 3. Hartman notes that she chooses not to reproduce Frederick Douglass's description of his aunt's beating (in his 1845 *Narrative of the Life of Frederick Douglass, An American Slave*), to contest the casual and careless circulation of such iterations of black suffering. My rather different choice, to display the image of Malcolm X's death, is with the caution that Hartman urges. And drawing out the affective connection at the edges of the photo, I suggest, is to present both loss and possibility in a productive manner.

109. Claire Jean Kim, *Asian Americans in an Anti-Black World* (Cambridge, UK: Cambridge University Press, 2023), 11.

110. In addition to Kim's work, see: Ellen D. Wu, *The Color of Success: Asian Americans and the Origins of the Model Minority* (Princeton: Princeton University Press, 2015); Lewis Gordon, *Her Majesty's Other Children: Sketches of Racism for a Neocolonial Age* (Lanham, MD: Rowman & Littlefield, 1997); Sylvia Zamora, *Racial Baggage: Mexican Immigrants and Race Across the Border* (Palo Alto, CA: Stanford University Press, 2022); Tanya Laterí Hernández, *Racial Innocence: Unmasking Anti-Black Bias and the Struggle for Equality* (Boston: Beacon Press, 2022)..

111. This is to change slightly Stuart Hall's famous line that "race is the modality in which class is 'lived.'" In "Race, Articulation and Societies Structured in Dominance," in *Sociological Theories: Race and Colonialism* (Paris: Unesco, 1980), 305–45, 341.

112. James Baldwin, "Notes of a Native Son," *Notes of a Native Son* (New York: Dial Press, 1963), 98. Christina Sharpe has also discussed these issues in *In The Wake: On Blackness and Being* (Durham, NC: Duke University Press, 2016), as has poet Dionne Brand in "On Narrative, Reckoning and the Calculus of Living and Dying," *Toronto Star*, July 4, 2020.

113. Wolfgang Binder, "An Interview with Piri Thomas," *Minority Voices* 4, no. 1 (Spring 1980): 63–78.

114. Fredric Jameson employed this term for rather different ends, to explain postmodern representation and economic–social systems, and that background bears on how I draw on the spirit of the term itself. See Fredric Jameson, "Cognitive Mapping," in *Marxism and the Interpretation of Culture*, ed. Lawrence Grossberg and Cary Nelson (Urbana-Champaign: University of Illinois Press, 1988), 347–60.

115. Charlottesville is also where students at the University of Virginia routinely study the razing of the city's once-flourishing Black district Vinegar Hill in the name of progress. See the documentary *That World Is Gone* (directed by Hannah Brown Ayers and Lance Warren, 2010). As many observers pointed out at the time and since, the right-wing white nationalists who marched in Charlottesville in 2017 were largely from outside the area, but they were tapping into a deeper history of social relations of the city and the region.

116. Walter Benjamin, *The Writer of Modern Life: Essays on Charles Baudelaire* (Cambridge, MA: Harvard University Press, 2006); Henri Lefebvre, *Writings on Cities*, trans. and

1. LANGSTON HUGHES'S HARLEM

ed. Eleonore Kofman and Elizabeth Lebas (London: Wiley-Blackwell, 1996); Marshall Berman, *All That Is Solid Melts Into Air: The Experience of Modernity* (London: Verso, 1982).

1. LANGSTON HUGHES'S HARLEM

1. Arnold Rampersad, *The Life of Langston Hughes*, vol. 1: *1902–1941: I, Too, Sing America* (New York: Oxford University Press, 1986), 51.
2. Already by 1952, just after the publication of Hughes's *Montage of a Dream Deferred*, literary critic Arthur P. Davis was writing that "one must bear in mind that with Langston Hughes Harlem is both place and symbol." "The Harlem of Langston Hughes' Poetry," *Phylon* 13, no. 4 (1952): 276–83, 283.
3. A notable exception is Edward J. Mullen, who writes in the introduction to his edited volume *Langston Hughes in the Hispanic World and Haiti* (Hamden, CT: Archon, 1977): "It was his contacts with the Spanish language and culture which reinforced and gave substance to his concept of *Negritude*. Furthermore, Hughes's acquaintance with the Hispanic world was more than a superficial encounter; it was a deeply-felt symbiotic relationship. His travels in the Spanish-speaking world not only provided the thematic underpinnings of some of his best short stories (*Spanish Blood* and *Tragedy at the Bath* are two examples) but they allowed him to deftly incorporate Spanish words and phrases in many of his poems and works of prose fiction" (38).
4. Valerie Babb, "Editor's Introduction," *Langston Hughes Review* 20 (Fall 2006): 1–2.
5. For one discussion of Hughes's literary and cultural working through of these dilemmas around Black subjectivity, see David E. Chinitz, *Which Sin to Bear? Authenticity and Compromise in Langston Hughes* (Oxford: Oxford University Press, 2013).
6. Langston Hughes, "Spanish Blood," in *Laughing to Keep from Crying* (New York: Henry Holt, 1952), 35–45, 35–36. This is the version to which I will refer in most of this chapter. As I expand on later, earlier manuscripts have some important differences. I have not been able to locate the original publication in print, in *Metropolis*, December 29, 1934, nor the succeeding one in *Modern Story* 1, no. 1 (October 1935); the version that appears in *Stag*, July–August 1937, 9–11, however, bears close resemblance to the edited manuscript, marked as due to appear in *Metropolis*, in box 353, folder 5709, Langston Hughes Papers, James Weldon Johnson Collection, Yale Collection of American Literature, Beinecke Rare Book and Manuscript Library (hereafter cited as Yale Hughes Papers).
7. See Alejandro de la Fuente and George Reid Andrews, *Afro-Latin American Studies: An Introduction* (Cambridge, UK: Cambridge University Press, 2018); Miriam Jiménez Román and Juan Flores, *The Afro-Latin@ Reader: History and Culture in the United States* (Durham, NC: Duke University Press, 2010); and Antonio D. Tillis, ed., *Critical Perspectives on Afro-Latin American Literature* (New York: Routledge, 2012).
8. Katherine McKittrick, *Demonic Grounds: Black Women and the Cartographies of Struggle* (Minneapolis: University of Minnesota Press, 2006), xiv.

1. LANGSTON HUGHES'S HARLEM

9. Amiri Baraka, "Return of the Native," in *The LeRoi Jones/Amiri Baraka Reader*, ed. William J. Harris (New York: Thunder's Mouth Press, 1991), 217.
10. A work of Hughes's time that touted "cultural pluralism" is Horace M. Kallen, *Culture and Democracy in the United States* (New York: Boni and Liveright, 1924).
11. As I will discuss later in this chapter, Hughes was in dialogue with Latin American writers. His relationship with Cuban poet Nicolás Guillén has been much discussed. See Carmen Alegría and Robert Christian, "Langston Hughes: Six Letters to Nicolás Guillén," *The Black Scholar* 16, no. 4 (1985): 54–60.
12. In using the term "worlded," I follow the example of literary scholar Djelal Kadir, who lays out an argument for its use in "To Compare, to World: Two Verbs, One Discipline," *The Comparatist* 34 (2010): 4–11.
13. I discuss how Harlem is represented in the Simple stories in "Langston Hughes and Simple: Across Form and Space to a Political Consciousness," in *Langston Hughes in Context*, ed. Vera Kutzinski and Anthony Reed (Cambridge, UK: Cambridge University Press, 2023), 62–71.
14. Langston Hughes, *Montage of a Dream Deferred* (New York: Henry Holt, 1951).
15. Langston Hughes, "Foreword: Who Is Simple?" in *The Best of Simple* (New York: Farrar, Straus, and Giroux, 1961), vii–viii. Hortense J. Spillers makes a sophisticated argument for understanding the discourses of the Simple stories through more literary formalist modes in "Formalism Comes to Harlem," *African American Review* 50, no. 4 (Winter 2017): 692–97. I hope not to gainsay this, as I propose understanding Hughes as having a kind of ethnographic impulse. Some evidence of his related interest in the documentary form can be seen in his friendship with photojournalist Henri Cartier-Bresson and *Ebony* magazine photographer Griffith J. Davis. See Sara Blair, *Harlem Crossroads: Black Writers and the Photograph in the Twentieth Century* (Princeton: Princeton University Press, 2007), 53.
16. Box 11, folder 2, Langston Hughes Papers, Vivian G. Harsh Research Collection of Afro-American History and Literature, Chicago Public Library (hereafter cited as CPL Hughes Papers).
17. See Brent Hayes Edwards's influential study *The Practice of Diaspora: Literature, Translation and the Rise of Black Transnationalism* (Cambridge, MA: Harvard University Press, 2003), as well as an earlier important work, Mullen's *Langston Hughes in the Hispanic World and Haiti*. *The Langston Hughes Review*, founded in 1982, has long featured articles about Hughes's travels abroad and how they affected his writings.
18. More general works on Black writers who traveled are numerous. Examples include: Cora Kaplan and Bill Schwarz, eds., *James Baldwin: America and Beyond* (Ann Arbor: University of Michigan Press, 2011); and Wendy Walters, *At Home in Diaspora: Black International Writing* (Minneapolis: University of Minnesota Press, 2005). It is also the case that such writers have been *read* and experienced as transnational; when I presented the ideas of this chapter in a lecture at the University of Chicago in 2015, one audience member, an African American photographer and school teacher in his seventies,

1. LANGSTON HUGHES'S HARLEM

remarked that reading Langston Hughes when he was in college, over fifty years before, had inspired him to travel abroad, to effectively trace Hughes's movements, as he developed a more pan-Africanist sensibility.

19. Vera Kutzinski, *The Worlds of Langston Hughes: Modernism and Translation in the Americas* (Ithaca, NY: Cornell University Press, 2012); Evelyn Scaramella, "Translating the Spanish Civil War: Langston Hughes's Transnational Poetics," *Massachusetts Review* 55, no. 2 (Summer 2014): 177–88; Ira Dworkin, "'Near the Congo': Langston Hughes and the Geopolitics of Internationalist Poetry," *American Literary History* 24, no. 4 (Winter 2012): 631–57; Anita Patterson, *Race, American Literature and Transnational Modernisms* (Cambridge, UK: Cambridge University Press, 2008); Brent Hayes Edwards, "Langston Hughes and the Futures of Diaspora," *American Literary History* 19, no. 3 (2007): 689–711; Jonathan Scott, "Home to Exile: Langston Hughes, Antillano," *Langston Hughes Review* 20 (Fall 2006): 3–16.

20. Langston Hughes, *The Big Sea* (New York: Hill and Wang, 1940) and *I Wonder as I Wander: An Autobiographical Journey* (New York: Hill and Wang, 1956). See also: Faith Berry, *Langston Hughes: Before and Beyond Harlem* (Westport, CT: Lawrence Hill, 1983); Rampersad, *Life of Langston Hughes*, vol. 1.; and Arnold Rampersad, *Life of Langston Hughes*, vol. 2: *1914–1967: I Dream a World* (New York: Oxford University Press, 1988).

21. Kutzinski, *Worlds of Langston Hughes*, 10.

22. Edward Said, *Out of Place: A Memoir* (New York: Vintage, 2000).

23. Isabel Soto discusses Hughes's profound engagements with Spain and the Spanish language in "'I Knew That Spain Once Belonged to the Moors': Langston Hughes, Race and the Spanish Civil War," *Research in African Literatures* 45, no. 3 (Fall 2014): 130–46.

24. Rampersad, *Life of Langston Hughes*, 1:50.

25. Rampersad, *Life of Langston Hughes*, 1:50.

26. Hughes, "Spanish Blood," 36.

27. Lise Waxer, "Of Mambo Kings and Songs of Love: Dance Music in Havana and New York from the 1930s to the 1950s," *Latin American Music Review/Revista de Música Latinoamericana* 15, no. 2 (Autumn-Winter 1994): 139–76. For a discussion of exchanges among Puerto Rican and African American performers, see Basilio Serrano, "Puerto Rican Musicians of the Harlem Renaissance," *Centro Journal* 19, no. 2 (2007): 95–118.

28. Quoted in A. Grace Mims, "SOUL: The Black Man and His Music," *Negro History Bulletin* 33, no. 6 (October 1970): 141–46, 146. See also: Josh Kun, "Bagels, Bongos and Yiddishe Mambos, or The Other History of Jews in America," *Shofar* 23, no. 4 (Summer 2005): 50–68; and Ruth Glasser, *My Music Is My Flag: Puerto Rican Musicians and Their New York Communities, 1917–1940* (Berkeley: University of California Press, 1995).

29. Juliet McMains, *Spinning Mambo Into Salsa: Caribbean Dance in Global Commerce* (Oxford: Oxford University Press, 2015); Vernon Boggs, *Salsiology: Afro-Cuban Music and the Evolution of Salsa in New York City* (New York: Excelsior, 1992); and Peter Manuel, "The Soul of the Barrio: 30 Years of Salsa," *NACLA Report on the Americas* 28, no. 2 (1994): 22–29.

1. LANGSTON HUGHES'S HARLEM

30. On dance as a performative practice that contends with the possibilities and difficulties of social life, see: Danielle Goldman, *I Want to Be Ready: Improvised Dance as a Practice of Freedom* (Ann Arbor: University of Michigan Press, 2010).
31. Hughes, "Spanish Blood," 36.
32. Dellita Martin-Ogunsola, introduction to *The Collected Works of Langston Hughes*, vol. 16: *The Translations: Federico García Lorca, Nicolás Guillén, and Jacques Roumain*, ed. Dellita Martin-Ogunsola (Columbia: University of Missouri Press, 2003), 3–4.
33. Doris Sommer, ed., *Bilingual Games: Some Literary Investigations* (Basingstoke, UK: Palgrave Macmillan, 2003), 1.
34. Sommer, *Bilingual Games*, 10.
35. Naoki Sakai, *Translation and Subjectivity: On Japan and Cultural Nationalism* (Minneapolis: University of Minnesota Press, 1997), 3.
36. Sakai, *Translation and Subjectivity*, 5.
37. Hughes, "Spanish Blood," 37.
38. Hughes, "Spanish Blood," 38.
39. "Possessed" was a word that Hughes changed. In both the 1934 draft manuscript and the 1937 version that appeared in *Stag*, the line read: "Most of his friends were Spanish-speaking, so he *learned* their language as well as English," but in the 1952 collection *Laughing to Keep from Crying*, it read, as I have noted, "he *possessed* their language." The 1934 manuscript is held in box 353, folder 5709, Yale Hughes Papers; the 1937 version was published in *Stag*, July–August 1937, 9–11; and the 1952 version was published in *Laughing*, 35–45.
40. Hughes, *Big Sea*, 50.
41. Michael North makes this argument in *Dialect of Modernism: Race, Language and Twentieth-Century Literature* (Oxford: Oxford University Press, 1994), 9.
42. Hughes, "Spanish Blood," 37.
43. Michel de Certeau, *The Practice of Everyday Life* (Berkeley: University of California Press, 1934), 122.
44. Box 353, folder 5709, Yale Hughes Papers; *Stag*, July–August 1937, 9–11.
45. Hughes, "Spanish Blood," 37.
46. José Piedra, "Literary Whiteness and the Afro-Hispanic Difference," *New Literary History* 18, no. 2 (Winter 1987): 303–32.
47. This is vividly brought into presence by Lisa Lowe in *The Intimacies of Four Continents* (Durham, NC: Duke University Press, 2015).
48. Hughes, "Spanish Blood," 36.
49. This is a bit different from how other Black intellectuals and writers of the time were discussing racial and spatial matters. James Weldon Johnson, for example, offered this description: "Harlem is not merely a Negro colony or community, it is a city within a city, the greatest Negro city in the world. It is not a slum or a fringe, it is located in the heart of Manhattan and occupies one of the most beautiful and healthful sections of the city. It is not a 'quarter.'" "Harlem: The Culture Capital," in *The New Negro*, ed. Alain Locke (New York: Albert and Charles Boni, 1925), 301–11, 301.

1. LANGSTON HUGHES'S HARLEM

50. Edward Ryan, "Only for Spanish," letter to the editor, *New York Amsterdam News*, October 5, 1927.
51. Geraldine Pratt and Victoria Rosner, eds., *The Global and the Intimate: Feminism in Our Time* (New York: Columbia University Press, 2012), 2.
52. Hughes, "Spanish Blood," 38.
53. Hughes, "Spanish Blood," 38.
54. Hughes, "Spanish Blood," 42.
55. McKittrick, *Demonic Grounds*, xviii, xiii–xiv.
56. In draft fragments of *The Big Sea*, the full quote reads: "A STORY ABOUT IT.... Fantastic days, these days of prohibition, bootleggers, gangsters, rum-runners, white sight-seers in Harlem, numbers and the New Negro Renaissance. About one aspect of those days, I wrote a story called: Spanish Blood." Box 11, folder 2, CPL Hughes papers.
57. See George Chauncey, *Gay New York: Gender, Urban Culture, and the Makings of the Gay Male World, 1890–1940* (New York: Basic Books, 1994); A. B. Christa Schwarz, *Gay Voices of the Harlem Renaissance* (Bloomington: Indiana University Press, 2003); William G. Hawkeswood, *One of the Children: Gay Black Men in Harlem*, ed. Alex W. Costley (Berkeley: University of California Press, 1996); Simon Dickel, *Black/Gay: The Harlem Renaissance, the Protest Era, and Constructions of Black Gay Identity in the 1980s and 90s* (East Lansing: Michigan State University Press, 2011); James F. Wilson, *Bulldaggers, Pansies, and Chocolate Babies: Performance, Race, and Sexuality in the Harlem Renaissance* (Ann Arbor: University of Michigan Press, 2010); Shane Vogel, *The Scene of Harlem Cabaret: Race, Sexuality, Performance* (Chicago: University of Chicago Press, 2009); and Hugh Ryan, *When Brooklyn Was Queer* (New York: St. Martin's Press, 2019).
58. Fiona Ngô, *Imperial Blues: Geographies of Race and Sex in Jazz Age New York* (Durham, NC: Duke University Press, 2014).
59. Shane Vogel, "Closing Time: Langston Hughes and the Queer Poetics of Harlem Nightlife," *Criticism* 48, no. 3 (Summer 2006): 397–425.
60. Claude McKay, *Home to Harlem* (New York: Harper and Brothers 1928); and *Fire!!: A Quarterly Devoted to the Younger Negro Artists* (Westport, CT: Negro Universities Press, 1970 [1926]).
61. Hughes, "Spanish Blood," 42. Gary Edward Holcomb, in "Langston Unashamed: Radical Mythmaking in Hughes's 1930s Short Fiction," *MFS Modern Fiction Studies* 61, no. 3 (Fall 2013): 423–45, makes an argument for seeing Hughes's short fiction of the 1930s as advancing certain radical socialist themes such as internationalism. He focuses on stories that are more explicitly international, but the perspective is helpful, I suggest, for understanding what Hughes is working out in "Spanish Blood."
62. Nella Larsen, *Passing* (New York: Alfred A. Knopf, 1929).
63. Hughes, "Spanish Blood," 38.
64. GerShun Avilez, in *Black Queer Freedom: Spaces of Injury and Paths of Desire* (Urbana-Champaign: University of Illinois Press, 2020), writes about queer Black bodies in "spaces of injury," linking desire and vulnerability.
65. Hughes, "Spanish Blood," 44–45.

1. LANGSTON HUGHES'S HARLEM

66. Hughes, "Spanish Blood," 40.
67. Hughes, "Spanish Blood," 42.
68. James Edward Smethurst, in *The New Red Negro: The Literary Left and African American Poetry 1930–1946* (Oxford: Oxford University Press, 1999), argues that in other works, particularly in his poems of the 1930s, Hughes develops a layered urban sensibility shaped by leftist politics.
69. This appears in *Stag*, July–August 1937, 11. The same language is in the manuscript in the Yale Hughes Papers, which is the final draft for the 1934 *Metropolis* print publication.
70. Edwards, *Practice of Diaspora*.
71. Hughes, "Spanish Blood," 45.
72. Zita Nunes, "The New Negro and the Turn to South America," chapter 4 in *Cannibal Democracy: Race and Representation in the Literature of the Americas* (Minneapolis: University of Minnesota Press, 2008), 115–44.
73. Juliana Góes, "Du Bois and Brazil: Reflections on Black Transnationalism and African Diasporas," *Du Bois Review: Social Science Research on Race* 19, no. 2 (Fall 2022): 293–308.
74. Langston Hughes, "The Negro Artist and the Racial Mountain," *Nation*, June 23, 1926, 694.
75. Chinitz, in *Which Sin to Bear?*, argues that Hughes was deeply concerned with questions of racial authenticity, but also had an expansive notion of what that meant, a "fluid notion of community" (5).
76. Quoted in Rampersad, *Life of Langston Hughes*, 1:40.
77. Hughes, *Big Sea*, 55.
78. Hughes, *Big Sea*, 40.
79. Racial passing, of course, was central to how so many Black writers were contemplating the boundaries of race: see Larsen, *Passing*; James Weldon Johnson, *The Autobiography of an Ex-Colored Man* (Boston: Sherman, French, 1912). For further critical treatment of the issue, see Allyson Hobbs, *A Chosen Exile: A History of Racial Passing in American Life* (Cambridge, MA: Harvard University Press, 2014); and Gayle Wald, *Crossing the Line: Racial Passing in Twentieth-Century U.S. Literature and Culture* (Durham, NC: Duke University Press, 2000).
80. Hughes, *Big Sea*, 50.
81. Mark Golub, "*Plessy* as 'Passing': Judicial Responses to Ambiguously Raced Bodies in *Plessy v Ferguson*," *Law and Society Review* 39, no. 3 (September 2005): 563–600.
82. "Riot Between Porto Ricans and Jews in Harlem Is Prevented by the Police," *Jewish Daily Bulletin*, July 28, 1926, 3.
83. "La zona puertorriqueña de la 110 a la 116, teatro de intense perturbación," *La Prensa*, July 28, 1926; "Los desórdenes de la calle 116," *La Prensa*, July 29, 1926. Lorrin Thomas provides a nuanced discussion of the Puerto Rican responses in *Puerto Rican Citizen: History and Political Identity in Twentieth-Century New York City* (Chicago: University of Chicago Press), 49–55.

1. LANGSTON HUGHES'S HARLEM

84. "Police Quell Riot Against Porto Ricans," *New York Amsterdam News*, July 28, 1926, 3. Testifying to the layers of transition, a Puerto Rican migrant writes about this period: "At that time the Jews who had concentrated there began to move out to better neighborhoods. The apartments they left behind were in good condition, and growing numbers of Puerto Ricans moved into them." *Memoirs of Bernardo Vega: A Contribution to the History of the Puerto Rican Community in New York*, ed. César Andreu Iglesias, trans. Juan Flores (New York: Monthly Review Press, 1984), 9.
85. "Harlem is Stirred by Riots," *Pittsburgh Courier*, July 31, 1926, 1.
86. "Colored Boy Steals Candy, Precipitates Fierce Harlem Riot," *Chicago Daily Tribune*, March 20, 1935, 2; "Police Shoot Rioters, Kill Negro in Harlem Mob," *New York Times*, March 20, 1935, 1.
87. Thomas, *Puerto Rican Citizen*, 75–83.
88. *The Complete Report of Mayor LaGuardia's Commission of the Harlem Riot of March 19, 1935* (New York: Arno Press, 1969; reproduced from *New York Amsterdam News*, July 18, 1936), 77. For that matter, when writing about the riot, Alain Locke does not mention Rivera's ethnicity either; see Locke, "Harlem: Dark Weather-Vane," *Survey Graphic* 25 (August 1936): 457–62, 493–95.
89. Claude McKay, *Harlem: Negro Metropolis* (New York: E. P. Dutton, 1940; New York: Harcourt Brace Jovanovich, 1968), 207.
90. Vega, *Memoirs of Bernardo Vega*, 180. Originally published as *Memoiras de Bernardo Vega: contribución a la historia de la comunidad puertorriqueña en Nueva York* (San Juan, PR: Ediciones Huracán, 1977). Vega did get the first name of Rivera wrong, however, referring to him as Leon instead of Lino.
91. Hughes, "Spanish Blood," 35.
92. James Weldon Johnson, ed., *The Book of American Negro Poetry* (New York: Harcourt, Brace, and World, 1959), 232–34.
93. Arnold Rampersad, introduction to *The Short Stories of Langston Hughes*, ed. Akiba Sullivan Harper (New York: Hill and Wang, 1996), xix.
94. Hughes himself dictated an attention to the autobiographical self when he reflected in 1945 on stories he had written with the fictional protagonist Simple: "It is just myself talking to me. Or else me talking to myself. That has been going on for a number of years, and in my writing, has taken one form or another from poetry to prose, song lyrics to radio, newspapers columns to books." "Simple and Me," *Phylon* 6, no. 4 (1945): 349–53, 349.
95. Anton Chekhov identifies the failure to resolve as a characteristic of the short story in the 1880 piece "Elements Most Often Found in Novels, Short Stories, Etc.," trans. Peter Constantine, *Harper's Magazine*, November 1997.
96. William Hogan, in "Roots, Routes, and Langston Hughes's Hybrid Sense of Place," *The Langston Hughes Review* 18 (Spring 2004): 3–23, discusses the Harlem that Hughes experienced as a "cultural crossroads, a place in the process of becoming, rather than as an established neighborhood with a fixed identity" (14). Though Hogan is concerned

1. LANGSTON HUGHES'S HARLEM

with the blendings of "north" and "south" in Harlem, and the connections across sites of the Black diaspora, his points relate to the way Hughes saw Harlem as open and diverse are similar to my approach in this essay. On the subject of Langston Hughes's rendering of place, see James de Jongh, "The Poet Speaks of Places: A Close Reading of Langston Hughes's Literary Use of Place," in *A Historical Guide to Langston Hughes*, ed. Steven Carl Tracy (Oxford: Oxford University Press 2004), 65–84.

97. Langston Hughes to Charlotte Mason, February 23, 1929, in *Selected Letters of Langston Hughes*, ed. Arnold Rampersad and David Roessel (New York: Alfred A. Knopf, 2015), 83.
98. Hughes to Mason, *Selected Letters*, 84.
99. "Interview of Ramona Bass," *Hughes' Dream Harlem*, directed by Jamal Joseph (2002), on YouTube, https://www.youtube.com/watch?v=OxMr46IUlDk&ab_channel=New HeritageTheatreGroup.
100. *Metropolis*, December 29, 1934; *Modern Story*, October 1935; *Stag*, July–August 1937, 9–11.
101. Lothrop Stoddard, *The Rising Tide of Color Against White World Supremacy* (New York: Charles Scribner's Sons, 1920); Franz Boas, "The Instability of Human Types," in *A Franz Boas Reader: The Shaping of American Anthropology, 1883–1911*, ed. George W. Stocking Jr. (Chicago: University of Chicago Press, 1974), 214–18.
102. Mikhail Bakhtin, *The Dialogical Imagination: Four Essays*, ed. Michael Holquist, trans. Caryl Emerson and Michael Holquist (Austin: University of Texas Press, 1981), 254.
103. Langston Hughes, "Little Old Spy," in *Laughing to Keep from Crying*, 163.
104. Langston Hughes, "Powder-White Faces," in *Laughing to Keep from Crying*, 113.
105. Earl Lewis, "To Turn as on a Pivot: Writing African Americans Into a History of Overlapping Diasporas," *American Historical Review* 100 (1995): 786–87, makes a good case for "overlapping diasporas." That formation is made especially vivid in tales about African American–Puerto Rican mixture or links between Latin Americans (who may or may not have been "Black") and light- and/or dark-skinned Cubans.
106. William H. Banks, Jr. ed., *Beloved Harlem: A Literary Tribute to Black America's Most Famous Neighborhood, from the Classics to the Contemporary* (New York: Broadway Books, 2005).
107. Banks, *Beloved Harlem*, xvii.
108. In a short explanatory note that introduces the story, Banks wrote: "'Spanish Blood' is a story set in East Harlem in the 1950s." Banks, *Beloved Harlem*, 206.
109. Kevin Lynch, *What Time Is This Place?* (Cambridge, MA: MIT Press, 1972).
110. Hughes, *I Wonder as I Wander*, 323.
111. Hughes, *I Wonder as I Wander*, 323.
112. In the essay "The Changing Same (R&B and New Black Music)," Amiri Baraka proposed this now-famous notion of the "changing same" of Black music and consciousness to highlight internal variation and continual adaptation. *Black Music* (New York: Da Capo, 1968), 180–211. Many theorists since then have drawn on this idea, including Paul Gilroy for the cultures of diaspora, in *The Black Atlantic: Modernity and Double Consciousness* (Cambridge, MA: Harvard University Press, 1993), and Fred Moten to discuss

1. LANGSTON HUGHES'S HARLEM

performance and improvisation, in *In the Break: The Aesthetics of the Black Radical Tradition* (Minneapolis: University of Minnesota Press, 2003).

113. As Guillén wrote in "El Camino de Harlem," "Hay que colocarse, pues, en el verdadero lugar en que nos han colocado; observar si ese es el que nos corresponde, por nuestra historia y por nuestro progreso. / We have to locate ourselves in the true site in which we are located; observing if that is the one that pertains to our history and our progress" (4). "El Camino de Harlem," *Diario de la Marina*, April 21, 1929, rpt. in *Nicolás Guillén: Prose de Prisa*, vol. 2 (Havana: Editorial Arte y Literature, 1975), 3–6. Later in the essay he specifically advises against any spatial containment of Blackness in a "*barrio negro*" like that of Harlem.

114. A number of works have problematized the exchange between Hughes and Guillén. See Vera Kutzinski, "Fearful Asymmetries: Langston Hughes, Nicolás Guillén, and 'Cuba Libre.'" *Diacritics* 34, no. 3–4 (2004): 112–42; John Patrick Leary, "Havana Reads the Harlem Renaissance: Langston Hughes, Nicolás Guillén, and the Dialectics of Transnational American Literature," *Comparative Literature Studies* 47, no. 2 (2010): 133–58; and Monika Kaup, "'Our America' That Is Not One: Transnational Black Atlantic Disclosures in Nicolás Guillén and Langston Hughes," *Discourse* 22, no. 3 (2000): 87–113.

115. Langston Hughes, *The Weary Blues* (New York: Alfred A. Knopf, 1926).

116. Langston Hughes and Arna Bontemps, *Popo and Fifina: Children of Haiti* (New York: Macmillan, 1932); Arna Bontemps and Langston Hughes, *Boy of the Border* (El Paso, TX: Sweet Earth Flying, 2009); Langston Hughes, Arna Bontemps, and Cheryl A. Wall, *The Pasteboard Bandit* (Oxford: Oxford University Press, 1997); Nancy Kang, review of *Boy of the Border* by Arna Bontemps and Langston Hughes, *Callaloo* 38, no. 2 (Spring 2015): 398–401.

117. Katharine Capshaw Smith, *Children's Literature of the Harlem Renaissance* (Bloomington: Indiana University Press, 2004), 235.

118. Langston Hughes, "My Early Days in Harlem," *Freedomways* 3, no. 3 (Summer 1963): 312–14, 314.

119. Langston Hughes, "The Harlem Riot—1964," in *Harlem: A Community in Transition*, ed. John Henrik Clarke (New York: Citadel Press, 1964), 214–20, 220.

120. Notably, the volume *Harlem: A Community in Transition* ends with this essay and these lines from Hughes.

121. Hughes, *Montage of a Dream Deferred*.

122. James De Jongh, *Vicious Modernism: Black Harlem and the Literary Imagination* (Cambridge, UK: Cambridge University Press, 1990); Bartholomew Brinkman, "Movies, Modernity, and All that Jazz: Langston Hughes's 'Montage of a Dream Deferred,'" *African American Review* 44, no. 1–2 (Spring/Summer 2011): 85–96; Günter H. Lenz, "'The Riffs, Runs, Breaks, and Distortions of the Music of a Community in Transition': Redefining African American Modernism and the Jazz Aesthetic in Langston Hughes' *Montage of a Dream Deferred* and *Ask Your Mama*," *Massachusetts Review* 44, no. 1–2 (Spring/Summer 2003): 269–82; Robert O'Brien, "Jazzing It Up: The Be-Bop Modernism of Langston Hughes," *Mosaic* 31, no. 4 (December 1998): 61–82; Jean-Phillipe Marcoux,

1. LANGSTON HUGHES'S HARLEM

"'Blues Connotation': Bebop Jazz and Free Jazz as Idioms Expressive of African American Culture in Montage of a Dream Deferred and Ask Your Mama," *Langston Hughes Review* 21 (Fall 2007): 12–29; David R. Jarraway, "Montage of an Otherness Deferred: Dreaming Subjectivity in Langston Hughes," *American Literature* 68, no. 4 (December 1996): 819–47.

123. Hughes, *Montage of a Dream Deferred*, 21.
124. Hughes, *Montage of a Dream Deferred*, 69.
125. Hughes, *Montage of a Dream Deferred*, 66.
126. Hughes, *Montage of a Dream Deferred*, 71–72. Reprinted by permission from the Langston Hughes Estate.
127. Hughes, *Montage of a Dream Deferred*, 66–65. Reprinted by permission from the Langston Hughes Estate.
128. Hughes, *Montage of a Dream Deferred*, 75. Reprinted by permission from the Langston Hughes Estate.

2. MAPPING PLACE

1. Claude McKay, *Harlem: Negro Metropolis* (New York: E. P. Dutton, 1940), 20.
2. A range of scholars in fields across the humanities and social sciences have stressed that an attention to movement is crucial to any project to map a space, including: Denis Cosgrove, ed., *Mappings* (London: Reaktion Books, 1999); Tim Ingold, *Being Alive: Essays on Movement, Knowledge and Description* (Oxford: Routledge, 2011).
3. Michel de Certeau's formulation, to which I drew attention in the introduction of this book ("what the map cuts up, the story cuts across"), is repositioned here, to go the other way, from story to map. Michel de Certeau, *The Practice of Everyday Life* (Berkeley: University of California Press, 1980), 129.
4. I distinguish my work on *Harlem: Negro Metropolis* from other recent projects that have brought McKay's unknown works to public attention. In 2009, Jean-Christophe Cloutier discovered a manuscript for the novel *Amiable with Big Teeth: A Novel of the Love Affair Between the Communists and the Poor Black Sheep of Harlem* in a minor archive. (It was eventually published under that title, edited and introduced by Cloutier with Brent Hayes Edwards, in 2017 by Penguin Random House.) And McKay's novel *Romance in Marseille*, ed. Gary Edward Holcomb and William J. Maxwell, was published by Penguin Random House in 2020; there were two manuscripts in the archives of the Beinecke and Schomburg libraries, but the novel had not been widely accessible to readers before Holcomb's and Maxwell's effort.
5. Jean-Christophe Cloutier has given sustained attention to *Harlem: Negro Metropolis* in his *Shadow Archives: The Lifecycles of African American Literature* (New York: Columbia University Press, 2019).
6. See Winston James's important work *Claude McKay: The Making of a Black Bolshevik* (New York: Columbia University Press, 2022). James identifies formative political

2. MAPPING PLACE

influences for McKay in Jamaica. While I do not disagree with the basic premise, I do want to raise the question of how an immersion in Harlem and its imaginaries developed in him a particular kind of politics of Blackness.

7. Claude McKay, *Home to Harlem* (New York: Harper and Brothers, 1928; Boston: Northeastern University Press, 1987); *Banjo: A Story Without a Plot* (New York: Harper and Brothers, 1929); and *Amiable with Big Teeth: A Novel of the Love Affair Between the Communists and the Poor Black Sheep of Harlem* (New York: Penguin Random House, 2020).
8. Claude McKay, *Banana Bottom* (New York: Harper and Brothers, 1933).
9. Here we might think of how Toni Morrison wrote that "the crucial distinction for me is not the difference between fact and fiction, but the distinction between fact and truth." "The Site of Memory," in *Inventing the Truth: The Art and Craft of Memoir*, ed. William Zinsser (Boston: Houghton Mifflin, 1995), 83–102, 93.
10. Claude McKay, *The Negroes in America*, trans. from Russian by Robert J. Winter, ed. Alan L. McLeod (Port Washington, NY: Kennikat Press, 1979 [1923]). Across chapters entitled "Labor Leaders and Negroes," "Negroes in Art and Music," and "Sex and Economics," McKay makes no mention of Harlem. These were early years in which the impact of the Harlem Renaissance might not yet have been understood by McKay, but the absence of an already concentrated space of settlement for Black Americans is still notable. A particular political agenda and perceived audience obviously shaped the conception and writing of this text.
11. Alain Locke, "The New Negro," in *The New Negro: Voices from the Harlem Renaissance*, ed. Alain Locke (New York: Albert and Charles Boni, 1925), 6–7.
12. Wallace Thurman, "Negro Life in New York's Harlem: A Lively Picture of a Popular and Interesting Section," in *Collected Writings of Wallace Thurman: A Harlem Renaissance Reader*, ed. Amritjit Singh and Daniel M. Scott III (New Brunswick, NJ: Rutgers University Press, 2003), 44. The essay originally appeared as a 1927 pamphlet in the Little Blue Books series published by socialist Emanuel Haldeman-Julius in a press he ran in Kansas.
13. W. E. B. Du Bois, "Two Novels: Nella Larsen, *Quicksand* & Claude McKay, *Home to Harlem*," *Crisis* 35, no. 6 (June 1928): 35, 102.
14. Cheryl Lynn Greenberg, *Or Does It Explode? Black Harlem in the Great Depression* (Oxford: Oxford University Press, 1997).
15. A prominent biographer of McKay, Wayne F. Cooper, outlines this argument in *Claude McKay: Rebel Sojourner in the Harlem Renaissance: A Biography* (Baton Rouge: Louisiana State University Press, 1987), especially chapter 11, "Looking Forward: The Search for Community, 1937–1940."
16. Biographical details from Cooper, *Claude McKay*.
17. Ambivalences about nationality persisted through McKay's life. In 1940 he became a citizen of the United States and at times wrote positively about its social arrangements even while continuing to explore the pulls of other places. See Claude McKay, "For Group Survival," *Jewish Frontier*, October 1937, 19–26. J. Dillon Brown discusses McKay's complex relationship to America in "Escaping the Tropics through New York: Eric

Walrond and Claude McKay in the American Grain," *Global South* 7, no. 2 (Fall 2013): 37–61.
18. Claude McKay, *Long Way from Home*, ed. Gene Andrew Jarrett (New Brunswick, NJ: Rutgers University Press, 2007), 231.
19. Claude McKay, "McKay Says Schuyler Is Writing Nonsense," *New York Amsterdam News*, November 20, 1937.
20. The period in which McKay was writing his autobiography, published in 1937, must at least partly overlap with the one when he was mulling over the material that he would develop into the 1940 *Harlem: Negro Metropolis*.
21. Claude McKay, review of *Home to Harlem* in James Clarke, ed., "Significant Books Reviewed by Their Own Authors," *McClure's*, June 1928, 81; quoted in Cooper, *Claude McKay*, 71–72.
22. McKay, *Long Way from Home*, 247.
23. Caroline Levine's interpretation of the multiplicity of forms coming together for social and political meaning in *Forms: Whole, Rhythm, Hierarchy, Network* (Princeton: Princeton University Press, 2015) has been influential for this line of argument, but I think that the weight of her discussion still lies in the sphere of the literary, with works of nonfiction at the edges. In a later piece, "Not Against Structure, but in Search of Better Structures," *American Literary History* 31, no. 2 (2019): 255–59, Levine writes: "I do not imagine a special role for the aesthetic . . . it seems to me that many ethnographic sociologies . . . also offer convincing accounts of multiple social forms. These, too, like *Bleak House*, are multiplot narratives with many characters interacting with overlapping institutions" (259). This comes at the end of the essay, almost as an aside, after she has discussed *Bleak House* and *The Wire*, the kinds of texts that literary and cultural critics are more comfortable discussing. Still, the reading of *Harlem: Negro Metropolis* that I am undertaking here should, I hope, realize the ambition to see a different kind of work, a nonfictional one, as holding the "multiple social forms" in which Levine is interested.
24. McKay was quite attentive to the visual: as I will discuss later, his texts brought to life the vivid and varied colors of peoples. It is also the case that he lived in a time of exchange between visual artists and writers who sought to represent Blackness. Cooper suggests that McKay was well-acquainted with, even adjacent to Jacob Lawrence and Romare Bearden; in fact, his West 125th Street apartment was across the hall from Bearden's studio. See Cooper, *Claude McKay*, 338, 349.
25. In the column "Backdoor Stuff" by Dan Burley, there is mention of McKay and Lewis facing a lawsuit for Lewis failing to gain permission from two men of whom he had taken a photo for the cover of *Harlem: Negro Metropolis*; it seems that this was later dropped. See *New York Amsterdam News*, November 30, 1940; and Bill Chase, "All Ears," *New York Amsterdam News*, December 7, 1940.
26. *Life in Harlem: A Documentary Film of America's Negro Metropolis*, produced by Edward W. Lewis (1940). Thanks to the Smithsonian National Museum of African American History and Culture for making a digital copy of this film available to me. Pearl Bowser discusses Lewis in "Pioneers of Black Documentary Film," in *Struggles for*

2. MAPPING PLACE

Representation: African American Documentary Film and Video, ed. Phyllis R. Klotman and Janet K. Cutler (Bloomington: Indiana University Press, 1994), 1–33. The exchange between McKay and Lewis recalls Sara Blair's discussion of close relationships between Black writers and photographers in *Harlem Crossroads: Black Writers and the Photograph in the Twentieth Century* (Princeton: Princeton University Press, 2007), particularly between Edwin Rosskam and Richard Wright for the photodocumentary work *12 Million Voices: A Folk History of the Negro in the United States* (New York: Viking Press, 1941). On the one hand, there is the undeniable dialogue between Wright and McKay specifically, and on the other, a more general set of influences for both writers, of the New Deal to document the life of poor and Black peoples; see Michael Denning, *The Cultural Front: The Laboring of American Culture in the Twentieth Century* (London: Verso, 1997); Jason Puskar, "Black and White and Read All Over: Photography and the Voices of Richard Wright," *Mosaic: an Interdisciplinary Critical Journal* 49, no. 2 (June 2016): 167–83; Lawrence P. Jackson, *The Indignant Generation: A Narrative History of African American Writers and Critics, 1934–1960* (Princeton: Princeton University Press, 2011).

27. Zora Neale Hurston, review of *Dusk of Dawn* and *Harlem: Negro Metropolis*, by Claude McKay, *Common Ground* 1, no. 2 (Winter 1941): 95–96, 95.
28. McKay, *Harlem: Negro Metropolis*, 15.
29. McKay, *Harlem: Negro Metropolis*, 16.
30. McKay, *Harlem: Negro Metropolis*, 21.
31. In the following chapter of this book I note how Vito Marcantonio mobilized "the slum" for popular and political effect.
32. Michael Keith, *After the Cosmopolitan? Multicultural Cities and the Future of Racism* (New York: Routledge, 2005), 10.
33. McKay, *Harlem: Negro Metropolis*, 22.
34. McKay, *Harlem: Negro Metropolis*, 29.
35. See Sandhya Shukla, "Little Indias, Places for Indian Diasporas," chap. 2 in *India Abroad: Diasporic Cultures of Postwar America and England* (Princeton: Princeton University Press, 2003).
36. McKay, *Harlem: Negro Metropolis*, 132.
37. McKay, *Harlem: Negro Metropolis*, 133.
38. McKay, *Harlem: Negro Metropolis*, 135.
39. McKay, *Harlem: Negro Metropolis*, 136.
40. McKay, *Harlem: Negro Metropolis*, 109.
41. By the time McKay was writing, "black belt" was also used for Black-majority areas populated by migrants from the U.S. South: Ernest W. Burgess referred to the "Black Belt, with its free and disorderly life" in his essay "The Growth of the City," in Robert E. Park, Ernest W. Burgess, and Roderick D. McKenzie, *The City* (Chicago: University of Chicago Press, 1925), 56. I would argue that the term still retained connotations to Southern plantation labor. For a discussion of these issues, see Allen Tullos, "The Black Belt," *Southern Spaces*, April 19, 2004, https://southernspaces.org/2004/black-belt/.
42. McKay, *Harlem: Negro Metropolis*, 135.

2. MAPPING PLACE

43. McKay, *Harlem: Negro Metropolis*, 137.
44. McKay, *Harlem: Negro Metropolis*, 137–38.
45. McKay, *Harlem: Negro Metropolis*, 29.
46. Hurston, review, 95. For Hurston, this quality of McKay's "achieves proportion," which I would take to mean balance and distance from the perspectives from within Harlem.
47. McKay, *Banana Bottom*, 4–5.
48. McKay, *Harlem: Negro Metropolis*, 29.
49. McKay, *Long Way from Home*, 109.
50. McKay, *Harlem: Negro Metropolis*, 29.
51. McKay, *Harlem: Negro Metropolis*, 30.
52. McKay, *Harlem: Negro Metropolis*, 30.
53. McKay, *Harlem: Negro Metropolis*, 30.
54. McKay, *Harlem: Negro Metropolis*, 31.
55. The unnumbered chapters of *Harlem: Negro Metropolis* are titled: "Harlem Vista," "The Negro Quarter Grows Up," "God in Harlem: Father Divine, 1935 A.D.F.D.," "The Occultists," "The Cultists," "Harlem Businessman," "The Business of Numbers," "The Business of Amusements," "Harlem Politician," "Marcus Aurelius Garvey," and "Sufi Abdul Hamid and Organized Labor."
56. For an important genealogy of the idea and its associations, see Svetlana Boym, "Theoretical Common Places," introduction to *Common Places: Mythologies of Everyday Life in Russia* (Cambridge, MA: Harvard University Press, 1994), 1–28.
57. Boym, *Common Places*, 19. Seanne Sumalee Oakley writes in *Common Places: The Poetics of African Atlantic Postromantics* (Amsterdam: Rodopi, 2011) that the differential common place "represents intrinsic intimacy and mutual relevancy within the diverse even as it relays difference" (2).
58. It is worth pointing out that women made up a large section of Father Divine's followers, while Garvey's movement was mostly male; see Beryl Satter, "Marcus Garvey, Father Divine and the Gender Politics of Race Difference and Race Neutrality," *American Quarterly* 48, no. 1 (March 1996): 43–76.
59. Robert Weisbrot, *Father Divine and the Struggle for Racial Equality* (Urbana: University of Illinois Press, 1983) and Jill Watts, *God, Harlem, USA: The Father Divine Story* (Berkeley: University of California Press, 1992) are the two major works on Father Divine. Watts, in particular, resists terming the Peace Mission Movement a cult, and takes seriously its religious content. As his book's title indicates, Weisbrot is interested in Father Divine as a kind of Civil Rights leader. Danielle Brune Sigler, in "Beyond the Binary: Revisiting Father Divine, Daddy Grace, and Their Ministries," in *Race, Nation, and Religion in the Americas*, ed. Henry Goldschmidt and Elizabeth McAlister (New York: Oxford University Press, 2004), 209–28, focuses on the tension between Father Divine's putatively "non-racial" self-identification and his undeniable (physically palpable) Blackness.
60. McKay began writing about Father Divine in the mid-1930s, with an article entitled "'There Goes God!': The Story of Father Divine and His Angels," *The Nation*, February 6, 1935, 151–53.

2. MAPPING PLACE

61. McKay, *Harlem: Negro Metropolis*, 39.
62. McKay, *Harlem: Negro Metropolis*, 39–40. The narration of *Home to Harlem* reads: "The broad pavements of Seventh Avenue were colorful with promenaders. Brown babies in white carriages pushed by little black brothers.... All the various and varying pigmentation of the human race were assembled there: dim brown, clear brown, rich brown, chestnut, copper, yellow, near white, mahogany, and gleaming anthracite.... And the elegant strutters in faultless spats; West Indians, carrying canes and wearing trousers of a different pattern from their coats and vests, drawing sharp comments from their Afro-Yank rivals." On the heels of this description, McKay writes: "Jake mentally noted: 'A dickty gang sure as Harlem is black, but—'" (289–90).
63. McKay's notebook contained a number of quotes on a page labeled on the top "Testimony," and then, further down, "Sunday: Rockland," which seems to concern an interview he did with Father Divine. See Claude McKay, Notebook, n.d., box 11, folder 338, Claude McKay Collection, Yale Collection of American Literature, Beinecke Rare Book and Manuscript Library (hereafter cited as McKay Collection).
64. McKay, *Harlem: Negro Metropolis*, 45.
65. McKay, *Harlem: Negro Metropolis*, 44.
66. McKay, *Harlem: Negro Metropolis*, 61, 69.
67. McKay, *Harlem: Negro Metropolis*, 74, 75.
68. McKay, *Harlem: Negro Metropolis*, 75.
69. McKay, *Harlem: Negro Metropolis*, 77.
70. McKay, *Harlem: Negro Metropolis*, 79.
71. McKay, *Harlem: Negro Metropolis*, 81.
72. See my discussion of these two sites in the introduction of this book.
73. McKay, *Harlem: Negro Metropolis*, 93.
74. McKay, *Harlem: Negro Metropolis*, 107.
75. McKay, *Harlem: Negro Metropolis*, 109.
76. McKay, *Harlem: Negro Metropolis*, 118.
77. McKay, *Harlem: Negro Metropolis*, 143.
78. McKay, *Harlem: Negro Metropolis*, 152.
79. McKay, *Harlem: Negro Metropolis*, 150.
80. McKay, *Harlem: Negro Metropolis*, 154.
81. McKay, *Harlem: Negro Metropolis*, 172.
82. McKay, *Harlem: Negro Metropolis*, 179.
83. McKay, *Harlem: Negro Metropolis*, 185.
84. McKay, *Harlem: Negro Metropolis*, 203.
85. McKay, *Harlem: Negro Metropolis*, 188.
86. Joel Nickels discusses the complex dialogue between McKay's political cosmopolitanism and racial nationalism in "Claude McKay and Dissident Internationalism," *Cultural Critique* 87 (2014): 1–37, as do Brent Hayes Edwards in *The Practice of Diaspora: Literature, Translation and the Rise of Black Internationalism* (Cambridge, MA: Harvard University Press, 2003) and Michelle Ann Stephens in *Black Empire: The Masculine Global*

2. MAPPING PLACE

Imaginary of Caribbean Intellectuals in the United States, 1914–1962 (Durham, NC: Duke University Press, 2005).

87. For the period beginning in the late 1800s until before World War II, there were, as historian Jeffrey S. Gurock notes, two Jewish Harlems, one east and one central/west, distinguished by class and ethnic origin, with the Jews in west Harlem largely German and middle-class, and on the east with more eastern European working-class peoples. Gurock's *The Jews of Harlem: The Rise, Decline and Revival of a Jewish Community* (New York: New York University Press, 2016) is the most recent work on this subject, an updating and expansion of an earlier book, *When Harlem Was Jewish* (New York: Columbia University Press, 1979).

88. "Jews and Negroes," *New York Amsterdam News*, February 14, 1923. Ambient stresses of the time—in which a majority of whites in Central Harlem were Jewish and African American populations were sorting through what cultural ownership of place meant vis-à-vis artistic and other movements and vis-à-vis national Black–white dynamics—were expressed in many kinds of conflictual encounters. One small but telling piece, "Resented Insult of Delicatessen Dealer," *New York Amsterdam News*, December 16, 1925, describes the claims of African American Sadie Powell that Ester Solomon, a Jewish woman, used a racial slur in response to her complaint about being shorted for an order of cheese, Solomon's accusation that Powell had punched her in the nose, and then the police's charge of a violation of the Sabbath law, with Powell as witness. The case was subsequently dismissed, but the reporting of this incident by the *Amsterdam News* reflects a keen interest in the contours of Black–Jewish relations and the specter of anti-Black racism within that field, as well as a growing awareness of the economic tensions of the place.

89. "Locke Compares Negroes and Jews," *New York Amsterdam News*, January 12, 1927.

90. "Horowitz Asks Truce of Negroes and Jews," *New York Times*, August 22, 1939.

91. McKay's personal papers are full of notes about the topic. In just one illustration, he transcribes an entire letter to the editor of the *Amsterdam News* from a Jewish man complaining about Black anti-Semitism among Garvey supporters. Claude McKay, "Transcription of letter printed in *Amsterdam News*," August 11, 1931 [*sic*], box 11, folder 338, McKay Collection. Original letter: Joseph Kirchner, "Offers Protest: A Jewish Reader Objects to Speaker's Remarks in Street; Cites Instances to Prove Error," *New York Amsterdam News*, August 19, 1931. The letter ends with: "I think that the average colored person knows that the Jew has always been his friend; has always helped him in every way. The same people who hate the Negro hate the Jew—and this applies to that woman from the West Indies who hates her own as well as my people" (8).

92. McKay, *Harlem: Negro Metropolis*, 200. McKay elaborated on these arguments in "Everybody's Doing It: Anti-Semitic Propaganda Fails to Attract Negroes: Harlemites Face Problems of All Other Slum Dwellers," *New Leader*, May 20, 1939; in that broadly anti-Communist publication as well as in the more progressive *New Republic*, he and Ted Poston, a Black journalist, debated McKay's assertion that Sufi was not anti-Semitic. See Claude McKay, "Claude McKay Replies to Poston on Solution of Negro Problems,"

2. MAPPING PLACE

New Leader, December 7, 1940; Ted Poston, "Harlem: Claude McKay's Book Sees Negroes' 'Way Out' in Economic Segregation," review of *Harlem: Negro Metropolis*, by Claude McKay, *New Leader*, November 23, 1940; and Ted Poston, "A Book on Harlem," review of *Harlem: Negro Metropolis*, by Claude McKay, *New Republic*, November 25, 1940, 732. McKay and Poston subsequently exchanged letters in "Correspondence," *New Republic*, January 27, 1941, 118–19, on the representation of anti-Semitism and segregation in *Harlem: Negro Metropolis*.

93. McKay, *Harlem: Negro Metropolis*, 207.
94. McKay, *Harlem: Negro Metropolis*, 208. Only eight years later, James Baldwin would discuss Black–Jewish relations in an important essay, "The Harlem Ghetto: Winter 1948," From the American Scene, *Commentary*, February 1948, https://www.commentary.org/articles/james-baldwin/from-the-american-scene-the-harlem-ghetto-winter-1948/.
95. McKay, *Harlem: Negro Metropolis*, 210.
96. McKay, "For Group Survival," 19–26.
97. McKay, *Harlem: Negro Metropolis*, 179.
98. The language that James Weldon Johnson uses to open his work on Harlem is noteworthy: "It strikes the uninformed observer *as a phenomenon*, a miracle straight out of the skies." *Black Manhattan* (New York: Alfred A. Knopf, 1930; New York: Da Capo, 1991), 4, my emphasis.
99. Johnson, *Black Manhattan*, 3–4.
100. See Michael Nowlin, "James Weldon Johnson's 'Black Manhattan' and the Kingdom of American Culture," *African American Review* 39, no. 3 (Fall 2005): 315–25.
101. Marcel Aurousseau, "Recent Contributions to Urban Geography: A Review," *Geographical Review* 14, no. 3 (July 1924): 444–55.
102. Park, Burgess, and McKenzie, *City*, 1.
103. Park, Burgess, and McKenzie, *City*, 3.
104. A few years before *Harlem: Negro Metropolis* came out, E. Franklin Frazier had published a piece on Harlem, "Negro Harlem: An Ecological Study," *American Journal of Sociology* 43, no. 1 (July 1937): 72–88, which focused entirely on empirical factors such as population characteristics and settlement, certainly without the kind of subjective inclinations that McKay's writing demonstrated.
105. Park, Burgess, and McKenzie, *City*, 153.
106. See Emory S. Bogardus, *Immigration and Race Attitudes* (Boston: D. C. Heath, 1928), as well as a more philosophically oriented work by Horace M. Kallen, *Culture and Democracy in the United States* (New York: Boni and Liveright, 1924).
107. St. Clair Drake and Horace R. Cayton, *Black Metropolis: A Study of Negro Life in a Northern City* (New York: Harcourt, Brace, 1945). Interestingly, Richard Wright wrote the introduction to *Black Metropolis*.
108. *New York Panorama: A Comprehensive View of the Metropolis, Presented in a Series of Articles Prepared by the Federal Writers' Project of the Works Progress Administration in New York City* (New York: Random House, 1938) assembles essays on a wide and curious array of topics. The essay by Wright and McKay appears on pages 132–51. The "guide book" does

2. MAPPING PLACE

not extend to all the areas of the city, nor are all ethnic and racial groups covered, and no authors are explicitly identified—the preface notes that those participating in the project were "naturally seeking no individual credit for their own part in a cooperative task" (v). See also J. J. Butts, "New World A-Coming: African American Documentary Intertexts of the Federal Writers' Project," *African American Review* 44, no. 4 (2011): 649–66.

109. This is not to deny the important work of Communist–Black exchange during this period, which William J. Maxwell discusses in *New Negro, Old Left: African-American Writing and Communism During the Wars* (New York: Columbia University Press, 1999).
110. Poston, "A Book on Harlem," 732.
111. John Dewey to Claude McKay, November 29, 1940, box 2, folder 61, McKay Collection.
112. When John LaFarge noted that McKay was "West Indian by origin: all the more significant, since he is completely objective in speaking of his own compatriots," he, perhaps unwittingly, affirmed the potential of Blackness to overcome differences in background. "No Black Butt for Benevolent Reds," review of *Harlem: Negro Metropolis*, by Claude McKay, *America*, May 31, 1941, 217.
113. C. G. Woodson, review of *Harlem: Negro Metropolis*, by Claude McKay, *Journal of Negro History* 26, no. 1 (January 1941): 120–21.
114. Woodson, review, 120.
115. Woodson, review, 120, 121.
116. Hilda A. Hill, review of *Harlem: Negro Metropolis*, by Claude McKay, *Journal of Negro Education* 11, no. 1 (January 1942): 75–77.
117. Hill, review, 75, 76.
118. Hill, review, 77.
119. Claude McKay, "Group Life and Literature," typescript, n.d., box 9, folder 287, McKay Collection.
120. McKay, "Group Life and Literature." Though there is no date on the manuscript of the essay, it would seem to have been written sometime during the 1930s, as it references his already-published (1928) *Home to Harlem* and (1929) *Banjo*.
121. A. Philip Randolph to Claude McKay, April 4, 1941, box 6, folder 173, McKay Collection.
122. Nella Larsen, *Passing* (New York: Alfred A. Knopf, 1929).
123. Simon Williamson, review of *Harlem: Negro Metropolis*, by Claude McKay, *New York Amsterdam News*, November 9, 1940.
124. These inclinations are particularly vivid in his piece "Where the News Ends," *New Leader*, June 16, 1939.
125. Though Carl Cowl refers to *Harlem Glory* as having been written after *Harlem: Negro Metropolis*, in the 1940s, Cloutier makes the convincing case that the more accurate period of work on the novel was 1936–1937. See Cloutier, introduction to *Amiable with Big Teeth*, xv.
126. Although Cowl's assertion implies a succession, with *Harlem: Negro Metropolis* coming first and *Harlem Glory* next, the point that he is making about McKay working in

2. MAPPING PLACE

different forms is not necessarily changed by learning of the probable simultaneity of the two texts.

127. The published version that resulted from the efforts of Hope McKay Virtue, Claude McKay's daughter, and Carl Cowl, ends with: "[Here the Manuscript Ends]." Claude McKay, *Harlem Glory: A Fragment of Aframerican Life* (Chicago: Charles H. Kerr, 1990).
128. Carl Cowl, preface to *Harlem Glory*, 7.
129. See an extended discussion of this project in the introduction to *Amiable with Big Teeth*. I do not disagree with the rich arguments that Cloutier makes, particularly as detailed in his article "Amiable with Big Teeth: The Case of Claude McKay's Last Novel," *Modernism/modernity* 20, no. 3 (September 2013): 557–76, about how McKay's novel can be seen as a kind of fruition of the archival impulse. But I do think that when Cloutier writes that the "nonfictional *Harlem* [:*Negro Metropolis*] could only go so far in fulfilling McKay's vision; without a novelization, the intensity of forces, the human interplay, the savory characters, would be lost to history, relegated to the 'unprocessed' archive" (572), he betrays rather different assumptions about nonfiction that the work of this chapter has sought to undo. As I have indicated throughout, I would like to suggest that the very qualities that are attributed to fiction (intensity of forces, the human interplay, the savory characters) appear to great effect in *Harlem: Negro Metropolis*. Moreover, the argument about the traffic in forms is made even more powerfully when we consider how McKay is making nonfiction do all kinds of political and imaginative work for him.
130. Nigel Thrift, "Intensities of Feeling: Toward a Spatial Politics of Affect," *Geografiska Annaler*. Series B, *Human Geography* 86, no. 1, (2004): 57–78.
131. Wayne Cooper's important edited volume of McKay's work is meaningfully titled *The Passion of Claude McKay: Selected Poetry and Prose, 1912–1948*, ed. Wayne F. Cooper (New York: Schocken Books, 1973).
132. Paul Gilroy, *Black Atlantic: Modernity and Double Consciousness* (Cambridge, MA: Harvard University Press, 1993). In somewhat related ways, Édouard Glissant provided an important theoretical template for the instantiation of Black historical experience in imaginative and material landscapes; see, among other works, his *Poetics of Relation* (Ann Arbor: University of Michigan Press, 1997).
133. Katherine McKittrick, *Demonic Grounds: Black Women and the Cartographies of Struggle* (Minneapolis: University of Minnesota Press, 2006), xiv, my emphasis.
134. Gilles Deleuze and Felix Guattari have written about the simultaneity of deterritorialization and reterritorialization with regard, especially, to the psyche in capitalism, but here I am conceiving of territory in rather more literal or geographic terms. Still, their emphasis on freedom (of representation and political subjectivity) resonates in the work that I see McKay as accomplishing. See Gilles Deleuze and Felix Guattari, *A Thousand Plateaus: Capitalism and Schizophrenia*, trans. Brian Massumi (London: Continuum, 2004).
135. Stuart Hall, "Race, Articulation and Societies Structured in Dominance," in *Sociological Theories: Race and Colonialism* (Paris: Unesco, 1980), 341.

3. CROSSINGS AT HOME AND IN THE WORLD

1. Peter Rofrano, interview by the author, April 5, 2005, New York, NY.
2. From conversations with a range of participants in New York, NY, 2005–present.
3. Michel Laguerre, *Minoritized Space: An Inquiry Into the Spatial Order of Things* (Berkeley, CA: Institute of Governmental Studies Press, 1999), 15.
4. Constance Grady discusses a lecture that Díaz gave at the National Endowment for the Humanities 2016 50th Anniversary conference "Human/Ties" at the University of Virginia. "Junot Díaz on Political Art and the Immigrant as Sauron," *Vox*, October 2, 2016, https://www.vox.com/culture/2016/10/2/12976156/junot-diaz-neh-human-ties-panel-sauron. See also Pnina Werbner, "Global Pathways: Working Class Cosmopolitans and the Creation of Transnational Ethnic Worlds," *Social Anthropology* 7, no. 1 (February 1999): 17–35; and Mike Featherstone, "Cosmopolis: An Introduction," *Theory, Culture, and Society* 19, no. 1–2 (April 2002): 1–16.
5. The charge of opportunism has been leveled against a number of these political formations, particularly as they have seemed to emerge from "outside" the area. It is worth mentioning the complicated relationship many African American activists and cultural figures had with regard to the Communist Party. For various perspectives, see: Mark Naison, *Communists in Harlem During the Depression* (Urbana: University of Illinois Press, 1983); Howard Eugene Johnson, *A Dancer in the Revolution: Stretch Johnson, Harlem Communist at the Cotton Club* (New York: Empire State Editions/Fordham University Press, 2014); Minkah Makalani, *In the Cause of Freedom: Radical Black Internationalism from Harlem to London* (Chapel Hill: University of North Carolina Press, 2014); William Maxwell, *Old Negro, New Left: African American Writing and Communism Between the Wars* (New York: Columbia University Press, 1999).
6. The authoritative, multifaceted text on Marcantonio is Gerald Meyer, *Vito Marcantonio: Radical Politician, 1900–1954* (Albany: State University of New York Press, 1989). Meyer has also written many other materials, including "Vito Marcantonio y El Partido Nacionalista Puertoriqueño," *Signos* 1, no. 1 (January–March 1980): 2–9; "Leonard Covello and Vito Marcantonio: A Lifelong Collaboration for Progress," *Italica* 62, no. 1 (Spring 1985): 54–66; and various pieces on the Vito Marcantonio website, such as "Italian Harlem: America's Largest and Most Italian Little Italy," http://www.vitomarcantonio.com/eh_italian_east_harlem.html. An earlier book, focused on political history, is Alan Schaffer, *Vito Marcantonio, Radical in Congress* (Syracuse, NY: Syracuse University Press, 1966); this is also the topic of Peter Jackson, "Vito Marcantonio and Ethnic Politics in New York," *Ethnic and Racial Studies* 6, no. 1 (January 1983): 50–72. See also Félix Ojeda Reyes, *Vito Marcantonio y Puerto Rico: por los Trabajadores y por la Nacion* (Río Piedras, PR: Ediciones Huracán, 1978); John Simon, "Rebel in the House: The Life and Times of Vito Marcantonio," *Monthly Review*, March 1, 2006, https://monthlyreview.org/2006/03/01/rebel-in-the-house-the-life-and-times-of-vito-marcantonio/.
7. Vito Marcantonio Papers: 1935–1953, Manuscripts and Archives Division, New York Public Library (hereafter cited as Marcantonio Papers).

3. CROSSINGS AT HOME AND IN THE WORLD

8. A number of individuals, including Marcantonio's most prominent biographer, Gerald Meyer, started the Vito Marcantonio Forum in 2011. This group has developed a website, http://vitomarcantonioforum.com/, with its own archive and organized activities to produce knowledge about Marcantonio as well as advocate for his importance. Fellow political activist and literary critic Annette T. Rubinstein collected Marcantonio's speeches in a volume entitled *I Vote My Conscience: Debates, Speeches and Writings of Vito Marcantonio* (New York: The Vito Marcantonio Memorial, 1956; repr. New York: John D. Calandra Italian American Institute, Queens College, The City University of New York, 2002). One point to make about these sources is that political sympathies with Marcantonio's project shape the collections: these are *curated* materials.

9. Some writings, though not as many as might be expected, have discussed Italian Harlem. The classic work, with a focus on religious history, is Robert Orsi, *The Madonna of 115th Street: Faith and Community in Italian Harlem* (New Haven, CT: Yale University Press, 1985). Jonathan Gill's synthetic history, *Harlem: The Four Hundred Year History from Dutch Village to Capital of Black America*, contains descriptions of Italian migrant formations in East Harlem, particularly vis-à-vis Jewish ones. Material on Italian Harlem can also be found in an earlier work: Workers of the Federal Writers Project, Works Progress Administration of the City of New York [FWP], *The Italians of New York: A Survey* (New York: Random House, 1938). Russell Leigh Sharman's ethnography *The Tenants of East Harlem* (Berkeley: University of California Press, 2006) has a chapter based on interviews with a longtime resident of Italian Harlem. Memoirs include Salvatore Mondello, *A Sicilian in East Harlem* (Amherst, NY: Cambria Press, 2005); and Kym Ragusa, *The Skin Between Us: A Memoir of Race, Beauty and Belonging* (New York: W. W. Norton, 2006). Also see three novels on Italians in Harlem by Garibaldi M. Lapolla: *The Fire in the Flesh* (New York: Vanguard, 1931), *Miss Rollins in Love* (New York: Vanguard, 1932), and *The Grand Gennaro* (New York: Vanguard, 1935).

10. According to Simone Cinotto in *The Italian American Table: Food, Family, and Community in New York City* (Champaign: University of Illinois Press, 2013), in the 1920s and 1930s, East Harlem was home to approximately eighty thousand first- and second-generation Italian immigrants, who accounted for 75 to 90 percent of the area's population. Meanwhile, according to Bill Tonelli in "Arrivederci, Little Italy" (*New York Magazine*, September 14, 2004), Little Italy in Lower Manhattan had only ten thousand Italian Americans at its peak in 1910.

11. Donna R. Gabaccia, "Inventing Little Italy," in *Journal of the Gilded Age and Progressive Era* 6, no. 1 (January 2007): 7–41. In this piece, Gabaccia also presents a rich archive of early sensationalistic fictional and dramatic representations of this and other Little Italys.

12. Jacob A. Riis, "Feast-Days in Little Italy," *Century Magazine*, August 1899, 491–99.

13. "Race Riot in Harlem Over Boys' Quarrel," *New York Times*, October 9, 1916.

14. Lapolla, whose fiction about Italian Harlem unfurled an informal community ethnography, began his 1935 novel *The Grand Gennaro* with a description of a typical multifamily house in the area: "In it three Italian families, all from different sections of Italy,

3. CROSSINGS AT HOME AND IN THE WORLD

were to meet, mingle, and separate, each bearing in charred burdens of memory the shock of their encounter" (3). The "encounter" could doubly signify, to refer to each family's encounter with the United States through migration, and with other families as a result of residential adjacency. America's national discourse for ethnicity, in turn, depended on constitutive nationality, so that for immigrants from various parts of Italy, as well as for Vito Marcantonio, to be Italian was to belong in the United States. The spatialization of that identity meant, too, that Italian Americanness was seen to constitute a population that corresponded to an enclave, as occupying territory was central to belonging. In all these ways, Italianness and Americanness were not necessarily in conflict: both national cultural ideology and Harlem massaged them together.

15. Benjamin Looker, *A Nation of Neighborhoods: Imagining Cities, Communities and Democracy in Postwar America* (Chicago: University of Chicago Press, 2015).
16. See Christopher Bell, *East Harlem Remembered: Oral Histories of Community and Diversity* (Jefferson, NC: McFarland: 2013) for a discussion of African American presence in East Harlem.
17. Vito Marcantonio, speech before the Seventy-Sixth Congress, August 3, 1939, in *I Vote My Conscience*, 109.
18. Fred Gardaphé, "The Consequences of Class in Italian American Culture," chap. 5 in *Leaving Little Italy: Essaying Italian American Culture* (Albany: State University of New York Press, 2003). See also David R. Roediger, *Working Toward Whiteness: How America's Immigrants Became White: The Strange Journey from Ellis Island to the Suburbs* (New York: Basic Books, 2005).
19. "Talk to Harlem Legislative Committee (VM chairman)," August 27, 1938, Audiotape 01735, Marcantonio Papers.
20. Jennifer Guglielmo discusses the complicated racial (and gendered) dynamic of Italians developing whiteness in *Living the Revolution: Italian Women's Resistance and Radicalism in New York City, 1880–1945* (Chapel Hill: University of North Carolina Press, 2015). See also Peter G. Vellon, *"A Great Conspiracy Against Our Race": Italian Immigrant Newspapers and the Construction of Whiteness in the Early 20th Century* (New York: New York University Press, 2014).
21. Rofrano, interview.
22. Peter Pascale, quoted in Nadia Venturini, "'Over the Years People Don't Know': Italian Americans and African Americans in Harlem in the 1930s," in *Italian Workers of the World: Labor Migration and the Formation of Multi-Ethnic States*, ed. Donna Gabaccia and Fraser Ottanelli (Urbana: University of Illinois Press, 2000), 196–213, 196.
23. Thomas A. Guglielmo discusses another example in *White on Arrival: Italians, Race, Color and Power in Chicago, 1890–1945* (New York: Oxford University Press, 2003).
24. It bears repeating that race was anything but stable in the United States during the period in which Marcantonio came of age; as Matthew Pratt Guterl points out in *The Color of Race in America, 1900–1940* (Cambridge, MA: Harvard University Press, 2001), immigration, religion, and social and racial science, as well as anti-Communism, confused the issues for both white and Black people in heterogeneous cultures. For an

3. CROSSINGS AT HOME AND IN THE WORLD

important discussion of racial ideology and white ethnic/immigrant groups, see: Matthew Frye Jacobson, *Whiteness of a Different Color: European Immigrants and the Alchemy of Race* (Cambridge, MA: Harvard University Press, 1999).

25. Rofrano was born in East Harlem and served as priest for Our Lady of Mount Carmel for many years, in the 1950s and 1960s and from 1986 until his death in 2007 at the age of ninety. He was a self-appointed chronicler of Italian Harlem, speaking often to the press as well as to researchers over the years. Although through his long life he participated in many projects and held a variety of views, in his last years he told a story of change that depicted Italians as victims of Puerto Rican incursions into the space. In 2005 he told me that East Harlem contained a mostly Italian population until the early 1930s, but that then "they had to get Italians out, so they brought in the Puerto Ricans from Puerto Rico, it was political.... Italians were pushed out of Harlem."

26. Gerald Meyer accesses data compiled by Irving Sollins in "A Socio-Statistical Analysis of Boys' Club Membership" (PhD diss., New York University, 1936) for his own discussion of diversity, "Italian Harlem: America's Largest and Most Italian Little Italy," Marcantonio: Defender of Human Rights [blog], August 26, 2012, http://vitomarcantonio.com/east-harlem/italian-east-harlem/.

27. Lapolla, *Grand Gennaro*, 3.

28. Mondello, *Sicilian in East Harlem*, 83.

29. Marcantonio, "Talk to Harlem Legislative Committee."

30. Bell writes about the influence on Marcantonio of a leftist history teacher named Abraham Lefkowitz in *East Harlem Remembered*, 59.

31. FWP, *Italians of New York*, 99. In fact, Marcantonio mentioned his desire to found a progressive weekly for East Harlem entitled *The People's Voice*, because of the Fascist-dominated Italian-language press. See Vito Marcantonio, "Note on 'The People's Voice,'" box 4, Marcantonio Papers.

32. Correspondence with Italian Welfare Association Local 118A, Workers Alliance of America, July 8, 1940, box 3, Marcantonio Papers.

33. Meyer discusses in detail Marcantonio's relationship with the Communist Party in chapter 4 of *Vito Marcantonio*. He notes that Marcantonio was not a Communist, but seldom disagreed with the party's positions. Moreover, it is clear that Marcantonio was a member or leader of many organizations and publications that were associated with the CP or with communist causes, such as the International Labor Defense, the Harlem Legislative Conference, the Harlem Victory Council, and numerous unions.

34. Marcantonio's papers are filled with close correspondence with members of the Harlem Legislative Conference, the Hispanic Progressive Club, the Harlem Center Civic Association, and similar groups. Marcantonio was also on the editorial board of *New Masses* and other left-wing publications.

35. Jim O'Grady, "City Lore: 'The Loneliest Man in Congress,'" *New York Times*, December 1, 2002. Rubinstein also notes in *I Vote my Conscience* that Vito Marcantonio "never lost his profound feeling of identification with his community" (1).

36. Reyes, *Vito Marcantonio y Puerto Rico*, 9. My translation.

3. CROSSINGS AT HOME AND IN THE WORLD

37. Stuart Hall, "Culture, Identity and Diaspora," in *Identity, Community, Culture Difference*, ed. Jonathan Rutherford (London: Lawrence and Wishart, 1990); and Gilles Deleuze and Felix Guattari, *A Thousand Plateaus: Capitalism and Schizophrenia*, trans. Brian Massumi (London: Continuum, 2004).
38. Robin D. G. Kelley's classic text *Hammer and Hoe: Alabama Communists During the Great Depression* (Chapel Hill: University of North Carolina Press, 1990) offers a rich account of Black and white Communist activists during the 1930s and 1940s
39. Wendy Brown, *States of Injury: Power and Freedom in Late Modernity* (Princeton: Princeton University Press, 1995).
40. A particularly rich discussion of the philosophical understanding of the concept can be found in Sally J. Scholz's *Political Solidarity* (University Park: Pennsylvania State University Press, 2008).
41. Discussions of racial *unity* appear across the works of thinkers such as W. E. B. Du Bois and Alain Locke, which could in turn be understood vis-à-vis labels of race *solidarity*.
42. Rousseau wrote in 1762 that "as men cannot engender new forces, but only unite and direct existing ones, they have no other means of preserving themselves than the formation, by aggregation, of a sum of forces great enough to overcome the resistance. These they have to bring into play by means of a single motive power, and cause to act in concert." *The Social Contract, Or, Principles of Political Right*, in *The Social Contract and Discourses*, trans. G. D. H. Cole (London: J. M. Dent and Sons, 1913), 14. And in 1893, Durkheim specifically used the term solidarity in *On the Division of Labor in Society*, trans. and ed. George Simpson (New York: Macmillan, 1933), 64: "Despite its immaterial character, wherever social solidarity exists, it resides not in a state of pure potentiality, but manifests its presence by sensible indices. Where it is strong, it leads men strongly to one another, frequently puts them in contact, [and] multiplies the occasions when they find themselves related" and "the more solidary the members of a society are, the more they sustain diverse relations."
43. Piri Thomas, chap. 6 in *Down These Mean Streets* (New York: Vintage, 1967).
44. Piri Thomas, interview by Christopher Bell, n.d., in *East Harlem Remembered*, 65.
45. Christmas greeting from the Harlem Center Civic Association, signed by Anita Piscopo, Leader, and Salvatore Cassataro, President, n.d., box 3, Marcantonio Papers.
46. Folio announcing the opening of the office and headquarters of the Harlem Legislative Conference, November 19, 1937, box 3, Marcantonio Papers.
47. "Manifesto." reel 2, microfilm 54, Marcantonio Papers.
48. Folio titled "Call for an Emergency Conference to the People of Harlem," box 3, Marcantonio Papers. The opening paragraph employs language of the left: "The real estate trust, the milk and food trust and other big monopolies have for the past two years been ganging up on the people. Now they are directing their fire at the unemployed and the subway riders of the City of New York. At the same time a vicious campaign of slander is being conducted against minority groups, particularly the Puerto Rican and Negro citizens of New York."

3. CROSSINGS AT HOME AND IN THE WORLD

49. Gerald Meyer notes that in 1945, the school population was 37 percent Italian, 13 percent African American, 9 percent Puerto Rican, and 41 percent "other" (presumed to include a significant portion of Jewish students). See Gerald Meyer, "When Frank Sinatra Came to Italian Harlem: The 1945 'Race Riot' at Benjamin Franklin High School," in *Are Italians White? How Race Is Made in America*, ed. Jennifer Guglielmo and Salvatore Salterno (New York: Routledge, 2003), 161–76, 161.
50. African American newspapers such as the more local *New York Amsterdam News* and national *Pittsburgh Courier* and *Chicago Defender* extensively covered Marcantonio's work on behalf of issues of racial justice throughout the 1930s and 1940s. A small representation of titles is as follows: "Marcantonio Is Backed in 20th: Gets Endorsement of All-Harlem Party," *New York Amsterdam News*, February 28, 1936; "Marcantonio Aiding Puerto Rican Heads," *Chicago Defender*, August 22, 1936; "Congressman Pays Tribute to Miller: Marcantonio Tells Parents of Colored Naval Hero His Action Will Speed the Day When the Race Barrier Will Be Broken," *Pittsburgh Courier*, March 21, 1942; "Marcantonio Issues Terse Letter to FDR: Congressman Calls on Commander-in-Chief to Aid Negro's Cause Now," *New York Amsterdam News*, July 3, 1943; and "Marcantonio in Parley with FDR on Negro Matters," *Chicago Defender*, February 26, 1944.
51. Marcantonio's personal papers are filled with correspondence with Powell, and many African American luminaries spoke at his memorial service.
52. Series II, box 3, Marcantonio Papers.
53. Mondello, *Sicilian in Harlem*, 83.
54. Vito Marcantonio, radio address on February 26, 1943, in *I Vote My Conscience*, 175.
55. Vito Marcantonio, speech before the House of Representatives, March 11, 1939, in *I Vote My Conscience*, 374.
56. There is a good deal of correspondence from those in Puerto Rico regarding these issues. See boxes 54–55 and reel 2, microfilm 54, Marcantonio Papers. Gerald Meyer's article "Vito Marcantonio, Congressman for Puerto Rico: 1934–1936, 1938–1950," Marcantonio: Defender of Human Rights [blog], August 26, 2012, http://www.vitomarcantonio.com/vm_congressman_for_puerto_rico.html contains a wealth of detail on Marcantonio's efforts on behalf of Puerto Rican workers. There is also quite a lot of important material in Reyes, *Vito Marcantonio y Puerto Rico*.
57. Olivor L. Chapman to Vito Marcantonio, March 26, 1940, reel 1, microfilm 54, Marcantonio Papers; Vito Marcantonio to Harold L. Ickes, March 18, 1940, reel 1, microfilm 54, Marcantonio Papers; Vito Marcantonio to José Kailan Melicio, March 18, 1940, reel 1, microfilm 54, Marcantonio Papers; and José Kailan Melicio to Vito Marcantonio, March 26, 1940, reel 1, microfilm 54, Marcantonio Papers.
58. Guadalupe Ruiz to Vito Marcantonio, n.d., reel 2, microfilm 54, Marcantonio Papers. Other correspondence concerning this case: Vito Marcantonio to Frederich R. Sacher, n.d., reel 2, microfilm 54, Marcantonio Papers; Vito Marcantonio to John H. Devitt, n.d., reel 2, microfilm 54, Marcantonio Papers; Frederich R. Sacher to Vito Marcantonio, n.d., reel 2, microfilm 54, Marcantonio Papers; William Cantwell to

3. CROSSINGS AT HOME AND IN THE WORLD

Vito Marcantonio, n.d., reel 2, microfilm 54, Marcantonio Papers; Vito Marcantonio to Diógene Ruiz, n.d., reel 2, microfilm 54, Marcantonio Papers.

59. Laura Briggs, *Reproducing Empire: Race, Sex, Science and U.S. Imperialism in Puerto Rico* (Berkeley: University of California Press, 2001); César J. Ayala and Rafael Bernabe, *Puerto Rico in the American Century: A History since 1898* (Chapel Hill: University of North Carolina Press, 2007).

60. Immanuel Wallerstein has made an economic argument for a category of the "extended Caribbean" to refer to a region from Brazil to Maryland, in *Modern World System II* (Berkeley: University of California Press, 2011). Lara Putnam has taken that concept to develop an understanding of Harlem as one point in a broader geography, through the Americas, of influence and habitation for Caribbean migrants, in "Provincializing Harlem: The 'Negro Metropolis' as Northern Frontier of a Connected Caribbean," *Modernism/Modernity* 20, no. 3 (September 2013): 469–84. See also Jason Parker's "'Capital of the Caribbean': The African American–West Indian 'Harlem Nexus' and the Transnational Drive for Black Freedom, 1940–1948," *Journal of African American History* 89, no. 2 (Spring 2004): 98–117.

61. See materials in boxes 54 and 55, Marcantonio Papers.

62. "10,000 Parade Here for Puerto Ricans," *New York Times*, August 30, 1936. The lead paragraphs read: "Ten thousand Puerto Ricans, representing a score of political and social clubs in the city, paraded for three hours through the streets of lower Harlem yesterday afternoon to protest the attitude of 'Imperialistic America' in making 'slaves' of the natives of the island. Spurred by the comment of Representative Vito Marcantonio, who recently returned from a two-weeks' visit to the island and denounced conditions there, the paraders shouted 'Free Puerto Rico!' and 'Down With Yankee Imperialism!' so loudly that thousands of other residents in the area, populated mostly by Negroes and Spaniards, leaned out of windows and over the edges of roof-tops and added their protests to those of the demonstrators."

63. See Daniel Acosta Elkan's fine PhD dissertation, "The Colonial Next Door: Puerto Ricans in the Harlem Community, 1917–1948," Bowling Green State University, December 2017, 45–74, for a discussion of citizenship for Puerto Ricans.

64. Jesús Cariel to Vito Marcantonio, June 23, 1939, box 55, folder titled "Puerto Rico–Citizenship," Marcantonio Papers.

65. José Ramón Sánchez, *Boricua Power: A Political History of Puerto Ricans in the United States* (New York: New York University Press, 2007), 115–18.

66. William Maddox to Vito Marcantonio, September 18, 1936, reel 2, microfilm 54, Marcantonio Papers; William Maddox to Vito Marcantonio, September 28, 1936, reel 2, microfilm 54, Marcantonio Papers; Vito Marcantonio to William Maddox, September 30, 1936, reel 2, microfilm 54, Marcantonio Papers

67. Pedro J. Biaggi to Vito Marcantonio, December 1, 1936, reel 2, microfilm 54, Marcantonio Papers.

68. Angelita Santaella to Vito Marcantonio, December 18, 1941, reel 3, microfilm 55, Marcantonio Papers.

3. CROSSINGS AT HOME AND IN THE WORLD

69. Angelita Santaella to Vito Marcantonio, November 5, 1941, reel 3, microfilm 55, Marcantonio Papers.
70. The full quote is: "Yo no estudié español en Salamanca, España. El español que conozco lo aprendí de labios remulos(?) y trabajadores humildes que sí hacer caron (?) a mi, buscando estuvierno (?) en disgracia. Mi español no nesdiatener [sic]. Mi español es del hombre común que trabaja y supere." Much of this is hard to understand in terms of clear, grammatically correct Spanish, but the way I would roughly translate it is: "I did not study Spanish in Salamanca, Spain. The Spanish that I know I learned from the lips of humble workers.... My Spanish is of the common man who works and prevails." Radio address, dir. Salvador Mercedo, with interviewer Alfred Barrea, Audiotape 01644, Marcantonio Papers.
71. Thomas, *Down These Mean Streets*, 42.
72. Marcantonio understood the importance of language and familiarity with Puerto Rico to his constituents, as did they. In a radio endorsement, the announcer begins by describing Marcantonio: "que habla hispaña, que ha vistado este país" (who speaks Spanish, who has visited this country), which draws on sources of connection. "Political Announcement," n.d. (prob. 1949, during mayoral campaign), Audiotape 01649, Marcantonio Papers.
73. Mikhail Bakhtin, "Discourse in the Novel" (1934–1935), in *The Dialogical Imagination: Four Essays*, ed. Michael Holquist, trans. Caryl Emerson and Michael Holquist (Austin: University of Texas Press, 1981), 271–72.
74. Marcantonio refers to some newspaper articles and other materials in Spanish-language papers in Puerto Rico, and there is no evidence in the correspondence of translations, suggesting at least a working fluency with Spanish. In a February 7, 1939 letter, Marcantonio writes to J. Enamorado Cuesta about having enjoyed a poem he wrote in *Prensa Libre*; see box 54, Marcantonio Papers.
75. Bakhtin, "Discourse in the Novel," 272. The full quote reads: "The authentic environment of an utterance, the environment in which it lives and takes shape, is dialogized heteroglossia, anonymous and social as language, but simultaneously concrete, filled with specific content and accented as an individual utterance."
76. Yasemin Yildiz, in *Beyond the Mother Tongue: The Postmonolingual Condition* (New York: Fordham University Press, 2012), suggests that a "post-monolingual" reading practice might be in order, as she, for a different set of cases, has questioned the conceptualization of monolingualism and multilingualism, pointing to the first as an ideology that studiously ignores the persistent experience of the latter.
77. Among other texts cited in the introduction of this book, see Susan Bassnett and Harish Trivedi, eds., *Postcolonial Translation: Theory and Practice* (New York: Routledge, 1999).
78. Randolph Bourne, "Trans-National America," *Atlantic*, July 1916, 86–97.
79. Vito Marcantonio, radio address, July 30, 1940, in *I Vote My Conscience*, 130.
80. In a July 13, 1939 letter there is an interesting discussion of human rights that extend beyond national belonging. Box 54, Marcantonio Papers.

3. CROSSINGS AT HOME AND IN THE WORLD

81. "Letter from Harlem Victory Council, dated March 28, 1942," "Minutes from Saturday afternoon meeting of Harlem Defense Conference, dated January 17, 1942," "Letter from Bernard Harkavy, National Secretary of Jewish Peoples Committee, May 26, 1942," box 2, Marcantonio Papers.
82. Salvatore J. LaGumina, "The New Deal, the Immigrants and Congressman Vito Marcantonio," *International Migration Review* 4, no. 2 (Spring 1970): 57–75.
83. "Citizenship Urged for Filipinos Here," *New York Times*, February 5, 1942.
84. Filipino War Workers Committee of Southern California to Vito Marcantonio, 15 June 1945, box 46, Marcantonio Papers.
85. See petition in folder titled "Electoral Democracy," box 49, Marcantonio Papers.
86. Vito Marcantonio, "Loyalty of Italian Americans," in *A Documentary History of Italian Americans*, ed. Wayne Moquin (New York: Praeger, 1975), 399–400.
87. Meyer, *Vito Marcantonio*, 246. This was yet another complicated case of the world and its turmoil bearing down on locality, which social relations registered. The global horizon of colonialism and race seemed close when fights broke out between area Italians and Black Harlem residents protesting the Italian invasion of Ethiopia ("Three Police in Harlem Hurt Fighting Mob," *New York Times*, July 13, 1936; "Mob of 400 Battles the Police in Harlem; Italian Stores Raided, Man Shot in Crowd," *New York Times*, May 19, 1936). In an incident that is fascinating for its expressed awareness of local racial, international, and economic conflicts, two young African American men were accused in 1935 of developing a "racket" that seized upon political differences to extort money from Italian merchants in exchange for not diverting anticolonial Black customers. Part of the evidence that was submitted included a book with details about the Italian-Ethiopian situation and the locations of Italian businesses in the West 117th Street area. The defense of the African American men, as reported in the newspaper, centered on an argument to discourage Mussolini's efforts in Ethiopia by raising the specter of a large-scale boycott of Italian businesses in Harlem. When announcing his sentence of the men to the City Reformatory, the judge remarked: "In this country we do not consider a man's race or religion, and the extorting of money will not be permitted." "2 Negroes Sentenced in Racket on Italians," *New York Times*, October 3, 1935.
88. Cheryl Greenberg, "Black and Jewish Responses to Japanese Internment," *Journal of American Ethnic History* 14, no. 2 (Winter 1995): 3–37; Lon Kurashige, *Two Faces of Exclusion: The Untold History of Anti-Asian Racism in the United States* (Chapel Hill: University of North Carolina Press, 2016).
89. Paul Susumu Seto to Vito Marcantonio, April 30, 1943, box 46, Marcantonio Papers.
90. For example, see George Yoshioka to Vito Marcantonio, April 6, 1942, box 46, Marcantonio Papers, where he notes: "As one evacuated from the Pacific Coast and now residing in a W. R. A. center . . . I believe that I am expressing the innermost feelings of all the 110,000 evacuees (70% of whom are citizens) in saying that we are greatly heartened and encouraged in the knowledge that you have the vision and courage to look at fundamental issues realistically, and that you have taken steps to correct an unjust condition that has existed for these many years." Also see "Move to Amend Nat. Act Introduced,"

3. CROSSINGS AT HOME AND IN THE WORLD

Manzanar [CA] *Free Press*, March 17, 1943; and "Editorial: A Bill for Americanism," *Heart Mountain Sentinel* (Cody, WY), March 13, 1943.
91. Vito Marcantonio to Clarence Reid, July 9, 1948, box 46, Marcantonio Papers. Many other letters during this period express the same sentiment.
92. Langston Hughes, *Montage of a Dream Deferred* (New York: Henry Holt, 1951).
93. Manning Marable, "Peace and Black Liberation: The Contributions of W. E. B. Du Bois," *Science and Society* 47, no. 4 (Winter 1983/1984): 385–405. Du Bois also discusses his peace activism in *In Battle for Peace* (New York: Masses and Mainstream, 1952).
94. Gerald Meyer, "Italian Harlem's Biggest Funeral: A Community Pays Its Last Respects to Vito Marcantonio," *Italian American Review* (Spring 1997): 108–20. The *New York Times* reports in "Tribute Is Paid to Marcantonio," August 13, 1954 that "a throng of 5000 from near-by tenements packed the sidewalks as a funeral service for Vito Marcantonio was held yesterday." "Private Masses Set for Marcantonio," *New York Times*, August 12, 1954, describes the scene thus: "Throughout yesterday and last evening, there was a steady flow of visitors to the funeral parlor. In the early evening, while about 125 persons were in line, two abreast behind police barriers; a light rain caused them to seek shelter. After the rain stopped, the line grew to a half-block in length. A funeral parlor spokesman said 20,000 persons had viewed the bier between 9 a.m. and 11:35 p.m. when the doors closed."
95. "Vito Marcantonio Memorial Program," December 7, 1954, box 80, folder 7, Marcantonio Papers; Funeral Pictures 1954, Photographs, Marcantonio Papers. See also Meyer's description of the funeral and service, *Vito Marcantonio*, 183.
96. This was the title of an essay in August 1954 in the magazine Paul Robeson ran, called *Freedom*, 1, which also appeared in Paul Robeson, *Paul Robeson Speaks: Writings, Speeches and Interviews: A Centennial Celebration* (New York: Citadel, 1978), 379–81.
97. Gilberto Gerena Valentín, *Soy Gilberto Gerena Valentín: Memorias de un puertoriqueno en Nueva York*, ed. Carlos Rodríguez Fraticelli (New York: Center for Puerto Rican Studies, 2013), 74.
98. "Private Masses Set for Marcantonio."
99. Meyer, *Vito Marcantonio*, 183.
100. Dorothy Day, "Death in August—Vito Marcantonio," *Catholic Worker*, September 1954, 1, 6; quote on 1.
101. Brian Massumi, "The Anatomy of Affect," *Cultural Critique* 31 (Autumn 1995): 83–109; Deleuze and Guattari, *A Thousand Plateaus*; Jonathan Flatley, *Affective Mapping: Melancholia and the Politics of Modernism* (Cambridge, MA: Harvard University Press, 2008); Sara Ahmed, *The Cultural Politics of Emotion* (New York: Routledge, 2004); Purnima Mankekar, *Unsettling India: Affect, Temporality, Transnationality* (Durham, NC: Duke University Press, 2015).
102. Flatley, *Affective Mapping*, 12.
103. Benedictus de Spinoza, *The Collected Works of Spinoza*, ed. and transl. Edwin Curley (Princeton: Princeton University Press, 1985); Henri Bergson, *Matter and Memory*, transl. Nancy Margaret Paul and W. Scott Paul (London: George Allen and Unwin, 1911).

3. CROSSINGS AT HOME AND IN THE WORLD

104. Joseph H. Loucheim, "Vito Marcantonio's Work," letter to the editor, *New York Times*, August 13, 1954.
105. Day, "Death in August," 6.
106. Raymond Williams, *Resources of Hope: Culture, Democracy, Socialism* (London: Verso, 1989), 242.
107. David Harvey, "Militant Particularism and Global Ambition: The Conceptual Politics of Place, Space and Environment in the Work of Raymond Williams," *Social Text* 42 (Spring 1995): 69–98, 81.
108. "Vito Marcantonio Falls Dead in Street," *New York Times*, August 10, 1954, 1, 14; quotes on 14.
109. In a *New York Times* article, "The Harlem Italians," of May 30, 1966, author Jonathan Randal writes of one community perspective: "There is a nostalgia for the time Marc—the late Vito Marcantonio—was the local Congressman or, as one resident put it, 'when our women could walk alone in the streets at night.' But the same people who live on these memories readily point out they often disagreed with Mr. Marcantonio's leftist views."
110. Orsi, "Religious Boundaries," 313–47, 329.
111. Geoffrey Pond, "Boys Fight Bias in East Harlem: After Trip to Puerto Rico Italian Americans Want to Help 'in Worst Way,'" *New York Times*, March 6, 1960.
112. Jonathan Randal, "The Harlem Italians," *New York Times*, May 30, 1966, 12.
113. Michael Stern, "East Harlem's Little Italy Gets Tinier Each Day," *New York Times*, October 15, 1968, 49, 93. In recent years, the church's candlelight procession and daytime march included Haitian women (from Brooklyn and other places inside and outside of New York), yet with mostly Italians holding the statue and in front. Few, if any, of these participants live in the East Harlem streets that the procession marks out, from 115th Street and Pleasant Avenue to Second Avenue, down to 110th Street, and back up again.
114. Elizabeth McAlister, "The Madonna of 115th Street Revisited: Vodou and Haitian Catholicism in the Age of Transnationalism," in *Gatherings in Diaspora: Religious Cultures and the New Immigration*, ed. R. Stephen Warner and Judith G. Wittner (Philadelphia: Temple University Press, 1998), 123–60.

4. SELFHOOD AND DIFFERENCE

1. Piri Thomas, *Down These Mean Streets* (New York: Alfred A. Knopf, 1967; repr. New York: Vintage, 1997), ix. Subsequent citations refer to the Vintage edition.
2. Claude McKay, review of *Home to Harlem* by Claude McKay, in James Clarke, ed., "Significant Books Reviewed by Their Own Authors," *McClure's*, June 1928, 81; quoted in Wayne F. Cooper, *Claude McKay: Rebel Sojourner in the Harlem Renaissance: A Biography* (Baton Rouge: Louisiana State University Press, 1987), 71–72.
3. Langston Hughes writes in his autobiography *The Big Sea* (Columbia: University of Missouri Press, 2002), "I went up the steps and out into the bright September sunlight. Harlem! I stood there, dropped my bags, took a deep breath and felt happy again" (83).

4. SELFHOOD AND DIFFERENCE

4. I mean here for the life story to be constituted by the totality of personal accounts (in writings and oral interviews) and performances (on the page and on the stage). Both Piri Thomas and Alaudin Ullah are in this sense constructing life stories. There are a number of debates in the fields of history and anthropology about how to understand particular forms, and the more theorized positions therein dispense with any expectation of empirical truths and focus on the constructed nature of the self. For thoughtful discussions of this topic, see: Charlotte Linde, *Life Stories: The Creation of Coherence* (Oxford: Oxford University Press, 1993); James L. Peacock and Dorothy C. Holland, "The Narrated Self: Life Stories in Process," *Ethos* 21, no. 4 (1993): 367–83; and Daniel James, *Doña María's Story: Life History, Memory and Political Identity* (Durham, NC: Duke University Press, 2000).
5. Mikhail Bakhtin, "Discourse in the Novel" (1934–1935), in *The Dialogical Imagination: Four Essays*, ed. Michael Holquist, trans. Caryl Emerson and Michael Holquist (Austin: University of Texas Press, 1981), 288.
6. Svetlana Boym, *The Future of Nostalgia* (New York: Basic, 2001), xvi.
7. Boym, *Future of Nostalgia*, xvi, 49.
8. Christopher Hayes, *The Harlem Uprising: Segregation and Inequality in Postwar New York City* (New York: Columbia University Press, 2021).
9. Daniel Moynihan, *The Negro Family: The Case for National Action* (Washington, D.C.: Office of Policy Planning and Research, U.S. Department of Labor, 1965).
10. See Claude Brown, *Manchild in the Promised Land* (New York: Macmillan, 1965). Carlo Rotella has wonderfully explored these questions in *October Cities: The Redevelopment of Urban Literature* (Berkeley: University of California Press, 1998).
11. Ralph Ellison, "'A Very Stern Discipline,'" interview by James Thompson, Lenox Raphael, and Steve Cannon, *Harper's Magazine*, March 1967, rpt. in Ralph Ellison, *Going to the Territory* (New York: Random House, 1986), 275–76. Years later he was even more critical, saying that describing Harlem as a ghetto was "one of the most damaging misuses of a concept that has ever come about in the United States" and noting the fundamental openness of the space: "In Harlem, in fact in most so-called Negro ghettos, a lot of Negroes do not spend most of their time there. They work outside. They work as domestics in white homes; they're cooking, they're taking care of children, they're teaching them their manners, they're changing their diapers; they are completely involved in America on that level." "An Interview with Ralph Ellison," interview by Richard Kostelanetz, *The Iowa Review* 19, no. 3 (Fall 1989): 1–10, 5, 6.
12. Johanna Fernandez, *The Young Lords: A Radical History* (Chapel Hill: University of North Carolina Press, 2020).
13. Michelle Joan Wilkinson, in "'To Make a Poet Black': Canonizing Puerto Rican Poets in the Black Arts Movement," explains: "The affirmation of a 'black aesthetic' encouraged assertions of a 'Nuyorican aesthetic'—a New York Puerto Rican aesthetic as defined by Miguel Algarín, the enterprising founder and director of the Nuyorican Poets Café since 1975. Yet, prior to the 1970s Nuyorican poetry movement, Puerto Rican poets were participating and collaborating in the development of the Black Arts Movement. In

4. SELFHOOD AND DIFFERENCE

New York City, where blacks and Puerto Ricans often lived adjacent to each other, the connection was particularly strong . . . a substantial number of Puerto Ricans and African Americans publicly promoted each other's agendas, providing the intergroup alliances that lent support to both social movements. For example, African Americans participated in the predominantly Puerto Rican Young Lords Party and Puerto Ricans participated in the Black Panther Party." In *New Thoughts on the Black Arts Movement*, eds. Lisa Gail Collins and Margo Natalie Crawford (New Brunswick, NJ: Rutgers University Press, 2006), 317–32, 319. See also James Smethurst, *The Black Arts Movement: Literary Nationalism in the 1960s and 1970s* (Chapel Hill: University of North Carolina Press, 2005); Urayoán Noel, *In Visible Movement: Nuyorican Poetry from the Sixties to Slam* (Iowa City: University of Iowa Press, 2014).

14. In *The Afro Latin Memoir: Race, Ethnicity and Literary Interculturalism* (Chapel Hill: University of North Carolina Press, 2023), Trent Masiki makes the argument that Thomas was particularly influenced by a "Black aesthetic" and his engagements with the Black Arts movement.
15. Raymond Chandler, "The Simple Art of Murder," *The Atlantic*, December 1944, 53–59, 59.
16. Philippe Lejeune, *On Autobiography*, ed. Paul John Eakin (Minneapolis: University of Minnesota Press, 1989).
17. One compelling example is Sharifa Rhodes-Pitts's *Harlem Is Nowhere: A Journey to the Mecca of Black Harlem* (New York: Little, Brown, 2013). As I indicated in the introduction, this is a notion that derives from Henri Lefebvre's discussion in *The Production of Space*, trans. Donald Nicholson-Smith (Oxford: Blackwell, 1991).
18. Alaudin Ullah, interview by author, September 21, 2016, New York, NY.
19. Jesse Hoffnung-Garskof, *Racial Migrations: New York City and the Revolutionary Politics of the Spanish Caribbean* (Princeton: Princeton University Press, 2019); Lara Putnam, *Radical Moves: Caribbean Migrants and the Politics of Race in the Jazz Age* (Chapel Hill: University of North Carolina Press, 2013); Virginia Sánchez Korrol, *From Colonial to Community: The History of Puerto Ricans in New York City* (Berkeley: University of California Press, 1994); Lorrin Thomas, *Puerto Rican Citizen: History and Political Identity in Twentieth-Century New York City* (Chicago: University of Chicago Press); Arlene Dávila, *Barrio Dreams: Puerto Ricans, Latinos, and the Neoliberal City* (Berkeley: University of California Press, 2004); Daniel Acosta Elkan, "The Colonia Next Door: Puerto Ricans in the Harlem Community, 1917–1948," PhD diss., Bowling Green State University, December 2017; and Gabriel Haslip-Viera, Angelo Falcón, and Félix Matos Rodriguez, eds., *Boricuas in Gotham: Puerto Ricans in the Making of Modern New York City* (Princeton, NJ: Markus Weiner, 2005).
20. "Harlem's Puerto Ricans," *New York Amsterdam News*, June 10, 1950. See also Dan Wakefield, *Island in the City: The World of Spanish Harlem* (Boston: Houghton Mifflin, 1959); Patricia Cayo Sexton, *Spanish Harlem: An Anatomy of Poverty* (New York: Harper and Row, 1965). Philippe Bourgois' ethnographic study *In Search of Respect: Selling Crack in El Barrio* (Cambridge, UK: Cambridge University Press, 1995) might be seen as a text

4. SELFHOOD AND DIFFERENCE

that is more self-conscious about the danger of stereotypical discourse on poor racial subjects in the city, though that is indeed a difficult feat to pull off when considering drugs and poverty, and when the author is not a local inhabitant (a classic dilemma of anthropological work on race and ethnicity).

21. In one example, a 1952 convention of sixty-six Puerto Rican and "Spanish-speaking" organizations in New York to discuss racial and economic betterment found some resolution in a council that would include African American groups, for the general goal of "banding together." "Sees Progress of Puerto Rican, Negroes in Unity," *New York Amsterdam News*, February 23, 1952.
22. Thomas, *Down These Mean Streets*, ix.
23. As Michel De Certeau writes: "His altitude transforms him into a voyeur. It places him at a distance. It changes an enchanting world into a text. It allows him to read it; to become a solar Eye, a god's regard. The exaltation of a scopic or a gnostic drive. Just to be this seeing point creates the fiction of knowledge." "Practices of Space," in *On Signs*, ed. Marshall Blonsky (Baltimore: Johns Hopkins University Press, 1985), 123–45, 123.
24. Thomas, *Down These Mean Streets*, ix.
25. Thomas, *Down These Mean Streets*, 24. In 1939, probably not too much earlier than the period that Thomas was representing (he would have been eleven years old, which seems like the right age for this encounter) the authors of the *New York City Guide* referred to a general understanding of "Spanish Harlem" and "Italian Harlem" continuing to exist simultaneously and with slightly different territories, with Italians inhabiting the area all the way east to the East River and Latinos living above Central Park North, east of Lenox, but west of Third Avenue. Federal Writers' Project, *New York City Guide* (New York: Random House, 1939), 253. The scene in the story, however, testifies to clearer, more carefully policed borders between the two ethnic areas.
26. Thomas, *Down These Mean Streets*, 24, 25.
27. Jacques Lacan, *The Four Fundamental Concepts of Psycho-Analysis*, ed. Jacques-Alain Miller, trans. Alan Sheridan (New York: W. W. Norton, 1978).
28. Thomas, *Down These Mean Streets*, 25.
29. Robert Orsi's "The Religious Boundaries of an Inbetween People: Street *Feste* and the Problem of the Dark-Skinned Other in Italian Harlem, 1920–1990," *American Quarterly* 44, no. 3 (September 1992): 313–47, discusses some of the cross-cultural exchanges on the border between "Italian" and "Spanish" Harlem that I refer to here. Other books on Italian Americans and race include Thomas A. Guglielmo, *White on Arrival: Italians, Race, Color and Power in Chicago, 1890–1945* (New York: Oxford University Press, 2003); and Jennifer Guglielmo and Salvatore Salerno, eds., *Are Italians White? How Race Is Made in America* (New York: Routledge, 2003).
30. Thomas, *Down These Mean Streets*, 30.
31. Thomas, *Down These Mean Streets*, 41–42.
32. Thomas, *Down These Mean Streets*, 43.
33. Thomas, *Down These Mean Streets*, 46.
34. Thomas, *Down These Mean Streets*, 46.

4. SELFHOOD AND DIFFERENCE

35. Thomas, *Down These Mean Streets*, 83.
36. Thomas, *Down These Mean Streets*, 83.
37. Thomas, *Down These Mean Streets*, 143.
38. Thomas, *Down These Mean Streets*, 1.
39. See: Yolanda Martínez-San Miguel's "Ethnic Specularities: Exploring the Caribbean and Latino Dimensions of *Down These Mean Streets*," *Latino Studies* 13, no. 3 (September 2015): 358–75.
40. Wolfgang Binder, "An Interview with Piri Thomas," *Minority Voices* 4, no. 1 (Spring 1980): 63–78. See Lisa McGill's *Constructing Black Selves: Caribbean American Narratives and the Second Generation* (New York: New York University Press, 2005) for a discussion of some of these issues, as well as Thomas's text.
41. Jesse Hoffnung-Garskof provides important insights about Schomburg's complicated identities in "The Migrations of Arturo Schomburg: On Being Antillano, Negro, and Puerto Rican in New York 1891–1938," *Journal of American Ethnic History* 21, no. 1 (Fall 2001): 3–49. Also see Earl Lewis, "To Turn as on a Pivot: Writing African Americans Into a History of Overlapping Diasporas," *American Historical Review* 100 (1995): 786–87, on overlapping diasporas, and Winston James, "The Peculiarities of Afro-Hispanic Radicalism in the United States: The Political Trajectories of Arturo Schomburg and Jesús Colón," chapter 7 in *Holding Aloft the Banner of Ethiopia: Caribbean Radicalism in Early Twentieth-Century America* (London: Verso, 1998), where a somewhat different argument about Schomburg's turn away from Puerto Ricanness is made.
42. Thomas, *Down These Mean Streets*, 69.
43. One example is the Harlem Legislative Conference; see folio "From the 'Office of Harlem Legislative Conference, 1484 First Avenue, New York, NY,'" December 13, 1947, box 3, Vito Marcantonio Papers: 1935–1953, Manuscripts and Archives Division, New York Public Library.
44. Thomas, *Down These Mean Streets*, 104.
45. Thomas, *Down These Mean Streets*, 121.
46. Thomas, *Down These Mean Streets*, 121.
47. Thomas, *Down These Mean Streets*, 159.
48. W. E. B. Du Bois, *The Souls of Black Folk* (Oxford: Oxford University Press, 2007 [1903]), particularly chapter 7, "Of the Black Belt," 53–64.
49. Thomas, *Down These Mean Streets*, 174.
50. Thomas, *Down These Mean Streets*, 174.
51. Thomas, *Down These Mean Streets*, 177.
52. Thomas, *Down These Mean Streets*, 177.
53. Thomas, *Down These Mean Streets*, 179.
54. See Adolph Reed Jr., "From Jenner to Dolezal: One Trans Good, the Other Not So Much," *Common Dreams*, June 15, 2015; Marquis Bey and Theodora Sakellarides, "When We Enter: The Blackness of Rachel Dolezal," *Black Scholar* 46, no. 4 (December 2016): 33–48; and Rogers Brubaker, "The Dolezal Affair: Race, Gender, and the Micropolitics of Identity," *Ethnic and Racial Studies* 39, no. 3 (2016): 414–48.

4. SELFHOOD AND DIFFERENCE

55. Thomas, *Down These Mean Streets*, 185.
56. Thomas, *Down These Mean Streets*, 186.
57. Richard Wright, *Native Son* (New York: Harper & Brothers, 1940); Eldridge Cleaver, *Soul on Ice* (Menlo Park, CA: Ramparts Press, 1968). Although *Soul on Ice* was published the year after *Down These Mean Streets*, its essays were written some years earlier, while Cleaver was in prison. The rough coincidence of these works and their sentiments, however, is what I want to point to here, particularly the sexualization of the white woman as a response to being traumatized by racism.
58. Thomas, *Down These Mean Streets*, 187.
59. Martínez-San Miguel has argued that the ensuing scene reveals how Thomas answers that dilemma with a diasporic consciousness, a representation in which "the Afro-Antillean man recovers his Hispanic and black identity to reject the specular image imposed on him by a white metropolitan imaginary." "Ethnic Specularities," 362.
60. See Marta Sánchez, *Shakin' Up Race and Gender: Intercultural Connections in Puerto Rican, African American, and Chicano Narratives and Culture (1965–1995)* (Austin: University of Texas Press, 2005), an excellent study of narratives that fills out this idea; and also Marta Caminero-Santangelo, "'Puerto Rican Negro': Defining Race in Piri Thomas's *Down These Mean Streets*," *MELUS* 29, no. 2 (Summer 2004): 205–26; and Eleuterio Santiago-Díaz and Ilia Rodríguez, "Writing Race Against Literary Whiteness: The Afro-Puerto Rican Outcry of Piri Thomas," *Bilingual Review/La Revista Bilingüe* 31, no. 1 (January–April 2012–2013): 12–29.
61. Thomas, *Down These Mean Streets*, 187.
62. Thomas, *Down These Mean Streets*, 188. Later in this passage the prostitute also speaks imperfect Spanish, which testifies to the widespread use of at least some Spanish communication in Texas. One could make a similar argument about how a kind of partial casual bilingualism functions in Harlem, evident in my analysis of "Spanish Blood" in chapter 2 and Vito Marcantonio's language use, which I discussed in chapter 3.
63. Thomas, *Down These Mean Streets*, 189.
64. Thomas, *Down These Mean Streets*, 189.
65. Thomas, *Down These Mean Streets*, 145.
66. Malcolm X and Alex Haley, *The Autobiography of Malcolm X* (New York: Grove Press, 1966).
67. Thomas, *Down These Mean Streets*, 290.
68. Langston Hughes, "Dream Variation," originally published in *The Weary Blues* (New York: Alfred A. Knopf, 1926), 43.
69. Piri Thomas, "Piri Thomas: An Interview," interview by Dorothee von Huene Greenberg, *MELUS* 26, no. 3 (Autumn 2001): 77–99; discussion of the origin of *Down These Mean Streets* appears on 80.
70. Thomas, *Down These Mean Streets*, 4.
71. Jonathan Randal, "The Harlem Italians," *New York Times*, May 30, 1966.
72. Richard Schechner, *Performance Theory*, 2nd ed. (New York: Routledge, 1988). Schechner reads sociologist Erving Goffman's project in evocative ways (e.g., "Goffman meant

4. SELFHOOD AND DIFFERENCE

that people were always involved in role-playing, in constructing and staging their multiple identities" [x]) that have influenced my reading *Down These Mean Streets* as a kind of performance, even though it is "staged" as writing. On bringing the language of performance to the study of literature, see an early article: Barbara Herrnstein-Smith, "Literature, as Performance, Fiction, and Art," *Journal of Philosophy* 67, no. 16 (August 1970): 553–63. See also Lynn C. Miller and Jacqueline Taylor, "The Constructed Self: Strategies and Aesthetic Choices in Autobiographical Performance," in *The SAGE Handbook of Performance Studies*, ed. D. Soyini Madison and Judith Hamera (Thousand Oaks, CA: SAGE, 2006), 169–87.

73. See J. L. Austin, *How to Do Things with Words* (Cambridge, MA: Harvard University Press, 1962), for an early example of bringing language and performance together.
74. Thomas, "An Interview," 85.
75. Thomas, "An Interview," 82.
76. Thomas, *Down These Mean Streets*, 198–99.
77. Thomas, "An Interview," 98.
78. Paul Gilroy's "planetary humanism," which he articulated in, among other publications, *Against Race: Imagining Political Culture Beyond the Color Line* (Cambridge, MA: Harvard University Press, 2000), draws criticism from Dan Robotham in an article for a special journal issue devoted to questions of race, "Cosmopolitanism and Planetary Humanism: The Strategic Universalism of Paul Gilroy," *South Atlantic Quarterly* 104, no. 3 (Summer 2005): 561–82. See also Gayatri Chakravorty Spivak, *Death of a Discipline* (New York: Columbia University Press, 2003).
79. Piri Thomas, *Down These Mean Streets* (New York: Signet, 1968).
80. James Nelson Goodsell, "From the Book Reviewer's Shelf: A New Voice for Spanish Harlem," *Christian Science Monitor*, June 15, 1967; Daniel Stern, "One Who Got Away," review of *Down These Mean Streets*, by Piri Thomas, *New York Times*, May 21, 1967.
81. See, for example, the title of the *New York Times* piece, "One Who Got Away."
82. See letters in box 1, file 14 and box 2, file 4, Piri Thomas Papers, Schomburg Center for Research in Black Culture, Manuscripts, Archives and Rare Books Division, New York Public Library (hereafter cited as Thomas Papers).
83. Thomas kept many of these letters in his personal correspondence; see box 1, folder 16, Thomas Papers.
84. Ruben Ramos Jr. to Piri Thomas, April 28, 1969, box 1, folder 14, Thomas Papers.
85. Box 1, file 20 and box 2, file 1, Thomas Papers.
86. Box 1, file 19, Thomas Papers.
87. Box 3, folder 12, Thomas Papers.
88. Gene I. Maeroff, "Book Ban Splits a Queens School District," *New York Times*, May 9, 1971.
89. Leonard Buder, "School District Bans a Book on East Harlem," *New York Times*, April 21, 1971.
90. *Indio*, script and performance by Allaudin Ullah, dir. Loretta Greco, Public Theater, New York, NY, June 28, 2005. In some cases, I refer to the performance that I attended, in others to the script that Ullah provided to me.

4. SELFHOOD AND DIFFERENCE

91. Thomas L. Webber, *Flying Over 96th Street: Memoir of an East Harlem White Boy* (New York: Scribner, 2004); and Irving Louis Horowitz, *Daydreams and Nightmares: Reflections on a Harlem Childhood* (Oxford, MS: University of Mississippi Press, 1990).
92. *Dishwasher Dreams*, script and performance by Allaudin Ullah, dir. Gabriel Vega Weissman, Castillo Theatre, New York, NY, October 26, 2018. This show is based on *Indio*, but also has some new material.
93. Vivek Bald, *Bengali Harlem and the Lost Histories of South Asian America* (Cambridge, MA: Harvard University Press, 2013).
94. The documentary film *In Search of Bengali Harlem*, directed by Vivek Bald and Alaudin Ullah (2022), is a lyrical exploration of Ullah's family story amid the "lost histories" of Bengali–South Asian migrants. See "Alaudin Ullah and Vivek Bald Interview for In Search of Bengali Harlem: APFF 2023," LRM Online, May 8, 2023, video, 26:52, https://www.youtube.com/watch?v=IaYZfXzqUpU.
95. See my discussion of Kochiyama's perception of Malcolm X in the introduction of this book.
96. *Harold and Kumar Go to White Castle*, directed by Danny Leiner (2004) and its film and television sequels; Aziz Ansari, *Master of None*, Netflix (2015–present); Hasan Minhaj, *Patriot Act with Hasan Minhaj*, Netflix, 2018.
97. *The Brother from Another Planet*, directed by John Sayles (1984).
98. *Dishwasher Dreams*.
99. *Indio*, manuscript in possession of the author.
100. See chapter 1, note 112.
101. Ullah has also been developing a play entitled "Halal Brothers" about a fictionalized exchange between Bengali and African American Muslims on the day of Malcolm X's murder in 1965, the occasion that opened *Cross-Cultural Harlem*.
102. *Indio*, manuscript, 8.
103. *Indio*, manuscript, 9–10.
104. *Indio*, manuscript, 11.
105. *Indio*, manuscript, 25.
106. *Indio*, Public Theater, June 28, 2005.
107. Many Indian migrants who came in the late 1960s or early 1970s, for example, told me of going to area Chinatowns for vegetables that were familiar to them before South Asian markets became more accessible. Fieldwork conversations conducted in the 1990s for Sandhya Shukla, *India Abroad: Diasporic Cultures of Postwar America and England* (Princeton: Princeton University Press, 2003).
108. *Indio*, manuscript, 32.
109. One can see the denigration of mother figures, who are anxious and unyielding in the face of economic and cultural insecurity, especially in favor of more supportive and, strangely, less policing fathers in early novels such as *Pride and Prejudice*, published in 1813, and the ethnic variant of that construction in a novel such as Amy Tan's *The Joy Luck Club* (New York: G. Putnam's Sons, 1989) or a film like *Bend It Like Beckham*, directed by Gurinder Chadha (2002).
110. *Indio*, manuscript, 41–42.

4. SELFHOOD AND DIFFERENCE

111. It is worth adding how careful Ullah is about presentation and representation. After a 2018 performance I attended, he asked if this term "kaloowa" or "kaluwa," a derogatory term from the nineteenth century, would be, like "nigger," seen as problematic to use in a public performance.
112. *Indio*, manuscript, 43.
113. Johanna Fernández makes the point that this sort of disagreement is a classic generational divide among immigrants and their children: those who have come from places with different maps for race and identity have a hard time comprehending the racial identification with Blackness that young people growing up in a U.S. urban context might feel. Fernández, *Young Lords*, 61.
114. Alaudin Ullah, interview by the author, September 8, 2016, New York, NY.
115. Ullah, interview, September 8, 2016.
116. Mel Watkins, *African American Humor: The Best Black Comedy from Slavery to Today* (Chicago: Lawrence Hill Books, 2002).
117. *Dishwater Dreams*, Castillo Theatre, October 26, 2018.
118. Ullah shared this last detail during a July 12, 2005 interview with the author, New York, NY.
119. Mikhail Bakhtin, *Problems of Dostoevsky's Poetics*, ed. and trans. Caryl Emerson (Minneapolis: University of Minnesota Press, 1984), 6.
120. *Indio*, manuscript, 57.
121. James Baldwin, "Notes of a Native Son," in *Notes of a Native Son* (New York: Dial Press, 1963), 76–102.
122. *Indio*, manuscript, 53.
123. *Indio*, manuscript, 54.
124. *In Search of Bengali Harlem*.
125. Ullah, interview, September 8, 2016.
126. Joseph Roach, *Cities of the Dead: Circum-Atlantic Performance* (New York: Columbia University Press, 1996), 39.
127. Lejeune, *On Autobiography*, 22.
128. Thomas, "An Interview," 82.
129. Paul John Eakin, *Touching the World: Reference in Autobiography* (Princeton: Princeton University Press, 1992), 24.
130. Raymond Williams, *Keywords: A Vocabulary of Culture and Society*, rev. ed. (New York: Oxford University Press, 1983), 126.
131. Wilson Harris, *The Radical Imagination: Lectures and Talks*, ed. Alan Riach and Mark Williams (Liège, BE: Department of English, University of Liège, 1992), 31.
132. Françoise Lionnet and Shu-mei Shih point to "lateral" networks in their coedited *Minor Transnationalism* (Durham, NC: Duke University Press, 2005), 1. I would read this as resembling the rhizome about which Gilles Deleuze and Félix Guattari have written in *A Thousand Plateaus: Capitalism and Schizophrenia*, trans. Brian Massumi (London: Continuum, 2004), even if Lionnet and Shih take issue with the notion of the rhizome, arguing that it assumes a dominant center. Édouard Glissant's notion of "relation" is another reference point. For this discussion, I am seeking to point to similar horizontal exchanges.

A CODA FOR THE STORIES

133. Charles Baudelaire, "The Painter of Modern Life" (1863), in *The Painter of Modern Life: and Other Essays*, trans. and ed. Jonathan Mayne (London: Phaidon, 1964), 1–40; Walter Benjamin, *The Arcades Project*, trans. Howard Eiland and Kevin McLaughlin (Cambridge, MA: The Belknap Press of Harvard University Press, 1991).
134. David Harvey, *Paris, Capital of Modernity* (New York: Routledge, 2003).
135. This is what Bart van Leeuwen has helpfully described as "moral" cosmopolitanism, in "If we are *flaneurs*, can we be cosmopolitans?" *Urban Studies* 56, no. 2 (2019): 301–16.
136. Karl J. Weintraub, "Autobiography and Historical Consciousness," *Critical Inquiry* 1, no. 4 (1975): 821–48. He writes: "The growing significance of autobiography is thus a part of that great intellectual revolution marked by the emergence of the particular modern form of historical mindedness we call historism or historicism" (821).
137. Ramón Sáldivar and Sidonie Smith have argued respectively for Chicano and women's writings of the self. Autobiographies by minoritized and/or disempowered peoples challenge dominant agents of history and develop productive literary spaces in which to rethink the social worlds by which they have been constructed. Ramón Sáldivar, *Chicano Narrative: The Dialectics of Difference* (Madison: University of Wisconsin Press, 1990); Sidonie Smith and Julia Watson, *Reading Autobiography: A Guide for Interpreting Life Narratives* (Minneapolis: University of Minnesota Press, 2010).
138. Michael M. J. Fischer, "Ethnicity and the Post-Modern Arts of Memory," in *The Poetics and Politics of Ethnography*, ed. James Clifford and George E. Marcus (Berkeley: University of California Press, 1986), 194–233.
139. Roach, *Cities of the Dead*, 6.
140. Ullah, interview, September 8, 2016.
141. Rotella, *October Cities*.
142. Piri Thomas, *Savior, Savior, Hold My Hand* (New York: Doubleday, 1972).
143. Thomas, *Down These Mean Streets*, 314.
144. Boym, *Future of Nostalgia*, xvi.
145. Boym, *Future of Nostalgia*, 50.

A CODA FOR THE STORIES

1. Roi Ottley, *New World A-Coming: Inside Black America* (New York: Houghton Mifflin, 1943), 54.
2. Ottley, *New World A-Coming*, 40–41.
3. Ottley, *New World A-Coming*, 50, 53.
4. "Media Alert," The Vito Marcantonio Forum, accessed June 9, 2023, https://vitomarcantonioforum.com.
5. Peter Rofrano, interview by the author, April 5, 2005, New York, NY.
6. Edward Said's work comes to mind, in *Culture and Imperialism* (New York: Vintage, 1993), as does Walter Mignolo's *Local Histories/Global Designs: Coloniality, Subaltern Knowledges and Border Thinking* (Princeton: Princeton University Press, 2000).

A CODA FOR THE STORIES

7. Richard Schaffer and Neil Smith, "The Gentrification of Harlem?" *Annals of the Association of American Geographers* 76, no. 3 (September 1986): 347–65, 347. See also the fine collection of essays: Andrew M. Fearnley and Daniel Matlin, eds., *Race Capital? Harlem as Setting and Symbol* (New York: Columbia University Press, 2018).
8. There are so many projects to identify here. Notable ones include the documentary film *Summer of Soul* (dir. Ahmir "Questlove" Thompson, 2021), about the 1969 Harlem Cultural Festival, which has been overshadowed by Woodstock, and a memoir by Paula Williams Madison about growing up with a Chinese-Jamaican mother in Harlem and returning to Jamaica to search for her Chinese grandfather: *Finding Samuel Love: China, Jamaica, Harlem* (New York: HarperCollins, 2015).

INDEX

Page numbers in *italics* refer to images.

Abdullah, Zain, 253n13
Abyssinian Baptist Church, 11
affect: vs emotion, 177
African Americans: the arts and, 55, 263n107, 272n112, 276n24, 295n13; and Italians, 292n87; Jewish, 11; and Jews, 122–23, 241–42, 280n88, 280n91, 281n94; LGBTQ 269n64; musical styles of, 272n112; national identity and, 192; politics and, 154–55; prejudice against, 40–41, 60, 63, 67, 71, 72–74, 82, 123, 170, 204, 224–25, 260n72, 280n88; and Puerto Ricans, 75–76, 107, 196, 198–200, 295n13, 297n21
Africans: as Harlem residents, 4, 10, 12, 114–15; national identity and, 192
Afro-Indigenous people: as Harlem residents, 5
Aladdin. *See* Ullah, Alaudin
Albarelli, Luigi ,144, 176

Algarín, Miguel, 295n13
Althusser, Louis, 262n12
Amiable with Big Teeth (McKay), 100, 132–33, 283n129
anti-Blackness. *See* racism
anti-Semitism, 122–23, 242, 280n91–92
Apollo Theater, 9
Asians and Asian Americans: as documentary subjects, 301n94; as Harlem residents/workers, 23–24, 29, 87, 108, 217–20, 223–26, 240–41, 301n107, 304n8; on Marcantonio, 173, 292n90; naturalization of, 172–73; prejudice against, 228–29, 260n72; the self and, 230
Audubon Ballroom (*also* San Juan Theater), 15
Aurousseau, Marcel, 125
autobiography, 185, 190, 229, 232, 271n94, 303n136–37; definition of, 209
Avilez, GerShun, 269n64

INDEX

Babb, Valerie, 46
Baker, George. *See* Father Divine
Bakhtin, Mikhail, 32, 82, 168, 169, 187, 227, 291n75
Bald, Vivek, 218, 253n13, 301n94
Baldwin, James, 42, 83, 228, 281n94
Banana Bottom (McKay), 109
Banks, William H. Jr., 73
Baraka, Amiri, 48, 272n112
baseball, 227–28
Bass, Ramona, 81
Bearden, Romare, 276n24
Bell, Christopher, 151, 255n24
Benjamin, Walter, 263n105
Biaggi, Pedro, 164–65
Big Sea, The (Hughes). *See under* Hughes, Langston
bilingualism, 57–58, 60
Black Arts Movement, 295n13
Black Manhattan (Johnson), 124–25, 281n98
Black Metropolis (Drake and Cayton), 126
Black Muslims, 206–7, 220; Malcolm X and, 251n2, 251n4. *See also* Islam
Black women, 47; geographies of, 67, 69; working, 121
Blair, Sara, 263n102, 277n26
Blumstein's Department Store, 9, 254n20
Boas, Franz, 82
Bontemps, Arna, 85–86
Bourgois, Philippe, 296n20
Bourne, Randolph, 170
Bowser, Pearl, 276n26
Boym, Svetlana, 112, 187–88, 236–37
Boy of the Border (Hughes), 86
Brother from Another Planet (film), 220
Brown, Claude, 236
Brown, Eugene. *See* Sufi Abdul Hamid
Brown, J. Dillon, 275n17
Brown, Wendy, 155
Burgess, Ernest W., 277n41

Caribbean, cross-culturality of, 17–18; extended (Harlem), 18–19, 91, 109, 162, 290n60
Caribbeans and Caribbean-Americans as Harlem residents, 15, 199–200, 290n60, 294n113
Carnegie, Charles V., 258n51
Cartier-Bresson, Henri, 266n15
Certeau, Michel de, 33, 34, 62, 263n103, 297n23
Chamoiseau, Patrick, 19, 20
Chandler, Raymond, 189
Charlottesville, Virginia, 43, 264n115
Chekhov, Anton, 271n95
Chinitz, David E., 270n75
Cinotto, Simone, 285n10
City, The (Park, Burgess, and McKenzie), 125
class, social: Marcantonio on, 146–47; and race, 69, 121, 135, 147; Ullah on, 217, 219, 222
Cleaver, Eldridge, 299n57
Cloutier, Jean-Christophe, 132–33, 274nn4–5, 282n125, 283n129
Columbia University, 14, 15–16
communism and leftism, 154–55; Hughes and, 269n61, 270n68; Marcantonio on, 151, 152–53, 176–77, 179, 287nn33–34, 288n48; McKay and, 121, 123–24, 126–27, 131, 135; resources, 282n109, 284n5, 288n38
Cooper, Wayne F., 275n15
Covarrubias, Miguel, 85
Covello, Leonard, 151, 158, 159, 176
Cowl, Carl, 132, 282nn125–26
cross-culturality, 17–18, 30, 87, 200, 240–41, 261n78, 266n10, 272n105, 302n132; Caribbean, 17–18; fictional representations of, 198–99, 200–203; Guyanese, 17; Harlem, 3–4, 6, 9–12, 19, 26, 31–32, 47–48, 61, 93, 94, 97, 103, 104–8, 110–11, 113, 122–24, 241, 253n13, 255n24,

306

INDEX

261n78, 271n96; W. Harris on, 17, 232–33; heteroglossia and, 32; vs interculturality, 258n45; interpreting, 141; Y. Kochiyama on, 25; language and, 169–70, 209–10, 223; Malcolm X and, 24–25; vs multiculturality, 16–17; social, 68, 69–70. *See also* bilingualism

Cullen, Countee, 79

culture: dominant, 17, 48; realism and, 28; R. Williams on, 263n101. *See also* cross-culturality

dance, 55, 113; as freedom, 70; as social explicator, 268n30

Dávila, Arlene, 253n13

Davis, Arthur P., 265n2

Davis, Griffith J., 266n15

Day, Dorothy, 176–77, 178

Deleuze, Gilles, 39, 154, 283n134

Dewey, John, 127

Díaz, Junot, 140, 284n4

"Digital Harlem" (mapping project), 254n16

Down These Mean Streets (Thomas), 189–91, 192, 193–213; ethnic identity in, 299n59; language in, 299n62; library bans of, 214–15

Du Bois, W. E. B., 97, 124, 173–74, 176; on Black-Asian solidarity, 24–25, 260n72

Durkheim, Émile, 155, 288n42

Eakin, Paul John, 232

East Harlem, 9–10, 11, 12, 15, 16, 145–46; compared to Harlem 148–49; compared to Italian Harlem, 157

Edwards, Brent Hayes, 132–33, 266n17, 274n4, 279n86

El Barrio (*also* Spanish Harlem), 3–4, 74, 193; physical boundaries of, 297n25; resources, 296n20, 297n29

Ellison, Fanny, 88

Ellison, Ralph, 88, 259n55, 295n11; on Harlem, 189, 295n11

emotion vs affect, 177

equality, 170–71; Marcantonio on, 158, 170–71; McKay on, 98

Father Divine (George Baker), 11, 112–14, 128, 278nn58–60, 279n63; McKay on, 278n60; resources on, 278n59

Federal Writers' Project, 126, 281n108

Fernández, Johanna, 302n113

Filipinos, 172–73

Flatley, Jonathan, 177

Ford, Henry, 122

Frazier, E. Franklin, 281n104

Futtam, Madame Fu, 115–16

Gabaccia, Donna, 145, 285n11

Garvey, Marcus, 11, 93, 278n58; McKay on, 118–19

Gilloch, Graeme, 263n105

Gilroy, Paul, 26, 134, 272n112, 300n78

Glissant, Édouard, 17, 18, 258n46, 261n78, 283n132, 302n132

globalism (*also* globality, globalization), 20, 43–44, 233, 261n78; Hughes and, 48–50, 52–67, 71–77, 80, 85; Marcantonio and, 140–41, 180–81; McKay and, 99–100, 104, 105–11, 114–19, 122–24, 130–31; Thomas and, 212. *See also* cross-culturality; place; space

Goffman, Erving, 299n72

Grady, Constance, 284n4

Guattari, Félix, 39, 154, 283n134

Guillén, Nicolás, 84–85, 273n113

Gurock, Jeffrey, 253n13, 280n87

Guterl, Matthew Pratt, 286n24

Guyana, cross-culturality in, 17

Hall, Stuart, 18, 135, 154, 264n111

Hamid, Sufi Abdul (Eugene Brown), 118, 119–22, 123, 132; spouse of, 115–16.

INDEX

Harlem: artistic depictions of, 47–73, 77, 83–84, 86, 88–92, 93, 131–33, 149–50, 185–202, 206–8, 212–13, 217–37, 279n62, 285n14, 304n8; "Blackness" of, 16, 18–19, 25, 29, 30–32, 48–50, 74–76, 100, 103, 106–9, 110–11, 114–15, 120–22, 129–31, 135, 242–43, 256n33, 268n49, 273n113; compared to Caribbean, 18–19, 91, 109, 162, 290n60; crime in, 292n87; cross-culturality of, 3–4, 6, 9–12, 19, 26, 31–32, 47–48, 61, 93, 94, 97, 103, 104–8, 110–11, 113, 122–24, 241, 253n13, 255n24, 261n78, 271n96; compared to East Harlem, 148–49; gentrification of, 13, 30, 244, 257n34; high cost of living in, 5, 257n34; indefinable nature of, 6–7, 9, 17, 18, 20, 27–28, 80, 103, 104–5, 185–86, 271n96, 295n11; map of, 8; photographs of, 101–2; physical boundaries of, 7, 8, 9, 14–15, 93, 104, 297n25; poverty in, 13–14, 145, 196–97, 296n20; as writers' haven, 83. *See also* East Harlem; El Barrio; Italian Harlem; *and under* Jews; Italians and Italian-Americans; Latinos; Puerto Ricans

Harlem Glory (McKay), 100, 133, 282nn125–26

Harlem: Negro Metropolis (McKay), 94–98, 101–35; critical reaction to, 127–28, 129–30

Harlem Renaissance, 32

Harris, Wilson, 22, 25, 27, 28, 30, 257n42, 258n44; on cross-culturality, 17, 232–33

Hartman, Saidiya, 40, 264n108

Harvey, David, 178, 233

Hill, Hilda, 128

Hoffnung-Garskof, Jesse, 257n39, 298n41

Hofmeyr, Isabel, 261n83

Hogan, William, 271n96

Holcomb, Gary Edward, 269n61

Holstein, Casper, 117

Home to Harlem (McKay), 131–32

Hughes, Langston, 31, 32, 37, 45–92, *46*, 48, 52, 73, 78–80, 88, 207; *The Big Sea*, 45, 50–51, 60, 68, 72, 269n56, 294n3; Blackness and, 47, 49–50, 53–54, 72, 73, 84–85, 86, 270n75; *Boy of the Border*, 86; and communism, 141–42, 269n61, 270n68; cosmopolitanism of, 52–53, 79; fiction of, 82–83; gay themes in, 68; on Harlem, 45, 49–50, 53, 81, 86, 87, 89–92, 265n2, 294n3; *I Wonder as I Wander*, 84; and Claude McKay, 109; language skills of, 52, 57, 60, 265n3; *Laughing to Keep from Crying*, 50, 82–83; *Montage of a Dream Deferred*, 88–92; *The Pasteboard Bandit*, 86; poetry of, 88–92; *Popo and Fifina*, 86; Simple stories, 50–51, 266n15, 271n94; *The Ways of White Folks*, 53; *The Weary Blues*, 85. *See also* "Spanish Blood"

Human Relations Area Files project, 258n44

Hurston, Zora Neale, on Claude McKay, 102, 109, 278n46

Hutchinson, George, 262nn94–95

identity (*also* the self, selfhood): created, 120; ethnic/personal, 18, 48–49, 56, 62–64, 67, 76, 99–100, 106–11, 147–48, 154, 187–201, 203, 211–12, 216–21, 234, 253n13, 286n24, 302n113, 303n137; generational differences in, 111, 302n113; national, 99–100, 111, 150; and nostalgia, 187–88; performances and, 114–15, 182, 190–92, 194, 196, 209–12, 216–21, 230, 230–32, 235–36, 253n13, 299n72; resources, 295n4

Islam: Kochiyama and, 251n4; Ullah and, 219–21, 229–30. *See also* Black Muslims

Italian Harlem, 9–10, 144–46, 149–50, 157, 182, 285nn10–11 and 14, 287n25, 294n113; physical boundaries of, 297n25; resources, 285n9, 297n29

Italians and Italian-Americans: activism by, 151–52, 157–58; and African Americans, 292n87; ethnic identity of, 147–48,

INDEX

286n20; as Harlem residents, 3–4, 9–10, 11, 140, 149–51, 285nn10–11, 285n14, 287n25, 294n113; Marcantonio and, 147–48, 172–73, 179–80; and Puerto Ricans, 181–82, 254n22, 287n25
I Wonder as I Wander (Hughes), 84

Jackson, John Jr., 253n13, 262n91
James, Henry, 79
Jameson, Fredric, 42–43, 264n114
James, Winston, 258n52, 274n6
Japanese and Japanese-Americans, 23, 173, 292n90
Jews: and African Americans, 122–23, 241–42, 280n88, 280n91, 281n94; Black, 11; depictions of, 90–91; as Harlem residents, 3–4, 10–11, 74–76, 122–23, 255n25, 280n87; and Puerto Ricans, 74–75, 215, 271n84
Johnson, James Weldon, 30, 79, 119; *Black Manhattan*, 124–25, 281n98; on Harlem, 268n49
Jones, Thomas Jesse, 255n24

Kadir, Djelal, 266n12
Kant, Immanuel, 19–20
Katan, Roger, 255n24
Keith, Michael, 104
Kelley, Robin D. G., 30, 288n38
Killens, John Oliver, 211
Kim, Claire Jean, 40
Kochiyama, Yuri, 20–25, *21*, 37, 40–41, 251n4, 263n104; African American influence on, 21; on on cross-culturality, 25; depictions of, *41*, 42, 251n3; and Harlem, 21–22; and Islam, 251n4; and Malcolm X, 1–3, *2*, 22, 23–24, 25
Koshy, Susan, 261n78
Kutzinski, Vera, 52, 273n114

labor agitation, 121
LaFarge, John, 127, 282n112

La Guardia, Fiorello, 10, 11, 153, 166, 256n30; and Marcantonio, 150–52
Laguerre, Michel, 139, 253n14
La Marqueta, 12, 197, 223
language, 57–58, 60; beyond communication, 32–33, 168, 198; as cross-cultural medium, 169–70, 209–10, 223; Harlem politics and, 166–69; literary, 187, 210; and racial/ethnic identity, 19, 57–61, 106, 107, 196, 197–98, 210, 223–24
Lapolla, Garibaldi M., 149–50, 285n14
Latinos, 63; and Africans/African Americans, 75–76, 107, 196, 198–200, 295n13, 297n21; the arts and, 55, 295n13; fictional depictions of, 45–72, 193–213; as Harlem residents, 3–4, 5, 10, 11, 15, 48–49, 64, 74–76, 78, 192–93, 252n11, 297n25; and Italians, 181–82, 254n22, 287n25; and Jews, 74–75, 215, 271n84; independence movements and, 162, 164, 290n62; Marcantonio and, 157, 158, 160–65; music of, 55; prejudice against, 5, 72, 221; racial beliefs of, 57; U.S. citizenship and, 163
Laughing to Keep from Crying (Hughes), 50, 82–83
Leeuwen, Bart van, 303n135
Lefebvre, Henri, 43, 263n103
Lejeune, Philippe, 190, 209, 231, 232
Levine, Caroline, 261n84, 276n23
Lewis, Earl, 272n105
Lewis, Edward W., 101–2, 276nn25–26
LGBTQ community, 11, 68; resources 256n30; vulnerability of 269n64
Life in Harlem (Lewis), 101
Lionnet, Françoise, 261n78, 302n132
Little, Malcolm. *See* Malcolm X
Little Senegal, 4, 10
Locke, Alain, 97, 108, 122, 271n88, 288n41
Looker, Benjamin, 146
Louchheim, Joseph H., 177–78
Lowe, Lisa, 253n12
Lynch, Kevin, 9, 84

309

INDEX

Malcolm X (Malcolm Little), 41, 42, 206–7, 263n104; assassination of, 1–3, *2*, 22; cross-culturality of, 24–25; depictions of, *41*, 42, 251n3; and Islam, 251n4; and Yuri Kochiyama, 1–3, *2*, 22, 23–24. *Also* Malcolm Shabazz

maps and mapping: cognitive, 42–43; movement and, 93–94, 105–11, 114–15, 274n2; non-territorial, 7, 254n16; personal, 233

Marcantonio, Vito, 32–33, 42, 137–84, *143*, 242; altruism of, 172; and Asian causes, 172, 292n90; and Black causes, 158, 159–60; death of, 174–77, *175*, 293n94; on equality, 170–71; and W. E. B. Du Bois, 173–74; ethnic/racial identity and, 149, 153–55; on Harlem, 140, 146–47, 148; on Italians and Italian-Americans, 147–48; language skills of, 166–69, 291n70, 291n72, 291n74; leftist politics and, 179, 287nn30–31, 287n33–34, 288n48, 294n109; locality and, 178–79; and Puerto Rican causes, 157, 158, 160–65, 166–67; respect of Harlem residents for, 175–79

Martínez-San Miguel, Yolanda, 299n59

Martin-Ogunsola, Dellita, 57

Masiki, Trent, 296n14

Mason, Charlotte, 81

Massey, Doreen, 261n80

McKay, Claude, 76, 93–135, 276n25, 282n112, 282n120; *Amiable with Big Teeth*, 100, 132–33, 283n129; and communism, 106, 121, 123–24, 126–27, 133, 135, 141–42; on Harlem, 93, 97–98, 100, 103–11, 113–16, 117–19, 123, 279n62; *Harlem Glory*, 100, 133, 282nn125–26; on historical fiction, 128–29; *Home to Harlem*, 131–32; and James Weldon Johnson, 124–25; *A Long Way Home*, 99; on national identity, 99–100, 111, 275n17; *The Negroes in America*, 96–97, 100; "Portrait of Harlem," 126–27; *Romance in Marseille*,

274n4; and social science, 125–29. See also *Harlem: Negro Metropolis* (McKay)

McKittrick, Katherine, 7, 47, 67, 134

Metropolitan Hospital, 15

Meyer, Gerald, 175, 176, 284n6, 285n8, 287n26, 287n33, 289n49

Miller, Warren, 236

Mondello, Salvatore, 150, 159

Montage of a Dream Deferred (Hughes), 88–92

Moten, Fred, 272n112

Mount Sinai Hospital, 15

Moynihan, Daniel Patrick, 189

Mullen, Edward J., 265n3

multiculturality vs cross-culturality, 16–17

Native Americans, 5, 262n10

Negroes in America, The (McKay), 96–97, 100

Ngô, Fiona, 269n58

Nickels, Joel, 279n86

nostalgia, 187–88, 236–37

Orsi, Robert, 179–80, 253n13, 285n9, 297n29

Ortíz, Fernando, 17–18, 258n47

Ottley, Roi, 240–42

Our Lady of Mount Carmel, 10, 182, 287n25

Park, Robert E., 125

Pascale, Peter, 149

Passing (Larsen), 31

Pasteboard Bandit, The (Hughes), 86

performance: identity and, 114–15, 182, 190–92, 194, 196, 209–12, 216–21, 230–32, 235–36, 253n13, 299n72; and literature, 299n72; and place, 108–9, 186–88; resources, 300nn72–73. *See also* ritual

photography, Harlem in, 101–2; resources, 277n26

Piro, Frank "Killer Joe," 55

place: common, 112, 278n57; ethnic segregation and, 253n14; beyond

INDEX

location, 178, 186–87, 259nn57–58; as story, 33, 261n80, 273n113. *See also* space
Plessy, Homer, 74
poetry, 295n13; Harlem in, 88–92, 194
Popo and Fifina (Hughes), 86
Poston, Ted, 127, 280n92
poverty, 13–14, 146–47, 182, 196–97
Powell, Adam Clayton Jr., 11–12
Pratt, Geraldine, 65
Pratt, Mary Louise, 252n12
Proto, Joe, 182
Puente, Tito, 11, 55
Puerto Ricans: and Africans/African Americans, 75–76, 107, 196, 198–200, 295n13, 297n21; the arts and, 295n13; fictional depictions of, 45–72, 193–213; as Harlem residents, 3–4, 10, 11, 74–76, 192–93; and Italians, 181–82, 254n22, 287n25; and Jews, 74–75, 215, 271n84; independence movement of, 162, 164, 290n62; Marcantonio and, 157, 158, 160–65; multiracial, 107; U.S. citizenship for, 163

racism: 40–41, 43, 71–73, 82, 86, 107, 123–24, 135, 242, 258n52, 264n115; artistic depictions of, 59, 63, 67, 83, 194–95, 199, 201, 204–5, 221–22, 224–25, 229
Rampersad, Arnold, 53, 79
Randolph, A. Philip, 129–30
Reddick, John, 263n107
religion: Catholicism, 10, 12, 176–77, 182, 254n22; Islam, 206–7, 220–21, 251n3; Judaism, 10–11; occult, 115–16; Protestantism, 11–12, 15
Reyes, Félix Ojeda, 154
Rhodes-Pitts, Sharifa, 262n91
Riis, Jacob, 145
ritual. *See* performance
Rivera, Lino, 75–76
Roach, Joseph, 230, 235, 258n45
Robeson, Paul, 260n62

Robotham, Dan, 300n78
Rofrano, Peter, 137, 148, 149, 287n25
Romance in Marseille (McKay), 274n4
Rosner, Victoria, 65
Rosskam, Edwin, 277n26
Rotella, Carlo, 236, 295n10
Rousseau, Jean-Jacques, 155, 288n42
Rubinstein, Annette, 153–54, 285n8, 287n35

Saint Cecilia Church, 12
Sakai, Naoki, 58
Sáldivar, Ramón, 303n137
Savoy Ballroom, 11, 55, 118
Schaffer, Richard, 244, 256n31
Schechner, Richard, 299n72
Schomburg, Arturo, 200, 298n41
Schomburg Center for Research in Black Culture, 11, 112
Senegalese, 4, 10, 113
Shabazz, Malcolm. *See* Malcolm X
Shih, Shu-mei, 261n78, 302n132
Sigler, Danielle Brune, 278n59
Smethurst, James Edward, 270n68
Smith, Katharine Capshaw, 86
Smith, Neil, 244
Smith, Sidonie, 303n137
solidarity, 19, 77, 84–85, 87, 123–24, 155, 288nn41–42
Sommer, Doris, 58, 263n97
Soto, Isabel, 267n23
South Asians. *See* Asians and Asian Americans
space, 261n80; components of, 9, 88, 130, 261n80; and memory, 188; movement and, 88–89, 274n2; narrative, 70–71, 79, 208–9, 303n137; racialized/ethnic, 18–20, 47, 61–65, 72, 74–78, 94, 97–111, 114–19, 124–26, 133–35, 139, 144–46. 148–50, 190, 195–202, 206–8, 212, 215, 217, 220–30, 233–34, 242–43, 253n14, 287n25; resources, 253n14, 254nn15–16, 261n80. *See also* place

311

INDEX

"Spanish Blood" (Hughes), 85; ethnic/racial identifications in, 47–50, 53–55, 56, 58–64, 77; role of Harlem in, 70–71, 77–78, 80; language in, 57–61, 268n39; role of women in, 66–67, 69; versions of, 62, 71, 81, 268n39

Spanish Harlem. *See* El Barrio

Spellman, Cardinal Francis, 176

Sufists, 121

Taylor, Monique, 253n13

Thomas, Lorrin, 76, 270n83

Thomas, Piri, 42, 167, 185, 187–216, 231–37; on Harlem, 193–98, 201, 236; identity and, 211–12; on Marcantonio, 157; performance and, 209–11; and Ullah, 191, 235; on writing style, 209–10. See also *Down These Mean Streets* (McKay)

Thrift, Nigel, 134

Thurman, Wallace, 97

travel, 34, 266n18

Ullah, Alaudin ("Aladdin"), 186–92, 216–37; cross-culturality in, 186, 216–31; *Dishwasher Dreams*, 217–18; on Harlem, 217–31; as documentary subject, 301n94; *Indio* 221–22; and Piri Thomas, 191, 235

Universal Negro Improvement Association, 11

Valentín, Gilberto Gerena, 176

Vega, Bernardo, 76, 271n90

Vogel, Shane, 68

Wallerstein, Immanuel, 290n60

Washington, Booker T., 124

Watts, Jill, 278n59

Ways of White Folks, The (Hughes), 53

Weary Blues, The (Hughes), 85

Weintraub, Karl, 234, 303n136

Weisbrot, Robert, 278n59

Williams, Raymond, 178, 232, 263n101

Wittgenstein, Ludwig, 58

Woods, Clyde, 7

Woodson, Carter G., 127–28

Wright, Richard, 126–27, 130, 277n26, 281nn107–8

GPSR Authorized Representative: Easy Access System Europe, Mustamäe tee 50, 10621 Tallinn, Estonia, gpsr.requests@easproject.com

www.ingramcontent.com/pod-product-compliance
Lightning Source LLC
Chambersburg PA
CBHW022034290426
44109CB00014B/855